MONOCACY

THE BATTLE THAT SAVED WASHINGTON

BY
B. Franklin Cooling

 White Mane Publishing Company, Inc.

This White Mane Publishing Company, Inc. publication was printed by:
Beidel Printing House, Inc.
63 West Burd Street
Shippensburg, PA 17257 USA

In respect for the scholarship contained herein, the acid-free paper used in this book
meets the guidelines for permanence and durability of the Committee on Production
Guidelines for Book Longevity of the Council on Library Resources.

For a complete list of available publications please write:
White Mane Publishing Company, Inc.
P. O. Box 152
Shippensburg, PA 17257-0152 USA

Library of Congress Cataloging-in-Publication Data

Cooling, B. Franklin.
    Monocacy : the battle that saved Washington / by B. Franklin
Cooling.
        p.   cm.
    Includes bibliographical references and index.
    ISBN 1-57249-032-2 (alk. paper)
        1.   Monocacy, Battle of, Md., 1864   I.   Title.
    E476.66.C86   1997
    973.7'36--dc21   97-6135
                                                                    CIP

PRINTED IN THE UNITED STATES OF AMERICA

DEDICATION

To the memory of Rudolf K. Haerle, whose friendship was more like that of family and whose discussions about the actual number of *Official Records* volumes and whether or not his fellow Hoosier's real name was Lew or Lewis Wallace enlivened many visits to his Indianapolis home and the Indianapolis Civil War Round Table.

TABLE OF CONTENTS

LIST OF ILLUSTRATIONS

Chapter Eight

LIST OF MAPS

PREFACE

Threads of Continuity

Growing up in Washington, D.C., one does not normally learn very much about a place called Monocacy. I remember as a youth passing a monument or two on the Frederick to Washington highway—one traveled that way by automobile before the advent of Interstate 270. My parents and I crossed bridges over a river and a railroad (much more fascinating to a young boy than endless farmland) on what is now Maryland Route 355. More importantly, we always encountered a tremendous thunderstorm just south of Frederick—about the time we crossed that river. I remember that more than anything else about the spot. Only later, when writing about defending Washington during the Civil War, and helping an old friend, Colonel Thomas Ware USA Retired, begin to treat a battle at this place called Monocacy—only then did I realize its significance in history.

Indeed, a small battle site nestles in the undulating farm country of upland Maryland. Its name comes from the Monocacy River that bisects adjacent hills and cornfields—now filling rapidly with suburban sprawl from the nearby city of Frederick. Overshadowed by better known battlefields like Antietam to the west and Gettysburg to the north, Monocacy may have been more important than either of them. One participant, Confederate Major General John B. Gordon, remembered that it was among the hardest fought contests of the war. Union civilian Registrar of the Treasury, Lucius E. Chittenden, suggested that because Monocacy delayed the onrushing Confederates and so saved the nation's capital at Washington, "it was one of the decisive battles of the world," and warranted "a more complete account than it has hitherto received." Yet, apart from Glenn H.

Worthington's account* (as a small boy, he had witnessed the battle from his father's cellar), relatively little has been done to analyze in depth what may be truly styled the Confederate victory that saved Washington.[1]

The Indians called the river Monoquacy, or Monnockkesy for "many big bends." Fed by streams coming from the Catoctin Mountains on the west, from Sugarloaf Mountain (the out-of-place eminence now passed fleetingly on Interstate 270 going to and from Washington) and the Linganore hills to the east on a similar thoroughfare to Baltimore, the river's source traces to a spring about six miles west of Cashtown, Pennsylvania—not that far from a place called Gettysburg. Monocacy thus forms a conduit to our history, not just for the Civil War period, but both before and after. It provided the setting for a vast influx of German refugee settlers in the eighteenth century, the birth of quaint city of church spires known as Frederick, and one can gain introductory knowledge to the river's story from the Reverend John Schildt's pleasant booklet, *Drums Along the Monocacy*.[2]

Cattle, grain, iron and fur were transported by early settlers down the Monocacy and thence via the Potomac to Alexandria, Virginia. Merchandise flowed in reverse to the upcountry for the hungry builders of early America. Fishing in those rivers provided both food and sport, while flour mills like the venerable Michaels Mill (1739) near Buckeystown, sprang up along the Monocacy's banks as water power was used for local commercial purposes. Subsequently, Conestoga wagons, railroad trains, and motor vehicles interrupted her sylvan quietude as usurpers for communication and travel. Today, the appellation "scenic river" aptly focuses a modern generation's regard for this most ancient of highways. Indeed, preservation has replaced utilization as the underlying philosophy in our desperate attempt to roll back the ruthless march of civilization known as urbanization and pollution from the Monocacy's banks.[3]

---

* In addition to Worthington's *Fighting For Time or The Battle That Saved Washington and Mayhap the Union* (Baltimore, 1932); see Brad Coker, *The Battle of Monocacy* (Baltimore, 1982); Albert E. Conradis, "The Battle of Monocacy; The Battle That Saved Washington From Capture," in Frederick County Civil War Centennial, Inc., *To Commemorate the One Hundredth Anniversary of the Battle of Monocacy, "The Battle That Saved Washington"* (Frederick, 1964); Robert E. Morseberger, "The Battle That Saved Washington," *Civil War Times Illustrated* (May 1974), pp. 12–17, 20–27; Benjamin Franklin Cooling, "Monocacy; The Battle That Saved Washington," *Blue and Gray Magazine* (December 1992), pp. 8–18, 48–56, 60, and *Jubal Early's Raid, 1864* (Baltimore, 1989), chapter 3; Walt Albro, "The Forgotten Battle for the Capital," *Civil War Times Illustrated* (January/February 1993), pp. 40–43, 56, 58, 60; and Joseph Judge, *Season of Fire; The Confederate Strike on Washington* (Berryville, Va., 1994) chapters VII–X.

But, this book is about something else. In a sense it is a story about a bridge—or really three bridges to be precise. One loomed larger than the others—whether the stone highway arch or the nearby railroad span both of which oriented on an axis for the Chesapeake port city of Baltimore. Even more auspicious for our story was the quaint covered wooden bridge that took the turnpike southward across the Monocacy to the nation's capital. "The bridges of Frederick County" might even be an apt title. But, in fact the book is a study of the battle at Monocacy for those bridges—a battle, like all battles, full of enigmas, ironies, and variations, not the least of which has been its under-appreciation through the generations. It is an almost forgotten, yet glorious chapter in our nation's history.

Swept up in general consideration of Confederate General Jubal Early's famous raid against Washington in July 1864, Southern contemporaries, for example, often rationalized away the whole episode, omitting the impact of any singular battle. Confederate engineer, artillerist, and staff officer, Brigadier General Edward Porter Alexander, always thought there had been a "much better play than the sending of Early on the raid to Washington," something he considered "purely bluff." He termed the very idea "absurd" that Washington could have been taken by Early's "little force" and pointed out that while the unbluffable Ulysses S. Grant had been reduced from seven to five corps pressuring General Robert E. Lee's Richmond-Petersburg defenses, the latter's own strength had shrunk by fully one-third (from three to two corps) through detachment of Early's force for the raid. Better, observed Alexander, had Early been sent to reinforce General Joseph E. Johnston above Atlanta. "It would not have been a bluff at all, but the very strongest play on the whole military board." In Alexander's account, at least, Monocacy was only a way station on a fruitless exercise going nowhere.[4]

As a soldier, Alexander surely would have concurred with civilian Chittenden's assessment that the importance of any battle "is determined by its ultimate consequences rather than its immediate result." In the case of Monocacy, the consequence and immediate result proved inseparable. The significance of Confederate victory on the field quickly evaporated in the time lost marching the victorious army to its ultimate objective, Washington, D.C. Failure to arrive in time—largely due to the twenty-four hours taken to engage in battle at Monocacy on July 9, rather than being able to rapidly traverse the forty miles to Washington and thus win the footrace for the Yankee capital—proved crucial.

On July 11, when Early's hot, dusty, and weary troops could not form a battle line to punch their way through ill-defended earthworks before the city, the irony of the Confederates' tactical success at Monocacy shone brightly. The so-called "battle of the sub-urbs," principally before Fort Stevens on the Seventh Street road, was thus dependent upon what the Union defeat at Monocacy accomplished in delaying Early. Neither protagonists then, nor historians since, have correlated these separate elements of the singular event other than by talking generally how the heat, dust, and distance prevented the Confederacy from securing its greatest coup. Monocacy and Fort Stevens form part of the whole—the latter might not have happened without the former.[5]

In isolation, both Monocacy and Fort Stevens were seen separately as minor episodes in a war of many battles, none of which, in and of itself, seemed especially decisive at the time. Yet, battles are part of a continuum of men and events in war. They must be viewed in that sense, not in isolation. Monocacy and Fort Stevens were part of a continuum that at one and the same time formed an embarrassment to the national government, thereby causing that government and its military arm to finally resolve the question of what to do about protecting Washington—symbol, sword, and shield of the Union. Monocacy was a catalyst that forced the issue of what to do about Mr. Lincoln's city and its corollary, the Shenandoah Valley, as both Lee's granary and covered invasion route to the territory north of the Potomac. This resolution occupied all of five months, and came at a crucial point for the political-military fortunes of both North and South. During those months, Lee and Early continued their audacious game of cat-and-mouse with Lincoln and his generals until the Union high command, led by Grant, ultimately employed overwhelming force to finally eradicate the threat in the famous Valley Campaign of 1864.[6]

Monocacy was also linked to another aspect of this continuum—the changing nature of the war itself. Not only was Monocacy illustrative of the onset of modern war—the application of technology to operations as shown by use of steamboat and railroad to rush reinforcements quickly to embattled sectors like the Monocacy and Washington. Rather, Monocacy and the summer of 1864 coincided with the escalation of total war against the populace, manifest during Early's sojourn in Maryland. What had begun earlier with Major General David Hunter's travesty at Lexington, Virginia and elsewhere in the Valley was carried north in the bosoms of Early's men seeking retaliation and retribution. Later, Hunter rekindled the inflammation in the so-called panhandle of West Virginia, before the new Union general in the Shenandoah, Philip H. Sheridan, carried the art to a new high with "The Burning" of the Shenandoah in the fall. Monocacy and the other pitched battles frankly pale in interest as this manifestation of war against civilians and their property better reflected what civil war had become by 1864. By this point, the American epic foreshadowed the twentieth century's experience with conflict involving not just the military but also the people.

At the time of Monocacy, New York diarist George Templeton Strong bemoaned the fact that he could see no bright spots, only "humiliation and disaster" as Early rampaged through Maryland. The London *Times* pontificated that the Confederacy seemed "more formidable than ever," while a Democratic editor at home opined that Lincoln was politically "deader than dead." Indeed, July was a dark time for Union fortunes, the fourth summer of a war that seemingly went on interminably. Yet, Monocacy and its surrounding events provided a wake-up call, a synergizing final surge of resilience and resolution to save the Union. By August and September it had come together in time for victories by Major General William Tecumseh Sherman at Atlanta and Sheridan in the Shenandoah to transform summer horrors to positive results in the national elections for Lincoln. Rather than seen as a chimerical rebel success on the battlefield (something hardly unique in the four-year struggle), Monocacy contributed to a legacy that ensured survival of the Republic. True, it was a close thing.[7]

To study Monocacy as a battle itself provides a reader with all the thrill and drama of personalities and events. A struggle for control of bridges, in fact, it resulted as much from a railroad president's concern for his prized iron span crossing the river as anything else. The battle produced two Medal of Honor winners for the defeated Union side, and horrendous casualties for key portions of Early's army. In fact, a question may be raised whether or not such losses seriously impaired the Confederate ability to overrun Washington's strong fortifications. Characterized by many participants as truly a soldier's battle because of how many company and field grade officers were cut down, the list of units included veterans and novices. They included vaunted VI Corps and Army of the Valley District professionals (as professionals went by the third year in a war of citizen amateurs), together with reserve troops and something styled the Ohio National Guard (thought to be militia because of their one hundred days' term of service). Indeed, the cast of characters further included a former vice president of the United States now clad in rebel gray, the son of the Union secretary of state as a regimental commander, two ever-controversial army leaders in Jubal Early and Lew Wallace (really a politician in uniform), and the staunchly regular Army of the Potomac brigadier James B. Ricketts. Their field of action included feints and flank attacks, the skirmish line and line of battle, combined arms teams and more. The strategic and tactical roles of railroad, steamboat, and telegraph (the technology of modern warfare), as well as tactical impact of combined arms on a napoleonic-style battlefield all traverse the Monocacy story.

For the ardent buff, Confederate artillery superiority won the day for rebel footsloggers in a hard-fought tussle between veteran infantry on both sides.

In the end, the abiding theme about Monocacy remains that of *time*. Indeed, Glenn Worthington appropriately captured that theme in the title of his classic book, *Fighting for Time*. Certainly, Monocacy equated with time gained to save Washington for the Union, as well as time lost for Early in his race to the capital and a daring scheme to liberate rebel prisoners at distant Point Lookout where the Potomac joined the Chesapeake Bay. This meaning was expressed most clearly when in 1931, the Maryland legislature passed a joint resolution and memorial that read:

> Whereas, this delay of twenty-four hours, caused by the battle fought at Monocacy to impede the progress of the invading army toward the National Capital, saved the Capital from capture and all the direful consequences thereof, and has for that reason been denominated "one of the decisive battles of the world."[8]

* * * *

Monocacy may never rank with Antietam, Gettysburg, Shiloh, or Vicksburg among the hallowed shrines of our civil war. Small battles with small casualty figures do not enrapture Americans more enthralled with annihilative events and the myths of history. Ironically, while Monocacy became a national battlefield park in 1934, it took fifty-seven additional years to secure its dedication and opening for visitation. Here again was another odd twist reflecting the fact that Monocacy and *time* will forever be entwined both in theme and in story. Especially, for Old Jube and thousands of men in blue and gray that hot July Saturday, it was, in fact, a moment when the clock stood still. Former president Ronald Reagan observed in his paean to the fiftieth anniversary of D-Day landings in Normandy during World War II that "war is an unpredictable mix of organized confusion, improvised ingenuity, and timeless courage."[9] The soldiers at Monocacy would have agreed. This book has been written in that spirit.

ACKNOWLEDGMENTS

Grateful thanks to those who have made this volume possible, including William J. Clipson for maps, and Walton B. Owen II for photographic support, as well as David E. Roth, publisher of *Blue and Gray Magazine* who provided key illustrations to enhance the text. Fred L. Rohrer of Fremont, California graciously sent a photograph of Alfred N. Sova, his great-grandfather who fought in the battle of Monocacy. Dr. Richard A. Sauers of Westover, Maryland guided me to the bounteous resources of *The National Tribune*.

Anne Calhoun of the Baltimore and Ohio Museum; Paul A. Carnahan from the Vermont Historical Society; Mrs. Bruce E. Lewis of The Seward House in Auburn, New York; Kermit J. Pike of the Western Reserve Historical Society; Gerold L. Cole of the Milner Library at Illinois State University; Bob Davis of Rockville, Maryland; Kevin C. Ruffner of Washington, D.C.; Peter Eisen and Bill Groff of Frederick, Maryland; John M. Gibson, Jr. of the Friends of Monocacy Battlefield—all provided leads and helpful comments that aided the research effort.

National Park Service representatives to be singled out include Susan Moore and Kathy Beeler at the Monocacy National Battlefield, Jody Morrison of the Technical Information Center at the Denver Service Center, David Nathanson of the Library, Archives and Graphics Research office at the Harpers Ferry Center, as well as Randy Biallas and Fred Sanchez at the Park Historic Architecture Division in the Washington headquarters.

Finally, a heartfelt thank you goes to Colonel Thomas A. Ware, USA Retired—longtime friend and fellow military historian with whom this work was originally to have been written in collaboration. That was not to be, but we can anticipate his own future analysis of the battle— written from a professional soldier's viewpoint. It will be pathbreaking in its own right. I have enjoyed his helpful advice and

comments on the present work, although like every author, I freely
acknowledge my own errors, omissions, and focus.

Note: *Monocacy – The Battle that Saved Washington* is the
fourth book in the author's series on the theme of defending
Washington during the Civil War. The others include *Symbol,
Sword, and Shield*; *Defending Washington During the Civil War*
(Hamden, Conn.: Archon, 1975 and Shippensburg, Pa.: White Mane
Publishing Company, 1991); *Mr. Lincoln's Forts: A Guide to the
Civil War Defenses of Washington*, written with Walton H. Owen
(Shippensburg, Pa.: White Mane Publishing Company, 1988); and
Jubal Early's Raid, 1864 (Baltimore: Nautical and Aviation Pub-
lishing Company, 1989), all of which are available from the pub-
lishers. Research files for these books have been placed respec-
tively at the Fort Ward and Historic Site in Alexandria, Virginia
and the Monocacy National Battlefield.

ONE

Old Jube Steals a March

The fields around the town of Staunton, Virginia were lush with wheat, corn, and clover. Orchards held ripening peaches, pears, and apples. Cattle and horses grazed contentedly, unbothered by the bustle of men and equipment nearby. It was Sunday, June 26, 1864—a typically hot summer day in the Old Dominion. Many of Virginia's native sons were moving into encampments with comrades from the Carolinas, Georgia, and Louisiana after an arduous fortnight of purging the Shenandoah Valley of Yankee invaders. Worn down by three years of war, reduced in numbers and forced consolidation of many of their prized units by bloody fights in the Wilderness, at Spotsylvania, and at Bethesda Church, the men in gray still retained their fighting spirit. They needed rest and reorganization, however. Pushed relentlessly by their new but nevertheless familiar commander, Lieutenant General Jubal Anderson Early, they simply needed to take stock of themselves, their arms, and their equipment.[1]

Early and his officers quickly began the task of culling out the enfeebled animals, the broken down wagons and artillery pieces and distributing an all-too-meager supply of new shoes and other gear sent up from Richmond warehouses. Quartermaster Major John Harmon and his commissariat counterpart Wells J. Hawks advised and supervised. The line and staff quickly had rankers out in the fields and orchards laying in stocks of ripened fruit and an early grain harvest. The general's aide, Lieutenant Colonel Alexander "Sandie" Pendleton, drew up orders scaling back the number of baggage and cooking utensil wagons to the barest minimum for the march ahead. Officers and men—even more pastoral types like Roman Catholic chaplain James Sheeran of the 14th Louisiana, grumbled and

1

groaned at the inconvenience. Early called the padre aside and bluntly told him that he, himself, had only one pair of underdrawers and had to do without them while they were being washed by a servant. Early wanted a lean force for the task that lay ahead. More anon on the man they dubbed "Old Jube."[2]

Expeditionary Preparations

The Staunton interlude also witnessed a revamping of the little army. Of possibly 15 or 16,000 officers and men* available to him, perhaps some 10,000 belonged to what a year before had been the pride and joy of Lieutenant General Thomas Jonathan Jackson's Second Army Corps. Later, it had belonged to Lieutenant General Richard Stoddert Ewell, one of "Old Jack's" pupils. Now it was Early's turn, the second of Stonewall's profane successors who had learned war at that calvinist general's knee. Early's command was augmented by some of the best units of Major General John Cabell Breckinridge's Department of Western Virginia. That impressive and influential Kentucky prewar politician as well as United States vice president and presidential candidate in 1860, would become Early's direct subordinate. Only five years separated those two lawyers in age (Early was forty-eight, Breckinridge, forty-three), and the Kentuckian received something of a provisional corps command since his well recognized experience derived from service in both eastern and western theaters during this war. Having cut his teeth on battles at Shiloh, Vicksburg, Baton Rouge, and Chickamauga, he had stymied at least one previous Yankee thrust in the Shenandoah that very spring.

The command arrangement might have been unsettling to some, but it placed an intermediary between the eccentric Early and his own variously temperamental division commanders. They included a sometime contentious and high-strung Georgian, Major General

---

* The "numbers game" has always bedeviled both contemporaries and historians. Early himself contended in 1881: "When I was detached from General Lee's army the whole corps did not amount to 9,000 effectives." He then cited an August 31, 1864, return that included: Breckinridge (2,104), Rodes (3,013),Gordon (2,544), and Ramseur (1,909), thus totaling 9,570 to which he added, "The strength of the cavalry and artillery is not given but both could not have exceeded 3,000." Thus, a total of 12,570 would stand after Early's return from his Maryland campaign. Possible attrition losses of 1,000 to 1,500 from that campaign suggest a figure of about 14,000 for its outset. Early concluded however that, "The force of infantry with which I moved on Washington did not, therefore, exceed eight thousand muskets, if it reached that number."

Early claimed: "My command consisted of what was left of the Second Corps, Army of Northern Virginia, with two battalions of artillery of three batteries each, attached to it; Breckinridge's division of infantry of three small brigades, four small

John Brown Gordon, Tar Heel Major General Stephen Dodson Ramseur, and two Lynchburg natives, Major General Robert Emmett Rodes and Brigadier General John Echols. Early's chief of artillery, Brigadier General Armistead Lindsey Long, also hailed from that Piedmont neighborhood (as did Early himself). Long was one of Army of Northern Virginia commander Robert E. Lee's favorite young officers. He had served some months as Lee's military secretary. Long yearned to take to the field, and his chief reluctantly let him go with Early. Lee knew that Old Jube needed a wise head to deploy the two good battalions of Second Corps guns plus a third battalion culled from Breckinridge's artillery—forty some guns in all.

Then there was the matter of the often unruly and inefficient cavalry. Another North Carolinian, recently assigned Major General Robert Ransom, took charge of that branch. Early really had wanted the current *beau sabreur* of the South, brigadier John Hunt Morgan, but that Kentucky cavalier, operating in southwestern Virginia with Brigadier General Samuel Jones since escaping from imprisonment in the Ohio Penitentiary, had undertaken a counter strike into the Federally occupied Bluegrass state in June. Thus Early received Ransom from the War Department instead. Early profoundly mistrusted what infantrymen termed "buttermilk rangers." Actually, buttermilk had little to do with the slur, for as one rebel horseman claimed later, for "the fact is that the cavalryman was more of a ranger for cane-reed whiskey and apple-jack." Rather, the mounted troops were a bit too free-wheeling, their commanders too lax to suit old line soldiers like Early. He preferred tighter and more orderly formations that could be brought to bear aggressively on standard battlefields of the day. Still, Ransom's horsemen would count four brigades and four batteries or fifteen light guns. Ransom, an old cavalry hand, could keep them in line, Early figured, and coordinate their widespread movements. Furthermore, that new cavalry "division" reported directly to the army commander.[3]

---

brigades of cavalry, and a small battalion of artillery attached to Breckinridge's command. In the three battalions of artillery I had nine batteries, neither of which had more than four field-pieces and some of them not that many. Besides these were one or two batteries of artillery, with the cavalry, the entire number of field pieces in all the artillery not exceeding forty." Early contended that a small contingent he had left at Winchester to collect stragglers had garnered some 1,500 by the time he returned from Maryland, and that "I had sustained a loss of some seven or eight hundred men in killed and wounded in some slight actions in the Valley before crossing the Potomac, and in the fight at the Monocacy." He went on to berate the Federals' overestimation of his strength and their own 14–20,000 men manning the works in his front at Washington. See Letter, J. A. Early to the editor of the *Republican*, "The Advance on Washington," n.d., *Southern Historical Society Papers* (July/August 1881), pp. 299–300, 301–305, 306.

Lieutenant General Jubal Anderson Early

Cantankerous commander of the Second Corps, Army of Northern Virginia and Army of the Valley District in July 1864.
U.S. Army Military History Institute

Major General Robert Emmet Rodes, C.S.A.

A Lynchburg native and graduate of Virginia Military Institute, he proved to be one of Early's finest division commanders during the Washington campaign. He was killed at Third Winchester the following September.
U.S. Army Military History Institute

Major General John Cabell Breckinridge, C.S.A.

This Kentucky Confederate general and former United States vice president, as well as presidential candidate in 1860, led a corps in Early's army during the Washington campaign. He was indicted for treason at the end of the war largely on the basis of this action.
U.S. Army Military History Institute

**Major General John Brown
Gordon, C.S.A.**

This brilliant and daring division commander from Georgia successfully broke the back of Union resistance at Monacacy. July 9, 1864.

U.S. Army Military History Institute

**Brigadier General John Echols,
C.S.A.**

This tall and imposing western Virginian rose from regimental to division command, ably serving Early as a second-line commander in the Washington campaign.

U.S. Army Military History Institute

Major General Stephen Dodson Ramseur, C.S.A.

Youngest West Pointer to receive a major generalcy in the Confederate army, he ably served Early as a division commander before being killed at Cedar Creek in October 1864.

U.S. Army Military History Institute

Major General Robert Ransom, C.S.A.

A solid but sluggish leader, he commanded Early's cavalry during the Washington campaign and proved incapable of exercising proper control over them.

U.S. Army Military History Institute

Brigadier General Armistead Lindsay Long, C.S.A.

Military secretary and artillery adviser to Robert E. Lee, he commanded Early's artillery in the Washington campaign but was overshadowed by the battlefield operational leadership of J. Floyd King.

U.S. Army Military History Institute

The army had an interesting assortment of personalities, ages, and backgrounds for its senior management. Early himself was West Point, class of '37, a veteran of the Seminole and Mexican Wars, but mainly a prewar rural lawyer from Rocky Mount, Virginia, member of the state's house of delegates—a commonwealth's attorney who had voted against Virginia's secession in a convention in April 1861. Scruffy, stooped, vitriolic, cantankerous, with a high-pitched voice, the bachelor citizen-soldier symbolized the rough stock he led. One soldier likened him to a country undertaker riding to a funeral. Another, George McCullogh Mooney of Company H, 5th Virginia, remembered that the boys in the ranks styled him "Old Lop Ear," because his ears were so big. To still others, he was simply "Old Jube," telling more than anything else that he was a true son of the Piedmont. He formed a contrast to the patrician Breckinridge—another lawyer who (like Early) had voted against secession, yet went with the Confederacy.[4]

The thirty-three-year-old John B. Gordon was the third lawyer. Hailing originally from Atlanta, he had raised his own company of north Georgia miners ("the Raccoon Roughs"), and rose quickly through successive levels of command. Prominent at Antietam, where he had been severely wounded, he was a striking and appealing leader of men. Tall, erect, superb in the saddle, he appealed to the men in the ranks. He had come close to helping the Confederate arms pull another Chancellorsville rout at the Wilderness, against some of the very Federal troops he would face in the coming campaign. After Spotsylvania, he ascended to the command of major general Edward "Allegheny" Johnson's division (Johnson having been taken captive in the battle), after proving a tenacious fighter once more.

Echols too was a peacetime lawyer, as well as commonwealth's attorney, and delegate to the state secession convention. A huge man, standing six feet four inches tall and carrying two hundred sixty pound on his forty-one-year-old frame, his amiability was legendary. He, however, always seemed to command reserve-type troops. Most of his war service took place in western Virginia, except for the Valley campaign of 1862 and the Cold Harbor battle.[5]

As for the others, Ransom, class of 1850, and Ramseur, nine years his junior and class of 1860, were both West Pointers. Both Tar Heels knew no other profession but soldiering. Rodes was class of 1848 at the Virginia Military Institute and a prewar civil engineer. Severely wounded at Seven Pines in the spring of 1862, he recovered after a long convalescence in time to distinguish himself in the Antietam campaign and led the van of Jackson's famous flank march at Chancellorsville. In the thick of the fighting from Gettysburg to the Totopotomy thereafter, the thirty-five-year-old Rodes would remain something of a cipher in the campaign ahead.

In appearance, they were all similar. Early, alone, wore a full and scraggly beard. Rodes, Breckinridge, Echols, Long, and yet another brigadier who would figure so highly in the upcoming campaign, cavalryman John McCausland (also VMI, class of 1857, and University of Virginia graduate the next year) all had mustaches. Gordon and Ramseur affected the French style of goatee and mustachio. In sum, this was a well-seasoned group of senior officers who had learned their trade on the job for the most part. So too for their brigade and regiment commanders; survivors, the lot. As for the men they led—they came in varying sizes, shapes, and states of dress and appearance. They hailed from Virginia, Maryland, North Carolina, Georgia, Alabama, Louisiana, and Tennessee—maybe elsewhere but credited to units from these states, at least. Their faded gray mingled with shadings of captured blue and homespun butternut. It was a veteran force, in fact and appearance.

In a controversial move, Early disbanded all reserve or home guard units in the Valley and probably exceeded his authority in so doing. At least, Secretary of War James Seddon protested as much to President Jefferson Davis. Early realized, however, that those over- and under-aged males could provide better service harvesting crops at home so that Confederate soldiers and civilians alike might eat the following winter. His preparations made, Lieutenant General Early led his re-created "Army of the Valley District" north from Staunton on June 28. The previous day's rain helped to assuage the sunburned veterans. That same day, off to the northeast, in distant Washington City, President Abraham Lincoln accepted nomination for a second term as president of the United States. The fates of the president and the general they called "Old Jube" were about to be joined.[6]

Genesis of the Maryland Campaign of '64

As the columns of men trudged northward on the Valley turn-pike that morning, most of them suspected their destination. If it was summer, it must be time to carry the war north of the Potomac once again, they joked. That had been the case for the past two years, with hopes and intentions eventually dashed at Antietam and Gettysburg. Now they were off again, presumably for a third try, and the reason was always the same: to relieve the pressure on the beleaguered Confederate government in Richmond and Virginia, and clear the enemy from the Shenandoah Valley—indispensable bread-basket for Confederate fortunes in the East. They were to buy time in that war of attrition and survival. Threaten Washington, cause the recall of the Army of the Potomac for its protection, and draw it away from Richmond. Raid up into the lush farmland of northern Maryland and Pennsylvania, carry the war to the enemy, and possibly garner support among both the ever-wavering border state secessionists, and at the courts of Europe. Then too, there was always a chance that capricious governments of Great Britain and France might yet seize upon some sign that the Southern Confederacy still breathed life and was thereby worthy of diplomatic recognition (with attendant military and economic help).[7]

Frankly, the days were past when Marylanders would have seceded from the Union. Moreover, by 1864, British and French politicians had lost their ardor for supporting disunion. Nevertheless it was a Northern presidential election year. If Early's army could somehow seriously embarrass the Lincoln government, cast doubts upon the ability of the North to break the bloody and inconclusive stalemate and thus finish off the rebellion—well then, there might just be a chance for Confederate survival after all. At least, those were the long shots, the hopes and ideas that floated about Richmond political circles, and translated into Lee's own strategy for coping with overwhelming Union pressure against the Confederate capital. Few of Early's men had those facts well thought out as they marched north on the twenty-eighth. The basics were on everyone's mind with implications for themselves, their families back home, and their new country.[8]

Early had been privy to the strategy ever since consulting with Lee near Richmond on June 12. Old Jube had been summoned that day to the army commander's headquarters from his reserve camp at the home of a Dr. Curtis near Gaines Mill. Lee told him about two missions. One was absolutely necessary. The second was a gamble, which evolved from the first; it was dangerous but holding great promise, he explained. First, said Lee, Early must take his army to the Shenandoah, where Breckinridge was holding off a persistent Union advance. The Kentuckian had been sent out earlier with his division. Initially, it had been Major General Franz Sigel who had been nettlesome until stopped cold at New Market on May 15. Sigel had retired with Breckinridge, unable to destroy his army. Then it had been Major General David Hunter's turn, and he had been too free with torch and intimidation of the Valley civilians to suit Lee. It would be Early's responsibility to help Breckinridge eliminate Hunter's bluecoats completely.[9]

Such success would relieve some pressure on the Richmond-Petersburg line, protect Lee's invaluable supply base and railroad center at Lynchburg, and thus free Early either to return to the main army or launch an independent raid into Maryland from the direction of Leesburg in Loudoun County. There he could threaten the Northern capital. It was an admitted gamble, and Early ruefully declared

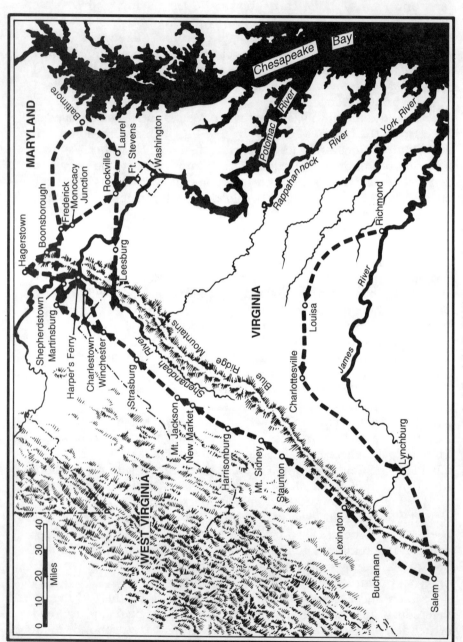

Map 1. Jubal Early's Raid, June and July 1864

after the war that in retrospect it seemed a forlorn hope. Timing and resources were everything. In June 1864, the mission was unquestionably vital to survival, so Old Jube accepted the assignment without hesitation. He was confident that he could accomplish both tasks. Initial written orders (now lost to history) arrived at his command post that evening.

As to the question of why Lee selected Early, the answer was simple. He was Lee's most logical and available choice for this independent assignment. Successor to the convalescing Ewell as Second Corps commander, Old Jube was no Stonewall Jackson, or James Longstreet for that matter. In fact, the succession had been stormy, Ewell not wishing to relinquish command, Early perhaps nudging the process so that he might ascend to that command. Yet, Early subsequently pledged fealty to Ewell even if the men of the Second Corps were not especially enamored of the transition to Early. Still, they knew he was a fighter. And, Early understood strategy well enough. How he responded to Lee's customary discretionary orders remained to be seen.[10]

Northward to the Potomac

As of mid-June, very few individuals knew about the whole scheme. The worn-down but unbowed Second Corps tramped westward to Lynchburg in mid-June dust and heat. That was part of their job. Home and family still took precedence over the "Cause." As newly promoted Georgia Brigadier General Clement Evans wrote his wife from a bivouac near Charlottesville on June 18: "It cannot be long before we will be with each other again." "Our enemies will soon give up their mad project of subjugation," he added, "and we will be at peace." Early's men successfully defeated Hunter just west of the city on June 17 and 18, and pursued the retiring Federal column to Salem where Early dropped the chase. Lee feared that Hunter "has not been much punished," (he told President Jefferson Davis on June 26), and could be reorganized and re-equipped and "repeat his expedition" unless the Confederates kept sufficient force in the valley to oppose him. Still, Lee thought Early's best move now lay with advancing to the Potomac and beyond. As of the twenty-sixth, the Confederate president and his principal general seemed more preoccupied with brainstorming a possible army-navy operation to liberate Confederate prisoners at Point Lookout, where the Potomac joined the Chesapeake. Early's army figured prominently in the planning. In this regard, as of three days later, Lee informed the chief executive: "There will be time to shape Early's course or terminate it when he reached the Potomac, as circumstances require."[11]

Indeed, eager to secure victory and acclaim, and never one to shirk the challenge of independent command, the feisty Early enthusiastically turned his expeditionary force northward at Salem. He became more convinced of the validity of the move with every step. Everywhere the Confederates found evidence of Hunter's passing: ruined houses and barns, and, when they reached Lexington, the destruction of Governor John Letcher's home and the Virginia Military Institute (under the guise that these facilities had been legitimate military targets). Even Stonewall Jackson's grave had been desecrated by the heartless enemy. The Confederates' collective ire was up. Spoiling for a chance to despoil Northern territory in turn, they pressed onward, spurred by a wild reception and supply of refreshment from citizens along the route of march.[12]

As early as June 16, Lieutenant Leonidas Lafayette Polk of the 43d North Carolina wrote his wife that she should not be surprised to see Early's army emerge in Pennsylvania, Ohio, Maryland, or anywhere else as they were on a sort of "wild goose chase." Everyone was in high spirits, flirting with local belles in a seminary at Botetourt Springs as well as every tiny hamlet and farm, paying homage to Jackson's grave site in Lexington, and visiting the Natural Bridge nearby before dropping from exhaustion into those rest camps for two days at Staunton. Then, with thoroughly lightened hearts and steps the resurrected Army of the Valley District marched forth on its new venture. Port Republic and Cross Keys, victory sites of the Jackson era, slipped by; "classic ground" as Maine-born, Louisiana Brigadier General Zebulon York in Gordon's division styled it. Now, every ranker in the army sensed they were going north of the Potomac, and their pace quickened. On June 30, Early fired off a telegram to Lee speaking of his high-spirited command, the wonderfully rich crops in the valley, and telling his superior that "I hope to do something for your relief and the success of our cause shortly."[13]

The pace was grueling on the macadamized Valley turnpike. They marched eighteen, sometimes up to twenty-four miles a day in the withering heat through Strasburg, Middletown, Kernstown, and other hamlets, recorded Georgia brigadier Clement Evans in his pocket diary. While citizens worried about their gardens and crops during a prolonged drought, the soldiery fretted about just making it to the cooling Potomac. Afternoon showers brought but fleeting relief. Early, himself, wondered about the absence of Federal opposition. In fact, no bluecoats appeared much before Captain George W. Booth's scouts from Brigadier General Bradley Johnson's cavalry brushed into them north of Winchester. The 31st Georgia held off an inquisitive band of Yankee cavalry coming into Middletown on the pike from the direction of Front Royal on July 1.

Brigadier General William Terry's Virginian brigade stumbled onto their first enemy about two miles from Martinsburg on July 3. Soon the Confederates fanned out toward Charlestown, Leetown, and Smithfield, and the expedition began to lose momentum. Early received a telegram from Lee on July 2 (the wires having been repaired behind the army as far as New Market), imploring him to remain in the Valley "until everything was in readiness to cross the Potomac and to destroy the Baltimore and Ohio Railroad and the Chesapeake and Ohio Canal" as far as possible. That re-direction caused delay, and suddenly too, the original eastward movement through Loudoun County to the Potomac seemed impractical.[14]

Meeting on July 2, with some of Lieutenant Colonel John Mosby's partisan rangers at Rectortown, just across the mountains to the east, Hugh Swartz, one of Early's quartermasters, learned that the locale lacked provisions for a large army. Swartz conveyed that information to Early at Winchester, whereupon the general decided (as he noted in his memoirs) that if he went through Mosby country, it "would have been necessary for me to halt and thresh wheat and have it ground, as neither bread nor flour could be otherwise obtained." That would occasion greater delay than if he kept straight north to the Potomac, taking provisions from the enemy and the countryside in Maryland, and getting on with Lee's instructions about the railroad and canal. Early was most conscious of the ability of that railroad to carry Federal reinforcements from the West either to relieve Washington or to harass his army's rear en route to the capital.[15]

After dark, Captain George W. Booth—a Marylander soon to be Bradley Johnson's cavalry brigade adjutant—located Mosby and informed him of Early's desire for cooperation. Notwithstanding the general's well known distaste for partisan cavalry, Mosby agreed to assist. The next day he concentrated some two hundred and fifty men and his newly acquired 12-pounder howitzer at Upperville. At mid-day they started to march towards the Potomac, plunder bags slung across their saddles. They bivouacked for the night near Purcellville, a village about ten miles west of Leesburg and only fifteen miles southwest of their objective. Dust and heat slowed the march, and just what role they would play in the Maryland campaign was unclear.

Early had promised Lee to hurry but a combination of circumstances conspired to make that impossible. One of Early's goals as he approached the Potomac was destruction of Major General Franz Sigel's reserve division guarding supply dumps as well as the Baltimore and Ohio Railroad. A revived Hunter, or any other Federal force in the area, could cut off Early's line of retreat using the railroad deployment. Early wasn't sure just where Hunter was at the moment, as he drew up plans to capture Sigel and destroy the rail link. Alarmed but undaunted by the advancing enemy force (nobody either in Washington or Grant's headquarters at City Point in the James River believed they were more than irregulars and other mounted raiders), Sigel's men, aided by Brigadier General Max Weber's contingent of infantry and cavalry shielding Harpers Ferry, managed to evacuate some warehouses, the rail yards, and other facilities just in time to escape capture. Other rear guard cavalry and infantry under Colonel James Mulligan and Brigadier General Julius Stahel kept Rodes, Ramseur and Johnson briefly at bay. While some people felt that the Federals had run off, Sigel and Weber really saved at least four trainloads of invaluable supplies and retired with only minor casualties to Maryland Heights across from Harpers Ferry after rendering the bridges impassable.[16]

Then Early's men succumbed to blandishments of an elated local populace, as well as festal boards provided by farsighted Federal quartermasters preparing Independence Day celebrations for their own soldiers at Martinsburg, Charlestown, and Harpers Ferry. Local diarists Luce Buck and Marcus Buck displayed their joy at Confederate "deliverance," while over at "Rose Hill" near Front Royal, young Nannie Buck, Julia Kiger, Bettie Wheatley, and Mary Richardson gathered to welcome passing Maryland Line cavalrymen only to find "not many called at the house." They were hurrying to close up with Early at Winchester. Countrymen stood all along the way with buttermilk, cold water, and all too often liquored punch in celebration. Junior officers hardly turned down pretty girls' offers of liquid refreshment, and Confederate surgeon and medical inspector, R. G. Coleman, complained irately after one frolic among the Yankee camps that "the soldiers in their unbridled license destroyed fifty times as much as they consumed." He blamed officers like Gordon for the disciplinary breakdown. So merrymaking combined with the heat and exhilaration over recent successes, as Early's force approached the Potomac crossings.[17]

The celebrations in abandoned Union camps and supply dumps went on all night of the Fourth. Of course, the Confederates felt entitled to it all. They had marched nearly two hundred miles since leaving the Richmond area. They had chased Hunter out of the Valley, then crossed that natural covered way northward, and had beaten a Federal garrison back from its supply cornucopia. Moreover, they seemed to be baffling the opposition much as Old Jack had done two years before. If Early had neither captured nor destroyed Hunter or Sigel, he was assuredly master of the Valley by the Fourth of July. What he had failed to do, of course, was to drive Sigel out of the direct line of passage to Washington. Lost in the confusion of the moment (and subsequently to many later students of the campaign), was the simple fact that Sigel and Weber now sat astride the main and direct route through Harpers Ferry to Frederick and the capital. Moreover, Early's force had probably lost several days' march toward that goal by those delays on the upper Potomac.

Early, himself, was acutely aware of that criticism, at least in retrospect. In his autobiography, he claimed that an examination of the facts from his narrative "will show that not one moment was spent in idleness, but that every one was employed in making some arrangement, or removing some difficulty in my way, which it was necessary to make or remove; so as to enable me to advance with a prospect of success." He particularly alluded to the problem posed by Sigel, stating that he could not cross the Potomac and the passes of South Mountain, until that Federal general "was driven from, or safely housed in," the Maryland Heights fortifications. What the Confederate leader failed to note was the delay occasioned by his own troops. Moreover, the cat was out of the bag. Federal authorities across the National Capital region began to suspect something more than a mere cavalry or guerilla raid was unfolding on the upper Potomac.[18]

Tardy Union Reaction

Lieutenant General Ulysses S. Grant, supreme commander of all the armies of the Union, for one, refused to believe that a major Confederate field force lay poised to cross the Potomac and invade Northern territory. As late as 5 P.M. on July 3, he wired Washington boldly: "Early's corps is now here. There are no troops that can now be threatening Hunter's department, except the remnant of the force W. E. Jones had, and possibly Breckinridge." That was the word brought by army scouts and Confederate deserters around Petersburg. Despite the telegraph link from Grant's headquarters at City Point, Virginia with the War Department in Washington, and from that central point to elsewhere in the field (whether upper Potomac or other theaters of operations), communication breakdowns were predictable. The fog of war generally hung thickly over all nineteenth-century military operations as a matter of course although faulty Union intelligence was as much to blame in this case. Furthermore, Grant had a plan of his own, and any unnecessary diversion or deviation from that scheme was not in his nature.[19]

Grant had been brought east in the winter of 1864 to take top command. Flushed with Western victories stretching from Forts Henry and Donelson two years before, through the capture of Vicksburg to the latest success the previous November at Chattanooga, Grant had his job cut out for him in the spring of 1864. President Abraham

Major General Henry Wager Halleck, U.S.A.

Chief of staff to the general-in-chief of all Union armies, he was most directly involved with planning and coordinating efforts to contain Jubal Early's 1864 invasion.

U.S. Army Military History Institute

Major General Franz Sigel, U.S.A.

Censured for a lackluster performance against Breckinridge at New Market in May 1864, he withdrew from the path of Early's invasion force at Martinsburg later that summer. But, his stand on Maryland Heights effectively denied the Confederates a direct route to the capital.

U.S. Army Military History Institute

Major General David Hunter, U.S.A.

A friend of Grant, and veteran of many campaigns, his conduct of war against civilians in the Shenandoah Valley drastically changed the tone of the war in the East. His burning and pillaging earned him the undying hatred of most Southerners and a grim determination by Early to exact retribution north of the Potomac in turn.

U.S. Army Military History Institute

Lincoln needed a winner in overall charge of Union land operations, and one who could work with the navy and the civilians in government. It was time to end the war, especially with an election in the fall, and with Peace Democrats and Copperheads becoming stronger and more militant. In short, the administration needed a unified and energetic military command structure, and Lincoln thought Grant was the man to achieve it. Shunning a desk in Washington where he would have been enmeshed in politics, Grant chose to accompany Major General George Gordon Meade's Army of the Potomac for the relentless pursuit of Lee, destruction of his army, and ultimate capture of the rebel capital, a mere 100 miles distant from Washington.[20]

That had proved to be a difficult 100 miles as the bloody spring campaign southward cost the Army of the Potomac 54,000 casualties in the Wilderness, at Spotsylvania, and on the North Anna River. In June, alone, an ill-fated frontal assault against well fortified Confederates at Cold Harbor slaughtered over 6,000 Union soldiers, which Grant claimed to rue the rest of his life. Grant, Meade, and a punch-drunk army really stood no closer to Richmond than had Major General George B. McClellan two years before. And that very same McClellan appeared headed toward the Democratic party's nomination for president in the 1864 elections. Then, on the same day that Lee had instructed Early to undertake his march to the Valley and beyond, Grant cut loose north of the James River, and moved his army to the south side, aiming to capture Lee's supply lines. Here was the task that focused Grant's attention. Raiders, partisans, and other diversions elsewhere had to be the responsibility of field commanders in those areas.

Not that Grant had been unaware of the role the Shenandoah Valley played in Confederate fortunes. Because he was new to the Eastern theater, he was hardly as sensitized to Lincoln's concern for the safety of Washington and the Valley's role as an invasion route north, as previous commanders of Eastern field forces had been. McClellan had lost his job, in part, over that issue. Meade should have briefed Grant, of course. Then too, he ought to have been counseled by Major General Henry Halleck, his predecessor as general-in-chief, as well as Secretary of War Edwin Stanton. "Old Brains," as Halleck was called, knew all about Grant from the West, and always harbored some suspicion as well as jealousy of his erstwhile subordinate's rapid rise to fame. As a professional officer, he accepted his own supplantation, and functioned as a chief of staff or go-between for Grant and other army commanders across the war-torn South. Thus, he should have made Grant acutely aware of the meaning of a rebel threat to the national capital region.[21]

Grant had set in motion the Sigel and Hunter thrusts to clear the Shenandoah and hold it, thereby implicitly protecting Washington as well as denying that breadbasket to the Confederacy. He delegated implementation to subordinates while he concentrated on overseeing Meade's task against Lee. It was Halleck's responsibility to keep matters sorted out in places like the Shenandoah and on the upper Potomac for his chief, just as he might do for other theaters of operations. Lincoln took himself out of the picture (probably much to the relief of long suffering generals), believing that Stanton, Halleck, and now Grant knew of his concerns and wishes and could forge the necessary team for military victory.[22]

Perhaps Grant was too confident that he could bring about a relatively quick victory to ponder the peninsula campaign of 1862 and McClellan's problems with Lincoln. He, like McClellan, had assured the president that sufficient protection would be left for the capital before the field army set off on its spring offensive. Indeed, well over 40,000 trained artillerists, infantrymen, and cavalry had been assigned to Major General Christopher Augur's Department of Washington, augmented by 789 heavy and 246 field guns early in 1864. Then, when the huge casualty lists sucked reserve troops from Washington's elaborate fortification system, Halleck had to remind Grant in early June that he had forwarded some 48,265 men from that department to reinforce the Army of the Potomac. June strength figures for the department still hovered at 33,289 officers and men. A large percentage of those were new convalescents and short-term state troops called "100-days men." They were quickly dubbed pejoratively "militia" by veterans (See Appendix 2).[23]

Lincoln remained loath to interfere as he had with McClellan. No Stonewall Jackson prowled the Valley this time, and everyone anticipated that Sigel and Hunter could accomplish the simple task of neutralizing the Shenandoah as a figure on the chessboard. That Sigel failed abysmally at New Market and then Hunter too seemed incapable of finishing the task at Lynchburg, hardly surprised Halleck. He had little confidence in many of the lesser Union generals, particularly politicians in uniform and those of foreign birth. Still, Old Brains hardly thought that those setbacks would evolve into a full blown Southern invasion to threaten Washington. There seemed to be a certain lethargy in the capital that summer generally, and one muses on whether or not Halleck's own personal disdain for Grant played some subtle role in the drama that was about to unfold.[24]

At least, the Union high command assumed that Hunter had remained in the upper Valley regrouping and consolidating previous gains after the Lynchburg failure. Then, by June 19, intelligence indicated that Confederates had reoccupied Lexington and Staunton, in Hunter's presumed rear. Halleck figured that the Federal force would have to retire through West Virginia. He and Grant then wasted another week speculating on Hunter's intentions, whereabouts, and line of retreat. Little was done to alert lower Valley reserve generals like Sigel or Max Weber, a pair of mediocre German emigré officers whose political value to the Lincoln administration for wooing fellow refugees far outshone their military prowess. Yet both of those Badeners had been soldiers in the old country, and so they turned to their own devices to receive whatever imprecise information was out there concerning Hunter's situation. On June 28, Grant wired Halleck to simply "put Gen. Hunter in a good place to rest" and as soon as possible start him for Charlottesville, east to the mountains "to destroy the Rail Road there effectively."[25]

Of course, this move was patently impossible, although nobody yet knew for sure that "Black Dave" (as soldiers liked to fashion Hunter after a head of hair so dark that it seemed to have been dyed), had taken himself off the playing field. Grant always retained a soft spot for Hunter, probably from early service under him in the West. Experienced and well trained at West Point, the sixty-two-year-old District of Columbia native was far too old for the ardors of field service. He had enjoyed a long army career, and had been one of Lincoln's early intimates. A bitter opponent of slavery, he became a thorn in the administration's side as he had tried to force independent emancipation, as well as recruitment of black troops. The Confederacy had even put a price on his head as a felon for such actions. Of course, his advocacy of harsh retaliation against civilians in the Valley had earned him further enmity. In some respects he simply offered something better than Sigel.[26]

At any rate, Grant was a little slipshod in how he monitored his subordinate's movements with the result that matters got out of hand in the two weeks following Lynchburg. The general-in-chief lost track of Hunter, the Valley situation, and a most dangerous Confederate force heading north to exploit the situation. The War Department was no better. The primitive intelligence services broke down, and the circuitous four-hundred-mile telegraph link (from Washington to Wilmington, Delaware, then down the Eastern Shore of Maryland and across the Chesapeake and the James to Grant's field headquarters at City Point, Virginia) did not help. Messages supposedly took only an hour to transit back and forth, but delays of three to six hours were not uncommon. At the early stages of the 1864 Valley crisis, it often seemed to take nine and one-half hours for Grant and Halleck to exchange wires.

Grant had to cross-check with Meade, and since their headquarters were not co-located, that also occasioned further delays. None of this was satisfactory for providing quick reaction in a crisis.

A smattering of reports from the upper Potomac noted increased rebel mounted activity, but as late as the twenty-ninth, Sigel sent word that his patrols had found no Confederate presence as far south as Cedar Creek near Strasburg. Then the situation changed dramatically. As Assistant Secretary Charles A. Dana recorded in his "recollections": "In the first days of July we began to get inquiries at City Point from Washington concerning the whereabouts of the Confederate generals Early and Ewell."[27]

One individual did not lose touch with the unfolding situation. He was not even an army officer but rather a prominent Baltimore citizen. A late evening telegram on June 29 from John Garrett, president of the Baltimore and Ohio Railroad, shocked the War Department with its contents. Rebel cavalry had struck his line and the telegraph near Martinsburg on the upper Potomac. Furthermore, said Garrett, Breckinridge and Ewell (who Garrett and others believed still commanded the Second Corps) were moving down the Valley in force, and "I am satisfied the operations and designs of the enemy in the Valley demand the greatest vigilance and attention." Stunned, Washington officials decided to await developments. Halleck always doubted skittish underlings like Sigel and Weber, although a man like Garrett warranted more attention. His railroad had been suffering under enemy operations since 1861. More dire news poured over the wires during the next several days.[28]

The Harpers Ferry region was a vital strategic point which commanded highway, rail, and canal passage through the mountains on the way to Washington. By July 2, Sigel and Weber reported quite accurately that at least three rebel divisions were headed their way, much too large an enemy force for his four Union infantry regiments plus 1,000 dismounted cavalry, and possibly another 1,800 mounted troopers, and several artillery batteries. Weber could contribute no more than 400 men of his own. Sigel soon learned too that no reinforcements would be forthcoming from Hunter's Army of West Virginia for another five or six days. So, the outnumbered pair had retired from Martinsburg and Harpers Ferry, dutifully informing the War Department of their actions.

Washington officials remained unimpressed by Sigel's wires, as Attorney General Edward Bates took the position that "Genl Segel [sic] got scared again, and incontenenly [sic] ran away from Martinsburg to Harper's Ferry and took safe refuge upon the Maryland heights." But, Halleck also dutifully informed Grant on the afternoon of July 1, that he had received various conflicting reports about conditions in the Valley, and observed: "It certainly would be good policy for [the Confederates] to destroy the Baltimore and Ohio Railroad, and make a raid in Maryland and Pennsylvania." Ironically, he fired off a telegram to

Hunter that same day, summoning the general to a Petersburg conference with Grant. At that moment, Hunter's footsore soldiers were recuperating beside the cooling waters of the Gauley River in distant West Virginia en route to the Ohio, and far out of touch.[29]

Sometime late on July 3, Halleck and Grant finally began to realize that something might be amiss in the Valley. The chief-of-staff particularly remembered the strategic importance of Harpers Ferry and how it had been forced to surrender ingloriously during the Antietam campaign in September 1862. To avoid a repetition of that disaster, Halleck sent forward three companies of extra artillery (perhaps 2,800 men) under Brigadier General Albion Howe to help Sigel and Weber defend the old arsenal town. Shortly after noon on Independence Day, Halleck wired Weber that everything should be prepared for the defense of his works, "and the first man who proposes a surrender or retreats should be hung." Halleck's wire reached Weber the next day, after he had evacuated the place.[30]

"It was time for the yearly 'skedaddle' which is as sure to come as Christmas itself," Corporal Charles Moulton of the 34th Massachusetts wrote his mother from the provost marshal's office at Harpers Ferry on July 18. According to that young newspaper printer, the Federals had parried thrusts all Independence Day before finally pulling back across the Potomac at dusk. Townspeople later told them that the small contingent of Confederates had looted the saloons and stores of the town, concentrating their wrath upon any Unionist property in the area. All that night Yankee cannon boomed shots from Maryland Heights on to sharpshooters and the celebrating Confederates in Bolivar and Harpers Ferry. Drunkenness prevented systematic pillaging and burning, but a lot of Federal property went up in smoke before Early's men departed.[31]

Howe's contingent arrived just in time to be bottled up with the rest on top of Maryland Heights. For a time the telegraph had gone dead. Weber and Sigel had lost touch with one another as the Southerners massed at Martinsburg and before Harpers Ferry. Mosby had determined that he could best assist Early's moves by attacking Federal communications downstream at Point of Rocks, which he did with 250 rangers and one cannon on the Fourth. Tension ran high until mid-evening that day, when Weber and Sigel finally linked forces. Still Mosby's actions further confused the already faulty Union intelligence that was passed on to Washington. Halleck advised Grant obliquely that conditions remained unclear, and that he had directed Hunter back to the line of the B & O but had received no reply. Of those officers on the ground the German-American pair, Sigel and Weber, as well as the Hungarian-American cavalry commander, Major General Julius Stahel, Henry Halleck damned with sarcasm by adding, "You can, therefore, judge what probability there is of a good defense if the enemy should attack the line in force." Ironically, Stahel had but recently distinguished himself in the little battle of Piedmont, further up the Valley, where on June 5, the Confederate force under Brigadier General William E. "Grumble" Jones had been routed and its commander slain. Stahel, hitherto regarded as merely an Hungarian dancing master and foreign poseur for hesitant action at New Market, would secure the Congressional Medal of Honor for his Piedmont deeds in 1893, twenty years after Halleck was in his grave.[32]

In any event, Halleck's wire to Grant was dispatched at 4 P.M., on July 3. It passed in transit Grant's 5 P.M. telegram (quoted earlier) that proclaimed Early was still in the Petersburg trenches. Even more bothersome than such erroneous information was Grant's opening line which suggested that Halleck, not he, was in a better position to direct Sigel's actions. Literally true, it displayed a disturbing disregard for the Valley's impact on what was going on before Richmond-Petersburg. Sometime later, however, Grant also began to have second thoughts and inquired of Meade, whence the intelligence had come about Early's supposed return to the Petersburg trenches from Lynchburg. Meade's answer proved marginally satisfying, and Grant remained unconcerned until the afternoon of Monday, Independence Day, when another deserter suggested that, indeed, Early's force had not returned from Lynchburg at all, "but is off in the Valley with the intention of going into Maryland and Washington City."[33]

Admitting that this was just the word of one deserter but that it was apparent that Early (or Ewell, for they persisted in ascribing the command to that Confederate general) was not in the lines, Grant directed Halleck to concentrate all possible forces about Washington, Baltimore, Cumberland, and Harpers Ferry, "ready to concentrate against any advance of the enemy...." Ever ready to take the initiative away from the enemy, Grant wanted subordinates on the scene to go on the offensive. Halleck did not receive Grant's wire until the morning of the Fourth. That afternoon he got to work, not with actions, but rather with suggestions and more observations, worthy of a staff officer but not the man of action apparently desired by Grant.

Official Washington continued to publicly expound the line that the situation was confusing but suggestive only of a cavalry or partisan raid. Halleck even told Grant as much. Yet he also noted that Maryland was virtually defenseless if this was truly anything more than a mounted raid. "As you are aware, we have almost nothing in Baltimore or Washington, except militia, and considerable alarm has been created by sending troops from these places to re-enforce Harpers

Ferry," he thought. Invalids and militia "are not of a character suitable for the field," although Halleck quickly added that he had no apprehension for the safety of Washington, Baltimore, Harpers Ferry, or Cumberland, since "if Washington and Baltimore should be so seriously threatened as to require your aid I will inform you in time."[34]

Thinking that Grant must have a large force of dismounted cavalry on hand since horses had worn out quicker than men in the recent campaign, Halleck advised that it be sent to Washington at once, for it could be remounted by "impressing horses in the parts of Maryland likely to be overrun by the enemy." At the very least, it would keep those steeds from falling to the rebels, although he did not say so to Grant. That veteran force could then be sent out confidently against the raiders. Grant's positive response noted that all the Army of the Potomac's dismounted cavalry plus Brigadier General James B. Ricketts's division of the VI Corps would depart City Point via steamer for Baltimore. He could send a whole corps if necessary, but the situation did not seem to require it, Grant privately told Meade when directing the 5,000 infantry and 3,000 dismounted cavalry northward. "We want now to crush out and destroy any force the enemy dares send north," proclaimed the general-in-chief boldly. On July 5, Hunter finally surfaced by communicating with Halleck from Parkersburg, West Virginia on the Ohio River. Grant, Halleck, and the rest realized that it was a race as to which side could get into position first for the contest over Maryland and the capital region.[35]

* * * *

Uncertainty and anxiety suddenly prevailed in Washington City. There had been hopes that Grant might successfully sortie at Petersburg in honor of the national holiday, but nothing happened. The heat and dust choked any enthusiasm for celebration in a city grown callous to war and patriotic sacrifice. A recent accident at the Washington arsenal cartridge factory had killed seventeen young women workers and disfigured others. So celebration took place only on the White House grounds where the city's African-Americans had been given permission to have their Sunday school picnic. The prosperous city Blacks arrived in all their finery. "Very quietly and decently behaved," was the way presidential secretary John Hay saw them, "but outside the grounds sat the underclass of the locale—contrabands in butternut, aliens and inferiors."[36]

The next day, the Navy Department hung out a large flag in honor of a sea victory. The USS *Kearsarge* had sunk the high seas raider CSS *Alabama* off Cherbourg in France. Then, that event too passed into memory as, with Congress in adjournment, residents prepared to depart on summer holiday. Out in the suburbs at Silver Spring, the family of old newsman and political confidant, Francis Preston Blair, prepared to leave for the Jersey shore. They had heard troublesome rumors about rebels on the upper Potomac and wondered what that portended for their neighborhood. Montgomery Blair was Lincoln's postmaster general, and together with his father, they had two adjoining farms out the Seventh street road that stood in direct line with any force coming toward the city from the north.[37]

If the fighting before Petersburg had slowed, political in-fighting at the capital had not. The city buzzed with gossip during the final days of the congressional session. President Lincoln had finally maneuvered his political rival, and secretary of the treasury, Salmon P. Chase, out of the cabinet. Chase had resigned in a huff before, with Lincoln always persuading him to remain. Everyone was caught by surprise when, this time, the president accepted his resignation. Maine senator William Pitt Fessenden succeeded Chase on July 1. The chief executive also signed several revenue measures including broadening the base of the income tax. There were public land and railroad bills from Congress requiring his attention, but on Independence Day he pocket-vetoed a harsh reconstruction bill that gave more power and initiative to the legislative branch rather than the presidency in the important area of restoring comity to a shattered land once the war had ended.[38]

Still, most people in the country had focused on Lincoln's chances in the upcoming elections and Grant's unending casualty lists from Petersburg. Lincoln suspended the privilege of the writ of habeas corpus, and proclaimed martial law in Kentucky on July 5. He claimed that many citizens of the border state had joined or helped the "forces of the insurgents." Of the situation in upper Maryland nobody knew or would admit much, as Secretary of the Navy Gideon Welles discovered when he visited the war department the next day. The city and administration slumbered on, awaiting developments. At that very moment, Jubal Early's men began crossing the Potomac at Shepherdstown ten miles upriver from Harpers Ferry. The water felt cool and refreshing, a welcome palliative to the carousing of the previous day and recent hot marches. It remained to be seen how the Old Line state—a borderland like Kentucky—would react to a third Confederate visit.[39]

TWO

The Third Confederate Invasion

Boteler's Ford near Sharpsburg, Maryland witnessed a third passage of Confederate soldiers in as many years on July 5, 1864. This time, however, while someone in the ranks took up the strains of "Maryland, My Maryland," the welcoming citizenry did not turn out, and Southern hearts beat less quickly with anticipation. On September 8, 1862, Colonel Bradley T. Johnson in Confederate gray had beseeched his fellow Marylanders to remember the cells of Fort McHenry and the dungeons of Forts Lafayette and Warren where Maryland secessionists had been incarcerated; the insults to wives and daughters, the arrests, and the midnight searches of houses by Federal authorities. "Remember then your wrongs, and rise at once in arms and strike for Liberty and Right," he had cried. Brigadier General Johnson didn't repeat that call in 1864. This time John Worsham of the 21st Virginia remembered only that sharp stones in the river bed "stuck in my feet at every step." Perhaps it was symbolic. Something seemed simply more perfunctory, almost dutiful, about that passage. No one really expected a wild reception in the Old Line state, and none was given. North and South alike had grown tired of soldiers and war.[1]

Destruction on the Upper Potomac

Unable to bag the blueclad defenders of Martinsburg and Harpers Ferry, Confederate officers had indulged their men's desire to sample the enemy's Fourth of July feasts, ransack the Martinsburg warehouses, and disable B & O railroad facilities. Thus, they sacrificed valuable time. Federal authorities had been alerted; relief

25

columns set in motion, and the initiative lost. Or, so it might have seemed. Jubal Early knew that time was precious. David Hunter might slip into his rear, and he still had to deal with Franz Sigel and Max Weber on Maryland Heights if he wanted to gain the most direct route to Washington. Stragglers had to be gathered in, convalescents returned to the ranks, and guards left for the caches of captured stores. Five companies of the 38th Georgia, "the Tom Cobb Infantry," they called themselves, served the latter purpose, but there was much to be done by everyone.[2]

Then, sometime on the afternoon of July 6, Captain Robert E. Lee, the general's son and namesake, rode into camp on the outskirts of Sharpsburg, and presented Early with a new wrinkle. Richmond superiors wanted the expeditionary force commander to detach a cavalry raiding force for a fast strike around Baltimore and Washington, and to cooperate with a naval expedition being sent to free prisoners at the Yankee prison pen at Point Lookout, where the Potomac entered Chesapeake Bay. One can imagine Early's profane response! Here he was miles from friendly territory, well embarked, but nowhere close, to his principal target of Washington. Suddenly, the government had come up with some scheme to march an additional one hundred miles beyond the capital to free prisoners! Of course, Lee desperately needed the 10–12,000 captured soldiers incarcerated at Point Lookout. Here were enough men to re-form a whole corps. Early recognized that fact. But, military logic suggested the impracticality if not outright impossibility of doing too many things with too few resources. Still, Old Jube was obligated to make the attempt.[3]

Concerned always about dwindling ranks—some of the men were dropping off constantly to visit family or friends, forage the countryside, or seek temporary relief from the dust and heat at farm wells and creeks—Early issued strict orders about such actions. In particular, he wanted no plundering or marauding on Maryland soil. The Confederates had always been very scrupulous about this in the past. The general instructed that Confederate currency or certificates of impressment would be used to pay for transactions. This assumed, of course, that recipients would accept such dubious forms of payment. But, that would be the Yankees' problem; Confederate officers and men would stand above reproach. In principle, at least, such measures would discourage pillaging, looting, and confiscation. On the other hand, some of the army's actions already augured ill in this respect.[4]

Brigadier General John Imboden's horsemen tried to disable the Baltimore and Ohio Railroad at Martinsburg before crossing the Potomac. And, they ranged upriver into the Maryland panhandle

Brigadier General John McCausland, C.S.A.

Perpetrator of the burning of Chambersburg,
Pennsylvania under Early's orders, his actions
reflected a decided turn in the war in the Eastern
theater.

West Virginia Department of Culture and History

Pillaging at Hagerstown

Early's Army of the Valley District wasted valuable time pillaging Union supply
dumps and creating general mayhem in honor of the national independence day
on the upper Potomac River.

Harper's Pictorial History of the Great Rebellion (1866), vol. II, p. 708.

under Major General Robert Ransom's orders. They did a commendable job cutting bridges, and destroying other railroad facilities all the way to Hancock, with particular success between Martinsburg and Harpers Ferry. Early always harbored mistrust of the forty-one-year-old lawyer and political figure who hailed from Staunton. He and his men clearly reflected the pernicious influence of "buttermilke [sic] rangers," in Old Jube's eyes. But, more like Mosby's partisan rangers than regular cavalry, they were most effective when raiding Union communications. Before Imboden took temporarily ill during Early's raid, his men were well on their way to repeating their previous year's success at wrecking the B & O. Meanwhile Major General John B. Gordon's infantry waged an equally fine campaign against the Chesapeake and Ohio canal's aqueduct over Antietam Creek, and they also burned barges that carried coal and other commodities down to Washington. The Antietam Iron Works also suffered demolition.

Ostensibly legitimate military targets, these facilities were still private property, so Hunter wasn't the only commander guilty of escalating the stakes to wage total war. In addition, Early sent Brigadier General John McCausland's troopers off to Hagerstown with specific directions to ransom that town for $200,000 and provide Early protection against any Federal interference from Pennsylvania. Their vanguard under Lieutenant George M. E. Shearer, Company A, 1st Maryland, engaged portions of a company of the 6th U.S. Cavalry under Lieutenant Hancock T. McLean, sent from Carlisle Barracks, Pennsylvania to resist rebel advances into the Cumberland Valley. McLean's troopers soon departed for the state line, as the Washington *Star* dismissed the Hagerstown altercation merely as "a bogus Harrisburg report."[5]

As it was, McCausland secured $20,000 from Hagerstown officials, the next day, despite problems with a misplaced decimal in his demand. But here again was something different from attacking military targets. True, the local Union quartermaster had fled north to Pennsylvania, leaving bulging warehouses, and the grayclad troopers quickly ravaged that facility. But, they also demanded 1,500 suits, pairs of shoes or boots, shirts, pairs of socks, and underdrawers from the citizenry. These items were to be delivered within four hours, or they would burn the town. Local banks raised the money—$10,000 from the Hagerstown Bank, while the Hagerstown Savings Bank and Washington County Bank of Williamsport chipped in $5,000 each. Business establishments partially supplied the clothing, although not enough and further hard negotiations were necessary to prevent the rebels from carrying out their threat. The raiders finally left town at dusk, headed for Boonsboro with 243 coats, 203 pairs of pants, 132 pairs of underdrawers, 737 pairs of stockings, 99 pairs of boots,

123 pairs of shoes, 830 hats, 225 shirts, 1,370 and one-half yards of piece goods, and "clothing, 70 pieces ass'd" which meant that Tiger Jack's mounted crew looked more like a traveling circus than a military outfit.

The next day more butternut outriders revisited Hagerstown, without incident, to be followed on July 8 by some 180 guerillas who pilfered more hat and shoe stores, set fire to government hay and the Franklin railroad depot and were about to destroy large quantities of oats and corn belonging to the U.S. government (stored in private warehouses). Citizens remonstrated with them, claiming they had fulfilled McCausland's demands, and that satiated the latest rebel thirst for destruction. Still, the irregulars forced Isaac Nesbitt, clerk of the court to post a $100,000 bond that the citizens would remove the grain and burn it themselves. The marauders made off with ten pairs of boots before finally leaving town. That evening blueclad cavalry reoccupied Hagerstown.[6]

From Shepherdstown to Williamsport, from Hagerstown to Sharpsburg and Boonsboro, druggist goods, hats, shoes, and other private stores—and, in several cases, more cash—departed with Early's Confederates or outriders. Despite the general's strictures, the perpetrators created great mayhem all over this part of western Maryland and vicinity. They called it retribution for Hunter's actions in the Shenandoah Valley. The propaganda value of their actions exceeded its practical value alone. Panicky reports about rebel depredations filled the Valley all the way to Pennsylvania. St. James College near Hagerstown conferred its degrees at an abbreviated commencement devoid of speeches. Citizens nearby were robbed of valuables; hundreds of men, women, and children filled the roads to Pennsylvania while farmers once again drove livestock to the mountains.[7]

Merchants from Chambersburg, Shippensburg, and Carlisle locked their doors and shipped goods and valuables to safety beyond the Susequehanna River in the central part of the state. Chambersburg declared a state of martial law and required passes to travel beyond city limits. The railroad shops there were stripped of machinery and taken to safety, while every northbound train likewise filled with refugees. Military quartermasters either abandoned their stores or frantically tried to dispatch them northward also. African-Americans hung close to government troops for protection, although, for the moment, Early's men were more concerned with remaining Yankee fighting forces on the upper Potomac, not in Pennsylvania.[8]

Early desperately wanted to repeat Stonewall Jackson's feat of capturing the entire garrison at Harpers Ferry just like two years before, but could not. Despite impressions such as those of Brigadier

General William Terry that during the day of July 6, "the march was somewhat retarded by a feeble resistence on the part of the enemy," reconnaissance of the Maryland Heights positions, and some heavy skirmishing told Early that he must push on, bypassing Sigel and Weber entirely. And so he did, for by July 7, his men were in motion on the hardpanned roadways via Keedysville, Boonsboro (also, apparently ransomed), Rohrersville, and Jefferson. Their immediate goal lay with those familiar South Mountain passes to the east. Frederick would be the next objective where the army could then gain the main highway to Washington.[9]

New shoes finally arrived (some via wagons Early had left behind to bring them forward once they reached railheads in the Valley from Richmond depots, probably some even from captured Federal warehouses). Now Old Jube felt more secure that his well-shod soldiers could finish the arduous trek to Washington. Yet, other obstacles persisted. Outriders increasingly encountered irate local farmers who objected to yielding their cattle and horses to the invaders, even under payment.

Seventy-year-old George Blessing at Highland, three miles east of Myersville, would prove to be one such burr under rebel saddles. Defying rebel overtures to surrender livestock and provender, Blessing, his son and two black laborers "bushwhacked" one band vowing to "let them see that there is one man who will stick to his house and defend it at all hazards." Such pluck earned Blessing subsequent fame in the pages of the New York *Tribune* as " The Hero of the Highland," to which Blessing snorted, " what nonsense, if they mean me!"[10]

At times, Early's passage took on more the appearance of a supply-gathering expedition, than a lightning move against an enemy capital. Part of Colonel Henry Cole's independent Maryland (Union) cavalry briefly stymied Confederate brigadier W. L. "Mudwall" Jackson's advance party near Keedysville, before Confederate infantry came up to stiffen the buttermilk rangers' resolve. Then, Lieutenant Colonel Harry Gilmor's portion (2d Battalion Maryland C.S.A.) of Brigadier General Bradley T. Johnson's cavalry ran into even more stubborn Yankee opposition just east of Middletown. This hamlet bridled at paying any more than $1,500 to the rebels, and Early's men soon received an additional surprise. Federal contingents from yet another military department had now entered the drama being played out in verdant Pleasant Valley. In any case, the threat they posed prevented rebel collection of any additional tribute from the outlying election district around Middletown.[11]

A Railroad President and His Bridge

The first countermoves to contain the Confederate raiding force had already been set in motion by the time Early's army splashed across the Potomac. President John Garrett of the Baltimore and Ohio was not a man to be trifled with. Scion of the Baltimore banking house of Robert Garrett and Sons, he had been educated at Lafayette College in Easton, Pennsylvania before passing into the family firm. Physically imposing, although suave in business manner, the burly railroad executive had carefully guided the B & O through prewar expansion into the midwestern markets. Avowedly pro-Southern at the time of the John Brown incident in 1859, Garrett had proclaimed his railroad "a Southern line" to fellow Baltimoreans in the heat of that moment. He subsequently became identified with Border state compromise as the nation moved to the brink of war two years later. Then, caught between the contending armies, his company suffered greatly from the war itself. In fact, on September 7, 1862, Confederates destroyed the center span of his bridge across the Monocacy near Frederick as well as the nearby turnpike bridge on the road to Washington. Still, the B & O remained a linchpin in the overall strategic communications of the Union.* Rapid transport of two Union army corps from Virginia to Tennessee in the fall of 1863 enabled the Lincoln government to keep the latter state from slipping back into the Confederate column. One of Lincoln's confidants, Garrett became acutely sensitized to Early's activities in the valley in June, and was among the first individuals to take action.[12]

Not only had the railroad president wired Washington twice on July 3 about events on the upper Potomac, and their threatened impact on his line, but, he had visited local Baltimore headquarters of Middle Department and VIII Corps commander, Major General Lew Wallace, the day before and requested action. As Wallace remembered the facts years later, he had come to appreciate the railroader's official calls "as significant of important business," and he braced himself accordingly. At this point, Wallace, too, knew nothing of events in the Shenandoah much less Hunter's repulse at Lynchburg two weeks before. Suddenly, he had standing before him one of the state's most prominent citizens asking for action—a citizen personally known to and trusted by Lincoln, with access to the administration in Washington, and a man prominent in the region.

---

* The original Monocacy railroad bridge was a wooden span 350 feet long, 24 feet wide and 38 feet above the water. It had three wooden arched deck trusses, rested on stone abutments, and piers reflected the well-known skills of its builder, German born and American trained Louis Wernwag, according to James D. Dilts, *The Great Road* (Stanford, 1993), pp. 80, 148.

32

John W. Garrett, President of the Baltimore and Ohio Railroad

The threat to his railroad by Early's raid prompted him to solicit aid from Lew Wallace at Baltimore and alert Washington authorities to the dangers of Confederate invasion.

Courtesy Maryland Historical Society

Major General Lewis "Lew" Wallace, U.S.A.

Veteran commander of the Middle Department-VIII Corps, Wallace sought to block Early's advancing army at Monocacy, and to gain time for reinforcements to reach Washington's forts. He also saw this as a way to redeem his own lost fortunes after tactical mistakes at Shiloh.

U.S. Army Military History Institute

Brigadier General Erastus Barnard Tyler, U.S.A.

Veteran commander of a brigade in Wallace's army and assigned to defend the Stone or Jug bridge which carried the National Road eastward from Frederick across the Monocacy River.

U.S. Army Military History Institute

Monocacy Railroad Bridge—July 1863

Shown here in a sketch by wartime artist Alfred Waud, the Baltimore and Ohio bridge across the Monocacy had been damaged by Confederates during the Antietam campaign two years before, but repaired to keep open the invaluable east-west supply route for national armies.

Courtesy Prints and Photographs Division, Library of Congress

34

Early's Confederates Sacking a Flour Mill

Harper's Pictorial History of the Great Rebellion (1866), vol. II, p. 708.

Early's Confederates Cutting the Chesapeake and Ohio Canal

Harper's Pictorial History of the Great Rebellion (1866), vol. II, p. 707.

Frederick Junction or Monocacy Station—1858

Courtesy Baltimore and Ohio Railroad Museum and Maryland Historical Society

**Post-Civil War Restored Covered Bridge on Washington Turnpike
across Monocacy River at Monocacy Junction**

Courtesy Baltimore and Ohio Railroad Museum, Baltimore, Maryland

**Stone or "Jug" Bridge—National Road Crossing over Monocacy
River East of Frederick, Maryland**

Marken and Bielfeld, Souvenir of Historic Frederick (1925), p. 20.

So, the general listened attentively as Garrett explained how his station agents between Harpers Ferry and Cumberland had notified him of the appearance of rebel detachments, and how such happenings in the past had been a forerunner of trouble.

Such events, in turn, had always impacted upon Washington's safety, Garrett implied, and the railroadman expressed his apprehensions about that poorly defended city. Couldn't Wallace and the Department of Washington's commander, Major General Christopher C. Augur, "unite in looking after the district of country between Harpers Ferry and Monocacy Junction?" he asked. Wallace felt that Garrett's anxiety related to an area beyond Wallace's jurisdiction, that extended only to the Monocacy River, just east of Frederick, and he told him so.* However, the mogul was more immediately concerned about his expensive, iron truss railroad bridge across that very stream. Wallace murmured that he had no cavalry to explore the situation beyond the mountains, and certainly could not impinge upon Hunter's department. Still, the presence of his blockhouse and its garrison on the eastern bank of the Monocacy just before the railroad bridge assured guardianship "of the structure from my end of it to the other." Therefore, said Wallace, Garrett's bridge would not be yielded without a fight. It was all spoken of very lightly, Wallace recalled forty years later when writing his memoirs: "I had not the faintest idea of ever being called upon to make the undertaking good."[13]

Garrett, for his part, took Wallace's promise much more seriously. He told the War Department the following afternoon that: "I have seen General Wallace, who states he can give no aid to Harper's Ferry, but will at once send the regiment of Maryland 100-days' men to strengthen the line at Monocacy and vicinity." Wallace, in fact, dispatched a more reliable reserve corps unit, the Third Maryland Potomac Home Brigade. He recalled later how serious and intense Garrett seemed to be, especially about Washington. Both men had agreed that the city's formal fortifications were tremendous, "with only a few post-guards to take care of them," as the general termed

---

*   Whatever Wallace's reason—desire to help Garrett, wish for combat glory or determination to retrieve a shattered reputation by once again commanding in the field, even the desire to protect Unionist citizens and government supply and hospital facilities in Frederick—once he reached the scene on the Monocacy, Wallace may have exceeded his authority at the time and pushed portions of his command some ten to fifteen miles beyond his jurisdictional boundaries. See Frank J. Welcher, *The Union Army: Organization and Operations, Volume I: the Eastern Theater* (Bloomington, 1989), pp. 18–19; Raphael P. Thian (John M. Carroll, editor), *Notes Illustrating the Military Geography of the United States, 1813–1880* (Austin and London, 1979 edition), pp. 91, 104.

them. He and a colleague had attempted the previous year to tour the whole system of forts that girded the city, but had only progressed from Alexandria upstream to Chain Bridge before tiring and adjourning "for oysters and coffee." It was public knowledge in 1864, said Wallace, that scarcely eight or nine thousand uninstructed garrison troops plus a melange of invalids and supply or administrative clerks in the city were all that was available to defend the place. So, Washington, if truly threatened as Garrett feared, was clearly incapable of defending itself. Still, Wallace wondered, could Washington be in danger, and if so, from whom? Thinking Hunter and Sigel surely had the situation well in hand, and would so inform the War Department should serious threat develop, Wallace tried to dismiss the matter. Frankly, thought the Baltimore commander, whatever the true situation, "it was not at all likely to reach and involve me or my department."[14]

Fresh information tweaked Wallace's further interest the next morning—July 3. Inquiring from an aide as to news of Hunter, Wallace was amazed to learn that newspapers had the West Virginia department commander located in the Kanawha Valley, thus opening the Shenandoah to enemy exploitation. Wallace and this aide, Lieutenant Colonel Samuel B. Lawrence, then spent the rest of the morning mobilizing the small forces "from the Monocacy River to the Chesapeake Bay, and beyond to the sea, with Delaware," for possible combat duty. "The operation was like gleaning in a lean field a second and third time," considering the small number of troops left by Grant for what should have been mere police duties in these two border states. About all the two men could muster were the 3d Maryland Regiment, Potomac Home Brigade, the 11th Maryland, seven companies of the 149th Ohio National Guard, three companies of the 144th Ohio National Guard, four companies of the 1st Maryland Regiment, Potomac Home Brigade, and a six-gun Maryland light artillery battery. The total force numbered scarcely 2,300 men.[15]

Wallace's units were clearly three-year volunteer regiments or 100-days contingents, but not militia. True, most of them had not seen a major battle, although the 1st Regiment Potomac Home Brigade had been at Gettysburg on July 2 and 3, 1863, the Baltimore Independent Battery Light Artillery had fought earlier in the Valley during that same campaign, and both the 1st and 3d Regiments Potomac Home Brigade had been captured at Harpers Ferry during the Antietam campaign. The latter had also seen minor action in western Virginia, and the artillery unit had also been captured at Winchester during Lee's march northward in June 1863. Otherwise, the two Ohio units had been organized only in May, the 11th Maryland scarcely two weeks before the news of Early's raid reached

Baltimore. Everyone had spent some time on railroad guard duty somewhere on the Baltimore and Ohio, or in the defenses of Balti-more, or elsewhere in the department. Yet, how would they fare against Army of Northern Virginia veterans on a major battlefield?[16]

Nevertheless, when additional intelligence filtered into Baltimore headquarters after lunch, Wallace ordered the first elements of his force westward via the B & O to Monrovia, not far from Monocacy junction, as a precautionary measure. Brigadier General Erastus B. Tyler, who commanded Wallace's first brigade at Relay House (where the Washington line branched off from the main line just south of Baltimore), took charge of the expedition. The forty-two-year-old Ohioan was a veteran of campaigns in western Virginia as well as Jackson's valley campaign in 1862. He had seen heavy action as a brigade commander at Fredericksburg and Chancellorsville, before being relegated to garrison duty at Baltimore at the end of June in 1863. Wallace was actually only staging his forward command at this time, for Tyler merely took the 3d Regiment Potomac Home Brigade with three days' rations and one hundred rounds of ammunition per man with him. The 11th Maryland replaced these troops at Relay House. Arriving at Monrovia, Tyler would further advance two com-panies to Monocacy Junction to construct rifle pits and improve the blockhouse defense against the as yet mysterious force rampaging on the railroad to the west. Tyler's mission was mainly one of prepa-ration and observation. Meanwhile, Wallace back at Baltimore is-sued additional instructions to subordinates from Annapolis to Dela-ware to be ready to send forward reinforcements at anytime. He also queried Department of Pennsylvania commander, Major General Darius M. Couch, as to information about Sigel, Weber, and others since the telegraph to Harpers Ferry seemed to be down. This done, "there was nothing for me to do but await developments," Wallace recorded in his memoirs.[17]

Wallace, like other Union commanders in the capital region, spent Independence Day glued to maps, studying strength reports, waiting and worrying. He dutifully sent numerous telegrams to Wash-ington, passing along Sigel's information about the situation and underscoring the seriousness of the situation. He received no re-plies. Wallace, like Franz Sigel and Max Weber, stood in poor repute at the War Department. Left to ponder and fret in his hot Baltimore office, he received additional word by Independence Day evening that the German generals had retired from Martinsburg and Harpers Ferry to Maryland Heights. Perhaps, thought Wallace, it might be propi-tious to personally join Tyler and establish a forward headquarters on the Monocacy. No stranger to combat, this Indiana native wanted to regain lost field command as well as favor in Washington.[18]

Wallace had served creditably in the Mexican War. He entered Hoosier politics and became a state legislator as well as state adjutant general. He raised a crack Zouave regiment at the onset of the Civil War, advancing to general officer rank based on his citizen-soldier abilities and political position. Then, however, his military career took a twist. He had saved Brigadier General Ulysses S. Grant's own budding fortunes by stymieing a rebel sortie at Fort Donelson in February 1862, thus forcing the post's surrender the following morning. Thereafter, petty jealousy of Wallace and a desire to shield their chief on the part of Grant's personal headquarters staff had intruded. Two months later, a misunderstanding of orders and a misturn at Shiloh gave Grant and an ungrateful War Department the opportunity to exile the Hoosier to administrative posts at Cincinnati and later at Baltimore. Serving capably in both assignments, Wallace nevertheless chafed to return to combat. He wanted to lead men in battle. He greatly feared that Secretary of War Edwin M. Stanton ("my implacable enemy," he called him), Major General Henry Halleck (who thought it "but little better than murder to give important commands to such men as Wallace") and a Republican administration were out to sack him. It did not help that he was a non-West Pointer, and that his political identity lay with the Democratic party even though the Lincoln government desperately needed all the Democratic support it could muster in the Old Northwest.[19]

Then, suddenly, fortune had smiled on the Hoosier when Lincoln sent him to command the Middle Department, largely to whip the wavering border state into line via military authority in time for the April 1864 primary. Abolition of slavery and Lincoln's reelection also needed to be assured there, Stanton told him bluntly, and when Wallace took charge at his Eutaw House headquarters in unruly Baltimore, he flatly declared: "Rebels and traitors have no political rights whatever." Hard enforcement of enfranchisement rules delivered Maryland into the Union column, Lincoln was pleased, and Wallace continued his clamp-down including an ill-fated attempt to confiscate all rebel property. The president put a stop to that, but Wallace shared the platform at the opening of the state fair on April 18 with Lincoln and Governor August Bradford, thus appearing as part of the administration's inner circle so far as Marylanders were concerned. When Wallace declined to speak at the festivities on the grounds that it was his function to fight, not to speak, Lincoln rejoindered that he "might soon get up a big fight for Wallace." Little did either of them realize that fight lay only months away.[20]

Lew Wallace surreptitiously slipped out of Baltimore aboard a special engine provided by his friend John Garrett, just after midnight, on July 5. The War Department knew nothing of his departure. He wanted it that way. Racing through the hot July darkness, and accompanied only by his personal aide, Major James R. Ross, the general reached Monocacy Junction, just across the strategic bridge, without incident. Alighting from the locomotive's cab, the pair dashed down "a soldier's breakfast," and prepared to evaluate the situation at first light. What Wallace soon discovered was a beautiful landscape of gently flowing river, rich farmland, and fields "golden with wheat just ready for the reaper." It was all reminiscent of some western prairie, he recalled later. The spires of Frederick in the distance caught his eye, and even at the time, Wallace shuddered at the thought of shattering such peaceful bliss with any notion of battle.

Wallace also quickly saw the attractiveness of the immediate terrain for a defensive battle. In addition to Garrett's railroad bridge, about two miles upstream lay a solid highway stone bridge—locally styled "the Jug Bridge" (from the huge demijohn that guarded its entrance)—that carried the famous National Turnpike east to Baltimore. One blockhouse on the east bank mounted a howitzer variously described as a 12- and 24-pounder, while a second smaller brass piece on a platform provided extra firepower. Perhaps a quarter-mile downstream from the junction lay a weather-beaten, wooden covered bridge across the Monocacy that bore the turnpike from Frederick to Washington. A second blockhouse guarded the approach to the covered bridge near the junction. More immediately, Wallace realized that he needed to concentrate his available troops, prepare his position, and, especially, reconnoiter the area to the west beyond Catoctin Mountain whence came news of the invaders. Then he must await the advance of those legions so as to ascertain their intended direction, whether to Baltimore or Washington. At least, he was now physically on the scene, and in a position to personally guard Garrett's railroad bridge. He did not inform the War Department of his presence, however, only that he had sent men forward. "I am doing all I can to concentrate my command," was the way a telegram on July 4 to Henry Halleck phrased it.[21]

Concentrating the Defenders

Assistant Secretary of War Charles A. Dana wired his civilian superior in Washington late in the afternoon of July 4, from Grant's headquarters at City Point, Virginia, that a Virginia deserter confirmed that Ewell's (Early's) corps had gone into Maryland. Momentarily, Grant wired Halleck the same information with the advice "to hold all of the forces you can about Washington, Baltimore, Cumberland, and Harper's Ferry, ready to concentrate against any advance of the enemy." That was precisely what Halleck, in a rather muddled sort of way, was attempting to do. In order to orchestrate or coordinate all of the diverse array of possible players—Hunter, somewhere to the west, Wallace at Baltimore, the Sigel-Weber concentration at Harpers Ferry, and Major General Darius Couch in Pennsylvania—Halleck attempted via the telegraph to erect a sort of cordon or blockage. More immediately, he prepared to send forward packets of reinforcement from Washington to Harpers Ferry, failing to realize that the Jubal Early's fast moving expeditionary force would quickly render such movements ineffectual. Still, such action would pour more bluecoats into the upper Potomac region, to be collected by Hunter for eventual combat against the raiders.[22]

Brigadier General Albion Howe's dismounted artillerymen as well as one or two battalions of dismounted cavalry from Washington's Camp Stoneman across the Anacostia River, went forward as infantry to Harpers Ferry by rail on July 3. Howe was to turn these men over to Sigel and Weber and return personally to the capital. Then, the telegraph link to Sigel went out suddenly on July 4, compliments of Colonel John S. Mosby and his band of partisan Virginia rangers. Washington defense commanders south of the Potomac received instructions to send part of their men to the northern fortifications of the city, and much of Independence Day passed in telegraphic traffic enumerating rebel cavalry depredations on the Baltimore and Ohio west of Harpers Ferry toward Cumberland, particularly at the south branch of the Potomac. Communiques from Couch and Pennsylvania Governor Andrew Curtin to Washington led to the conclusion that the Keystone State must call out its militia since there were no Federal troops available to help that community. Apparently some of Sigel's wagons and skulkers passed eastward through Frederick spreading more rumors. That same day, Lieutenant Colonel David L. Clendenin, commanding the veteran 8th Illinois cavalry, received orders to take six troops of his regiment (leaving one in quarters at Washington), and proceed by the shortest route to Point of Rocks or vicinity, and ascertain who had cut the telegraph to Harpers Ferry, the enemy's position, force, composition, "and generally acquire any information concerning him which will be of interest." Ultimately, Clendenin went forward with only five companies.[23]

Much of what the War Department was hearing at this point came from Garrett and his energetic master of transportation, William Preston Smith, based on their chain of agents along the rail line westward. They kept Stanton and Halleck well informed concerning the various concentrations of both Union and Confederate forces, the threats to their railroad, as well as other unfolding developments. The railroaders particularly worked hard to rapidly remove locomotives and rolling stock east and west of Early's invasion to avoid their destruction. Tracks and ties could be rapidly replaced; engines and cars could not. Mosby's activities seemed especially troubling since they widened the overall span of rebel operations. In essence, Early's destructive capabilities now extended all the way from the south branch of the Potomac and Patterson's Creek close to Cumberland on the west, to the Maryland-Pennsylvania line north of Hagerstown in the Cumberland Valley, downstream to Mosby's activities at Point of Rocks, Berlin, and Sandy Hook below Harpers Ferry. Tyler reported that even Frederick was threatened on July 4, the result of the partisan rangers' activities against Union local defense troops near the mouth of the Monocacy River where it entered the Potomac.[24]

Perhaps Tyler's reports as well as Garrett's information, concerning Mosby's close-in threat to the railroad, expedited Wallace's decision to go to the front in person. He certainly stopped all forward movement of Howe's reinforcements so as to free trains for his own concentration on the Monocacy line. Whatever troops came from Washington were unloaded at the bridge, then returned to Monrovia, and helped Tyler's men throw up earthworks at Monrovia and Mount Airy "to protect themselves against cavalry." The justness of Mosby's threat may be difficult to ascertain at this late date. On balance, however, his rangers triggered a wake-up call in Washington and the dispatch of more of the 8th Illinois Cavalry upriver. For the moment, however, Point of Rocks commanded everyone's attention on Independence Day.[25]

Federal authorities had established a military post at Point of Rocks on the north bank of the Potomac to protect the vulnerability of the B & O at this point. A weak fort and outlying rifle pits were manned by a semi-present garrison of Company G (Captain F. H. Hardesty) and Company H (Captain Robert C. Bamford) of the 1st Regiment Potomac Home Brigade Infantry—perhaps one hundred forty-five men under Bamford's direct command. Weber also dispatched two companies of a local Unionist mounted unit styled the Loudoun Rangers which had been organized in June 1862 by authority of Secretary of War Edwin M. Stanton. These Rangers were primarily of German stock, who had settled in Loudoun County, Virginia and were bitter enemies of the Mosby band. Their purpose was to patrol along the Potomac and to counter guerillas. Most Virginians considered them traitors, and Mosby's men held them in low esteem as fighters—something of a "caste and class" issue. As ranger John H. Alexander observed, "We could never get close enough [to them] to levy our attachment." At any rate, perhaps eighty of them were present on the Fourth of July, forming Company A under twenty-six-year-old Captain Daniel M. Keyes, and recently organized Company B, led by Captain James W. Grubb. Keyes commanded the Rangers, and his men brought the total Union garrison to about two hundred twenty-five soldiers.

On the morning of July 4, Bamford received the disquieting news that a portion of Early's command was at Leesburg. By noon, a Loudoun County Unionist, Mahlen James, brought word that a large rebel force was headed Bamford's way. Bamford alerted his men, and placed pickets on an island in the river to command its ford. The rest of his infantry went into the earthworks and rifle pits. At 1:30 P.M., Bamford reported that Mosby, with about three or four hundred infantry and cavalry plus a section of artillery had appeared on the south bank. The "Gray Ghost," as Mosby was called, then announced his arrival by wading into the river, drawing the fire of the Union pickets. Satisfied as to the enemy's strength and location, Mosby placed his sole howitzer on high ground and ordered First Lieutenant Sam Chapman, the battalion adjutant, who commanded the piece, to commence firing.

Mosby also directed Lieutenant Albert Wrenn, commanding twenty-five carbineers, to dismount and drive off the pickets on the island. Finding one annoying Federal sharpshooter firing unhindered from a bridge over the Chesapeake and Ohio Canal on the Maryland side, Mosby inquired of one of his dismounted cavalryman, Emory Pitts: "Pitts, can you stop that Yankee over there from sucking eggs?" Pitts allowed as how he would try, and breast deep in the water felled his opponent with one shot. The other pickets soon scurried from the island, which was then used by Wrenn's men to pin down the main defenders on the north bank. Chapman's howitzer carried on a noisy, if inaccurate fire, that added to the enemy's discomfort. It was now time for Mosby to administer the "coup de main."

Most of the Rangers had remained mounted throughout these preliminary actions, awaiting their chance. Mosby now ordered Captain Adolphus "Dolly" Richardson's First Squadron to rush the outmanned Union defenders, who quickly retired to their fortified camp. The Loudoun Rangers removed the planking of the bridge spanning the canal, but Richardson pressed on, pulling down a decrepit building to use as substitute planking. Ranger Harry Hatcher sprinted into the Union camp and captured the garrison flag, and after a quick consultation among Captains Bamford, Hardesty, and Keyes, the Federals conducted an "orderly retreat" toward Frederick, under orders from Weber to retire if attacked by superior force. Accounts vary, with Mosby claiming later to have routed the Yankees, capturing camp equipage, supplies, etc. The regimental historian of the Loudoun Rangers merely observed, by contrast, that the defenders put up a stiff defense, but lacking artillery, suffered some disadvantage. Mosby's men suffered not a single casualty in the affair.[26]

The Partisan Rangers now turned to plundering the village as a railroad train approached Point of Rocks from Harpers Ferry at this point. Chapman's howitzer sent a shell screeching overhead to

convince the engineer to halt the train. Then, according to some accounts, local townspeople convinced Mosby not to burn the train in
front of their homes. So, the cavalry leader directed engineer Elliott
to pull it down the line between the Curtis American and St. Charles
Hotel, before reputedly setting it afire. Supposedly the tracks were
badly twisted, but other accounts simply have the train escaping by
backpeddling toward Harpers Ferry. At any rate, the rebels did heavy
damage to the enemy camps, canal boats and the five civilian stores
in the hamlet ("which seemed to be their principal mission on this
raid," wrote one Union chronicler). Store owner, Lewis Meems, convinced Mosby that he was a Southern sympathizer and so his purloined goods were returned to him. But every Ranger left town that
evening with food, clothing, whiskey, and dry goods in sacks slung
over their saddles. Looking like a "parade of Fantastics," in civilian
bonnets and draped cloth around their shoulders, they re-crossed
the Potomac to celebrate and sleep off their singular marking of the
nation's birthday.[27]

The rangers bivouacked for the night along the road to Leesburg.
Indulging in some of the liberated whiskey and a huge pound cake
shaped like a spread eagle which they had found in the Yankee officers' quarters in the Point of Rocks camp, the war probably seemed far
away to Mosby's men. The next morning the colonel got three wagons loaded with the booty and then ordered Walter Bowie and Joe
Nelson with small detachments back across the Potomac for a deeper
raid against telegraph lines in Maryland. Mosby also wrote out a
message for Jubal Early and handed it to Fount Beattie and Harry
Heaton, instructing them to seek out the general, rumored to be
somewhere around Sharpsburg. Then, with the rest of his command,
probably no more than 150 men, he moved back toward Point of
Rocks, intending to recross in person. He discovered though that
soldiers from the 8th Illinois cavalry were now there in force. The two
sides dueled across the river, accomplishing little more than killing a
villager, Ellen Fisher, before the Confederates pulled out, heading
south to the vicinity of Leesburg once more.[28]

Admittedly, the railroad had been little affected by Mosby's actions of the fourth, but the telegraph was wrecked. William Shock,
the telegraph operator, escaped with his telegraph instrument, and
during the night met with B & O track walker, Frederick Stunkle.
They reconnected the wire, and telegraphed the news to Baltimore.
The next day, two trains of troops were sent up, while over night
Peter B. Stouffer, railroad foreman, took his men out to Point of Rocks
to begin track repairs. Mosby later claimed his little foray greatly
aided Early's movements. Early claimed otherwise. In truth, it may
have been little more than a typical partisan raid, and localized

internecine conflict against home guards like the hated Loudoun Rangers. Partisans were notorious during the war for temporarily teaming up with major military operations, but hovering on the flanks conducting irregular, highly independent feats, which in the end, proved more nettlesome than anything else for their Yankee opponents. Whichever the case, July 5 dawned with Lew Wallace surveying the situation out on the Monocacy amidst these resports of raiders rampaging in the neighborhood.

The Hoosier general learned from Tyler about Mosby's foray at Point of Rocks and that Weber and Sigel were indeed safe on Maryland Heights. The countryside was filled with stragglers, said Tyler, and, indeed, some three hundred of them seemed to have wandered all the way to Annapolis on the Chesapeake Bay. Further conversation between Tyler and his chief developed the fact that no one really knew where the enemy raiders were, how many, or their intent. Tyler had scouts out all over the place with men like W. H. Engler of the 3d Regiment Potomac Home Brigade infantry operating in small details from Monrovia on the railroad, impressing horses and seeking sightings of the enemy. Wallace then secured the services of a half-dozen local citizens to go westward across Catoctin Mountain, on the pretext of business, and uncover what they could of the rebels. Even before they had returned unsuccessfully late at night, Wallace had determined to bring forward the rest of his fighting command, the 11th Maryland, the Baltimore battery, and sundry other detachments from Annapolis as well as the Monument City, like one hundred mounted infantry from the 159th Ohio National Guard, commanded by a mustering officer, Captain Edward H. Leib, 5th U.S. Cavalry.

"The situation was as yet too indefinite," Wallace recalled, and fighting was not yet under consideration. The Middle Department commander, however, summoned key staff officers forward from headquarters, and he sent word through that office that guards on the bridges of the Baltimore and Wilmington Railroad over Bush, Back, and Gunpowder rivers north of the city should be "constantly on the alert," and kept as strong as possible. He switched his own command post at the Monocacy bridge from the blockhouse to a small, one-story frame structure beside the tracks nearby, a house ostensibly owned by a man named Lyeth, incorrectly identified as a captain in the rebel 1st Maryland. Then, having done what he could do for the day, "I spent the rest of it seated on a bench near the bluff overlooking the river and the valley off to the distant mountains," Wallace noted in his memoirs.[29]

Union activity proved equally fragmented elsewhere. The day had started with great indecision in Washington as to the strength of

the enemy raiders. "Thus far it seems to be a raiding expedition by
some of the partisan robbers that infest that region, and who have
joined together," Stanton wired Pennsylvania Governor Andrew G.
Curtin at 6 A.M. on the morning of July 5. Indeed like Imboden,
Captain John McNeill's partisans had remained pesky on the B & O
above Harpers Ferry in upper Maryland and West Virginia. Five hours
later, the secretary of war increased the threat alert by noting how
deserter reports from Petersburg had caused Grant to warn about
Ewell's corps leaving there to cross over into Maryland. Stanton hesitated, however, since the report conflicted with earlier situation estimates by the general-in-chief. He suggested that Curtin and Couch
merely organize their militia for any emergency, amending that with
yet another missive by mid-afternoon, which suggested President
Lincoln wanted 12,000 militia for 100-days "to serve at Washington
and its vicinity." The governor and Pennsylvania commander both
responded that when necessary they would turn out the requisite
number "to serve in Pennsylvania and Maryland." They were already
receiving scattered reports of rebel outriders advancing north of
Hagerstown, in the Mercersburg vicinity.[30]

Stanton sought similar aid from New York Governor Horatio
Seymour. He suggested that his emergency troops probably wouldn't
be needed for service exceeding sixty days. Seymour said that he
would do what he could. Governor John Brough of Ohio did likewise,
but when Halleck wired the departmental commander at Columbus,
Ohio seeking transfer of a Veteran Reserve regiment from the Rock
Island Illinois prison camp, feisty old Major General Samuel P.
Heintzelman fired back: "There is not a soldier who can be spared
from this department." Heintzelman had seen these scares to the
capital before. Besides, he had been rough handled by Halleck's bureaucrats for his earlier association with the McClellan clique that
headed the eastern army two years before. Heintzelman felt comfortable in ducking this latest challenge. So Halleck had to wire the Iowa
adjutant general directing militia to take over at Rock Island, thus
freeing the Veteran Reserve unit there for duty at Washington.[31]

The question paramount in everyone's minds—where was David
Hunter and his army? At 9:10 A.M. that morning, Stanton seized the
reins and wired the missing department commander via Pittsburgh
and Parkersburg, West Virginia. Testily pointing out that rebels had
been operating for two days against Martinsburg, Harpers Ferry, and
other points on the Baltimore and Ohio Railroad, the secretary of war
bluntly stated: "These points being within your department you are
expected to take promptly such measures as may be proper to meet
the emergency." Stanton directed Hunter to immediately report his

whereabouts, and acknowledge receipt of the telegram. Five hours later came word from the general that he was pushing his command as fast as possible toward Martinsburg. Some forty carloads of infantry had left that very morning from Parkersburg for New Creek. In a separate missive to the army's adjutant general, Hunter waffled a bit more, suggesting merely that 1,300 troops had departed to reinforce Brigadier General Benjamin F. Kelly at Cumberland, that everything depended upon how fast the railroad supplied rolling stock for the movement, but that Sigel's force "if properly managed," was amply sufficient to have driven back the enemy. Surely Hunter knew better, if he recalled his own misfortune at Lynchburg.[32]

By evening on July 5, Halleck and Grant had exchanged several more messages that suggested great relief in finally hearing from Hunter. "As Hunter's force is now coming within reach, I think your operations should not be interfered with by sending troops here," commented Halleck. Grant had volunteered in the early afternoon to send a full army corps back if necessary—a dispatch received in Washington at 6:45 P.M. But, Halleck, at least, thought the dispatch of excess dismounted cavalry, to be remounted by impressing horses in parts of Maryland likely to be overrun by the enemy, would suffice at this point. Officials at the capital still wanted to believe that the invading force was merely cavalry and partisans. Having no "apprehensions, at present about the safety of Washington, Baltimore, Harper's Ferry, or Cumberland," Halleck wired Grant at 10:30 P.M., these points "cover our supplies, and raids between cannot effect any damage that cannot soon be repaired." By this time, Grant had changed his mind. "I think now there is no doubt but Ewell's corps is away from here," he wired Halleck ten minutes before midnight on the fifth. He had already directed Meade to send in all the dismounted cavalry on hand, plus a good infantry division, Grant said, and looked to quartermaster concentration of transport vessels in the James River to effect the movement.[33]

Much depended upon Meade and Hunter, and how quickly their troops got into position. Men like Stanton, Grant, and Halleck could merely assess the situation, issue directives, and hope for their timely execution. Out in the triangle of operations—from Cumberland to Harpers Ferry, and to the Monocacy—other men held the issue more squarely in their hands. Closer in, preliminary concerns about the state of undergrowth and brush on the somewhat neglected forts at Washington might cause Department of Washington (XXII Corps) officers to shift units about the northern perimeter to police the works, but Major General Christopher C. Augur's principal concern was Howe and getting the vanguard of his Harpers Ferry relief group—the 170th Ohio National Guard—as well as the dismounted artillery serving as infantry pushed forward as far as possible. Ironically, the War Department had already received word of the possible Point Lookout raid, for Augur told Camp Stoneman (the cavalry remount center in D.C.) commander, Colonel William Gamble, on the fifth, to send a small detachment to the vicinity of Upper Marlboro in Prince George's County to watch the roads down into southern Maryland, with a similar column doing likewise from Port Tobacco closer to the Potomac in Charles County. A new prison camp commander, Brigadier General James Barnes, was sent to the Point Lookout pen, and 2,000 of its captives dispatched northward to Elmira, New York for safekeeping.[34]

Indeed, in some ways, John Garrett's railroad still held the key to Union success at this juncture. The War Department considered crucial the expeditious movement of Hunter's army eastward. Of course, this depended upon the amount of damage done by McNeill's and Imboden's men, as far as St. John's Run. Benjamin Kelly's troops at Cumberland had repulsed rebel attacks on the North and South Branch as well as the Patterson's Creek bridges, Garrett wired Lincoln in the evening of the fifth. His railroad gangs had begun repairs on the Patterson's Creek bridging quickly, although the South Branch trestle had been damaged, he noted. Kelly, reporting through Garrett's railroad agents in western Maryland, sounded more optimistic, suggesting that only thirty feet of trestle were damaged on the South Branch, and that the iron span was all right. He undertook personal supervision of the repair effort, as he, like everyone else, expected Hunter to move rapidly eastward over the course of the next few days. Meanwhile, repair crews, reinforcements, and normal traffic would use the Chesapeake and Ohio Canal for movements.[35]

The situation to the east, however, remained more garbled on July 5. Commanding sufficient rolling stock to convey Howe's men to Harpers Ferry as well as Wallace's contingents to the Monocacy was daunting enough from the logistical point of view. Mosby had continued to hover about Point of Rocks, firing from the Virginia shoreline on several random engines and trains sent up to Harpers Ferry. Then too, Weber had ordered the firing of the 273 feet of wooden trestle linking the Maryland shore with the town when he had evacuated that place the previous night. Garrett fretted that the great iron spans would fall prey to further military destruction. He could do little about rebel destruction of railroad trackage west of that point. But he ranted more about Union destruction of his property. Garrett's continuous supply of information to Lincoln and the War Department certainly provided reasonably current data from the field at this time. However, it also added to the "fog of war" since the situation remained so fluid in western Maryland, and so many interests were involved.[36]

* * * *

Former Secretary of the Treasury Salmon P. Chase recorded in his diary on July 4: "Cries of all kinds except cries of pain filled the air this morning, with explosions of cannon, ringing of bells, and whiz-whiz snap-snap of crackers [they] and awaken me." It was the "Anniversary of the Independence of the United States," he continued, but how little most celebrants seemed to be thinking of the difference between the "United States which declared it and the United States which celebrate it." Thirteen original states battling for independence and Union, now twenty-three struggling with divided counsels to compel obedience to the constitution and laws, he commented, with eleven others "in which counting all classes and colors there is a majority of loyalists, but a majority controlled by the master class," with the African-American portion of both, treated by the United States government as inferiors and aliens rather than as equals in natural rights and as citizens. What will be the end of it all, he asked rhetorically, "it is hidden from me.[37]

Union forces began to assume blocking positions against the Maryland invaders by July 5, as the supreme command suddenly realized that this was no mere foray by cavalry and partisans. The Confederates still busied themselves west of South and Catoctin mountain ranges, with the heat and dust slowing movements for them as much as for their Federal opponents. Matters remained indefinite, and the heat in downtown Washington similarly stifled the mental alertness and actions of Stanton, Halleck, and the Washington department command. Out in the suburbs, Elizabeth Blair Lee wrote her husband, the rear admiral, that she had stirred the rumor pot by telling her father, old Francis Preston Blair, "all my Secesh rumors" concerning the attack upon Harpers Ferry. But, the old man had been so preoccupied with a planned hunting expedition that he had been unaware of such developments.

Suddenly, the elder Blair had immediately rushed across the street to the White House, but missed the president, who was at the War Department nearby. Then, said daughter Elizabeth, her brother, Montgomery (the Postmaster general), had arrived to console his sister that the rebels had been checked and held on the upper Potomac, and that Hunter's command was "en route to face the foe." Returning to their country place the next day, Elizabeth Blair Lee made ready to take her mother off to catch the sea breezes on the New Jersey coast, just as the male Blairs undertook to depart on their own expedition. That was fine with her, for it left "us womankind more free [to] skidadle [*sic*] into the city." As yet, it seemed that no one anticipated skedaddling from an onrushing enemy. Escape from the nation's capital for the fortunate few was prompted more by heat and humidity than worries about Old Jube and his raiders.[38]

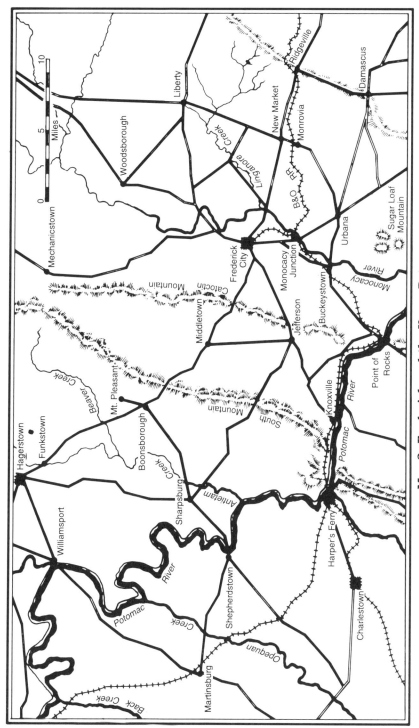

Map 2. Frederick and the Upper Potomac

THREE

Three Days of Overture

Midway through the first week in July, the Confederates had finished their river crossings, concluded their business at Hagerstown and vicinity, and skirmished on John Garrett's railroad line to the west at Sir John's Run and Big Cacapon Bridge. They also had expended valuable time probing Franz Sigel's and Max Weber's positions atop Maryland Heights opposite Harpers Ferry. Confederate prisoners of war as far off as Fort Delaware, on the Delaware River south of Wilmington, and Point Lookout, Maryland (where the Potomac empties into the Chesapeake Bay), "believed that Gen. Early would capture Washington City and release all the prisoners in reach," when they heard of the advance into Maryland, remembered Lieutenant John Blue of the 11th Virginia cavalry, one of those prisoners. Down near Richmond, General Robert E. Lee focused upon his increasing deficiency in useful cavalry (he had bluntly told President Jefferson Davis that inability to secure horses would affect "our Southern communications" with dire results). He also mused about European intransigence, telling his chief executive that Confederate safety depended solely upon its own efforts, and whether or not the young nation could defeat or drive enemy armies from the field, thus securing peace.[1]

Sometime on July 6, Fount Beattie and Harry Heaton rode into Early's Sharpsburg camp with a message from the partisan leader, Colonel John Mosby. In essence, Mosby would obey any order that Early would give him. The two rangers claimed later that Old Jube seemed to have been drinking heavily when they met him, an assertion later used by the "Grey Ghost' in his postwar quarrel with the general about his own participation in the Maryland campaign, among other things. Whatever the case, since spirits seemed to flow freely throughout Early's Maryland campaign, Old Jube flatly told the scouts that his targets were Frederick and then Washington, D.C. They carried that information back to Mosby the next day. Meanwhile, on the afternoon of the sixth, another courier arrived to see Early. It was none other than General Lee's son and namesake, and he bore something far more critical than a message of cooperation from a partisan.[2]

Robert E. Lee, Jr. had committed the contents to memory, in case of capture, and the dispatch is now lost to us. But, it had to do with a new twist in Old Jube's mission. The details seem as fuzzy now as they must have been at the time. The estimated 15,000–20,000 incarcerated Confederates at Point Lookout invited a rescue attempt. Lee needed the manpower. They were being poorly guarded by U.S. Colored Troops. Some sort of combined joint Confederate naval-land operation was thought to be the way to liberate them. Newly minted Maryland brigadier Bradley T. Johnson and his cavalry would provide the land contingent. Navy commander John Taylor Wood with several gunboats would slip through the union blockade off the Virginia capes and rendezvous with Johnson at Point Lookout.

Timing was remarkably tight—the twelfth was the appointed hour of liberation. While Lee had long been privy to this scheme, other correspondence that has survived indicates some tone of skepticism as to the scheme's viability, largely due to his fear that the plan had become common knowledge in Richmond, and hence susceptible to Union interception. But, initially, Lee told Davis: "I think the guard might be overpowered, the prisoners liberated and organized, and marched immediately on the route to Washington." So, Lee's son apparently transmitted this information to Early and after predictable oaths from Old Jube about the imbecility of deviating from his mission, the general settled down to figure out how to accomplish the task.[3]

Indeed, it was a great time for rumination in the summer heat. Washington officials alternately worried about the mysterious doings in western Maryland, and President Abraham Lincoln's unpredictable decision to declare martial law in guerilla-plagued Kentucky. Lieutenant General Ulysses S. Grant and his staff at City Point, Virginia, still pondered Lee's activities, although by the sixth, claimed Assistant Secretary of War Charles A. Dana, Grant was convinced Washington was the raid's objective. Dana would go back to the capital from City Point three days later, "in order to keep Grant informed of what was going on." The Frederick, Maryland *Examiner* talked about the rebels staging another raid on the Baltimore and Ohio Railroad. "The general opinion is, that they will make us a visit, but we think not," claimed its editor. And, Major General Lew Wallace, reputedly taking a place on a makeshift bench overlooking the brown-flowing Monocacy River just outside that city, tried to unravel what lay "back of the distant, semi-transparent blue wall of mountains" to his west. At least some answers would be forthcoming during that day.[4]

July 6—A Day of Watchful Waiting

Wednesday, the sixth of July, dawned warm and bright on the upper Potomac. Several things became more apparent that day. By mid-afternoon, Grant freely admitted: "I think there is no doubt but Early's corps is near the Baltimore and Ohio road." Finally, getting the enemy commander's name straight, he suggested that if that corps could be caught and broken up it would be highly desirable to do so. Of course, this admonition did not reach the War Department until the next day due to telegraphic delays. But, Grant's words also expressed his customary expectation that subordinates should look past the immediate and on to the ultimate goals, whereby "it is important to our success here that another raid be made up the Shenandoah Valley, and stores destroyed and communications broken."[5]

Grant was not about to absolve Major General David Hunter of his previously botched mission to ultimately ravage the Valley and then move on to Charlottesville and environs closer to Richmond and Petersburg. For the moment, however, Grant's missive crossed a telegram from the chief of staff, Major General Henry Halleck, that simply confirmed the enemy's activities at Martinsburg (Sigel's fault because he failed to send out scouts to ascertain the Confederate approach), the wild estimates of rebel numbers (7,000 to over 30,000 according to Sigel, with other figures in the 20,000–30,000 range), and the fact that, if true, "the invasion is of a pretty formidable character." Whether viewed from Washington or City Point, Hunter was the key player, all other subordinates were second-rank in quality and importance, and Halleck especially asked if Grant might send back a "good major-general to command in the field till Hunter arrives?" The chief of staff did not want Washington commander, Major General C. C. Augur, to leave his post for such a task at this critical moment.

Down on the James River, Army of the Potomac veterans that Grant intended sending to the capital region were glad to go, recalled Sergeant J. Newton Terrill, later regimental historian of the 14th New Jersey. "They were tired of lying in the sand," and heat at Petersburg. It took all day to muster them and get them aboard troop transports like the *Sylvan Shore*, before departing about 4:00 P.M. Then, "being on the cool river is a great transformation we much appreciate—Hallelujah," rejoiced Captain Lemuel A. Abbott of the 10th Vermont in his pocket diary. Captain George C. Davis remembered the Union soldiers telling themselves: "In Maryland we shall find pure springs of water, ice-houses, property, vegetables, blackberries, fruit and pies that are neither sewed nor pegged!"[6]

Grant told army commander Major General George Gordon Meade that these troops "need not take teams, ambulances, or ammunition" except what they carried personally, for "I expect them back here so soon that there is no necessity for transporting the teams back and forth." Besides, there were easily six hundred teams available in Washington anyway. Grant even expected the dismounted cavalry that he sent back would speedily return fully mounted and equipped.

Not only was the general in chief overly optimistic, but also dangerously unrealistic about what might be transpiring north of the Potomac. There were even mixed signals as quartermaster and transportation officials at City Point scurried around readying the expedition. How many men were going back? Cavalry chief, Major General Philip H. Sheridan, told Halleck he was sending 2,496 sick, dismounted, and mostly unarmed troopers; the chief quartermaster of the Army of the Potomac enumerated Brigadier General James Ricketts' 5,000 infantrymen and about 3,000 dismounted men of Sheridan's cavalry. To what destination? It seemed to be the port of Baltimore rather than Washington, according to most estimates. Indeed, Grant may have been thinking the troops were destined directly for Washington, while Halleck seemed to be operating under the idea of funneling them directly by rail to besieged Harpers Ferry. Confusion would befuddle the Union high command in the critical days ahead.[7]

Meanwhile, Brigadier General Albion P. Howe reached Harpers Ferry from Washington in the predawn hours and by mid-morning, had reported back that his 2,800-man relief force had reinforced the Maryland Heights position. Howe, a 46-year-old West Pointer and artilleryman had earlier commanded an infantry brigade and division in the Army of the Potomac. Since late 1863, he had served as inspector of artillery and commander of the Artillery Depot in Washington. He must have been pleased to once again take to the field even though his relief column was a mixed bag of troops. The 170th Ohio Infantry, for example, was a 100-days outfit commanded by Colonel Miles V. Saunders. Three batteries of artillery went along as infantry, and a battalion or two were made up of assorted dismounted cavalry. Howe's orders had been to go by rail in three separate increments on July 5, rendezvous with a veteran cavalry unit at Point of Rocks, and proceed to Harpers Ferry by rail if the way was clear. If the track was destroyed or blocked, then he was charged with clearing or repairing it in order to reach Weber and Sigel. Howe and the mounted cavalry would then return to

Washington. In actuality, however, once he reported back from Harpers Ferry, Halleck instructed him to remain and assist in the defense of Maryland Heights.

In the capital, Augur suggested to Halleck that Grant really should return a full regiment of heavy artillerists to stiffen the militia in the city's forts "as the latter are not sufficiently instructed in the use of heavy batteries." Later in the day, Augur also instructed Colonel Moses Wisewell, commander of the District of Washington in the city, to run a security check of arrangements at the Potomac bridges and to report what guards he had visited, the hour, and the precise condition of defense at each point. It turned out that while the defenses themselves were sufficient, the guard force was not.

Augur similarly ordered additional reconnaissance out toward Manassas Junction and Thoroughfare Gap by Colonel Charles R. Lowell's 2d Massachusetts Cavalry, based at Falls Church in northern Virginia. He did not want any rebel surprises springing from that direction. On the other side of town, the Baltimore and Ohio's Master of Transportation, at the railroad's Camden Station headquarters in Baltimore, W. P. Smith, pressed the War Department to increase guards on the railroad bridges between the cities. Augur, for one, at least recognized that somebody had better think more about Washington's close-in protection rather than dispatching everything upstream to Harpers Ferry. So, he held back Captain Albert W. Bradbury's 1st Maine Battery and Captain Frank C. Gibbs' Battery L. 1st Ohio Light Artillery at the artillery instruction camp, Camp Barry, in the District. They would not go to Harpers Ferry.[8]

B & O president John Garrett, Sigel, and Brigadier General B. F. Kelly, commander at Cumberland, Maryland kept the telegraph wires buzzing with information about Hunter's whereabouts and progress. Although Halleck anticipated some delay in that army's eastward passage due to damage to the railroad, Kelly was much more optimistic. He had driven partisan John H. McNeill's raiders from the line near New Creek, and thought that advance elements of Brigadier General Jeremiah Sullivan's division from Hunter's army would be in Cumberland by nightfall. Units like the 2d Maryland Potomac Home Brigade, the 2d Maryland Eastern Shore and Ohio National Guard regiments would keep the line clear and operable. The War Department remained hopeful that an aggressive Hunter could incorporate the Maryland Heights troops with his own and mount a serious threat to the Confederate rear once he had returned to the region. The crisis would all end quickly, Secretary or War Edwin Stanton assured Ohio Governor John Brough, when the politician reported that his whole military organization was now in service, and that any emergency calls might drastically affect his state's ability to

Brigadier General Bradley T. Johnson, C.S.A.

Trusted Marylander in the Confederate service, he was sent by Early to free Confederate prisoners held at Point Lookout, Maryland but dallied in his ride around Baltimore suburbs.

U.S. Army Military History Institute

Major Harry Gilmor, C.S.A.

Local Maryland Confederate hero, his exploits in the Baltimore suburbs temporarily cut rail and telegraph communications between Washington and the northeast but did little permanent damage.

U.S. Army Military History Institute

Lieutenant Colonel David R. Clendenin, U.S.A., 8th Illinois Cavalry

This intrepid midwesterner provided intelligence to Lew Wallace's force and successfuly harried Early's march on Frederick.

U.S. Army Military History Institute

Old Toll Gate—Braddock Heights
Area of Clashes between Clendenin and Johnson/Gilmor Forces.
July 7, 1864
Mark & Bielfeld, Souvenir of Historic Frederick (1925), p.13.

Battlefield of July 7, 1864, Looking toward Frederick. Old National Road at Right

Oscar Bray, "A Proposed Road on the Monocacy Battlefield," April 26, 1940
Courtesy National Park Service, Harpers Ferry Center Library

Battlefield of July 7, 1864, West of Frederick. View toward Monocacy Junction, Old National Road (Old Route 40 in foreground)

Oscar Bray, "A Proposed Road on the Monocacy Battlefield," April 26, 1940
Courtesy National Park Service, Harpers Ferry Center Library

meet government calls for longer-service men to be used elsewhere in the war. In the long run, Halleck proved correct: Hunter's movement eastward would not be rapid.[9]

Pennsylvania Governor Andrew Curtin and his military counterpart, Major General Darius Couch, proved equally unresponsive. Curtin, Stanton, and Couch could not agree on legalistic terms for mustering Keystone State militiamen, and wasted valuable time wrangling about pay status, and protocol. Not that the Cumberland Valley was past danger. Indeed, Couch had placed Chambersburg under martial law, and designated that town as the assembly point for "old soldiers" and militia to gather. Some five hundred rebels were reported at Greencastle, closer to the Maryland line, although reports held the main body closer to the Potomac. Lieutenant Hunter McLean then returned to scout the Hagerstown situation, finding only a few rebel stragglers that he quickly dispersed. He found more around Sharpsburg and Funkstown, but did not test them. The Pennsylvania Reserves were supposedly turning out en masse, and Curtin promised Stanton, somewhat ambiguously, that afternoon that: "An organized force of 10,000 men in this department, and 12,000 at Washington, will give substantial aid to the government."[10]

More irritating were returning Hagerstown refugees who claimed that the city fathers should never have paid money to McCausland's bandits. All things considered, however, Lew Wallace's sector on the Monocacy proved to be the cusp of the day's action (combined with the skirmishing going on between Sigel and Early's advance near Maryland Heights where the Georgia brigadier noted in his "Valley Campaign Diary" that his men "cut a road with pocket knives and attacked enemy in rear"). A fifty-man roving patrol from the 1st Maryland Potomac Home Brigade under the aggressive Frederick post commander and provost marshal, Major Jonathan I. Yellott, was roughed up by rebel cavalry videttes near Middletown in Pleasant Valley.

Nonetheless, Yellott's people brought back word that "a large portion of Ewell's corps are in the neighborhood of Boonsboro." Hired civilian scouts also confirmed that the area west of South Mountain was thick with rebels and that no civilian traffic could pass that way. Yellott heard nothing from Sigel, but declared that he was evacuating stores from Frederick by a 300-wagon train escorted by 200 troopers, and had established a stragglers camp at the town. Independently, Wallace received a dispatch from Sigel (which he relayed to Washington), that portrayed an enemy numbering a corps plus three divisions, and 3,000 cavalry, that "appears to be moving in strong force toward Frederick." This news suggested to Wallace, at least, that the enemy was coming at him in great force. Later, he learned that Halleck, upon receipt of this message, down-played the news due to its source with Sigel. Nonetheless, Wallace proceeded forward with his own preparations.[11]

Wallace ordered Yellott to hold Frederick proper but if forced to retire to do so on the Baltimore turnpike so that he might defend the east bank of the Monocacy at the stone bridge. Meanwhile, Wallace looked to move his own command forward from Baltimore. Indeed, an early alert call had gone out several days before, but left city garrisons in camp. Captain Frederick W. Alexander's Baltimore Light Artillery Battery, and Colonel William T. Landstreet's 11th Maryland Volunteer Infantry (Maryland's only 100-days regiment) proceeded to muster on the third, thereby disturbing pleasant summer reveries with family and friends. Thus ended the good time so near home, noted cannoneer Frederick W. Wild, "where we could go three or four times a week, and get a square meal, have a good bath, and change clothes, go to the theater and other amusements." They had watched the firework displays over the city from their camps the next day, before boarding a troop train at 9:00 P.M. on the fifth.

Stepping groggily off the cars at dawn of the sixth, they went into camp on the banks of Bush Creek, near Gambrill's Mill, south of the river. Many were soured to the point that bookkeeper-turned-soldier Sergeant William H. James of the 11th jotted petulantly in his diary, "we spent the day in the broiling sun." Such a feeling may have conditioned Wallace's own later remembrance that they were a "good looking, clean body of city men, but like their commander, green to a lamentable degree." He was singularly unimpressed with Landstreet's casual salute of his superior "with a ludicrous defiance of the approved military habit." "As the officer is, the command will be," was the Hoosier's dismissal of these Marylanders.[12]

Then, Wallace's day improved greatly with the chance appearance of Lieutenant Colonel David L. Clendenin and 230 troopers of the veteran 8th Illinois Cavalry. This regiment was one of the more experienced and better mounted units in the Army of the Potomac. In 1863, while a part of Brigadier General John Buford's excellent cavalry division, the Illini soldiers claimed to have fired the first shots of the battle of Gettysburg. Even Mosby's cocky band accorded them begrudging respect. Their tall, thirty-one-year-old commander hailed from Morrison, Illinois. He had risen to his present rank and command (without promotion due to the regular commander, Colonel William Gamble, commanding a cavalry brigade without relinquishing the 8th Illinois colonel's slot), but his promising career had nearly ended in late June 1863 when he was formally accused of cowardice on three counts in actions at Kelly's Ford (May 8), Beverly Ford (May 9), and Upperville (June 2) during the early stages of the Gettysburg campaign. Deeply offended and humiliated, Clendenin was sent back to command dismounted cavalrymen concentrated in Alexandria. Clendenin's primary accuser, apparently, was a competitor for his job, Major John L. Beveridge. Acquitted by a court-martial, Clendenin nonetheless had missed Gettysburg (where the regiment performed under Beveridge, who himself left the service with an honorable discharge and organized a new 17th Illinois Cavalry). Then, Clendenin regained his position in time for the spring and summer campaigns of 1864.

Augur had ordered Clendenin out on July 4 with six companies (he actually took only five), to find out just who had interrupted telegraph communication from Washington with Harpers Ferry, "and ascertain the enemy's position, force, composition," as well as any other useful information. The men had been only too happy to exchange provost, escort, and picket duty at the capital for more active service. The Camp Relief barracks on Seventh Street in the city had been stifling, and the unceasing round of funeral escort, provost patrols, interdicting smuggling operations and battling bushwhackers between Point of Rocks and the Occoquan River below Washington for much of the summer had sapped their ability to function as a unit. It was "a long line to picket," observed 1st Sergeant Silas D. Wesson of Leland, Illinois in his pocket diary. Fortunately, he had been able to purchase a Roman candle from a sutler for Independence Day, and, "had fun shooting it at the boys." Now, light of heart, with three days' rations for men and horses, and no encumbering wagons, they set forth at 7:00 P.M. on July 4, bound for the upper Potomac.[13]

The Illinois troopers marched nearly twenty miles through upper Montgomery County before halting just after midnight. Clendenin wanted them well rested for the next day's action. By noon on the fifth, they had reached Point of Rocks, in time to be welcomed by shells from Chapman's howitzer, firing from across the river. A hot skirmish consumed the afternoon as Mosby's people attempted to recross into Maryland, both at Point of Rocks and Noland's (Nolan's) Ferry downstream near the mouth of the Monocacy. He penned a note to Early on that matter although the general claimed after the war that he had received absolutely no information from the Ranger during his Maryland campaign. Meanwhile, Mosby kept the rest of his command circling over hill and dale on the Virginia shore to deceive the Federals and deter their crossing in turn. Finally, by 10:00 P.M., both sides broke off the action, claiming to have repulsed the other.

Clendenin's cavalrymen then rested for three hours before sunrise on the sixth. Later that morning, he sent a squadron upriver to Berlin and Sandy Hook (the latter just east of Maryland Heights) where yet another skirmish ensued with Mosby's band. These were small detachments under Walter "Wat" Bowie and Joe Nelson that got across the Potomac at Edward's Ferry near Leesburg, moved up the Chesapeake and Ohio Canal towpath, destroying a couple of canal boats and clipping telegraph wires before encountering Clendenin's men. Nelson's people got farther, plundering shops and cutting down telegraph wires at Adamstown, six miles below Frederick on the railroad before escaping around Sugarloaf Mountain and back across Noland's Ferry. Finally, a wire from Howe at Harpers Ferry directed the Illinoisans "to repair to Frederick and ascertain the force of the enemy reported in the vicinity of Boonsborough" west of South Mountain. It seems that the cavalry's actions had permitted Howe to join with Weber's force on Maryland Heights by late afternoon that day. If Mosby had damaged the B & O tracks at Point of Rocks (his claim to have interdicted the line for forty-eight hours seems exaggerated), neither Clendenin, Howe, nor the railroad's executives mentioned any problem. An engine from Sandy Hook, manned by a brave crew, sped through Point of Rocks about noon. Neither Chapman's cannon nor Mosby's small arms could hit it.[14]

Arriving at Frederick at 8:00 P.M. on July 6, Clendenin was met by a messenger from Wallace. Would he please come to the junction for consultation? The Illinois cavalryman obliged, and the two veteran warriors immediately took a liking to one another. "That he was a Western man had a great deal to do with my confidence," Wallace recorded in his autobiography years later. Needing cavalry to scout across the mountain, Wallace sought to induce the Illinoisan to help out on the Monocacy rather than reporting at Harpers Ferry. Clendenin did not disappoint him. Wallace promised to detach two of Alexander's guns for Clendenin's use, and then explained the mission very simply. If Washington was truly Early's target, and nobody knew for sure at this point, Wallace remembered telling the cavalrymen, "How can we here in his front hope ever to be excused if he pockets the great prize through our failure to unmask him?" Clendenin quite agreed, and said he could be ready "directly, the horses are baited," as they had not been unsaddled. It took the rest of the night to prepare the artillerists for Clendenin's expedition, possibly because, like Landstreet's infantrymen, Alexander's people also had endured a tiring overnight trip from Baltimore. At any rate, nothing much could be accomplished before daybreak of the seventh anyway.[15]

Wallace then settled back to read the dispatches forwarded from Baltimore where Lieutenant Colonel Samuel B. Lawrence was covering for him. Loyal, politically attuned Union Leagues were busy turning out their home guard contingents to protect the city, said Lawrence, but he wanted to know what to do with "over 300 skulkers from General Sigel's army" then at Annapolis. They could soon be back on the road to help against Early, joined by four companies from the Eastern Shore of Maryland, the 149th Ohio Volunteer Infantry as well as Captain E. H. Leib and the mounted infantry of the 159th Ohio. Then, everyone thought better of sending Sigel's malingerers anywhere, and Colonel A. R. Root at Annapolis received orders to retain them for guard duty at the parole camp, and send instead six militia companies, with fresh attitudes and stamina.[16]

July 7—Skirmishing on the Mountain

Clendenin departed at daybreak, with Wallace's enjoinder to send back a messenger every fifteen minutes, "if you strike the rebels." While passing through Frederick, the cavalryman received word from Halleck formalizing the ad hoc arrangement whereby he would report to Wallace. An early morning message from Yellott also noted that he had just returned from a night's scout, with three companies of the 1st Maryland Potomac Home Brigade and the Loudoun Independent Rangers, and they had driven back about one hundred rebels at Middletown. "I am confident that the force in Maryland does not exceed 300 marauders," he noted. Meanwhile, Wallace opened the morning with a command conference in line with his principle of getting better acquainted "with whom he may chance to be associated in duty." While further confirming his skepticism about Landstreet, the council at least (in Wallace's memory) surfaced Colonel Charles Gilpin of the 3d Maryland as a patriarchal leader, and Captain Frederick W. Alexander of the artillery as a professorial figure of good breeding, competence, and eagerness in Wallace's eyes. Best of all, he had that fine battery of six 10-pounder Parrott rifled cannon.

Colonel Allison L. Brown's 149th Ohio Volunteer Infantry had been reorganized at Camp Dennison in that state on May 4, from companies of the 27th Ohio National Guard from Ross County. The 55th Ohio National Guard Battalion from Clinton County renamed and mustered into U.S. service, were still virtually militia. Nonetheless, Wallace entrusted to Brown and Gilpin the vital defense of the stone or jug bridge on the Baltimore Pike. As the Hoosier explained to them, if that span remained undefended, "we should have the enemy upon our backs—provided he appeared." Brown also received orders to place a company to guard Crum's Ford, an intermediary crossing between the railroad junction and the stone bridge. It was about ten o'clock when this "social" function concluded, and Wallace returned to his perch atop the bench near the blockhouse above the river.[17]

The general sat musing about the cloudless sky and shimmering sunshine, the wheat fields, houses, barns, and Frederick's church spires, Wallace noted in his reminiscences. "The report of a distant gun, muffled, to be sure," but from the right direction "seemed dropped from the sky, high up," and he knew that Clendenin had found the enemy. Within the hour, a courier rode up with a 10:15 A.M. message from the cavalryman. He had met the rebel's videttes about halfway between his present position in the crotch of the Catoctin Pass called Solomon's Gap and Middletown. He had driven them back, only to be stopped and forced to retire in turn by superior numbers of Confederates. A half-hour later another messenger brought word that Clendenin's worst fears had come true about being outflanked in the pass and that he had inadequate numbers both to combat the infantry skirmishers advancing directly upon him, and horsemen working their way around his flanks. "Am falling back towards Frederick," he reported to Wallace; "I think a force has gone through on Harper's Ferry Pike." He would be back in Frederick in two hours.[18]

The details of the morning's action went something like this. Clendenin, with a section of Alexander's battery attached, had left Frederick about 5:30 A.M., marching deliberately toward Middletown. Companies A and B of the Loudoun Independent Rangers had scattered the enemy pickets up on Catoctin Mountain, skirmishing with them all the way to Middletown and incurring three wounded. In turn, Yellott's men had been blunted by Major Harry Gilmor with the 1st and 2d Maryland Confederate Cavalry battalions, leading the van of Bradley Johnson's equally cautious advance toward Frederick. By 7:00–7:30 A.M., Gilmor's men had deployed on a rise just east of Middletown. Yellott's retiring force and Clendenin's people took position about one and one-half miles east of town, essentially commanding the bridge crossing over little Hollow Creek (Gilmore termed it "a large stream") at Motter's tavern. Brisk skirmishing ensued with three or four Marylanders cut down, both battle lines swaying back and forth indecisively, as the 8th Virginia Cavalry (arriving as reinforcements) was particularly hard hit by the "pretty shooting" of Clendenin's artillery piece. In graphically recounting the effects of one shell burst on the formation, J. Kelly Bennette flatly declared: "Since the beginning of this war I have seen death in many of its horrid forms but never have I seen so *frightful* a wound" as provided by that one shot. Gilmor dismounted his men and moved to outflank the pesky opposition only to be stopped temporarily by a timid Ransom.[19]

Eventually, Ransom changed his mind and permitted Gilmor and Johnson to attempt the flanking movements. By this time, however, Clendenin sensed the move and withdrew back to the summit of Catoctin Mountain. Johnson detached a Virginia contingent from the main column as it passed the Fairview toll gate. It quickly made its way to the Harpers Ferry road off to the south, and managed to push Yankee pickets almost to Frederick's outskirts at Rizer's barn,

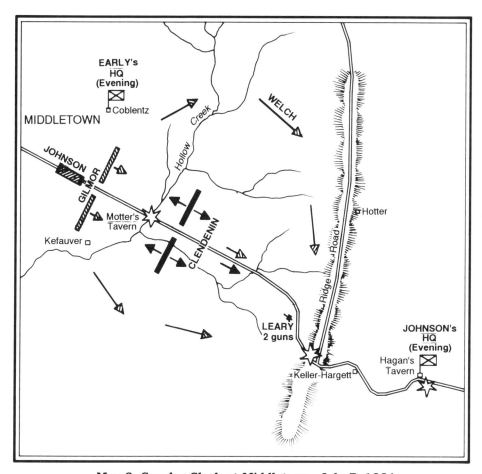

Map 3. Cavalry Clash at Middletown, July 7, 1864

even passing close to the Mount Olivet cemetery near the Georgetown or Washington turnpike south of the city. By this point, however, Clendenin had withdrawn back to Frederick suburbs, and Ransom's fears that the enemy would be reinforced and his desire to await arrival of supporting infantry and artillery stifled Johnson's fondest wish—to liberate his home town. Still, noted Gilmor, "we had a lively fight at long range, but 'nobody hurt' except by artillery" of which he claimed his side employed eight and the Yanks six guns. Bennette recounted going into line of battle both on the macadamized turnpike and in the fields to the south, as renewed skirmishing pushed Federals out of houses and barns in the area about two miles west of the city.

Hearing the morning gunfire in the distance, Wallace had dispatched Brigadier General Erastus B. Tyler with Gilpin's 3d Maryland, Leib's 159th Ohio (only lately arrived from Baltimore), and three more of Alexander's guns. They took position to cover the confluence of the Hagerstown (National Road) and Harpers Ferry turnpikes west of Frederick. Gilpin had orders to evacuate the city only as a last resort and then retire by way of the stone or jug bridge to the east. All of these reinforcements went up from the junction by train, accompanied by locomotive whistles and bells to announce their arrival. In turn, the cars evacuated supplies and convalescents from facilities in town. Wallace also ordered the erection of an earthwork on the high ground just east of Garrett's railroad bridge in which he emplaced a brass howitzer from one of the blockhouses.[20]

Bits and pieces of stray commands from all over the upper Potomac now straggled into the Monocacy area. On July 2, Lieutenant Joseph Lane of Company C, 22d Pennsylvania Cavalry, had started a 175-wagon train (guarded by something like 200 men) from Martinsburg to Frederick. He delivered his wagons, watched the train guard desert in droves, but reported to Wallace who put him on provost duty, gathering stragglers, before sending him off to work with Clendenin. Wallace, however, brushed aside Tyler's suggestion for deploying 300–400 of Sigel's stragglers that Yellott had collected in Frederick. The Hoosier felt that if they had deserted Sigel, they would do so again. Besides, his own command had only twenty-five rounds of ammunition per man, due to supply foul-ups in Baltimore. Perhaps unwisely, for he needed every soldier he could find, Wallace even refused to give them rations. So "they took possession of the wooded hills to the east, and the smoke of their fires was plainly visible through the day," he inserted in a footnote to his postwar reminiscences. Preoccupied now with the impending battle, conscious of his inadequate strength, but determined to accomplish his mission of uncovering the purpose and strength of the enemy, Wallace returned to his musing while awaiting developments. Years later, he remembered wondering at the time if what he was doing was "right, morally speaking." He was subjecting his men to the perils of combat when the situation seemed increasingly doubtful of positive result.[21]

Wallace could not worry long about the morality of his decisions. Arrival by noon of odds and ends under a veteran major of the 1st New York Cavalry, plus dispatches from Baltimore put an end to his ethical quandary. Word from Lawrence mentioned release of some political prisoners in the city, and the fact that Camp Parole stragglers and ammunition would be coming out on the railroad very soon. One particular message caught Wallace's attention more than the others. It was from John Garrett, and it read simply: "A large force of veterans arrived by water, and will be sent immediately." Wallace jumped to the telegraph and directed Lawrence to rush them forward. It turned out that the colonel knew nothing of these men, and most of the afternoon passed at Baltimore headquarters trying to find more information about them from the B & O president. By 2:00 P.M., however, heavy skirmishing on the western outskirts of Frederick demanded Wallace's attention. Bradley Johnson had begun a determined push to capture the town. "A battle now taking place at Frederick, with a fair chance to whip the enemy," he wired Baltimore at some point. "I shall hold the bridge," he proclaimed, asking Lawrence to so inform Garrett.[22]

Fighting surged back and forth from about mid-afternoon and into the evening, as Johnson butted heads with Clendenin's dismounted troopers, Leib's and Gilpin's infantry, and others sent forward from the junction by Tyler and Wallace. Johnson wanted to break through his opponents' position, even outflank it by cutting across country to the Washington turnpike south of town at Mt. Olivet cemetery and to dash into town behind the defenders. However, Ransom continued to restrain such enthusiasm. The hesitant cavalry chief was both ill and unsure of the opposition at this point.

The apex for the Federal defense became the juncture of the roads leading out of Frederick to Harpers Ferry and Hagerstown. Local promontories such as Hagan's (or Hogan's) and Prospect Hills, also a rise styled by some as "Red Hills," figured in the action which spread across corn and wheat fields, as well as wooded lots belonging to the Rizer, Zimmerman, Wilheneas, and Burgess families. The battlefield formed a rough quadrangle bounded by the Harpers Ferry, Burnt Mill, and Almshouse Roads and the Hagerstown Pike. Rebel artillery—actually a four-gun battery from Baltimore that took position on a hill near John Hanan's (Hagan's?) new barn about a mile from town according to local resident Jacob Engelbrecht—joined the dual with their Monument City counterparts in Alexander's Battery by 4:30 P.M. Some civilian spectators caused confusion when they wouldn't move out of the danger zone. Engelbrecht, in fact, viewed the whole affair, especially the firing at Rogers' barn and farmyard, from an elevated spot on South Street.

By 5:00 P.M. a panicky Gilpin sent word to an equally concerned Wallace that Clendenin's men were running out of ammunition, that the telegraph operator had run away, and he asked excitedly: "What shall we do in the emergency?" Earlier, he had supposed only eight hundred enemy confronted him. Then, at 6:15 P.M., he told Tyler that unless reinforced with both men and ammunition, he was falling back to the Monocacy as the rebels seemed to be trying to outflank him "to get onto the National Road," to the south. He particularly wanted Sharps carbine ammunition for Clendenin, as "our men fight well." All of this led Wallace to anxiously wire Baltimore a half-hour later, "I think my troops are retiring from Frederick," gaining in return a promise from Lawrence to push forward what men and ammunition he had on hand. But by 7:30 P.M. Wallace had to inform Clendenin that no Sharps ammunition was available.[23]

Somehow, the Federals held their ground. Perhaps it was due to good shooting by Alexander's guns, or Clendenin's veteran horsemen that steadied the resolve of the Maryland militia. Maybe it was Wallace's message telling Gilpin to give his men the news that "veterans from Grant [were] landing at Baltimore, and they will be up some time tonight." Certainly Wallace understood that reinforcement from either the meager numbers at the stone bridge or the junction would endanger those positions. So, he instructed: "The fellows fighting you are only dismounted cavalry, and you can whip them. Try a charge on them." Gilpin did as suggested, and it worked, or so the Union side believed. It is more likely that Ransom's order to Johnson to pull back for the night had the desired effect. Alexander's gunners again had wrought havoc among the enemy, said the unit's historian later. One shot supposedly caught a group just emerging from some woods and killed or wounded eighteen of them plus their horses at one stroke. The guns, said the historian, were manned by "the boys from Havre de Grace" (where the Susquehanna River empties into the upper Chesapeake Bay), and these were "expert duck hunters which gave them that calm, yet quick and accurate sight, without getting excited." Such characteristics, he said, "are so essential to a good artillery man." At any rate, the blue-coats drove the Johnnies back up Catoctin Mountain at a cost of some twelve killed and fifty wounded rebels. Half that number of bluecoats were casualties, with dead cows and damage to farm property the heaviest toll. Perhaps more importantly, Alexander was using up artillery ammunition that should have been reserved for the major upcoming confrontation.[24]

A brilliant victory having eluded him, Bradley Johnson abandoned his command post on a low range of hills not far from the house of George William Smith, and, acting under Ransom's orders, broke off the action about 9:00 P.M. Confident that his flankers could have knifed into Frederick via South Market Street, and thus combined with another flanking force working from the northwest via the reservoir road to rout the opposition in his front, Johnson was chagrined with Ransom's constraints and sundown order to withdraw from the fighting. So chastened, Johnson established headquarters for the night in Hagan's (or Hogan's) Tavern. An elated Wallace wired Lawrence at Baltimore headquarters: "Think I have had the best battle of the war. Our men did not retreat, but held their own. The enemy were repulsed three times." He also sent a slightly briefer statement to Halleck, stating that a portion of his command had "handsomely repulsed" a band of rebels. Halleck never replied directly to Wallace's wire although the War Department had the telegram in hand by 11:00 P.M. Wallace also sent Garrett the news at 8:53 P.M., and the railroad president in turn passed the dispatch to Halleck so that it arrived at 9:30 P.M. Lawrence, at least, welcomed the news and asked if Wallace wanted it passed to the press.[25]

Finally, Halleck telegraphed Wallace at 9:40 P.M. telling him to impress all horses in Maryland and the border counties of Pennsylvania. This move would keep them from rebel hands, but also help remount the blue-clad cavalrymen being sent by train and canal boat to the mouth of the Monocacy. Both sides, as usual, sought remounts. As Gilpin told Tyler at 4:00 P.M. that day, "we have sent all the horses we can obtain." The rebels seemed to be doing a better job of corralling horses west of South Mountain, read the sketchy scouting reports sent to Couch's headquarters at Harrisburg. By late evening, however, it became apparent in all sectors that this was not merely some raid for horses.

Interrogation of a Lieutenant George M. E. Shearer of Bradley Johnson's staff and two other captives from his 1st Maryland Cavalry, convinced the provost marshal's office at the Pennsylvania state capital of two things, at least. First, Longstreet's and Ewell's corps of Lee's army had left their Richmond fortifications and "are undoubtedly somewhere in the neighborhood of the Potomac River." Second, that their design was not upon Pennsylvania but upon the city of Washington. Suddenly, the wires buzzed with the name Bradley Johnson and his Maryland and Virginia horsemen. Even City Point headquarters had to supply what it knew about this contingent. Either the fighting near Frederick, or intelligence about a rumored raid on Point Lookout prison had the Union War Department aflutter in this regard.[26]

Higher headquarters, thanks to B & O president John Garrett, also realized by evening that local commanders such as Wallace, Tyler, and Couch hesitated operating across jurisdictional boundaries. Accordingly, at 9:00 and 10:00 P.M., respectively, Halleck issued orders to Middle and Pennsylvania department commanders not to worry about strict departmental lines. Wallace was already doing so by default. Mostly, however, the War Department and rear echelon headquarters focused upon getting Army of the Potomac veterans back to the capital region, under some capable overall commander, and quickly inserted into the equation. Grant initially thought that Couch might handle the responsibility pending Hunter's reappearance. Halleck wanted Major General Quincy Gillmore, however. Everyone was sure that Sigel needed to be replaced.

Indeed, Special Orders 230 from Washington did just that, supplanting both Sigel and Julius Stahel with Howe. Their troops remained inert on Maryland Heights, continuing to thwart Early's direct passage downriver en route to Washington from that direction. Hunter, meanwhile, was nowhere close to the chess board and Curtin and Couch continued their hassles with Washington about troop call-up. So the capital region's safety continued to depend upon Sheridan's dismounted cavalrymen and especially Brigadier General James B. Ricketts' infantry division getting back as the corset-stays for reserve troops and militiamen before the rebels overwhelmed them. By late evening, the high command, from Lincoln through Grant and Meade, assumed that 8,000–10,000 veteran troops had been directed to concentrate at the "mouth of the Monocacy," and that supply officers and transportation officials had set the transfer in motion.[27]

A central problem remained. Such concentration was not taking place either smoothly or fast enough. Refitting dismounted cavalry at the Giesboro Depot in Washington was a hurdle, but then there was the matter of sending upcountry blacksmiths, forges, and quartermasters with money to pay for the impressed horses. The greatest bottleneck proved to be Baltimore where a gigantic mixup between commissary, ordnance, and transport personnel (including John Garrett's hard-pressed railroad officials), threatened to delay and frustrate the whole scheme of placing Ricketts' arriving troops onto rail cars headed west. The B & O was already clogged with trains chugging back and forth with provisions, ammunition, and other supplies for Wallace's troops. Even that operation had become snarled, due to the transfer of ammunition from Fort McHenry magazines to a nearby rail siding.

Then as the army's transports hove to at Locust Point, a message came that none of the troops could disembark until Ricketts himself appeared to give the order. Consternation swept over Lawrence, Garrett, and others. They immediately bombarded the War Department with requests to countermand that directive. Garrett, in particular, had his locomotives fired up and ready to move. It took until 9:00 P.M. to get the necessary guidance from Stanton. Finally, sometime after that, with ordnance, commissary, and all other support officials actively working to get this latest column in motion, Colonel William S. Truex's brigade was the first to move westward by rail to Monocacy Junction with five days' rations in their haversacks. They had been waiting aboard their transport *Columbia* since noon to disembark, finally doing so at 6:00 P.M.[28]

The race against time continued as another night of warm darkness spread across the capital region. Men rushed about in Baltimore getting other men aboard rail cars and off to the fighting. Lawrence, acting under Wallace's orders, told Brevet Brigadier General William W. Morris to hold all of his troops in the city in a state of readiness, gather all stragglers, and prepare the meager defenses of the city accordingly. One set of returns had less than 1,000 men left in town for such duty. Over in Washington, local commanders surveyed and readied the northern defense line of that city by having their men clear brush and trash from overgrown earthworks. Responding to B & O master of transportation W. P. Smith's continuing anxiety, other contingents were sent out to guard the bridges and culverts on the Baltimore and Washington branch of the B & O. At Monocacy Junction, on the main stem to the west, an ever alert Lew Wallace plotted his next move and sent a complementary dispatch forward to Gilpin on the battle-line west of Frederick about 8:40 P.M. "You have behaved nobly," it read, "endeavor to hold your ground, but make no movement to drive the enemy from your front." Let the enemy remain where they are, suggested Wallace, as "I will endeavor to put a force in their rear tonight." An overly-optimistic Wallace anticipated eight thousand veteran troops would be on the ground by 1:00 in the morning. Sometime after dark, he sent for a young volunteer aide, Lieutenant E. Y. Goldsborough (a Frederick native who had recently retired from active service with the 8th Maryland because of poor health to be the state's attorney in his hometown). Goldsborough's mission was to determine Gilpin's exact state of affairs. What Wallace wanted to do was run the first arrivals from Baltimore out on the railroad toward Harpers Ferry where they could get into Bradley Johnson's rear and do damage. No such troops arrived in time, however, as he recalled in his autobiography, and "the wisdom of the enterprise was not put to test." Rather, out there in the darkness, on the side of Catoctin Mountain the rebels themselves sank down into makeshift bivouacs, the mystery of their numbers and their intent unsolved.[29]

At some point, earlier that day, Lee had written President Davis from Petersburg giving him a detailed accounting of what he knew of Federal movements based on scouting reports and published information in the New York *Herald*. The intelligence was very sketchy, but the Army of the Northern Virginia commander had a pretty good idea about Yankee troop movements on the James, Hunter's movements in West Virginia, and public knowledge of Early's activities at Martinsburg and vicinity. Building upon reports of cheering blue-coats passing downriver on the steamers, the precise encampments of Union cavalry just south of Jordan's Point on the James River, and the fact that some sixty-eight enemy regiments were to be discharged that month—"the probabilities are that they are troops bound for Washington, and if Hunter is brought up the Ohio and around by railroad Early may be opposed by a force too large for him to manage," the general told Davis. He promised to warn Early so that he could be on guard, but, although Lee did not say so, it might be too late. Now, Confederate as well as Union high authority had something to worry about, for Lee, like Grant knew that his opponent had detached much-needed troops from the Petersburg operation, even though the size, destination, and purpose of these troop redeployments remained unclear.[30]

July 8—The "Battle of Frederick"

Brigadier General James B. Ricketts, commanding the Third Division, VI Corps, wired Halleck at 12:45 A.M., on July 8, that he and "the greater part of my division" had arrived at Baltimore, and awaited further orders. The rest of the command "will be here by evening"; transportation and ammunition train having been left behind at City Point. To the west, an all-pervading hush settled across the Monocacy Valley, although the fitful Wallace and his staffers arose time and again, listening anxiously for the sound of the first train from Baltimore. Garrett's people had one moving at 12:50 A.M., carrying Truex's brigade, with a second starting at 3:20. Finally, as Wallace dozed on a simple pallet of boards by the door of his makeshift quarters ("bare as Mother Hubbard's cupboard," he remembered years afterward), one of Leib's troopers acting as an orderly, awakened the general. A train was coming from the east. Wallace directed Major James R. Ross to stop the cars before they reached the iron bridge and bring the senior officer to him. This proved to be Colonel William W. Henry of the 10th Vermont. Overcoming vexation at interruption of his passage to Harpers Ferry, the pragmatic Henry soon acceded to Wallace's request that he reinforce the battle line at Frederick.[31]

Henry's manner suggested to Wallace a shrewd, brave, and conscientious soldier—an "Ethan Allen and the Green Mountains"—whose missing finger on one hand seemingly symbolized a combat wound. Henry informed Wallace that his division commander would be up by "one-o'clock to-night," and Wallace quickly advised that the Vermonters partake of breakfast before joining Tyler's battle line west of town. Lieutenant Goldsborough had already reported Gilpin in need of help, and Tyler, too, had sent word back early that morning that the Marylanders had gone forward at daylight to probe the enemy on the side of Catoctin Mountain. Everyone had plenty of ammunition, suggested Tyler, although Alexander needed his battery forge for horse shoeing. At any rate, Wallace determined to rush forward the rest of the artillery, the 11th Maryland, and the ten companies of the 144th and 149th Ohio. He most certainly wanted Henry's Vermonters to bolster Tyler's weak left

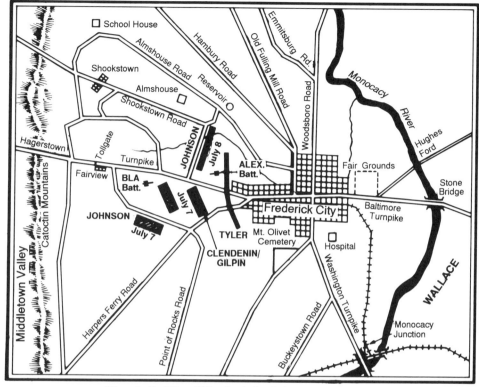

Map 4. Battle of Frederick, July 7 and 8, 1864

flank, since it lay closest to the main concentration of his little army at Monocacy Junction.[32]

The Vermonters were ready after an hour with fire, skillet, and coffee pot. Counting one hundred rounds of ammunition stuffed into each man's cartridge box and pockets, they re-boarded the train. Leaving Lieutenant Colonel Lynde Catlin to supervise things at the junction, Wallace took a seat next to Henry as the locomotive and cars swayed slowly up the branch line into town. On the way, the Hoosier stressed to Henry the need to "give as large an impression of your numbers as possible," to the peering eyes of the enemy. The experienced veteran nodded, "I have practiced that before; if the ground is broken, it is easily done." The two men parted at the Frederick station, on the corner of All Saints and South Market Streets. Off went the Vermonter with his troops to find Tyler. Wallace and his staff, meanwhile, waited for orderlies to bring up their horses before likewise going to the western outskirts of town and the impending combat.[33]

Wallace and Henry both found Tyler, Gilpin, Alexander, and Clendenin ready to renew the fight. The terrain was favorable for defense, the soldiers' spirits bright (as Wallace rode about congratulating everyone on the previous day's success). They all watched with interest as clouds of dust about a mile or two out on Catoctin Mountain indicated the advancing Confederates. Still, the renewed fighting remained fragmentary as Johnson and Ransom showed little energy before 10:00 A.M. Even the Maryland and Ohio reinforcements from the junction recalled later that they had not made the march to town and gotten into line much before noon. Clendenin and Alexander went out once more to probe Confederate positions on the Hagerstown, Harpers Ferry and, some said, Mountain or Snookstown roads. Henry's people began their hours of marching and counter-marching around the little hill near the battleline that for years would provide for yarn-swapping tales at regimental reunions as "Deception Peak."

Indeed, Colonel William S. Truex, commanding Ricketts' First Brigade, decided to deceive what he thought were Early's signal corps' observers on Catoctin Mountain by parading back and forth to create an illusion of strength. He even rode his old gray war horse at the head of a column over one hilltop, while next to him an orderly prominently displayed the brigade banner—a white painted banner sporting the Greek Cross of the VI Corps. He considered it a good thing that Early should know the Army of the Potomac veterans were now present. So the Army of the Potomac veterans kept marching around what some have suggested was the modern Linden Hills on the old national road, although it may well have been the hill located about a mile west of town and south of the Hagerstown pike—opposite the modern state police station. At any rate, they performed a steady left turn movement so that the enemy could always see them as they emerged on the north and west sides before slipping south and east through gullies to repeat the maneuver.[34]

Clendenin's activity proved equally brash. Some of his men, accompanied by a cannon, apparently got into Johnson's rear and nearly to Middletown at one point. They noticed the carnage and fresh graves from the previous day's fight before Harry Gilmor's Maryland Confederate battalion arrived to "clean them out." J. Kelly Bennette, the 8th Virginia Cavalry's medic, remembered how one of Alexander's shells actually cut in twain a rebel rider and his horse, and the action was bloody but brief. Clendenin was more successful in stampeding the rebel command post at secessionist-owned Hagen's tavern on the Middletown road. However, superior numbers gradually forced the Illinois horsemen back down the mountain to the main battle line at Frederick. By mid-afternoon, this pressure threatened even Wallace's composure. Then a messenger arrived with a wire from Howe at Harpers Ferry (Mosby's telegraph wrecking operations apparently having been transitory). Neither general knew one another's specific situation, but Howe wanted Wallace to march and join forces with him. The Hoosier guickly fired back a reply that it would be "injudicious to advance from Frederick" until he had replenished supplies, and, more importantly, until he had better intelligence about the moves of the enemy "said to be retiring towards Boonesborough." He asked for Howe's help in that regard so that a "concentrated action can be had between my force and that at Harper's Ferry."[35]

Wallace realized, what Howe (and his predecessors) could not know by remaining holed up on Maryland Heights: Any shift from Frederick would open the roads and railroad to Baltimore and Washington—a situation he was sworn to prevent. So, he watched the growing contention between skirmishers that went "languidly on," broken occasionally by artillery fire that amused his lounging militia and the Frederick citizen onlookers. Joseph Urner's grandfather had clamored up into the cupola of the new courthouse and watched the first mounted Confederates come over the brow of Linden Hill to the west. Then, about 4:00 P.M., his binoculars disclosed what he had been awaiting—three long, continuous yellow cloud-lines, on as many roads, coming his way. It was Early's main force, now moving eastward in earnest.[36]

Major General Robert Rodes' column had traversed Crampton's Gap in South Mountain marching towards Jefferson on the Harpers Ferry pike, while Major Generals Stephen Ramseur, John B. Gordon, and John C. Breckinridge were moving from Boonsboro towards Middletown on the Hagerstown Road. Brigadier General William Lewis's brigade of North Carolinians brought up the rear, hauling salvageable supplies from Harpers Ferry. Having left the town the night before, they also had burned the trestle work of John Garrett's railroad bridge across the Potomac at that point. The colorful Gordon and his mounted party rode to the old Antietam battlefield so that he could regale his youthful staff with past glories. Then the scenery and heat began taking their toll all along the rebel march columns as men fell out to seek shade, fresh fruit, and, as always, water.[37]

Rest stops at hamlets like Rohrersville, Jefferson, and Shookstown helped the marchers. The "very uncomfortable heat" proved daunting, however, as Captain Robert Park of the 12th Alabama recalled. Still, the countryside was beautiful; neat, tidy, and unspoiled by war. To the older men in the ranks it was again reminiscent of the Sharpsburg campaign two years before. The column soon had a huge train of liberated horses, cattle, as well as harvest from berry patches and orchards. North Carolinians like Billy Beavans and George Wills of the 43d Infantry, and Sergeant Major John G. Young of the 4th Regiment State Troops, subsequently boasted that they had lived handsomely on cherries, apple butter, milk, and "the fat of the country," during this third campaign in Maryland. Army quartermasters took stock of some 1,000 horses and cattle secured in one day's foraging alone. Nobody worried about the burden of this booty for the march to Washington. By the time that Early's army reached Frederick on July 9, Young estimated that the army's wagon train alone stretched for nine miles along the highway. As of the previous afternoon, everyone was having too good a time plundering or cursing the heat. That serious fighting lay somewhere ahead bothered few of the marchers.[38]

The Confederate build-up by late afternoon caused sharp escalation in the fighting before Frederick. The Confederates were clearly in strength—estimates reached Wallace of upwards of 30,000 veterans in the enemy force, and he watched every shift on the firing line for some additional sign of intent. The occasional rush by Johnson and his horsemen was merely the deception of an advance guard, he decided, but he hinted to Tyler that withdrawal would have to occur that night. In the meantime, under the watchful eye of Frederick citizens, the blue-coats kept the Johnnies at bay. Despite warnings from the solicitous Wallace, these civilians refused to move to safety. A Confederate battery dropped a few shells into the city, including one that smashed through the roof of the Presbyterian church on Second Street, plunging through the floor of the chancel and burying itself harmlessly in the cellar. Joseph Urner's grandfather beat a hasty retreat from the courthouse cupola at this point, and some rebel sympathizers even came near losing their lives to "friendly fire" in the fray. Only sundown ended the fighting—and entertainment.[39]

Suddenly, early that evening, Clendenin thought he spotted a Confederate move toward the Buckeystown crossing of the Monocacy that led to Urbana on the turnpike to Washington. Clendenin sent word to Wallace. Catlin corroborated the intelligence a few minutes later by telegram from the junction, with additional word from deserters that Breckinridge and 12,000 men were "marching in the direction of Harper's Ferry," with more of the enemy on the road between Berlin and Point of Rocks. In one sense, this was the indicator that Wallace wanted—the rebel target was Washington, not Baltimore. On the other hand, any such flanking move would seriously endanger the Federals' advance position west of Frederick. Wallace remembered later that he had ordered Clendenin to take his command across the river "at the first ford below the wooden bridge on the Washington pike," and hold it against the enemy until further notice. "Take care of my left as best you can," he told the Illinoisan. Wallace also told Tyler to retire the little army across the river that night and prepare for the inevitable battle on the morrow.[40]

The fight for Frederick was over. Wallace and Tyler withdrew through town under cover of darkness. Covered by the 8th Illinois and Leib's men, a much chagrined Colonel Truex and his staff hastily abandoned a chicken and waffle supper laid out for them by the black kitchen servant of a loyal Unionist just outside of town. An orderly rushed up with Wallace's retirement order and the hungry officers (who had not eaten since leaving Baltimore the night before) "were compelled to leave without enjoying the evening repast," noted the regimental historian of the 87th Pennsylvania. In town, quartermasters tried to save the last government stores from the warehouse district near the railroad station. Then everyone moved eastward toward the jug bridge crossing. Many claimed to have been led by treacherous, or at least ignorant, guides into various mishaps. Some of Alexander's artillerymen lost their way in the darkness, stumbled over the stone bridge and down country lanes, losing a cannon and lumber in a ravine when a thunderstorm struck suddenly. They retrieved it with the help of some infantrymen, then continued up a blind path into a farmer's barnyard before eventually gaining Monocacy Junction and much needed rest near dawn.[41]

Pickets from the Pennsylvanians as well as the 14th New Jersey were also misled and bumbled around for a while. They had been spread out from north of Boonsboro or National Road to south of the pike to Jefferson. Concentrating them all took time. Lieutenant William Craig of Company D of the 14th remembered well how their baptism to the service had occurred two years before in campsites at Monocacy Junction. But now he had to perform the delicate task of extricating skirmishers using only whispers. They encountered shadowy, gray-clad figures that they took for Maryland militia and eventually scampered back through Frederick. Some of Clendenin's horsemen were the last Federals to leave town. Meanwhile, Wallace personally rode back, projecting a nonchalant air so as not to disturb the townspeople who had gathered asking about the retreat. Many of them had placed barrels of drinking water on street corners for the hot and tired government troops. Wallace felt truly sad to be abandoning them to the rebels, but he had little choice. His self-appointed mission was to uncover the size and intent of the enemy, as well as delay them; he now had to save his own troops. "There could no longer be room for doubt," he noted in colorful reminiscences later, "what I saw were columns of infantry, with trains of artillery." They were good strong columns too, he added, "of thousands and thousands." It would be suicide to fight them in the streets of Frederick.[42]

Wallace broke his self-imposed silence to Washington by wiring Halleck at 8:00 P.M., before leaving Frederick: "Breckinridge, with strong column, moving down the Washington pike toward Urbana, is within six miles of that place. I shall withdraw immediately from Frederick City and put myself in position on the road to cover Washington, if necessary." Indeed, the first sentence was slightly premature, despite feints and movements to Tyler's left all during the fighting on the eighth, an obvious indication of what the morrow portended. Then too, Wallace sounded a bit self-serving—possibly for Halleck's benefit—since his official obligation hardly lay with screening Washington. Still, Halleck had told him not to worry about departmental boundaries, and no matter how badly outnumbered, somebody had to blunt the rebel drive. Then too, Garrett's railroad bridge and the junction lay south, not east, of the city. Wallace's line of communications was the B & O and his base of operations at Monocacy or Frederick junction near the turnpike to Washington south of the city where it crossed the Monocacy. So, dutifully and professionally, he opted to defend the way to the capital, not the direct roadway back to Baltimore.[43]

For the moment, Wallace's immediate needs lay with reconcentrating his meager strength and succoring his men. He had sent four telegrams during the day to Baltimore concerning subsistence, as his supplies were stretched thin. But, confusion reigned in that city, unbeknownst to the Hoosier general. Lieutenant Colonel Lawrence tried to rush supplies forward by rail only to conflict with the need for transportation to carry Ricketts' men to the front. Lawrence had the first subsistence train ready at 5:00 A.M. that morning; another at noon. Garrett's priorities, however, came from the War Department in Washington. In actuality, the B & O president sent six troop trains out to the Monocacy during the day, starting at 12:50 A.M., with Truex's people aboard. A second left at 3:20 A.M., a third at 7:45 A.M., a fourth at 8:30 A.M., a fifth at 9:40 A.M., and the final train at 4:00 that afternoon. All of the veterans started with only the food in their haversacks. They would get more at Monocacy Junction, they were told. Halleck further confused the situation by wiring Ricketts to draw upon the chief of ordnance and the quartermaster general at the capital if Baltimore storehouses proved incapable of support. At any rate, Wallace needed both Ricketts' men and the food. He also needed more ammunition, artillery, and some entrenching shovels. It lay with logisticians to sort out the problem.[44]

Forty miles to the south, in Washington, the day had passed anxiously but placidly. Officials bustled about shifting resources to cover the unfolding threat from north of the city. Veteran Reserve Corps convalescents went out to man the northern defense line particularly where the road from Frederick entered the lines. Veteran commander of the 1st Vermont Heavy Artillery, Colonel J. M. Warner, took charge of the area and tried to drill the newcomers in the ways of managing heavy ordnance. Rumors came in about rebel scouting parties at Brookville—north of Silver Spring out the Seventh Street Road and scarcely seventeen miles northwest of the Baltimore and Ohio station at Laurel on the Baltimore-Washington line. Similar reports had rebel horsemen, possibly Mosby, at Falls Church in Virginia.

From Pennsylvania came word of 30,000 men and 125 pieces of artillery comprising the invasion force, as well as horse thievery and brazen looting in the Hagerstown-Boonsboro region. Couch and the War Department continued to tarry about mobilizing the Pennsylvania militia, although Department of the East commander, Major General John A. Dix, dispatched the convalescent 10th Veteran Reserve Corps regiment from New York City during the day. By now just about everybody except the B & O's Garrett had given up on getting Hunter's army back through West Virginia in time to be a factor. Halleck and Grant haggled about the top general's desire to have Major General E. O. C. Ord, not Quincy Gillmore, as the overall commander stopping the invasion. "I do not wish, however, to change any order that may have been made," Grant acquiesced. In all, the day's activities were hung up on the differing impressions of affairs upriver. Only by early afternoon had some clarity begun to appear in Henry Halleck's thinking, at least, in Washington.[45]

Halleck wired Grant, at 2:30 P.M., about the state of affairs. Impending arrival of Army of the Gulf veterans from New Orleans for service with Meade and Grant suggested additional reinforcements that could be re-directed to Washington. Ricketts' division had reached Baltimore and had gone forward to the Monocacy, but Sheridan's dismounted cavalrymen were mostly so sick that barely 500 could take the field. Halleck dismissed Hunter's presence as coming too slowly over a broken railroad. He recounted the enemy activity all over the area, and the "considerable alarm" in Washington, Baltimore, and Pennsylvania. By 1:30 P.M., the picture was even bleaker.

Halleck now had Wallace's dispatch about rebel movements toward Urbana on the Washington turnpike plus information from Sigel and Couch based on scout, prisoners, and citizen reports. Enemy strength estimates ranged between 20,000 and 30,000. Hunter was completely out of the picture, and "until more forces arrive we have nothing to meet that number in the field," Halleck declared. The militia wasn't reliable enough even to hold forts at Baltimore and Washington. One third of Lee's army was north of the Potomac, and if Grant wanted to cut off the raid and not merely to secure depots, "we must have more forces here." In a dramatic reversal, Halleck now requested that troops be sent from the James to Washington, not Baltimore. "I think ... that very considerable reinforcements should be sent directly to this place," were his words.[46]

* * * *

It had been a tiring day for everyone. It was an especially tough one for Clendenin's hardworking Illinois troopers. Silas Wesson penned in his diary, " Been fighting and marching night and day," as "the country is full of rebs." He noted the loss of a comrade, Charley Greenville, who had been born in Finland and served in the Czar of Russia's army during the Crimea. "He was a good soldier," said Wesson simply. He went on to observe how the Confederates had outnumbered the blue-coats and that all they could do was fall back. The Maryland home guards came to help them, but they were no good, he sneered. Down at old Francis Preston Blair's Silver Spring mansion, just north of Washington, daughter Elizabeth Blair Lee wrote her admiral husband that they could hear cannon fire all day, although some family members dismissed the sound as mere thunder. Assistant Secretary of the Navy Gustavus Fox had assured her that the Confederates had retreated back to the Shenandoah Valley. But, she did not quite believe him. The officials' silence seemed ominous, she scoffed, and she was anxious to be off with her mother to the Jersey shore "where I can sleep more than I can here."[47]

In town, President Abraham Lincoln issued a strong proclamation on the eighth underscoring a constitutional amendment to abolish slavery. He also declared that he would not support Congress's contention that only that body had the authority to eradicate that national blight—an underscoring of his pocket veto four days before of the so-called Wade-Davis reconstruction bill. The chief executive intended to remain flexible about how different states chose to prepare themselves for returning to the Union.

Out in Loudoun County, Virginia, ranger Mosby extracted his wily partisans from their raid on Point of Rocks, and bivouacked that night near Waterford, Virginia. They were returning to protect their corner of the Confederacy against a rumored raid from the 2d Massachusetts Cavalry. They had not accomplished much, possibly only briefly disrupting Union communications on the Maryland side of the river but contributing no sustained service to Jubal Early's expedition. Mosby—like most partisans—was too busy protecting his own lair. Perhaps Early was right about "buttermilk rangers," at least he remained bitter for years about Mosby's lack of true cooperation in the Maryland campaign.

At the Charles Coblentz farm just ouside Middletown toward the western foot of Catoctin Mountain, Old Jube set up his headquarters. His army bivouacked on the other side of Hollow Creek, where the Fountaindale subdivision sprawls today. He had ransomed tiny Middletown for $1,500 during his passage but he had hoped for $8,000. The next day would be pivotal to his further success. He needed to pass Frederick quickly, and make time down those forty-odd miles to Washington. Suddenly, however, there was this added Point Lookout mission from Lee. Up on Catoctin Mountain, a miserable Bradley Johnson awaited directions in a drizzly rain.[48]

FOUR

Monocacy—Morning Rendezvous

An overnight thunderstorm deluged the Confederate bivouacs in Middletown Valley and atop Catoctin Mountain. Maryland brigadier Bradley Johnson was especially miserable. The damned Yankees occupied his hometown and he could do nothing about it. Proud scion of a local Frederick family, his uncle had been Governor Thomas Johnson, and he himself had been states attorney in 1851. As delegate to the 1860 Democratic convention, he had supported Kentuckian, now Confederate general, John C. Breckinridge, for president. That night, Breckinridge was somewhere down the mountain at Jubal Early's headquarters, second-in-command of the army to which Johnson was assigned. Johnson, meanwhile, was being restrained by his immediate superior from reaching his home at North Court and West Second streets in Frederick and freeing his family from Yankee oppression.

Then at some point during the evening, Johnson was called to Jubal Early's headquarters and told that he and his troopers were to be entrusted with the Point Lookout mission. Supposedly on June 26, Robert E. Lee had declared to President Jefferson Davis that Johnson was the most suitable person to lead the expedition. "Bold and intelligent, ardent and true," were the words he had used about the Marylander, although Lee admitted that he was unable to say if Johnson had all the requisite qualities, for everything "in an expedition of the kind would depend upon the leader." In any event Frederick's liberation would be the responsibility of others as Early fretted the whereabouts of David Hunter from the west and kept a 140-man contingent from McNeill's Partisan Rangers with Imboden's cavalry busy scouting and watching—"sometimes 5 or 6 miles in the rear," according to Henry Truehart. Meanwhile, the rest of the army restlessly awaited the dawn of yet another hot day.[1]

Saturday, July 9, dawned without a cloud in the sky and a cool freshness to the air after the overnight rain. Shifting wet blankets across already sore shoulders, the gray-clads breakfasted quickly while the first skirmishers, led by Major Henry Kyd Douglas of Early's staff, moved slowly down the mountain, probing their way into Frederick. The scene was glorious for early risers like Virginian J. Kelly Bennette who saw the town's spires "rising far above the hills glitter like silver and gold in the burning sun." Others like Tar Heel Sergeant Major John G. Young looked for something far different. Frederick, he was told, contained any number of pretty girls, "most of them I believe secesh," he recorded. Friends of the invaders soon alerted Early's men to the Federal evacuation, then cheered lustily as the rebels moved into the city.[2]

From the Confederate perspective, the city's reaction seemed quite friendly. Father James Sheeran, the 14th Louisiana's chaplain, lost control of his horse in the clamor, much to the rankers' glee. Cary Whitaker, an officer with the 43d North Carolina, penned in his diary how a captain in his unit told him that there was much "waving of handkerchiefs, handing out of water on the streets and other indications of friendship for the Confederate cause" when they marched through town that morning.

Local secessionist Peter Bahm presented Douglas with a pair of spurs as thanks for "deliverance," while Alabama Captain Robert E. Park recalled later that John Greenlief Whittier's heroine, the "mythical Barbara Frietchie," was nowhere in evidence as supposedly she had been when Jackson marched through town two years before. He was unaware even then that the ninety-seven-year-old Frietchie had died two months after Antietam, hence could not have been present to taunt the rebels again in 1864, even had she actually done so during their previous visit. Indeed, Frederick had a strong nationalist streak. Three hundred forty-one of her citizens had voted for the Union, compared to only 117 for secession, and city voters in 1860 went with southern Unionist candidate John Bell for president instead of county and statewide preference for state's right Democrat John Breckinridge. On July 9, however, Unionists remained behind shuttered windows.[3]

Frederick City

Founded by German immigrants like Thomas Schley and Joseph Brunner (who built the famous local farmhouse Schifferstadt), around the middle of the eighteenth century, English settlers also helped identify Frederick as a frontier market town. Frederick hosted an April 1755 meeting between British general Edward Braddock and colonials George Washington and Benjamin Franklin as well as the Maryland provincial governor Horatio Sharpe to plan the ill-fated attempt to take French Fort Duquesne in western Pennsylvania. Braddock's men encamped five miles to the west on the mountain slopes at a natural spring—a locale known to this day as Braddock Spring on Braddock Heights. Ten years later the first rebellion against England's despised Stamp Act occurred in Frederick as twelve local judges called "the 12 Immortals" repudiated that act. Local youth then went off to aid the minutemen besieging Boston while stone barracks erected by British prisoners during the Revolution signaled American determination "to remove as far as possible the necessity of quartering troops in private houses"—one of the grievances that had led to confrontation with the mother country in the first place. Local businessman and banker Casper E. Cline supplied the limestone for those barracks from his quarry, located about a mile south of town. Hessians taken at Trenton, Saratoga, and Yorktown supplied the labor. One of those prisoners stayed on in Frederick after the war and sired Jacob Engelbrecht, who by the 1860s was a local tailor, businessman, and inveterate diarist.[4]

Subsequently, Revolutionary patriot and first state governor, Judge Thomas Johnson, John Hanson (the first "President of the United States in Congress Assembled" in 1781), and local attorney-turned-writer, author of the "Star Spangled Banner," Francis Scott Key, as well as controversial Chief Justice Rodger Brooke Taney (of Dred Scott litigation fame), all called Frederick home. During the turbulent secession winter of 1861, a refugeed Maryland legislature met briefly in Kemp Hall (later a Federal supply facility) when violence and rioting disrupted Baltimore and Annapolis, causing the Lincoln administration to send troops to place those cities under martial law. From their Frederick session, however, the legislators solemnly declined to carry the state out of the Union—adhering to conventional Southern wisdom of the time that only a specially elected convention could do that and that this was inexpedient given expanding Union military occupation of the Old Line State. The politicians denounced both occupation and the war as unconstitutional, vowed Maryland neutrality on the issue of coercing seceded states back into the Union and actually called for recognition of the Confederacy as an independent nation.

Still, this too passed, and if many of Early's men had kinsmen and friends in the area in 1864, so too, did soldiers of the Union! Frederick and environs truly reflected a "house divided" by civil war. The city streets and roads beyond had subsequently felt the tramp and rumble of feet, hooves, and wagon wheels of both armies going to and from the killing

Frederick, Maryland Court House

This structure replaced an earlier court house dating to 1784 but mysteriously destroyed by fire in 1861. The replacement was completed a year later, although county officials did not move in until 1864.

Marken and Bielfeld, Souvenir of Historic Frederick (1925), p. 2.

Street Scene, Carroll Creek Crossing, Looking East. Frederick, Maryland

Marken and Bielfeld, Souvenir of Historic Frederick (1925), p. 3

Confederate Soldiers on Patrick Street in Frederick, Maryland, September 1862

Two years later rebel troops once more marched through this city en route to the battle of Monocacy. Their numbers were less but their valor and determination were undiminished.

Frederick County Historical Society

Old Baltimore and Ohio Railroad Freight Depot in Frederick

Such facilities plus warehouses and hospitals provided a supply base for Union forces operating in Maryland and Pennsylvania during the war.

Marken and Bielfeld, Souvenir of Historic Frederick (1925), p. 29.

Lew Wallace's Headquarters at Monocacy Junction

Turn-of-century view looking northwest, Washington turnpike bridge in distances to left, Baltimore and Ohio Railroad bridge on right—house no longer standing.

Courtesy The Historical Society of Frederick County, Inc.

View from Tyler's Position, Jug Bridge Sector

Looking toward Hughes Ford. Monocacy River in trees in center scene of final action in late afternoon, July 9, 1864. Photograph circa 1940.

Oscar Bray, "A Proposed Road on the Monocacy Battlefield," April 26, 1940
Courtesy National Park Service, Harpers Ferry Center Library

Remains of Union Trenches

Overlooking covered bridge crossing of Monocacy River on Washington Turnpike, photograph circa 1940.
Folder, Monocacy Battlefield Reports, Harpers Ferry Center Library, Harpers Ferry, W.Va.

Scene of McCausland's Encounter Battle with Ricketts' Veterans

Looking northwest across Araby farm toward Brooks Hill on left, Worthington farm on right. Note wheat shocks much as they would have been on July 9, 1864. Photograph circa 1940.

Oscar Bray, *"A Proposed Road on the Monocacy Battlefield," April 26, 1940* National Park Service, Harpers Ferry Center Library

Jug Bridge Sector Battlefield

Looking west toward Rodes' battleline on crest of ridge. All-day skirmishing took place in fields to front. Jug or urn now resides in city park beyond scope of photograph.

Courtesy The Historical Society of Frederick County, Inc.

grounds of South Mountain, Antietam and Gettysburg. Robert E. Lee, Stonewall Jackson, George Gordon Meade, even President Abraham Lincoln himself (visiting a wounded general after Antietam in a house still standing on court square) had visited Frederick. Taking their lead from Lew Wallace's postwar observation that the city and vicinity "had been a playground for the game of war from its first year," Frederickans Paul and Rita Gordon offer a pleasant introduction to these tumultous times. Through it all, however, the little city had been spared destruction. The "clustered spires" of the old churches that inspired Whittier's poetry similarly refreshed the spirits of soldiers and civilians, blue and gray alike, who loved the pretty upland Maryland community.[5]

Throughout the years then, the key to Frederick's importance lay both as a market town and county seat, but also because of long distance highways that transited the town. In the earlier part of the century, the echo of "wagon wheels west" had sounded in her streets with settlers migrating toward the alluring land beyond the mountains to the west. The colonial road to Cumberland soon became part of what was known as the federally funded National Road that eventually linked Baltimore with the Mississippi valley. Just east of town stood a magnificent stone bridge which carried that road over the Monocacy. Built in 1807–1808 by well-known Frederick countian Leonard Harbaugh at a cost of $55,000 to the turnpike company, it was meant to stand the test of time. Harbaugh also constructed the three locks at Great Falls of the Potomac to make the river navigable for long boats, and similar facilities at Harpers Ferry on the Shenandoah River. He similarly built other stone buildings in Baltimore, Georgetown, and the District of Columbia including "the President's house before it was burned by the English in 1814," according to one local historian. Here, at Frederick's stone bridge in December 1824, town citizens greeted the Marquis de Lafayette and escorted him to their fair city. "There are few if any finer specimens of bridge-making in America," declared one awe-struck young New Yorker who first saw the edifice at the time of the Monocacy battle in 1864. "It is still as firm and beautiful as when erected [in 1808]," he declared after the struggle. He took note particularly of "the great stone decanter or cruise on the eastern end, placed there probably to indicate the plenty known to abound in Frederick county." Locals affectionately dubbed it "the Jug bridge."[6]

Yet, before the war, the highway already enjoyed competition from the young Baltimore and Ohio Railroad that crossed the river just to the south of Frederick. The city itself escaped railroad tracks in its midst except for the spur from Frederick or Monocacy Junction that terminated at the passenger station at All Saints and South Market Streets. A similar freight facility wasn't far away. Campaigns north of the Potomac in 1862 and 1863 spawned development as a regional supply and hospital rehabilitation center with storehouses rented by military authorities while a barracks hospital, designated General Hospital Number 1, regularized ersatz care of sick and wounded in local churches and schools following Antietam and Gettysburg. Maryland's strong Roman Catholic heritage was reflected in the hard work performed by Sisters of Charity in Frederick military hospitals. On the one hand, Frederick's mercantile and agrarian surroundings and its railroad and turnpikes seemed fatefully linked even before the great rebellion. Yet, nowhere did this become more apparent, however, than during those three fateful July days in 1864. Ironically, even Jubal Early was familiar with Monocacy junction and environs. His brigade had bivouacked there on the night of September 6, 1862, en route to Antietam.[7]

Ransoming Frederick

Physician and slaveholder, Richard Hammond, welcomed Old Jube who immediately set up temporary headquarters with his host at Second and Market Streets. He did not think that Frederick held the rich treasure trove that had been uncovered in Martinsburg and Harpers Ferry. Informers swore that Wallace's two days of delaying tactics, plus the slow Confederate advance, had permitted Union citizens to hide their personal property, especially horses. The banks had also made arrangements and the Internal Revenue collector had sent $70,000 in funds to Washington for safekeeping. Government warehouses had been emptied the night before, and railroad officials had withdrawn all locomotives and cars east of the Monocacy. Nevertheless, Early wanted to ransom the city, and immediately sent his supply officers to present town fathers with an ultimatum. They were to impose a financial levy, or burn down the city. He wanted this border-state community to feel his wrath "in retaliation for similar acts by Federal forces within our borders," Early told his officers. Privately, he assured the Hammonds that "you need not fear, as timely warning will be given you to leave with your family" if any burning took place.[8]

Hammond and his wife preserved the little walnut drop-leaf table upon which Early supposedly wrote his demand for tribute. Yet, the surviving document was signed by four of the general's supply officers, asking for a "contribution" from town fathers. Early's emissaries included Lieutenant Colonel William Allan, ordnance chief; Major W. J. Hawks, commissary chief; Major John A. Harmon, quartermaster; and Dr. Hunter McGuire, chief surgeon. They presented Early's demand for $200,000 "in current money for the use of the army," or $50,000 in material goods at current prices for each of their respective departments. The officers also demanded 20,000 pounds of bacon, 6,000 pounds of sugar, 3,000 pounds each of coffee and salt, and 500 barrels of flour. A brawny guard of rebel soldiers stood by during the negotiations, ready to burn Frederick to the ground if the mayor and council failed to comply with Southern demands. As friendly citizens entertained the transiting army, and Early prepared to battle Wallace south of the city, the supply officers haggled over these terms with Mayor William G. Cole and as many of the Board of Aldermen and Common Council as could be found. The wily civilians negotiated long and hard, in what the Confederates decided were stalling tactics.[9]

Allan claimed later that the civilians had stalled pending some resolution of the combat with Wallace. Indeed, the wily Cole, forty-nine-year-old brother of *Maryland Union* editor Charles Cole, had been around local politics since 1838. He had been first elected mayor as a Democrat in 1859 and then reelected on the Union ticket in 1862. He asked Allan and the other officers for time to consult with aldermen John Sifford, James Whitehill, David J. Markey, James Brunner, and Daniel Derr. He also wanted the advice of council members David C. Winebrenner, George Metzger, Edward Sinn, Thomas M. Holbruner, John A. Simmons, James Hergesheimer, and William Derr. In the end, however, his advisers proved to be Judge Richard H. Marshall (one of Taney's former law students, and himself longtime Associate Judge for the Circuit Court); Lawrence J. Bringle, former Maryland state legislator; R. H. McGill; and Joseph Baugher. Together, the townsmen advised Cole to play upon Confederate sympathies and sense of fairness. The assessment for a town of only 8,000 residents was "onerous," they decided, a sentiment soon incorporated in a formal petition to Early. After all, they noted, "the entire basis of the City does not exceed Two million, two hundred thousand dollars, that the tax now levied at the rate of $37^1/2$ cents on the 100$ produces 8000$, as the annual corporate tax of the City." Other assessments in Maryland had been far less (they apparently knew of the Hagerstown and Middletown demands), they added. Advancing that Hagerstown's tribute had been but one-tenth of that demanded of Frederick's citizens (news of their neighboring town's fate had made its way east rather quickly), Cole's delegation asked that Old Jube reconsider his demands.[10]

Early would not comply and the impasse continued all morning and into early afternoon. The Confederates' overall familiarity with the local community's wealth from previous visits mitigated against the civilian position. Then the general's twenty-four-year-old adjutant, Alexander "Sandy" Pendleton (whose father, a brilliant staff officer with Lee at Petersburg had been a prewar rector of All Saints Episcopal church in Frederick), joined the Confederate delegation with news of success in the battle raging just south of town. Finally, the mayor's party relented as officials of the Farmers and Mechanics, Franklin Savings, Frederick County, and Central Banks, along with the Frederick Town Savings Institute, came up with the cash (as a "loan to the city," they claimed). The latter institution produced $64,000; the Central Bank, $44,000; the Frederick County Bank, $33,000; the Franklin Savings Bank, $31,000; and the Farmers and Mechanics Bank $28,000 for the project. In all, Early's ransom reduced Frederick coffers by one-quarter of their capital. Major J. R. Braithwaite, the only bonded quartermaster officer in Early's whole force, gave Cole a receipt "in full payment," and a gentleman's agreement was reached that all property in the city, including that belonging to the Federal government would be spared. Braithwaite then reputedly hauled the money away in a wicker basket like some ancient nobleman receiving tribute from his serfs. John Murdock, a local freeman, claimed that at the last minute he had contributed $2.35 to cover a shortfall in the amount, and thus saved Frederick from burning.[11]

With the negotiations ended, Pendleton and the other elated staffers discovered a friendly restauranteur who plied the group with champagne and ice cream on that hot afternoon. Somehow, none of this would have impressed the struggling men in the ranks, by this time locked in mortal combat with the Yankees. That mattered little to Early's staff officers, of course. Other rebel foragers, mostly cavalrymen, brazenly walked into Frederick stores and liberated whatever they found in bins and on shelves, leaving only worthless rebel scrip in payment. No wonder local businessman Jacob Engelbrecht penned in his diary: "These are awful times, one day we are as usual and the next day in the hands of the enemy."[12]

Later, the Confederates found unevacuated warehouses brimming with quartermaster supplies. 380,872 cubic feet of space in seven locations plus ten or twelve of the finest and best equipped hospital buildings contained upwards of $262,500 worth of government property at the moment of Early's arrival, was cited by plaintiffs many years after the war. Bakeries with 10,000-loaf daily capacity, a forage house for 8,000 barrels of corn, corral and stables for over 300 horses were also noted, plus government workshops such as blacksmith shops, wagon repair facilities, paint shops, "and in fact everything needed for the use of a well equipped army—amounting in value at a fair estimate from $1,000,000 to $1,500,000" claimed attorney Edward Goldsborough in 1902.[13]

But Allan and his brother officers discovered this fact long after execution of the agreement with the town leaders. Duty bound to honor the arrangement and protect such property, the facilities and supplies returned to Union hands over the next several days when the men in blue came back to the city. Meanwhile, rebel scavengers undoubtedly liberated some of the materiel. On July 9, 1864, however, few residents in Frederick either recognized that fact or worried about the consequences. They were much too pleased to be spared Early's torches.[14]

Battle Preliminaries

The Federals, encamped on the Monocacy, suffered through the thunderstorm and restless night as did their opponents. Yet, they awoke, noted W. T. McDougle of Company K, 126th Ohio, years later, to a "halo of sunshine and beauty," birds singing joyfully (something

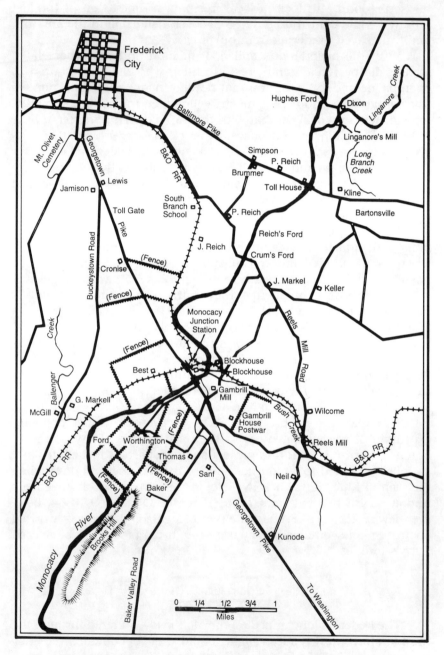

Map 5. Field of Monocacy, July 9, 1864—Pre-Battle

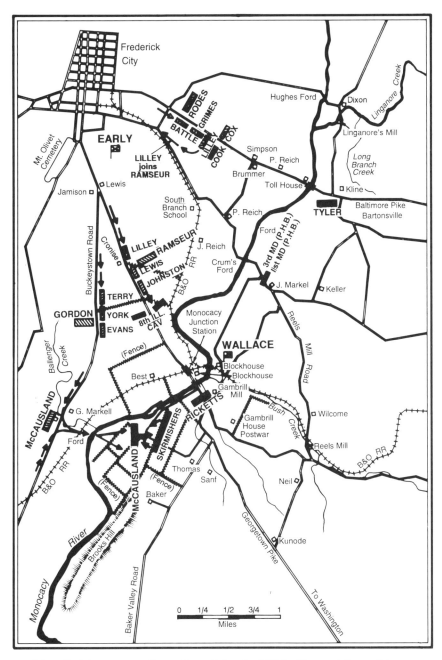

Map 6. Monocacy, Saturday, July 9, 1864—Troop Disposition, 8:00 A.M. to Noon.

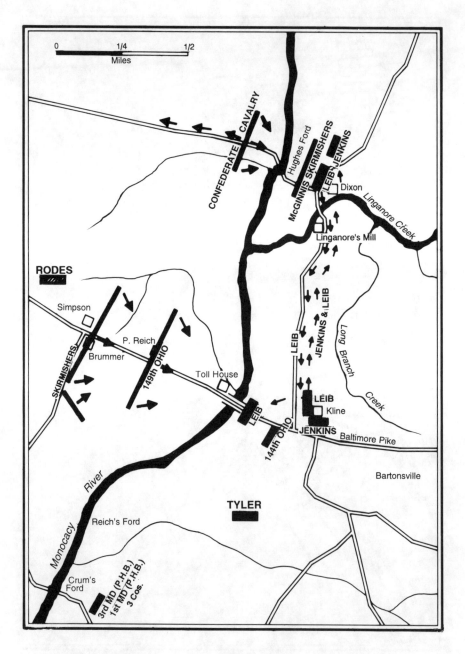

Map 7. Monocacy, July 9, 1864—Stone Bridge Sector, 8:00 A.M. to Noon.

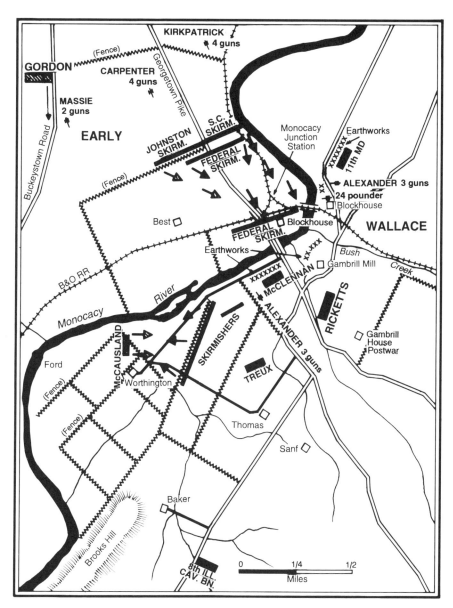

**Map 8. Monocacy, July 9, 1864—Junction Sector,
8:00 A.M. to Noon.**

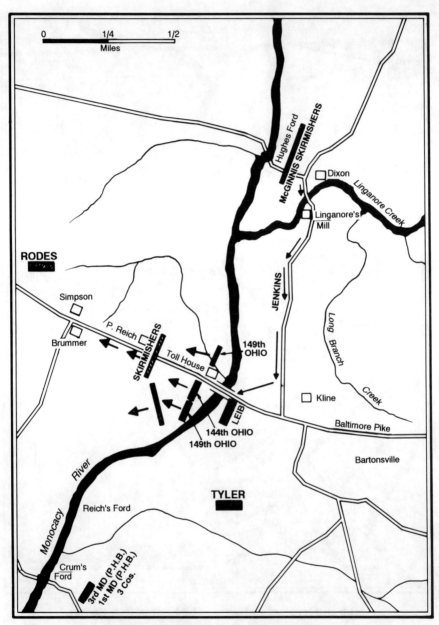

Map 9. Monocacy, July 9, 1864—Stone Bridge Sector, Noon to 2:30 P.M.

long absent from VI Corps veterans' experience before Petersburg), and the veritable "paradise" of the Keefer Thomas "Araby" farm with its fields and livestock. "We could scarcely believe it possible that before the setting of the sun this beautiful place would be the scene of such deadly strife. Still, refugees were streaming in, the rumble of distant firing could be heard in the direction of Harper's Ferry, and, at length," noted McDougle, "the clouds began to gather."[15]

Others saw it differently. Clendenin's cavalrymen from the 8th Illinois had left Frederick about one or two o'clock in the morning. They had reached Monocacy Junction via the Baltimore pike and a farm road about daylight. Barely having time to make coffee, and lacking sleep, "they were obliged to enter upon the duties of the day," recalled their unit historian. In actuality, they were able to catch several hours rest before Clendenin rousted them out. "There is to be a battle sure," jotted Silas D. Wesson during this lull before one squadron (Companies B and I) went across the covered bridge and up the Georgetown Pike toward Frederick looking for the enemy. At the same time, Captain Edward Leib's company of mounted infantry from the 159th Ohio departed upstream to report to Colonel Allison Brown at the Jug Bridge while Company C of the 8th went in the opposite direction toward Buckeystown to burn a bridge and picket several fords. Clendenin and the remainder of the regiment rode out the Baker Valley Road to engage a Confederate mounted force said to be aiming at enveloping Wallace's left.[16]

Simply awaiting developments proved the course for others in Wallace's army. Alexander's Baltimore batterymen took time to have "our regular soldier's breakfast of boiled salt pork, hardtack, and coffee which tasted good after a night's march," especially as horrendous as theirs had been in the rainstorm. They then fell asleep around their guns. For the 14th New Jersey, this was home turf, since its members recalled nostalgically "fourteen months have passed" since the regiment had left their Monocacy bridge campground they had styled "Camp Hooker." At that time, they had come out from Baltimore by train, encamped in the northwest angle between the junction and the turnpike on September 4, 1862, and then had been whisked back to Elysville near Baltimore two days later when news arrived that Confederates had crossed the Potomac. Indeed they had, as the New Jerseymen discovered when returning to Monocacy Junction on the seventeenth. They had found the middle span of the railroad bridge destroyed and all facilities burned at the junction. Nearby (ostensibly north of the junction, and about one-quarter mile east of the turnpike, directly in front of one time Maryland governor Enoch Louis Lowe's "Hermitage" house), lay the wooded grove where Lee's famous "Lost Order" had been found by Federal soldiers just prior to the battles of South Mountain and Antietam, although the location would remain controversial.[17]

The Jerseymen then spent the next nine months at Monocacy Junction defending the railroad line, providing details for provost duty in Frederick, and enjoying the Maryland countryside. Major Peter Vredenburgh, Jr. regularly went quail hunting with Colonel Keefer Thomas of Araby. He even had a hunting dog sent to him from home. Periodically, Vredenburgh and his men were called out to check on suspicious events in the neighborhood—reports of guerillas, spies, and contraband goods passing southward to Virginia. But, generally, the time passed pleasantly with visits to local Unionist families, sightseeing along the Potomac, and only occasional moments of anxiety when heavy skirmishing toward Williamsport or Sharpsburg suggested something more serious was about to occur behind the lines.[18]

This relatively quiet service permitted men like Vredenburgh to ponder events other than combat. He wrote his father on October 7 that he expected there would be bitter fighting before the war was over, and that Lincoln's preliminary emancipation proclamation "will have the effect of repelling the border states besides having a bad effect abroad." Indeed, he had been correct, Vredenburgh told his father just before the new year, for "men here, who were good Union sympathizers before are now on the other side." The proclamation would ruin them, they had told the young major, and the border states would not submit to it. Strictly speaking, Lincoln's action might be right, Vredenburgh concluded, but it would be unwise to enforce it since so many ignorant and prejudiced people bluntly stated that if the government was going to take their slaves away, they would not stand for it. Eighteen months later, the Jersey troops had little time to worry about implications of either the Emancipation or the emancipationist president's chances in the upcoming fall elections. On July 9, they were too busy worrying about their own fate.[19]

To some of the Jerseymen, the Monocacy scene looked quite natural, but to others their old camp ground was scarcely recognizable due to "grass and weeds." Lieutenant Colonel Caldwell Kepple Hall, their commander, erected a huge fly tent at their new position facing the wooden bridge near the Thomas farm south of the river. He wanted to shield his officers from the rising sun, since he thought everyone would surely have ample time to prepare for the day's activities. Hall and Vredenburgh actually took breakfast with Thomas (including several drinks, Vredenburgh wrote his mother several days later), before returning to the bridge, and then back to the Thomas' front gate where the 14th took its post. Every move was done slowly and deliberately in anticipation of the extremely hot day.[20]

Over northeast of the railroad junction and the river, Will James of the 11th Maryland remembered encamping in a clover field after the scrap on the eighth, taking a bath in a small stream nearby, and scrounging supper from comrades before being called to march and countermarch to reach bivouac just south of the railroad at the Junction. He cursed the wet socks he got crossing a brook during the night march, a soaking that plagued him for days thereafter. Several companies of the 9th New York Heavy Artillery that had arrived during the previous day's fighting had then aided Alexander's men in retrieving their lost caisson and ammunition during the pitch-black night march. Their sister regiment, the 87th Pennsylvania, had similarly helped right an overturned gun at one point. Bone tired, these infantrymen stumbled into makeshift rest areas near James Gambrill's house and large mill south of the river near the junction about dawn.[21]

Major General Lew Wallace personally reached the Junction slightly before midnight, the result of having a half-lame horse, "requisitioned" from a Frederick City physician. Met by an anxious Lieutenant Colonel Lynde Catlin, Wallace went to his makeshift headquarters in John Lyeth's house beside the railroad, and assessed the situation. He now had Truex's first brigade from the Army of the Potomac—five regiments of about 2,000 men according to Catlin's estimates. Ricketts was supposed to arrive about 1:00 A.M., and Wallace quickly called for pen and paper to prepare a detailed assignment plan for both veteran generals. Roughly speaking, then, all the area north of the railroad, especially the sector of the stone or jug bridge that held the key to the army's highway retreat route to Baltimore, belonged to Tyler. South of the railroad would be Ricketts' domain, "upon whom I thought the extreme of the fighting would fall," explained Wallace later. Or, in other words, said Wallace, "the raw men to Tyler; the veterans to Ricketts."[22]

Wallace also needed to restrict civilian traffic in and out of his defense lines. Refugees already clogged both the National Road and the Washington Turnpike. So, he ordered curtailment of civilian movements, and established that both Tyler and Ricketts were to forward morning field returns for their commands, to include communication and transportation assets. The Hoosier seemed to be settling down for a prolonged wait beside the Monocacy. Events would prove otherwise. For now, however, he folded his coat for a pillow and stretched out on the rough floor to catch some sleep. But, thoughts intruded of the three mile line to be defended with meager resources, his right as a commander to expose subordinates to threat to life and limb, and most of all the impact upon his personal career of what, for all intents, appeared to be a forlorn hope against great odds. It was all very melodramatic as Wallace told it in his memoirs, nearly a half century later.

Suddenly, a train whistle announced Ricketts' 1:00 A.M. arrival. There was no ceremony between the two men beyond the usual handshake, "no asking after health or news, no gossip, no apologies," just business. Their conversation turned quickly to numbers, objectives, and duty. Between them, Wallace and Ricketts estimated that they had 7,500 effectives with which to confront three or four times that number of the enemy. Wallace then explained his three objectives, and how he was doubtful that one had been attained— uncovering Early's true goal of Washington. Ricketts asked the distance to the city, Wallace estimated about sixty miles or two days forced march. Then he offered the thought that Early had already lost his reputation as a good soldier, for he should have easily been in the capital by now. Why? asked Ricketts. "He had only to cross the Potomac at Edwards Ferry below Harper's Ferry," for "no power on earth could then have saved the city from him." As it was, Old Jube had "fooled away his time and chances," an opportunity "which, if now lost by him, the Confederacy can never hope for again," replied Wallace. Ricketts chuckled.[23]

Wallace then explained his second objective—to brush aside the curtain of mystery as to Early's numbers. This information had defied Union commanders for several weeks. Wallace also defined still a third objective, which was "by hook or crook [to] get thirty-six or forty hours on Early." That, when added to the two days of forced marching required to reach Washington, would permit Grant to send a corps or two back to defend the city, he claimed. Wallace then injected a gratuitous slap at Halleck by telling Ricketts how Grant's chief of staff had remained so out of touch with the real situation on the upper Potomac as to feed all reinforcements into Harpers Ferry where they then became bottled up and useless (or at least inert) atop Maryland Heights.

The troops at Harpers Ferry were "of no more account in the defence of Washington than so many stones," claimed Wallace. He added that he and his Baltimore contingents had been in place for three days, and Halleck "has not so much as wired me a word of intelligence respecting the enemy, or in the way of encouragement." Ricketts might well have interceded with the orders he had received from Halleck concerning concentrating and cooperating with Wallace on the Monocacy, but no mention of such a comment occurs in Wallace's own postwar account of their conversation in the predawn darkness of July 9. Whatever the full story, Wallace continued about Halleck's own directive for him to go to Harpers Ferry and join the useless force on Maryland Heights.

This observation immediately aroused Ricketts to thunder: "What! And give Early a clear road to Washington! Never—never! We'll stay here. Give me your orders." Here was precisely what Wallace hoped to hear, and proceeded to outline his battle plan for the Army of the Potomac veterans—across the pike behind the wooden bridge, "because it is the post of honor. There the enemy will do his best fighting." The two generals shook hands and parted, and, recalled Wallace, "I lay down and slept never more soundly."[24]

Wallace got up early, walked out to the bluff by the railroad bridge and noticed that "sooty perfume" from cooking fires all over the valley erased the smell of new mown hay from the yellowing stubble fields. Local farmers and their workers were out early, too, gathering wheat despite the threat of battle. North of the river, over on the road to Buckeystown at Lime Kiln, William Jarboe Grove's father had him, a lad of eleven at the time, and a black helper handling wheat when the first signs of a battle seemed in the offing. The helper wanted to flee, but the elder Grove persuaded him to finish unloading the hay wagon, unhitch the horses, and secure everything first. Similarly, slaves John Ephraim Tyler, and Thomas Palm on the hay fields at John T. Worthington's "Clifton," or "Riverside Farm," told one another that circling buzzards meant trouble ahead. The harvesting stopped by 8:30 or 9:00 as Worthington, and his neighbor, Colonel C. Keefer Thomas, sent their hands with the farm animals to the nooks of nearby Sugarloaf Mountain. Neither landowner wanted to lose precious livestock or crops to either army. But, sharp-eyed rebels eventually spotted the mountain hiding places, and Thomas, proud owner of "Araby" farm suffered large financial loss.[25]

Actually, Thomas had recently moved back to his native Frederick County from Baltimore, purchasing Araby in 1860. The two hundred forty acre farm, with its 1780s period house stood on land that had been granted in colonial times to James Marshall, a Scottish immigrant. The farm also lay astride an ancient Indian trail that came north from the Washington, D.C. area, passed Sugarloaf, and crossed the Monocacy behind the Gambrill Mill at the mouth of Bush Creek. At this point, thirty-nine-year-old James Gambrill had a flourishing business, purchased from George W. Delaplaine in 1855 and expanded earlier in 1864, to a value of $10,000. His mill was a large and well-known one in the area, and familiar to many of the Federal soldiers from earlier visits. None of this meant much when sounds of blue and gray picket fire disturbed the serenity of the peaceful scene that morning. Families from these farms quickly scampered to house cellars to await the outcome.[26]

Later, when combat truly opened in earnest, Mrs. Gambrill took her two sons, Richard and Staley, to join the Thomas family and that of railroad agent Frank Mantz in the sanctuary of the Araby cellar. The Worthingtons stayed behind closed shutters, and Gambrill chose

to remain behind at his mill, later amiably chatting with Ricketts on
the porch of adjacent Gambrill home. At some point, early that morning, members of the 9th New York Heavy Artillery noticed two attrac-
tive young women flitting from place to place, obviously searching in
a distressed vein for something or someone. Last viewed, they were
passing across the railroad bridge westward. In fact, it may have been
young Alice Thomas and her friend, Mamie Taylor, searching for two
beaus and Thomas's brother, missing for several days and presumed
impressed into Federal ranks. Indeed, the young men had come out
from Baltimore to court the girls on the Fourth of July. Subsequently
rounded up by Landstreet's Marylanders, given arms, and pressed
into emergency service, Julius H. Anderson, Hugh M. Gatchell, and
Samuel Thomas participated in the skirmishing west of town until
one alert officer warned that their civilian attire might be taken as
proof they were spies or rebels. He advised that they simply slip away,
which they did, ending up with the group on Gambrill's porch that
morning. They subsequently retired to the mill when the battle swirled
around them later.[27]

Breakfast finished, Wallace and his staff rode over to collect
Ricketts and inspect the troop positions. Essentially laid out by
Wallace's senior aide, Major James R. Ross, neither general saw any
reason to alter the disposition. Arrayed in two lines, with a seventy or
eighty yard interval between, Ricketts' command faced north, paral-
leling the Monocacy. The right flanks extended a short distance northeast of Gambrill's Mill and the left flanks stood on high ground southwest of the Georgetown Pike. Supported by three of Alexander's guns,
Ricketts' veterans commanded approaches to the "gray-stained roofed,
wooden bridge," that carried the macadamized turnpike across the
Monocacy. Farther to Ricketts' left were Clendenin's cavalrymen, bent
as much upon getting around the enemy's right flank as guarding
Wallace's own left. Company B, under Lieutenant George W. Corbit,
took charge of a farm ford on the Worthington property. But, Wallace's
cavalry were stretched thin, and his extreme laft flank lay well up in
the air out to the southwest toward the Thomas, Worthington, and
Baker farmplaces.[28]

Still, Wallace had the preponderance of his force situated to
block the axis route to Washington, not Baltimore. It was almost as if
he fully expected Early to move in that direction, not withstanding
the melodrama of suspense he protrayed in his autobiography. Up
around the stone or jug bridge, carrying the National Road across
the Monocacy, Colonel Allison L. Brown's Buckeye infantry (144th
and 149th Ohio National Guard) defended that axis. Brown set out
his picket line west of the bridge on a ridge crest toward Frederick.
Fearing a flank attack via the unprotected Hugh's Ford crossing just

to his north, the Ohioan dispatched Captain Charles W. McGinnis's Company C, of the 149th to block that approach. It wasn't much for protecting his primary avenue for retreat, however, no matter what happened elsewhere along the front. Besides, there was no way to demolish the stone bridge should the enemy effect a breakthrough.[29]

Between Ricketts and Tyler lay two critical points, the east side of the river at the railroad bridge, and Crum's Ford closer to the stone bridge upstream. Colonel William T. Landstreet and eight companies of the 11th Maryland, noted Sergeant William H. James in his journal, "occupied the extreme right of our line, to the north of the railroad, and just behind the brow of a hill upon which was stationed Alexander's Baltimore battery." Directed to support the battery, they were compelled to lie down out of sight of the enemy at this point. Three of Alexander's 3-inch rifles, plus a 24-pounder howitzer (removed from the nearby railroad blockhouse and placed in a crude earthwork) constructed by Captain William H. Wiegel of Tyler's staff, provided superb enfilading fire for any enemy advance southward on the Georgetown Pike across the river. At Crum's Ford, Colonel Charles Gilpin took charge of the 3d Maryland Regiment (Potomac Home Brigade) and three companies of her sister unit, the 1st Maryland (Potomac Home Brigade). Positioned "along the base of a hill," they commanded approaches to the crossing. At some point, Captain Charles J. Brown's company of the 1st Potomac Home Brigade accompanied Clendenin's videttes out to the upper reaches of the Best farm, about a mile out from the Junction on the Georgetown Pike to observe the Confederate advance.[30]

So there it was, a Federal battle front stretching from the Baker farm southwest of the turnpike to Washington all the way northward to Hugh's Ford beyond the stone bridge. A three mile line, defended by less than 7,000 men and seven cannon. Veterans (cavalry, infantry, and artillery) were supplemented by relatively untried reserve troops, led by a mixture of West Pointers and citizen soldiers. A river to its front, but with bridges and fords to defend, Wallace's little scratch force awaited events while the ever-present fog of battle continued out to its front.

Battle Actions—Jug Bridge and Further South

At this point, Wallace also expected arrival of several additional regiments of the 2nd Brigade, VI Corps. En route by rail from Baltimore, B & O officials assured the general that they would be on the ground by 1:00 P.M. The fact that they never got beyond Monrovia, eight miles to the east, would not be known until too late. Meanwhile, Wallace and Ricketts scanned the horizon for signs of Confederate advance. According to Allison Brown's after-action report, "the enemy made his appearance at 6:00 A.M." on the National Road east of town. The vanguard of Brigadier General Robert D. Lilley's brigade of Stephen Ramseur's division "threw out his skirmishers, who soon became engaged with my men." Skirmishing intensified after 8:00 A.M., as Robert Rodes' division supplanted Lilley's men, probing eastward from town.[31]

Ironically, two years earlier, the stone or jug bridge had been the center of another firefight preparatory to the battles of South Mountain and Antietam. Buckeyes had been there then also—the 11th, 28th, and 36th volunteers, of Colonel George Crook's 2d brigade, Brigadier General Jacob D. Cox's Kanawha division, IX Corps. With a rush, they had captured the bridge from the east, dispersed rebel defenders and pushed on to liberate Frederick. As Chaplain W. W. Lyle of the 11th Regiment had recorded: "Flags were waving from every house, and hats and handkerchiefs from every balcony and window," when they reached the city. "Cheer upon cheer went up with such a genuine 'ring,' that no one could doubt either the loyalty or lung-power of Frederick's sons and daughters."[32]

Now, however, it was 1864, and Buckeyes defended the bridge in reverse. It wasn't long either before Wallace and Ricketts spotted Confederate columns approaching on the Washington Road from Mount Olivet Cemetery just south of town. "Two regiments, as regiments on both sides now go," supposedly muttered the VI Corps veteran officer. These were Ramseur's men, and Clendenin and Captain Charles J. Brown's 1st Maryland Potomac Home Brigade quickly engaged them along with a company of the 11th Maryland, two companies of New York "Heavies" and a company of the 10th Vermont. Landstreet's company soon passed back down the roadbed of the branch line rail spur, back across the iron railroad bridge spanning the Monocacy, and after a mile and one-half, took position in what appeared to be old mill-race, more like a natural formation, thought Sergeant James, "in groups of from four to six" men. They were directed to remain quiet and keep a lookout for rebels as their strong position gave them favorable outlook against the anticipated Confederate attempt "to turn the right of our army which occupied the position around the railroad bridge."[33]

James considered the location afforded his men excellent protection from their natural, five-foot high breastworks and a large number of trees. Apparently Confederate observers, too, thought the Crum's Ford sector too strong for a crossing. Within an hour, however, long range artillery fire opened between Alexander and Confederate gunners on the Cronise farm, perhaps close to Cline's quarry, and eventually across the turnpike on the Best farm. "We could not see their guns," recorded artilleryman Frederick W. Wild of the Baltimore Battery, "and for every shot fired we received two in return." Outgunned, the Federal battery provided some relief to the Union skirmishers as fighting escalated in front of Monocacy Junction.[34]

Soon, as more Confederates came in view, so too, did their artillery. Veteran gunners, probably from Kirkpatrick's Amherst (Virginia) battery found the range of Yankee troop concentrations around Gambrill's Mill. They dropped their first shells upon the unsuspecting, breakfasting bluecoats. The latter had been munching on supplies brought up by train from Baltimore and distributed about 7:30 A.M. The first rebel fire mortally wounded two men from the 151st New York, while several others in the 87th Pennsylvania were likewise severely wounded. Still others fell closer to the mill itself, and the scene was soon bedlam with troops falling into ranks, much shouting and bugle calls, amidst the screeching shells. The scene was quite grisly when, a short time later, Wallace checked on the makeshift hospital arrangements at the site. In fact, his own mounted party became a target. Whether or not Wallace chose this moment to change headquarters remains unclear. In any event, both the eastern blockhouse as well as the Lyeth house soon became an impact area for Confederate artillery fire just like Gambrill's mill and the structures at the railroad junction. Neither Wallace nor Ricketts had much confidence in Alexander's 3-inch guns for suppressing the enemy artillery, preferring instead Wiegell's more authoritative howitzer. But, the enemy's sixteen or so Napoleons, together with the quickly rising temperature, made for a hot morning in this sector. By this point, Lew Wallace could surely deduce that Washington, not Baltimore, was Early's target.[35]

As the first rebel shells impacted upon the drowsy defenders near the mill and junction ("although we did not forsake our hardtack and 'sowbelly,'" coolly observed W. L. Gardner of Company K, 110th Ohio), the engineer of a Baltimore and Ohio train decided to leave the junction, taking with him the telegrapher and other railroad employees. Wallace was irate when he learned of the event later, for it robbed him of telegraphic contact with his Baltimore headquarters (and, hence, Washington). Held for a while just beyond the hills across the river to the east in order to evacuate battle wounded, the train's departure underscored the escalating fighting near the junction. Ramseur's men had the mission of testing Union positions at the junction and turnpike bridge crossings. While not pressing an attack, at this stage, they nevertheless edged closer to the wooden bridge as the morning progressed. Wallace later called this activity before 10:30 A.M. "little more than a warm skirmish and experimental cannonading."[36]

First Lieutenant George E. Davis with Company D, 10th Vermont, Lieutenant Chauncey Fish of Company B and Captain A. S. Wood with Company M, both from the 9th New York "Heavies" assisting Brown's Marylanders in countering the gray-clad skirmishers thought otherwise. Wood recalled later that he had marched up the pike toward Frederick that morning, "anticipating a pleasant day on picket," when suddenly "a rebel skirmish line opened full upon us." Another party, including the division surgeon, assistant surgeon, and Chaplain Edwin M. Haynes from the 10th Vermont were similarly caught off guard. Riding toward Frederick to partake of breakfast, they had to scurry for cover when the first whiz of minie balls indicated the opening of the battle. Warm skirmishing and experimental cannonading notwithstanding, some 300 to 500 Federal riflemen spent the next few hours contesting Brigadier General Robert D. Johnston's veteran brigade of North Carolinians probing the turnpike approach. Wallace later admitted to Davis directly (in a postwar letter dated March 29, 1889) that he and Ricketts witnessed the Confederate deployment of skirmishers. "Their movement was like the opening of a fan, and when it was finished, their line on both flanks was much in excess of yours." At various points, the rebels effectively utilized not only the Best barn, but also haystacks and other cover to batter the bluecoats, and even intimidate Wallace, Ricketts, and their staffs impatiently prowling the south bank of the stream.[37]

The first Federal and Confederate prisoners were taken between 7:00 and 8:00 that morning, and included Hospital Steward W. G. Duckett of the 9th New York "Heavies." Captured about midway between Frederick and the junction, the feisty New Yorker was hauled before Brigadier General John G. Echols, who could not contain himself at the shock of finding Army of the Potomac veterans confronting the Confederates along the banks of the Monocacy. "Damn that 6th corps," swore the Virginian, "we meet them wherever we go." Unimpressed by general officers, the disrespectful Duckett responded that his adversary would soon find the whole corps present to welcome the rebels "with bloody hands to hospitable graves." Duckett tried to mislead Echols "and I believe they were more cautious than they would have been had they known our real strength, and we were saved from greater disaster," he claimed.[38]

Meanwhile, at the stone bridge, Brown saw rebel cavalry moving toward Hughes' Ford about 10:00 A.M. They may have been the outriders of Brigadier General Bradley T. Johnson's liberation force, testing Wallace's right flank and providing token support for the main battle. At any rate, to counter this thrust, the Ohioan rushed two companies (Captain Thomas B. Jenkins' Company E, 149th Ohio, and Captain Edward H. Leib's company of 159th Ohio Mounted

Infantry) to the ford, where, according to Leib, they "drove the rebels off." No sooner had this occurred than Rodes sent his own skirmish line knifing into the left side of Brown's defenders west of the stone bridge. About 11:30 A.M. Brown's men buckled; the Ohioan requested help from Tyler, who dispatched Companies B, G, and I of the 144th Ohio to the rescue. Brown's initial counterattack with only Company B, 149th Ohio, failed, but a bayonet assault by their sister units recovered the ground lost earlier. Brown now extended his line to encompass what was termed "Reich House Ridge," while reporting that his losses in the attack had been sharp since "the enemy was posted behind a fence, while my men were compelled to charge across an open field, up the hill in fair view, and within short range of his guns." Leib's dismounted men participated in Brown's counterattack and, altogether, the Buckeyes retained possession of this position the rest of the day. McGinnis' company of the 149th continued to defend Hughes' Ford.[39]

Early eventually rode forward by late morning to see how the advance progressed. Rodes' demonstration seemed to be faring well to the east, but valuable time had passed on the turnpike to Washington. The July sun arched ever higher in the hot sky, and Old Jube remained unsure about both terrain and opposition. Friendly townsfolk assured him that mere militiamen guarded the bridge crossings. Yet, they were fighting hard, and some way around them had to be found quickly. If he could outflank the Union position, then he might regain the Washington road easily and be on his way before nightfall. It was critical to find some ford or crossing downstream. If only he had not been forced to relinquish Johnson's cavalry for that Point Lookout raid. For that matter, what was wrong with that bunch of buttermilk rangers under McCausland, thought Early. His orders to them the day before had been distincly pointed toward securing the Monocacy crossing even before reaching Frederick. Wasn't it ever thus with the undependable cavalry?

"Buttermilk Rangers" to the Rescue

The fact that Ramseur, reinforced by Major General John B. Gordon's division, and supervised by the able Major General John C. Breckinridge, might have simply blasted across Crum's Ford against the Maryland reserve troops and fanned out to disperse Wallace's defenders, was not self-evident at this time. Similarly, the fact the whole army might have simply side-slipped down the Frederick-Buckeystown Road seems not to have caught anyone's eye either. Had Johnson not departed on the Point Lookout raid, and been present to advise the generals with his knowledge of the home neighborhood, Early might have simply crossed the Monocacy at Buckeystown against mere mounted videttes, and reached Wallace's rear at Urbana by early afternoon. But, Early strictly focused on the direct road south to Washington.[40]

Brigadier General John McCausland's horsemen had been directed the day before to capture the junction itself and get on the Union left flank downstream from the junction while cutting the telegraph and railroad between Maryland Heights and Baltimore. But, they never left their bivouacs near Jefferson until dawn on the ninth. Guided by local resident D. Calvin Bready, the column then turned right at a tollgate atop Catoctin Mountain, descending into a neighborhood styled "Carrollton Manor" after its original colonial era grantee. They passed the Red Hill schoolhouse and rode until they reached the Point of Rocks or Manor Road. They next turned left and continued toward Frederick until part of the band split off to the right, reaching the Buckeystown-Frederick Road at Lime Kiln. Here they paid Thomas R. Jarboe (who resided at Gayfield, a nearby 388-acre tract), several hundred dollars for a young mare, a bargain for Jarboe who thus left other horses at his place from the acquisitive cavalrymen. Moving now toward Frederick in parallel with comrades on the Manor Road, McCausland's two wings eventually reunited at Griffen Taylor's spread near the covered bridge over Ballenger Creek on the Buckeystown Road, across the road from the Markell farm. A year earlier, Union Major Generals Joseph Hooker and George G. Meade exchanged command of the Army of the Potomac at this spot before Gettysburg. Now, aided by a dragooned Unionist farmer, Simon Cornbise, McCausland's scouts quickly found the farm ford at the mount of Bellenger Creek, leading to the Worthington property. An elated Early suddenly realized that his maligned "buttermilk rangers" had redeemed themselves. They had discovered the answer to his problem. Heavy fighting still might be avoided.[41]

Some of McCausland's 900 to 1,000 motley-attired troopers (the total could have been higher, given the imprecise records) used the local lime kilns for lookout posts, recalled eleven-year-old William Jarboe Grove later. They too, may have uncovered the crossing from such perches. At any rate, Lieutenant George W. Corbit's B Company, 8th Illinois, gave the Confederate riders an initial rebuff at the crossing, but his numbers were too few to do much. Getting out of the way was Corbit's only option, Wallace supposedly told Ricketts when he spied what was happening through binoculars. Corbit fell back to the Baker Valley Road near Araby, then lost control of that artery, and, for the moment, portions of Clendenin's command were separated by a hostile force. Four of his companies had reinforced a fifth under Major John M. Waite guarding the Buckeystown-Urbana axis, and these men were now cut off from Wallace's main position.

The Illinois troopers fell back sullenly to the Baker Valley Road near Araby and took position to cover the extreme left flank of the army. For the moment, Clendenin's command was split and mostly cut off from Wallace.

Clendenin's men were used to tight places. They had fought rebel artillery at close quarters the year before at Brandy Station prior to Gettysburg. Their leader knew how to reconstitute his command when necessary. At the Monocacy, he now calmly directed the downstream squadron to continue its demolition work, dispatched another under Major John M. Waite to protect the vital Buckeystown-Urbana Road leading to the Washington Turnpike several miles to Wallace's rear, and swung back around McCausland to reposition the remnant near where the Baker Valley Road met up with that turnpike, thus shielding Ricketts' left flank. A skeptical Lieutenant Lemuel Abbott of the 10th Vermont (the left flank infantry in line) noted: "Having little faith in our cavalry, I feared a cavalry charge from the enemy down the pike to my left." But, McCausland soon had his hands full with the VI Corps veterans, and exploitation of his success against Corbit quickly evaporated.[42]

Upon the first sign of Confederate crossing at the Worthington property about 10:30 A.M., Wallace had alerted Ricketts to the danger. Ricketts, like Clendenin, was an old pro at tight places in combat. An artilleryman by trade, he had begun the war by commanding a battery overrun at First Bull Run. Promoted to brigadier general of volunteers "for gallant and meritorious conduct" at that disaster, he later commanded a division at Cedar Mountain, Second Bull Run, and Antietam, where he had two horses shot beneath him, and was himself severely injured when the second fell on him. Invalided to the court-martial proceedings for Major General Fitz John Porter, his possible controversial position regarding that officer's conduct in the Second Bull Run campaign may have earned him the enmity of Secretary of War Edwin M. Stanton and the War Department's inner circle. It was with some degree of irony that he joined an equally disfavored Wallace. Still, as one who would fight under him at Monocacy (and earn a Medal of Honor in doing so), Vermont Captain George F. Davis said later of him: "Having seen so many political Generals who were promoted to high commands solely upon political influence, it is refreshing to know personally a General as true, modest, and capable as James B. Ricketts, U.S.A." So, it was certainly a seasoned fighter, whose small third division of the VI Corps now responded to the general's perception of the correct thing to do in facing the threat posed by McCausland.[43]

Ricketts quickly swung his left flank around to compensate for McCausland's developing threat. This may have been the move that led Wallace to recall after the war that he had exclaimed to his staff at the time: "Look at that line of battle—there isn't a straggler on it." This, according to Captain Robert T. Cornwell, the general's aide, but the general still must have wondered at that time, where were Ricketts' reservers—that elusive, anticipated third brigade. Certainly, Ricketts' move now subjected his line to an enfilading fire from Confederates posted across the river, especially in the Best farm vicinity. The movement, however, generally extended Ricketts' line south on the Washington Turnpike, arching north of the Thomas house to the Baker Valley Road. From Clendenin's cavalry on the extreme left, Colonel William Truex's brigade fell in line from left to right: 10th Vermont, 87th Pennsylvania, 14th New Jersey, 106th and 151st New York. They sought out every natural protection they could find on this generally open terrain, the Jerseymen hovering behind a hawthorn hedge on the lawn just north of Araby house. Basically, to their front lay a wheatfield filled with shocks of wheat also used by the defenders. When Ricketts redeployed Truex's brigade, Colonel Matthew B. McClennan's Second Brigade held its ground, except for fifty men of Lieutenant Charles J. Gibson from Companies B and C, 122d Ohio, whom the general sent forward to strengthen the skirmish line near the Worthington house about 11:00 A.M.[44]

By this point too, Ricketts' men were suffering from overshoots from the brisk skirmishing north of the river. The Best barn, west of the turnpike and north of the railroad had become a rebel sharpshooter's nest, and Private Frederick Wild of Alexander's battery recalled that they had had difficulty locating where these marksmen were "until one of our officers noticed small puffs of smoke from under the shingles of a barn, half mile or more away!" Finally, Alexander's and Wiegel's fire got the building's range, set it afire, and, observed Wild, "we had the satisfaction of seeing some of [the enemy riflemen] being carried away on a litter, and put in an ambulance." A veteran of the Loudoun Rangers observing the action also noted that a few well-directed shots from the artillery "set the barn on fire, with several wheat and hay stacks, burning the premises and compelling the enemy to seek other quarters." But, as the Confederates continued to side-slip down the Buckeystown Road, and position supporting batteries accordingly, Wallace would eventually have to send more of Alexander's guns to Ricketts on the left.[45]

Meanwhile, McCausland, having dismounted his men in the Worthington yard, now advanced them over a post and rail fence and through waist-high corn toward a walnut and locust tree lined divisional fence separating the latter property from Araby. He and his men anticipated an easy victory, and horseholders took the mounts back across the river to safety. Silently, in ambush, the Federals watched the cavalry come at them on foot with guidons waving and the shrill "rebel yell" yip-yip on their lips. Suddenly, Ricketts' men rose to their feet, rested their muskets on the fence rails, and delivered a blinding volley into McCausland's men. When the smoke had cleared, the corn field seemed to hide the dead, dying, and cheerless living crawling back to safety out of range of the deadly Yankee muskets. Civilian John Worthington, himself a Southern sympathizer, could not believe his eyes. What fools to advance when he himself could see clearly from his shuttered upstairs windows how strongly Ricketts' men had been posted along the boundary fence. Not so the poor rebels down on the ground, and they understandably blamed their leaders for the calamity. Clearly then, these were not militia, realized everyone up to and including Jubal Early at this point—as Major General John B. Gordon admitted years after the war (when, as US Senator from Georgia, he told Wallace at a chance meeting). By the same token, one of the Confederates captured by the 106th New York during his attack was the lieutenant colonel of the 17th Virginia Cavalry who had proclaimed that Early had 20,000 infantry, cavalry and artillery with him, thus perpetuating Federal contention for years that the expedition was far more than a mere raiding force.[46]

McCausland's panicky survivors ran past the Worthington house before regrouping near the riverbank. Yankee skirmishers, emboldened by the success, returned to the disputed area. Although timing in this battle was never precise, it was now the noon hour apparently. "Nothwithstanding the attacks received," Wallace recalled colorfully in his memoirs, "we were exactly as in the morning." He ticked off five hours gained in this "fighting for time," against Old Jube. Indeed, his outnumbered little army seemed to be acquitting itself well and the Hoosier warrior counted himself lucky as he sat munching on a lunch of sardines and crackers. An aide reminded him of a bottle of wine that some Baltimore admirer had sent him, but "I disposed of his suggestion that we tap it then by thoughtlessly telling him to keep it for supper." Indeed, the afternoon would bring a different twist of fate, but for the moment, Wallace enjoyed his success. He considered wiring Halleck and Washington, but, then decided that while he had now uncovered the direction of rebel intent, he still did not have an accurate feel for their numbers. He decided to wait awhile.[47]

The Confederates then seemed to increase their pressure all across his front. If the Maryland home guard position on high ground at Crum's Ford stood defiant, Rodes' men made life so miserable for Brown's men near the stone bridge that "to even show their heads above the hilltop" was dangerous. Watching this action was Lieutenant Colonel Theodore O'Hara, a Kentuckian serving with the 12th

Alabama in Brigadier General Cullen A. Battle's brigade held in reserve at this point. O'Hara had penned the poignant "Bivouac of the Dead" soon after the Mexican War, a fitting verse to later dominate national cemeteries of the Civil War. For the moment, at Monocacy, however, he was but a witness to the desultory but deadly skirmish fire near the jug bridge. Ramseur's pressure against the covered bridge position on the Washington Road was also strong at that time, and Wallace had room for concern.[48]

Sharp action and sharp losses on the skirmish lines in Ramseur's area north of the junction were as important to the holding action here as at stone bridge. Catching sight of three sycamore trees that seemed to obstruct the Union battery fire from north of the railroad, Brigadier General Erastus Tyler (whom Wallace characterized as "a man of intelligence, and brave") directed volunteers from the 3d Regiment Potomac Home Brigade to cross the river quickly and cut them down. David Winter of Company F and a comrade proceeded to the task, came under heavy sharpshooter fire, and the second man soon cowered, claiming a wife and children at home. Winter undauntingly completed the task, returned to win Tyler's discharge from further duties for two hours that day, only to resume his place on the firing line, combating the very skirmishers that had tormented him earlier.[49]

Nonetheless, superiority in numbers and firepower slowly constricted the Union defenders back toward the river. Vermont Major Charles G. Chandler, the senior officer on this portion of the line, had unaccountably returned across the river, leaving the novice, Maryland Captain Brown in charge. Brown became so flustered at his inability to recognize advancing rebels clad in captured Union garb, that he readily relinquished responsibility to Lieutenant Davis of the Vermonters. Davis, in turn, was taken off guard at being thrust "into such a responsible position, where authority must be used, and great risk taken." Yet, he did not shrink from his responsibility, and he quickly aligned his men with Ricketts' position across the river, using the fire of the main body to avoid being outflanked and cut off from his line of retreat to the bridges. Sharpshooters in copses of trees remained ever troublesome, while the "boom of rebel artillery firing mainly toward the Thomas farm" continued unrelentingly. Other events now occurred that severely compromised Wallace's ability to contain Ramseur's slow, but steady progress toward the bridge crossings.[50]

The sequence of events is not clear. At some point, a green crew member accidentally spiked Wiegel's howitzer. Wiegel tried everything to unspike it. He tilted the barrel forward, attempted to pour powder down the vent to fire off the piece, but nothing worked, and this invaluable ordnance was now lost to the defenders. Then, the special train that had been retained behind the eastern hills for evacuating the morning's wounded (there being no field ambulance service available), steamed off without warning when its engineer was spooked by the heavy incoming artillery fire. Wallace, already denied direct telegraphic communication between Monocacy Junction and his Baltimore headquarters, now lost his remaining link with the outside world. "Indeed, could hands have been laid upon him, I think yet [that] I could have stood quietly by and seen the cowardly wretch hanged," Wallace wrote forty years later. The Hoosier grieved now for the wounded that he would be forced to leave behind in the inevitable retreat that impended. And, he still wondered where Ricketts' remaining 1,000 men might be when he so desperately needed them. By one o'clock in the afternoon, the spiked howitzer, the missing reinforcements, and the departed train underscored Wallace's suddenly deteriorating situation.[51]

It also remains unclear just when and why Lew Wallace directed the burning of the Washington Turnpike covered bridge. One 9th New York observer thought that the order came at 12:30 P.M. from his regimental commander, Lieutenant Colonel William Henry Seward Jr. (son of President Lincoln's secretary of state). Lieutenant Davis suggested that word arrived "in the early part of the noon attack" by the Confederates. Wallace himself declared that he made his decision about 2:00 P.M. Whatever the timing, the New Yorkers had gathered wheat sheaves from a nearby field, and placed them beneath the southeast corner of the shingled roof of the bridge. Then, Privates A. N. Sova, Samuel R. Mack, and Sergeant Albert L. Smith soon had a blazing fire started "which wrapped the roof in flames like magic." Covered bridges were tinder boxes anyway, and the New York skirmishers closest to the structure withdrew quickly, everyone assuming the rest of the Federals north of the river would do likewise. Wallace tardily remembered his men out on the skirmish line at the last minute, and dispatched an aide to rescue them. The burning bridge forced him to turn back. Davis and his men, caught unaware by the burning of the bridge, continued to hold the Confederates at bay north of the Monocacy most of the afternoon.[52]

* * * *

As the battle on the Monocacy reached its critical mass early on the afternoon of July 9, the outside world knew little of what was taking place. Assistant Secretary of War Charles A. Dana noted in his memoirs that when he reached Washington on the ninth, both the capital and Baltimore were in a high state of excitement, and filled with refugees. Damage to private property "done by the invaders was said to be almost beyond calculation." Mills, workshops, and factories were reportedly destroyed, he commented, and twenty-five to fifty miles of the Baltimore and Ohio wrecked. At 1:00 P.M., Major General Henry Halleck wired Lieutenant General Ulysses S. Grant from Washington that if the XIX Corps troops, then in transit from the Gulf of Mexico, arrived in time, they should be sent on to Washington rather than disembarking them in lower Virginia. Hunter reported that only one of his divisions had passed Cumberland, Maryland, owing to low water in the Ohio, continued Halleck, but nothing else of note had occurred. Indeed, it was only by afternoon on the ninth that communiques of the day before and the normal stirrings of hot summer had begun to engage War Department attention.[53]

All Washington knew about Wallace related to events of the previous day, and that the Hoosier as well as Ricketts had been poised for a more decisive battle on the ninth. Basically, all reinforcements and supplies had been sent forward to the Monocacy from Baltimore, although officials scurried about that city organizing militia, Union League volunteers and 100-days recruits for self-defense. It was mainly a morning of waiting and watching forty miles away at the capital. Military units there continued to shift about, as by that time, brevet major general, and chief engineer, John Gross Barnard, had returned from temporary duty with Grant and Meade, and solemnly pronounced that "in view of any conceivable probability of an attack on Washington," he recommended sending back the heavy artillery regiments at Petersburg. These gunners were "at best worth only so much infantry to General Grant."[54]

The "Heavies" were experienced and skillful gunners who knew the armament and terrain in front of Washington's fortifications. "The remnant of these regiments would furnish a full complement of experienced gunners to all the forts, and impart confidence to the militia troops now in the forts, and give to the defense a reliability which it cannot have, do what we may without them," said Barnard. He specifically cited the 1st and 2nd Connecticut Heavy Artillery whom, along with a few others, Barnard regarded as superior even to Seward's 9th New York. Ironically, at 10:55 A.M., Halleck ordered the commanding officer at Baltimore to stop "any part" of those New Yorkers which had reached the city and to send it to Washington instead. At that very moment, Seward's men stood facing an oncoming enemy on the Monocacy.

Otherwise, Colonel Charles R. Lowell reported matters quiet over at Falls Church in northern Virginia, while Major D. W. C. Thompson, of the 2nd Massachusetts Cavalry at Muddy Branch camp in Montgomery County, Maryland, prepared to cope with any Confederates should they breach the Monocacy line. Commanders on Maryland Heights learned from a local Sharpsburg canal boat captain that 1,000 to 1,500 rebels were guarding a quantity of supplies collected in the area at or near Shepherdstown. Brigadier General B. F. Kelly at Cumberland reported his informants had Confederate cavalry brigadier John Imboden with some 1,500 men moving toward Sharpsburg, and only small squads of rebels as far north and west as Hagerstown.

Indeed, observers all over western Maryland avowed that small bands of raiders were foraging and confiscating livestock, particularly horses. Everyone seemed powerless to stop them. Pennsylvania officials were hopelessly deadlocked with the War Department concerning mustering of militia as that state's adjutant general declared: "In this state the middle of the harvest season is not a favorable period to recruit men for service requiring them to leave their homes." Major General John A. Dix at New York echoed the difficulties, "There is a very bad state of affairs here," suggesting three reliable regiments of state troops "are indispensable to the preservation of order and for the security of public property."[55]

Part of the trouble continued to be the wildly inflated strength figures attributed to Early's invaders. They ranged from a low of 20,000 to a high of double that figure. Federal reaction was virtually paralyzed in consequence. At least Wallace now recognized that he was outnumbered three to one, but that the pressure against Ricketts on his left indicated "the undermeaning of which was Washington." By burning the wooden turnpike bridge and holding on until five or six o'clock, his antagonist could not possibly move his army before the morrow. Twenty hours—even, twelve—would add to Old Jube's timetable, thought Wallace, and "would be ample for General Grant to land his interfering corps" at Washington. So, by high noon that hot July Saturday, Lew Wallace had "resolved to hold on the Monocacy."[56]

FIVE

Monocacy—Afternoon Climax

Message traffic at the War Department telegraph office was brisk during the day on July 9. Immediate concerns, however, were more strategic than tactical. The fog of war had descended upon events in upper Maryland. Major General Henry W. Halleck, chief of staff, wired general in chief Ulysses S. Grant at 1:00 P.M. about the XIX Corps veterans coming east from Louisiana by boat. Halleck wanted them sent to Washington, rather than disembarking them at Fort Monroe on the lower peninsula below Richmond. Major General David Hunter's troops, transitting from West Virginia, had been slowed by low water in the Ohio River. Otherwise, he noted: "No important change reported since my telegram of last evening." Grant acceded to the request (which would reach Washington at 7:30 that evening), but he wanted these XIX Corps veterans from the west sent to him by July 18 or 20 to participate in an offensive against the Weldon railroad (lifeline to the besieged Confederates in the Richmond-Petersburg lines). Still, Grant was flexible: "If the rebel force now north can be captured or destroyed I would willingly postpone aggressive operations to destroy them and could send in addition to the Nineteenth corps, the balance of the Sixth Corps."[1]

Other communication between the two Union leaders would come later that day. Meanwhile, Halleck continued to engage in futile wrangling with Northern authorities about mustering 100-days troops, the lack of surplus arms and equipment to supply the same, and the purging of Philadelphia hospitals as well as Veteran Reserve regiments from New York City and Elmira, New York to be sent immediately by train to bolster the forts around Washington. Especially disheartening was Major General Darius M. Couch's dispatch that he had only about 130 cavalry, 200 infantry, and four pieces of artillery available in the Cumberland Valley of Pennsylvania for falling upon Early's flank and rear. Elsewhere some further shifting of units and mobilizing manpower continued both in Washington and Baltimore. But, from Major D. W. C. Thompson (2d Massachusetts Cavalry) at the Muddy Branch cavalry camp in Montgomery County, to Major G. F. Merriam, chief of artillery at Fort Duncan on Maryland Heights above Harpers Ferry; to Lieutenant Colonel Samuel B. Lawrence, the assistant adjutant general at Baltimore, little more could be done than watchful waiting.[2]

News of the battle occurring on the banks of the Monocacy was particularly slow in reaching both Washington and the rest of the North. Even John W. Garrett, railroad president and intrepid communicator with Halleck, could not glean much information due to Wallace's self-imposed silence (the Hoosier did send information about the previous day's combat that reached Halleck about the time Wallace's skirmishers had begun scoring the rebel advance east and south of Frederick in the early morning). Apparently a New York *Tribune* reporter, "D. R.," got off a dispatch to his editor, Sidney H. Gay, that recounted events down to, and including, the early morning skirmishing. Approved by Wallace, it passed through Garrett's Camden Station office at Baltimore about 9:45 A.M., but, as incorporated into the railroader's larger dispatch, never reached Washington before nightfall. Wallace's reticence with respect to Halleck, the flight of the telegrapher and other railroad personnel, the preoccupation with fighting the battle, and general dislocation of a combat zone all confounded the issue. Wallace, Ricketts, Tyler, and the Confederate counterparts all fought in isolation at the Monocacy River.[3]

Horatius at the Bridge

According to his memoirs, Wallace spent a great deal of time counting the hours that he had delayed Early and trying to discern his opponent's exact strength. Considering himself outnumbered three to one, the Hoosier resolved to hang on until late afternoon, for such a stalemate would preclude the Southerners moving toward Washington before the next morning. Still reluctant to disclose to Washington his somewhat unexpected presence on the Monocacy and engagement in major battle, while undoubtedly swept up in the drama of that action as well, the Hoosier tarried in not alerting Halleck and the administration to Early's intentions as soon as pressure mounted from Ramseur and then McCausland in the Washington turnpike sector. Moreover, given a time line on dispatches actually

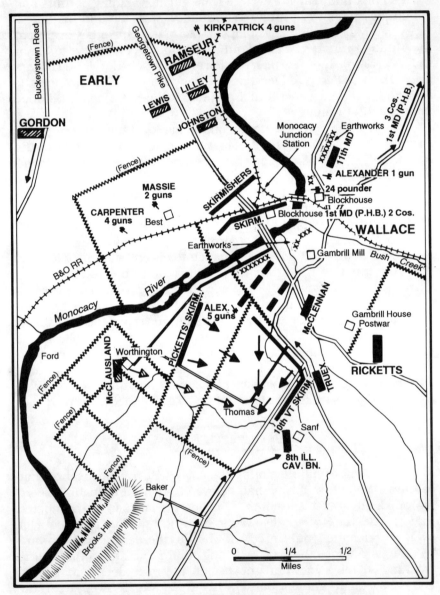

**Map 10. Monocacy, July 9, 1864—Junction Sector,
Noon to 2:30 P.M.**

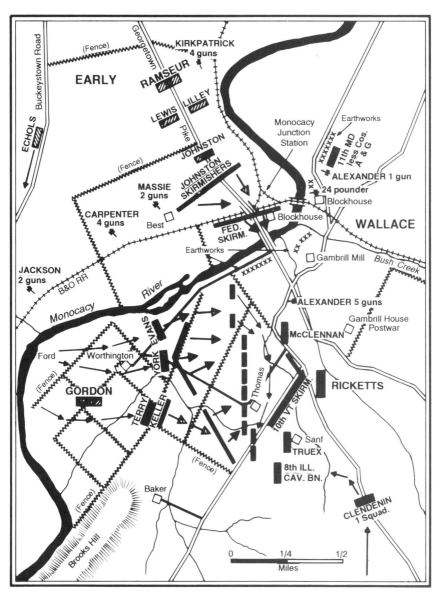

**Map 11. Monocacy, July 9, 1864—Junction Sector,
2:30 P.M. to 4:30 P.M.**

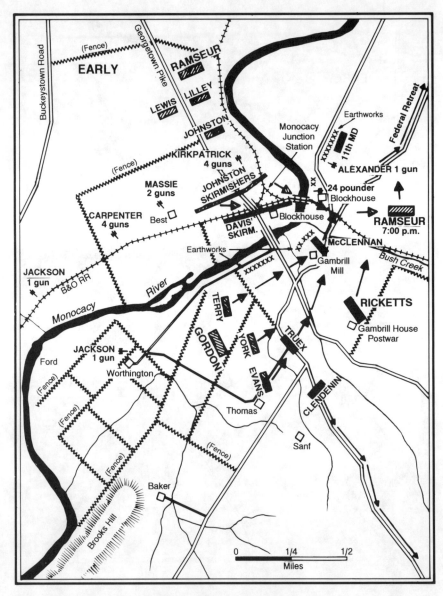

**Map 12. Monocacy, July 9, 1864—Junction Sector,
4:30 P.M. to 7:00 P.M.**

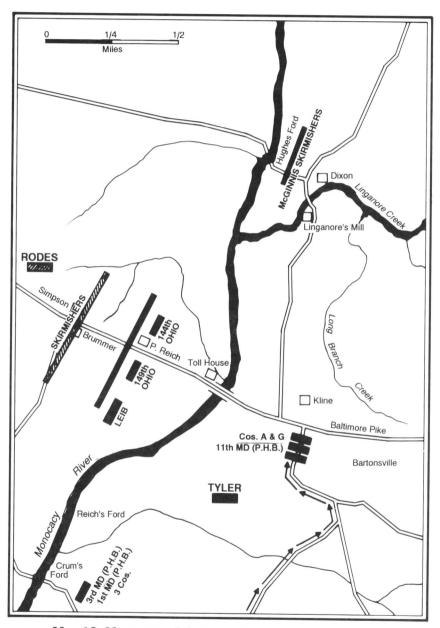

Map 13. Monocacy, July 9, 1864—Stone Bridge Sector, 2:30 P.M. to 4:30 P.M.

130

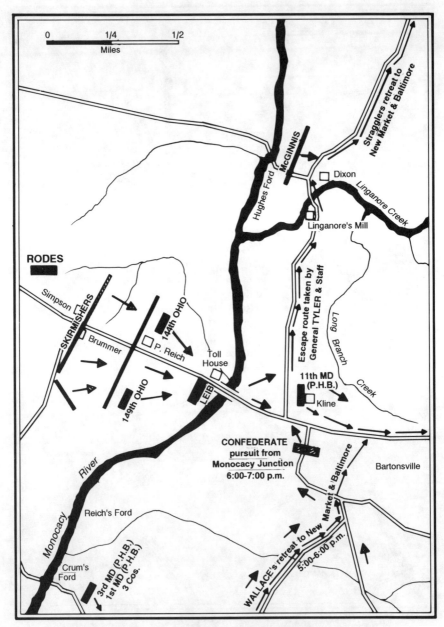

**Map 14. Monocacy, July 9, 1864—Stone Bridge Sector,
4:30 P.M. to 7:00 P.M.**

Araby House of Colonel Keefer Thomas

Center of firestorm that raged during afternoon of July 9, 1864, between the forces of Ricketts, McCausland, and Gordon.

Photograph by Charles A. Davis in 1893
Courtesy Vermont Historical Society

"Araby" Porch Showing Shell Damage in 1893
Photograph by Charles A. Davis
Courtesy Vermont Historical Society

Araby Farm Battlefield

Looking toward Brooks hill; Confederates advanced across right face of hill past Worthington farm, *top center.*

Marken and Bielfeld, <u>Souvenir of Historic Frederick</u> (1925), p. 34.

Brooks Hill from Baker Valley Road

Photograph by Charles A. Davis in 1893
Courtesy Vermont Historical Society

Washington Turnpike Highway Bridge

Site of Covered Bridge in July 1864, burned by Ricketts' men to prevent Confederate crossing.

Photograph of postwar highway bridge taken by Charles A. Davis in 1893
Courtesy Vermont Historical Society

Washington Turnpike Bridge

Site of Covered Bridge in July 1864, burned by Ricketts' men to prevent Confederate crossing. Union positions on high ground to left of photograph.
Photograph taken by Charles A. Davis in 1893
Courtesy Vermont Historical Society

**Private Alfred N. Sova,
9th New York Heavy Artillery**

One of the men who set fire to the
Monocacy covered bridge.
*Courtesy Fred L. Rohrer,
Sova's great-grandson,
of Fremont, California*

**Brigadier General James
Brewerton Ricketts, U.S.A.**

Stalwart commander of Third Division,
VI Corps, who reinforced Wallace and
bore the brunt of McCausland and
Gordon assaults on July 9.
U.S. Army Military History

Scene of 10th Vermont Skirmisher Battles North of Monocacy

Baltimore and Ohio Railroad tracks in foreground, railroad cut to left out of photograph, highway in background.

Photograph by Charles A. Davis, 1893
Courtesy Vermont Historical Society

Araby Hill Farmland

Site of heavy fighting between Ricketts and Gordon, late afternoon, July 9, 1864.

Photograph by Charles A. Davis, 1893
Courtesy Vermont Historical Society

View from Thomas' Hill Field

Looking toward Washington turnpike with Monocacy junction (water tanks) and railroad in left center. Scene of decisive Confederate breakthrough on afternoon of July 9, 1864. From a photo circa 1940.

Oscar Bray, "A Proposed Road on the Monocacy Battlefield," April 26, 1940
Courtesy National Park Service, Harpers Ferry Center Library

Gambrill's Mill

Site of Union hospital and final action in sector south of Monocacy on July 9, 1864.

Photograph by Charles A. Davis, 1893
Courtesy Vermont Historical Society

Washington Turnpike Crossing

Postwar view of wartime covered bridge as seen from Wallace's headquarters. Brooks Hill in background, Worthington and Thomas farms to left, skirmishers' battlefield in foreground.

U.S. Army Military History Institute

View from Tyler's Position

Jug Bridge Sector, Monocacy River in trees in center. Reich's farm on left. Scene of final action late afternoon, July 9, 1864. Photograph, 1940.

Oscar Bray, "A Proposed Road on the Monocacy Battlefield," April 26, 1940
National Park Service, Harpers Ferry Center Library

sent, it took many hours to relay messages back via the Eastern Shore through Baltimore to the capital, a fact that probably eluded Wallace at that moment. Aside from Wallace's post-war reminiscences, however, which make those intentions more readily apparent than they actually were at the time, he hung back, and the railroaders' (including telegraph personnel) flight eclipsed any opportunity for earlier alert of the capital. Suddenly he was confronted, too, with scores of wounded, who could not be evacuated due to the train's departure. Profoundly shocked by such perfidy, the undaunted commander now realized retreat was only a question of time.[4]

The lull in the conflict continued as Wallace and his staff lunched on sardines and crackers provided from a nearby storehouse by the redoubtable VIII Corps commissary, Lieutenant Colonel Alexander Bliss. Major James R. Ross, Wallace's senior aide-de-camp, brought word that Brigadier General Erastus Tyler had matters under control at Crum's Ford (about a mile upstream) where the steep bluffs on the Union side of the stream deterred rebels ostensibly massing for attack. Of course, this was actually part of Rodes' overall demonstration against Colonel A. L. Brown's contingents at the stone bridge and Hughes ford farther north. The Confederates pressured but did not assault Wallace's defenders in the area, although Colonel Bradley T. Johnson's raiding column may have brushed fairly hard against the Ohioans and particularly Captain Edward Leib's mounted infantry at Hughes ford as they traveled out the Libertytown Road en route to Baltimore. Even this was transitory and merely calculated to help Early keep Wallace off guard and the defenders spread too thin to properly defend the Washington turnpike sector. Still, Wallace was pleased that Brown had succeeded in repelling several enemy charges, "and was in odd spirits." But, where were Ricketts' missing regiments, still en route from Baltimore, he wondered. They had been due by 1:00 P.M.[5]

Just then the pace of the action picked up about 2:00 or so. Wallace and his staff noticed a group of mounted men, whom they took to be officers, riding leisurely along the far side of the Monocacy surveying the Union positions. Their precise identity could not be ascertained, although Wallace remarked, "there will not be much more delay," for yonder seemed to be "the man in chief command reconnoitering us." Whether or not the enemy riders included Jubal Early remains unclear (more likely it was Breckinridge and Gordon and their staffs), but having sampled the hospitality of local secessionists, and satisfied that his supply officers were successfully ransoming the city, the general surely rode out to see what was slowing his army's progress. Ostensibly, he established some sort of command post at John Loats' farmhouse across from Mt. Olivet cemetery. He needed to quickly clear the Washington turnpike if his schedule was to be maintained. Johnson's cavalry had orders to rendezvous with the Point Lookout prisoners two days hence before the Washington forts, and so time was vital. Just then, both Wallace and Early were surprised by a renewal of McCausland's assaults from the vicinity of the Worthington property. If nothing more, the butter-milk rangers showed Early where he might send heavier infantry columns to outflank the unexpectedly stiff resistance at the junction and covered bridge.[6]

Repulse of McCausland's Second Attack

McCausland's chastened rebels had been whipped back into fighting form by their surviving officers using oaths and the flats of their swords. The shame at having been bested earlier by what they took to be rag-tag Yankee militia irked the rebels. Reinforced by their horse-holders, who had been left earlier with all the mounts north of the river, the dismounted troopers splashed across the river once more and surged anew up through the Worthington property around 2:00 P.M. Possibly 900 to 1,000 men may have now constituted this new wave. Across the Monocacy, the lounging ranks of Breckinridge's infantry watched and cheered expectantly from temporary rest positions beside the Buckeystown Road. McCausland's added strength virtually overlapped Ricketts' left flank along the Thomas-Worthington property line, a fact quickly picked up by Wallace's binoculars. No longer able to employ his 24-pounder howitzer's 1,300–1,400 yard killing range against such danger to his flank, the army commander merely sent Lieutenant Colonel Lynde Catlin to warn Ricketts of the danger, and urge him to place his whole command in one elongated line to equalize the front with the Confederates.[7]

Ricketts was caught off guard by the latest rebel maneuver. Masked by the terrain, the dismounted cavalrymen had passed south-east of the Worthington house, knifing between that structure and Brooks Hill, and toward a section of the boundary fence to the left of Ricketts' skirmishers. The latter scampered back to adjust to the new threat, but to no avail. Frantically, the Union brigadier sent a message to Wallace; something about enemy artillery enfilading his flank, cavalry in his rear, "What should I do?" This did not sound like a veteran commander, accustomed to the variables of the battlefield. McCausland's movement now achieved a new axis, pointing directly at the Thomas house. Carpenter's and Jackson's batteries from across the river peppered the VI Corps troops with harrowing artillery bursts as they swung to face the new threat. Wallace said of these bursts years later that "the horrible hissing, screeching they made in going were more dreadful to the imagination than were their explosions in fact." The soldiers on the scene, however, were more aghast at the extent of this latest attack. To Lieutenant Lemuel Abbott of the 10th Vermont, "if this was an average sized brigade in Early's army then half the truth as to its numbers has not been told." First spotted coming over the end of Brooks Hill, Abbott recalled that they came down the long slope, through a wide little valley out of sight, "all the while shouting their ominous defiant battle cry." Then, appearing out of the defilade in excellent order, "on they came, swinging first one way and then another, keeping us in breathless suspense," while the defenders were "determined to hold our ground as long as possible when the shock of battle should come."[8]

Alexander, at Wallace's instruction, shifted more guns to the pastures above Araby house in an effort to counter this new threat. Many of the novice Marylanders blanched as they passed the ersatz field hospital set up at Gambrill's Mill. Although organized and in the service since August 1862, they simply lacked the long exposure to combat possessed by Ricketts' VI Corps men. Now, they stood face-to-face in a bloody confrontation with Southern pros, even if Early regarded his cavalry as a rather shiftless lot. McCausland's drive quickly overran the Thomas house itself (the residents and others cowering in the basement as the tumult raged overhead). Ricketts' line reformed behind the road embankment of the Washington turnpike where it passed the Araby farm on the east. Then, suddenly, it was the Confederates' turn to be rebuffed.[9]

It was load and fire for both sides now locked in stiffer combat than before. The melee caused Southern gunners to relax their fire for fear of hitting friendly troops, and McCausland's men suddenly found themselves outgunned in the Thomas yard. Nathaniel Harris recalled that his 16th Virginia Cavalry was badly cut up, and that the lieutenant colonel of the sister 17th Virginia called for a volunteer to climb atop his shoulders "and from that elevation look down on the enemy's line so as to find out what was going on." No sooner had the pair straightened themselves up that a volley from the defenders cut them down. Unsupported, the Confederates wavered. Wallace caught sight of the change from his observation point near the eastern blockhouse. Quickly, he sent Ross again to Ricketts, this time suggesting a counterstroke.[10]

Ross met Captain W. H. Lanius, aide to Colonel William H. Truex, commanding Ricketts' embattled first brigade. The young captain grasped at the suggestion without bringing Ricketts into the deliberation. Defying enemy sharpshooters, he galloped to the positions occupied by the 87th Pennsylvania and 14th New Jersey, and directed them to "charge across the fields and take position, with the right resting at the Keefer Thomas house. The two regiments went forward up Araby's front lane and over the yard, routing McCausland's men from around the main house. Joseph G. Stonesifer of Company I of the 87th reputedly reached the house first, while Spangler Welsh of Company F and comrades quickly took up their own sniping positions at some of the windows. A Confederate shell crashed through the dining room scattering knives, forks and spoons on a table, and the Federals quickly dispersed toward the barn where they were taken captive by the retiring rebels. Then, the beaten cavalrymen sullenly retired once more to the Worthington property with Union skirmishers close on their heels.[11]

McCausland's last attack ended the fighting between his people and Ricketts' veterans. It had taken scarcely twenty or thirty minutes for the Confederates to take the Thomas house. They held it for another twenty minutes, from approximately 2:25 until 2:45, according to one observer, Glenn Worthington, who as a boy had witnessed the fight from his father's cellar. Other interpretations have the second McCausland attack completed by 2:30 P.M. In any event, Ricketts had reestablished Union control over Araby farm by mid-afternoon. In the process, gunfire from carbines and muskets, as well as two of Alexander's guns providing fire support for the defenders, had riddled the brick structure itself. Clendenin's Illinois horsemen now parceled themselves back onto Ricketts' left flank as best they could, given their inadequate numbers. Other portions of that command continued their scouting and bridge destruction off down the Baker's Valley Road toward Buckeystown. At least they provided rudimentary screening for the army's flank, even though they had no direct impact upon what was fast becoming a more major battle.[12]

Worst of all, McCausland's two attacks, plus the need to provide counter-battery fire against Confederate guns and activities across the river had drained Alexander's ammunition. "A single Union battery on the field was 'pumping away' over our heads," recounted Osceola Lewis of the 138th Pennsylvania, referring to Alexander's work, "but without any apparent effect." Once more, the VI Corps boys deplored the absence of "McKnight's or any other 6th Corps battery" for had they have been present "the day could have been saved." But, Captain James McKnight's Battery M, 5th U.S. Artillery, had been left back at Petersburg along with other division artillery and wagons—thought to be too taxing to the hard-pressed transportation system. Infantry alone from the Army of the Potomac would have to suffice against Early's raiders. Alexander may have wished that less ammunition had been expended up on Catoctin Mountain or outside Frederick over the past few days. Certainly, Wallace must have wondered why his Baltimore logisticians had failed to send forward more supplies to the Monocacy.[13]

Temporary Stalemate

Whatever Early thought of the twenty-nine-year-old McCausland personally, the southwest Virginian had "solved the problem for me," he said, enabling Old Jube to exploit a farm ford to finish off the enemy. He told Breckinridge to send forward the veteran division of Georgian John B. Gordon. There was something more than militia beyond the river, and Early needed them eliminated in order to regain his timetable for reaching Washington. Brigadier General John Echols' less experienced second division would remain north of the river in reserve. Gordon had already brought his command from the vicinity of Mount Olivet cemetery to the Buckeystown Road, and posted division on a hillock overlooking the unfolding battlefield. Similarly, Brigadier General Armistead L. Long advanced twelve of his guns. As Private Henry R. Berkeley of the Amherst Virginia artillery noted in his diary: "We first took a position on the left of the Washington Pike and afterwards crossed over to the right and put our battery on a hill fronting a still higher hill held by the Yanks." Thus in position by about 1:00 P.M. on the Best farm, these cannoneers were joined by the Allegheny (Carpenter's) four guns and a section of the Fluvanna (Massie's) artillery.[14]

Some officers, like brigade commander William Terry, chafed at the delay, citing that his troops had arrived about a mile south of Frederick at 8:30 that morning and then had stood and waited six hours for something to happen. The men in the ranks had other impressions, however. Delighted to just "*look* at a battle," rather than participate for once, "we made ourselves comfortable and lay down under the shelter provided." They sent up cheers every time one of their sharpshooters or artillerists scored a hit on their opponents. Such spectator sport proved short lived. When Breckinridge's orders to advance arrived (sometime after 2:00 P.M.), most of Gordon's soldiers bridled at having to leave blankets, oilclothes, and "articles we had captured in some former battle." Dutifully, however, they formed ranks and trudged off in the heat to follow McCausland's pathfinders. Turning left off the Buckeystown Road just after crossing the little covered bridge over Ballenger's creek they took a farm lane between the McGill and Markell houses to what was called the McKinney-Worthington ford.[15] Apparently, Breckinridge preceded Gordon across the Monacacy setting up his command post at the Worthington house.

Brigadier General William Terry told his brigade of Virginians to remove their shoes and wade the Monocacy barefoot; others claimed Gordon himself gave that order, still others noted they were told not to waste time but splash across fully shod. I. G. Bradwell of the 31st Georgia in Clement A. Evans' brigade recalled that as they neared the ford, Gordon called out: "Plunge right in, boys; no time for pulling off clothes." Once across, Terry at least, reminded his men to take time to securely retie their shoes, recounted Private James Hutcheson of the 2d, 4th, 5th, 27th, and 33d Virginia Consolidated Infantry Brigade. Evans then rode along the line of battle telling what he expected the men to do. Noting that they were on enemy's flank, "you must advance quietly until you strike them, then give a yell and charge!" Indeed, the Federal line stood scarcely seven hundred yards across fields studded with grain stacks and wheat sheaves. Everyone, observed Gordon in his reminiscences, "must have known before we started" that the attack could become "tangled and confused." So, the Georgia veteran took time to properly congeal his attack, using the fields around the Worthington house and intervening woodland between there and the defenders, to screen his preparation. Apprehensive that he was operating beyond the support of the rest of the army, Gordon claimed after the war that he knew that if any soldiers in the world could win victory against such adverse conditions, "those high-mettled Southern boys would achieve it here."[16]

Meanwhile, near the junction and bridges, Union commander Lew Wallace watched as Ramseur's skirmishers launched a heavier effort to dislodge bluecoats north of the river. Lieutenant George Davis' cat and mouse game in the corn, wheat, and clover fields and the spiking of the howitzer must have made him wonder just how much longer Union lines could hold in that sector. Somewhere in the noon hour, Wallace concluded that he needed every man to help Ricketts with what could only be ever-increasing Confederate pressure on that flank. Riding to the wooden bridge with the intention of burning that structure so as to free up the defenders there for work elsewhere, he noticed the Union skirmishers north of the river. He directed Ross to ride out to warn them, but the aide decided the distance was too great and "they will retreat at sight of the smoke."[17]

Dismissing pangs of guilt at deserting them by thinking of the offsetting threat to Ricketts, Wallace, about 12:30 P.M., directed Lieutenant Colonel William Henry Seward (son and namesake of the current secretary of state), to set the bridge afire. Seward had already ordered Lieutenant Chauncy Fish, and B Company of the 9th "Heavies" "to move down to that bridge and hold it at all hazards." Clinging stubbornly to their position all morning amidst rebel artillery fire, attempting to rake the bridge structure, Fish now had the distasteful duty of burning it. Privates Alfred Nelson Sova, Samuel R. Mack, and Sergeant Albert L. Smith had already gathered sheaves of wheat from a nearby field and placed them into holes previously cut in the roof.

Now, Sova shinnied up a wood beam and applied the torch. The bridge was quickly consumed, flaming embers falling, hissing into the cool river. With all this taking place to their backs, few if any of the skirmishers north of the river probably realized they were cut off from the army.[18]

Wallace realized that his remaining time on the Monocacy was limited. About 2:30 P.M. he sent a hasty message to the commander of the long-missing VI Corps contingent, thought to be somewhere back on the railroad around Plane No. 1. "Hurry up your troops; I am greatly in need of them," read the note. The absent officer was to "send train of empty cars; also telegraph operation." Then, at some point that afternoon, Baltimore and Ohio president John W. Garrett received word that the wires had been cut east of Monocacy at 11:00 A.M., and, as he told Washington late in the day, two trainloads of Ricketts' division had been at Plane Number 4, thirteen miles east of that river ever since that time. Garrett himself wired the officer in command of those troops about the battle raging to his west, and that "arrival of your re-enforcements is deemed of great importance." He queried, would it not be proper for him to proceed at once either by foot or rail? A subsequent telegram from Garrett to President Lincoln indicated that this officer was well aware of the battle in progress at 1:00, but other evidence pointed to great laziness in moving forward as required. None of this did Wallace much good, waiting and hoping as the battle continued into the mid-afternoon.[19]

At 3:00, Wallace broke his own self-imposed silence with higher authorities. He dictated two messages to aides, Majors Ross and Max Woodhull, which he wanted sent by fast rider to Monrovia and thence by wire to Washington and City Point. In them, Wallace outlined how he had been fighting Early at Monocacy Junction since seven o'clock that morning, had repulsed two assaults, but that a third, and heavier one, was impending. He stated bluntly that the Confederate force numbered 18,000 to 20,000 men, plus a corps reserve, "with field artillery in proportion." "If you have not already strengthened the defensive force at Washington," he warned Grant not too subtly, "I respectfully suggest the necessity for doing it amply and immediately." Years later, he claimed that he particularly wanted to provoke a "constitutionally slow, if not timid" Henry Halleck to action. Such autobiographical bravado notwithstanding, nothing official survives to suggest that either Wallace sent such messages or that they were received.[20]

Equally unclear, but just as plausible, however, was the ostensible mid-afternoon meeting between Wallace and Ricketts concerning the increasing enemy buildup. Ricketts reached Wallace's command post overheated and with hair, beard, and uniform covered with dust. Remaining mounted, the VI Corps officer chatted freely with Wallace about the missing reinforcements, the strength of the rebel flanking column, and what should be done about retreat. "Awhile longer," Ricketts suggested, since Early could no longer move until morning now that the clock stood at 3:30 P.M., and, "if what I am told is true, that the ford is very rocky, it will be noon before he can get his artillery across the river." The plucky Ricketts had been in tight places many times before and he was not about to run away, having thwarted two rebel assaults so far. So, the pair agreed to stay as long as possible, and then retire by country roads north to the National Road and thence towards Baltimore. His ammunition running low, Ricketts turned stoically to the task of stopping the full and final test from one of Early's crack divisions.[21]

Gordon's Assault

Wallace watched the Confederate mass just then emerging from the shadows of the Worthington farm woods. "They are coming," he shouted to aides, calling for horses since "we may have to ride." "How long that line is," someone else noted apprehensively, and Wallace suddenly realized that this particular Confederate assault would undoubtedly overlap Ricketts' defense. Actually more nearly equal in strength than any participant on either side wanted to admit then or later, Confederate superiority rested largely with more artillery, ammunition, and what Gordon himself subsequently claimed that he saw in "my brave fellows" that afternoon—"an enthusiasm which amounted almost to a martial delirium." At any rate, preceded by a thin line of skirmishers, the solid ranks of butternut and gray threaded their way through obstacles of farm fencing and wheat sheaves, eliminating pesky Yankee sharpshooters as they came. One such unfortunate bluecoat was later found dead behind a wheat sheaf with a dozen wounds in his body.[22]

Gordon's advance began by brigades, *en echelon*, from the right. Evans on the right, Terry on the left, with a shrunken, consolidated brigade of Louisianans under brigadier Zebulon York in the center, they quickly passed across the Worthington front yard, brushed Brooks Hill on their right, and by 3:30 P.M. emerged from the woods in full battle array (two or three lines, preceded by skirmishers), ready to strike Ricketts' command. According to Early, writing after the war, the whole affair was now under Breckinridge's "personal superintendence," as the Kentuckian joined Gordon in Worthington's front yard. From that vantage point, the former United States vice president calmly monitored the rest of the battle. By contrast with the bullet-scarred Thomas place, John Worthington's equally sturdy brick structure largely escaped major damage from hostile fire. Distant from the main firestorm, this centerpiece, the Confederate staging area, soon became a field hospital, as would virtually every other farm on both sides of the river.[23]

The inimitable "yelp, yelp, yelp" of the distinctive rebel yell arose from the mass, Wallace remembered in his memoirs. Evans' Georgians headed directly towards the Thomas house and outbuildings, and the five defending regiments of Truex's brigade that had borne the brunt of the sector's fighting thus far. The 138th Pennsylvania and one battalion of the 9th New York Heavy Artillery had been sent from Colonel Matthew McClennan's brigade to assist Truex and took position on the extreme left of the division. "We advanced," recorded Evans after the war, "under the embarrassment of the interspersed *wheat shocks* which stood in our way." York's skeletal units aimed at the seam between Truex and what remained of McClennan's command, the 9th New York "Heavies," and the 110th New York closer to the river. Terry's Virginians keyed on the left flank of the latter units (the New Yorkers commanded, incidentally, by Secretary of State William Henry Seward's son and namesake), pulled off their river anchor by the strength of this new rebel drive. Gordon's heavy battle array caused Wallace much concern when he detected this leftward shifting, but he could do little without reinforcements.[24]

Evans' men first encountered the full fury of Ricketts' determined defenders near a large oak tree about one hundred yards from the Yankee lines. McCausland's dejected troopers had been more than happy to see the infantrymen's arrival even if the latter's officers had taunted, "Come on Georgians, follow me—we will show these cavalrymen how to fight, these are only one hundred-days men and they can't stand up against our troops," as they passed through the retiring horse soldiers. The jubilant rebels soon learned otherwise. A bloody conflict raged in and around the Araby buildings, hotly contested by Truex's men. Young Mamie Tyler recalled years later that huddled with the other noncombatants in the Thomas's cellar, the six hours of conflict above them were "hours of suspense, anxiety, and at times of terror, though there were some amusing episodes during the long hours of confinement. One of those seeking shelter was an old colored 'mammy,' who became quite indignant with the younger inmates for feeling the pangs of hunger." Frequently the black matron remarked, 'Honeys, say your prayers, dis is no time to eat; pray de good Lord to deliver us from this dreadful battle.'" Tyler continued for her rapt postwar listeners: "You can imagine how strange the sounds outside those walls, 'minie' balls slashing the shrubbery, while the larger missiles of war's fearful instruments twisted huge limbs from the trees, leveled chimneys, and tore out an angle of the house."[25]

Private G. W. Nichols of the 61st Georgia claimed that in this fighting, "Our brigade suffered as bad as it ever did in battle for the amount of men and length of time engaged," citing that it would bave been worse if they hadn't been ably supported by York's Louisianans on their left. "All that we could shoot at was the smoke of their guns, they were so well posted," referring to Ricketts' men. It was called a victory, he claimed after the battle, but a costly one cutting down over five hundred men of Evans' brigade. If these were raw troops facing them, he decided, "I never saw old soldiers shoot better." Scarcely fifty-two muskets out of 150 in his unit could be stacked when it ended; the 12th Georgia losing fully half of its complement. Much of this could be attributed to both volley fire and expert sharp-shooter aim.[26]

Union and Confederate marksmen alike vied for likely targets. A bluecoated sniper was effective from a wheatstack until he, too, was cut down by eighteen balls. Sergeant Lyman B. Pike of the 10th Vermont had particularly good luck from his Baker Valley Road-Washington Turnpike culvert until he too dropped dead from an enemy's bullet. Evans went down with several nasty wounds ("fell a hard stunning fall," he phrased it), right in front of his old 31st Georgia regiment, one bullet ripping apart his pocket sewing kit, driving pins and needles into his side which plagued him for a decade thereafter. Colonel Edmund Atkinson of the 26th Georgia took over for him. Gordon's younger brother, Captain Eugene Gordon, spurred his mount along the line rallying the men forward and was wounded at some point. The popular, young Colonel John H. Lamar of the 61st Georgia as well as his second-in-command, David Van Valinburg, and 98 of the 152 men engaged, were similarly cut down as was Lieutenant Colonel John Baker of the 13th Georgia. Six consecutive flag bearers of the 12th Georgia battalion were shot, including the last, Lieutenant James Mincy, who survived a nasty lung wound and a Union surgeon drawing a silk handkerchief through the wound to cleanse the path of the bullet. Virtually every saddle was emptied of officers, leading I. G. Bradwell to conclude years later that the fight was made by "private soldiers of our brigade without leadership." Poor Tom Nichols of the 61st Georgia simply sat down, wiping his brains from his temple with his hand, and lingered for twelve agonizing hours, muttering how he was going to go back to Virginia, procure a horse and ride home to Georgia to fight no more.[27]

Much of the loss could be attributed to accurate shooting by the 14th New Jersey and 87th Pennsylvania. A nasty flanking fire was similarly laid down by Colonel William Henry's 10th Vermont, positioned with the rump of Clendenin's horsemen by the Baker's Valley Road. "Wait boys, don't fire until you see the C.S.A. on their waist belts and then give it to 'em," importuned the Vermonter. They did, and Bradwell, at least, was convinced that barely 800 to 1,100 brigade members survived. Crashing into Truex's roadside ditch position on the turnpike—"as fine breastworks as I ever saw," was the way Georgian George W. Nichols put it, "our brigade suffered as bad as it ever did in battle for the amount of men and length of time engaged." Evans' brigade was stopped cold, and the weight of Gordon's attack shifted up the line to York's men. Of course, Colonel Thomas' house suffered even more damage from the combat around it.[28]

The forty-four-year-old Zebulon York, a transplanted Down-Easter from Maine who had gone south to amass a cotton fortune, took Stafford's consolidated Pelican brigade (scarcely 250 men said one participant) into action just north of the Thomas house. Ground configuration permitted the Louisianans to move forward relatively unnoticed by Truex's preoccupied defenders. So, York's Tigers sprang forward to exploit the seam between Truex and McClennan. Once again, dogged Yankee defense cut down scores of Southerners. As York confessed to a Richmond friend after the battle, Monocacy was one of the "fiercest and bloodiest that my command has ever been engaged in, considering the numbers." He cited loss of "more than one-quarter of the number I took into the fight" or about 163 killed, wounded, or missing. The bluecoats also absorbed increasing punishment. Three color-bearers of the 126th Ohio went down, as well as a like number of Jersey standard bearers. Altogether, the latter unit lost three officers and 140 men on the very terrain they had earlier used as a training ground when first entering service several years before. This was the field visited by Father James B. Sheeran after the fight to find a regular line of Yankee dead—"lying in every direction and position, some on their sides, some on their faces, some on their backs with their eyes and mouths open, the burning sun beating upon them and their faces swarmed with flies."[29]

Araby house eventually settled into Confederate hands, the refugees from the battle continuing to huddle in the cellar. But, before it did, Major Peter Vredenburgh of the 14th New Jersey rushed into the upstairs at one point, looking frantically for the family that had befriended him when his unit had been encamped nearby two years before. He found them in the cellar "frightened to death," and brought them a bucket of ice water, as well as the family silver which he had discovered on the vacated dining room table. He locked the drawers and some of the doors to the house to prevent vandalism. Mamie Tyler recalled years later how they had conversed with the young officer about the course of the battle. "Of course, he expected to drive the rebels back in short time, at which we very boldly expressed deep regret, and also requested to let us have a wounded Confederate, who was lying outside of the cellar window inside with us—'wouldn't you rather have a live prisoner than a dead one,' this wounded man received our most devoted attention; our handkerchiefs were used in bathing the wounds with ice water." He also informed Vredenburgh "that Lee with his army was on our left at Urbana and that Early's corps was fighting our troops. The major left hastily to pass that news to Ricketts "in order that we might get orders to retire."[30]

Before its capture, Araby house came under pointblank Confederate artillery fire when Major William McLaughlin and Lowry's battery rumbled across the Monocacy and set up to blast Union sharpshooters from the structure. The cannoneers were "supervised" by the Worthington family rooster, who like the chickens, had been left to run freely in the yard when the family retreated to the cellar. Now with every cannon discharge, he crowded lustily as if to approve every shot directed at the enemy. Another Worthington animal was also pressed into service, apparently. Captain Randolph Jones Barton, one of Terry's aides, fearing the loss of his pet mare, "Mary Stuart," in the impending attack, purloined a spare horse that he spotted either in a field or stable (accounts differ). Covered with mud from wallowing, Barton claimed later, the mount reminded him of a rhinoceros. Supposedly he was John Worthington's carriage horse, "Old Davy," exempted from being taken off to Sugarloaf. This cost the horse his life, for he was soon shot from beneath Barton; the young captain received only "a blow upon my sword belt" from a spent bullet. Years after the war, Barton, by then a prominent Baltimore lawyer, would encounter Worthington's son, Glenn, by this time Judge of the Maryland Court of Appeals, who reminded Barton that he owed the jurist the cost of the horse. At one point, too, Barton claimed to have encountered Keefer Thomas' daughter, Alice, and thinking the horse had belonged to her family, offered recompense. Alice, by this time a grown woman, declined the offer, expressing, instead, "her satisfaction at being able to contribute in any way to the Southern cause."[31]

In any event, by this time what had started as a battle for fence rows, had become a typical slugfest between old foes in the overheated fields and yards between the Worthington and Thomas houses. At this point, Gordon may well have realized that he faced Army of the Potomac veterans, not militia. He dispatched couriers back to Breckinridge at the Worthington house, requesting reinforcements. John Echols' division still lazed about watching the fighting from the McGill farm across the river. They were available. There was no time to dally while they got across the stream, however, so Gordon turned to Terry's Virginians to break the back of the stubborn Yankee resistance. The choice proved a good one as Terry's people could change front and assault the portion of Ricketts' line closest to the river, it was decided. Observing after the war that his division "had passed the forest of malign wheat-stacks," climbed a second fence and was in close proximity to Wallace's first line of battle that appeared little hurt and standing firmly, Gordon was a role model for men in the ranks like John Worsham. "He was sitting on his horse as quietly as if nothing was going on, wearing his old red shirt, the sleeves pulled up a little, the only indication that he was ready for the fight," the soldier recalled. Then, the attackers surged once more across the Worthington and Thomas fields.[32]

The actual sequence was lost in the smoke of battle. Having gone only a few steps, the Confederates came in view of what apparently were Lieutenant John A. Walcott's skirmishers from Company F, 151st New York. They lay behind a post-and-rail fence that divided corn field from pasture about 125 yards away. They had been out there all day screening cannoneers and 3-inch guns of Alexander's battery. "On going into the fight we went on a run, left wheel by regiment," recalled color bearer George C. Pile of Company A, 37th Virginia. Terry halted his precipitous advance by yelling at his men to take it easy "or you will break yourselves down and will not be able to fight the enemy when you get to them." But their pause was only momentary, for then, at "right-shoulder-shift" they plunged over and through the line of enemy skirmishers and took the fence. Men in front shouted "at 'em boys," but Gordon turned in his saddle calling, "keep quiet, we'll have our time presently," and asked the troops to pull down the fence so that everyone might easily pass through. With Gordon in the lead, the Confederates moved out into the Thomas pasture north of Araby house and close to the river. Ahead lay yet another fence line and an abandoned road cut, defended not only by Abbott's survivors but the major complement of the 9th New York "Heavies" and the 110th Ohio—protecting the pasture and Thomas' hill field. A savage fight then ensued.[33]

Their erstwhile rifle pits of no further use since they faced the river, not the direction of the Confederate attacks, the bluecoats still put up a stiff fight. To break the stalemate, according to childhood observer Glenn Worthington, Terry dispatched Colonel J. H. Funk's consolidated 2d, 4th, 5th, 26th, and 33d Virginia to find the hollow through which the Worthington Spring discharged into the Monocacy. Thus hidden by the terrain, these remnants of the old Stonewall Brigade "flanked" the Federal line and enfiladed it from a sudden and unexpected quarter. Cannon across the river added to this enfilading fire. In fact, one battery seemed to single out color bearer George Pile of the 37th Virginia for special attention, "the balls striking very close." Later, the young artillery lieutenant would cross the river to apologize in person to Pile.[34]

Fellow Virginian James A. Hutcheson recalled walking to one fence, behind which the Yanks were "shooting at us for all they knew how." His comrades stuck their own muskets between the rails and put a volley into them, and those Federals who did not get shot jumped up and ran like wildfire, with the Johnnies close on their heels. "That volley settled the Monocacy fight," thought Hutcheson. Indeed, it was the most exciting fight he ever witnessed, claimed John Worsham. Terry's men rushed forward as "the men were perfectly wild when they came in sight of the enemy's column," he claimed. Now bested, the veteran 110th Ohio folded, as did Seward's less experienced New Yorkers from the Finger Lakes region of upstate New York—having little military experience beyond garrison duty in Washington's fortifications. As Confederate leaders watched expectantly, the full pressure of Gordon's division now drove against Federal positions all along the Washington Turnpike line. Soon, the portion situated in the Thomas hill field above the Bush Creek Valley disintegrated, and was forced down "over the sloping field to the Washington road."[35]

New Jersey major Vredenburgh told his mother by letter three days later how the rebels followed them closely, "and it was really magnificent to see how heroically they charged." He had never seen "so bold a movement before." Low on ammunition, Alexander's gunners could do nothing to stem the tide, in fact limbering up their pieces and withdrawing by 4:00 P.M. ostensibly under Wallace's orders for a general withdrawal as soon as the Hoosier had spotted the extent of Gordon's assault. Once again the veteran infantry of the Army of the Potomac rued the absence of their regular artillery support. Now, back across the Thomas property they went, and abruptly down into the Bush Creek valley around Gambrill's Mill. "Elevate your pieces, men; elevate your pieces," shouted Colonel Mat McClennan, in an effort to have what was left of his Second Brigade hit targets in the hill field above them, from which Gordon's infantrymen poured point blank fire down upon the shattered Federals. The staying power of the Army of the Potomac veterans simply could not withstand Gordon's final onslaught. Futilely, officers like First Lieutenant Daniel B. Harmon of Company H of the 9th New York unconsciously shouted the refrain from George F. Root's popular "Battle Cry of Freedom"—"rally 'round your flag, boys," but to no avail. The order now came to "shift for ourselves," recounted that unit's historian, with the result that disorder, even rout in places took over. Wallace's control of the battle evaporated.[36]

In fact, all the Federals now suffered from insufficient ammunition resupply and combat fatigue. Yet, individual acts of bravery occurred as some units fought back bitterly. Both Seward and his second-in-command, Major Edward P. Taft, went down wounded. Seward wore a private soldier's uniform that day, and feigning death, he eventually escaped by bridling a stray mule with his silk pocket handkerchief. Taft was captured, robbed of personal possessions, but regained his freedom the next day when Federal mounted patrols re-took Frederick and released all the wounded captives left there by Early's departing army. Even Gordon, too, had his horse shot from beneath him. Astonished by the ferocity of this fight in the July heat, he later claimed that one small stream of water ("probably the one flowing across the Thomas lawn toward Gambrill's Mill and Bush Creek," suggested local authority Glenn Worthington), ran red with the blood of dead and dying. "Nearly one half of my men and large numbers of the Federals fell there," Gordon concluded after the war. The victorious Confederates swept all before them, although, said Georgia private I. G. Bradwell, "our ranks were pretty thin— hardly a good skirmish line—but ranged along the higher ground we continued for a while to exchange shots at the heads of the enemy in the road below us."[37]

Ricketts, having been forced to elongate his already overextended line by the weight of Gordon's attack on the Araby house and outbuildings, now watched as his base units on the right collapsed. His maneuver and concentrated enemy artillery fire had cost the battle. If only his third, missing brigade had come up; if only there were more ammunition; if ...! Now, he was faced with completing one of the most difficult military maneuvers—extricating a command under victorious enemy attack. Orders came from Wallace about 4:00 P.M. per their earlier agreement, and, at some point, the Hoosier had also ordered the burning of the blockhouses. Wallace contended later that the VI Corps troops "were not whipped, but retired reluctantly, under my orders," but this spanked of typical officer post mortems.[38]

Many of the participants viewed it differently, with rebels claiming complete rout, their opponents suggesting they tried to "send as good as we received," for the most part. Bradwell recalled years later that the Yankees fled "faster than did Ben Hur in that celebrated chariot race" alluding to Wallace's famous postwar novel. Louisiana brigadier York waxed ecstatically a week after the battle to a Richmond friend that "the victory was perfect, the rout as disgraceful as the Yankee army could make—they ran like sheep having no shepherd." Hutcheson, one of Funk's veterans, contended that York's people "must have been crowding them about that time [Terry's attack], for it was about fifteen or twenty minutes from the time we drove them from the fence till the whole force was in full retreat." Still, Alexander's artillerymen moved off the field in good order at a walk while enduring heavy enemy fire. They crossed the railroad and fought off the spiked 24-pounder howitzer and the mountain howitzer as well. So it might not have been a complete rout after all.[39]

Whatever the actual case, organized Union defense had broken on the southern portion of the battlefield. Gordon's overwhelming assault (particularly the final thrust by Terry's Virginians), the enfilading enemy artillery fire from King's guns and Funk's riflemen, the unrelenting pressure from Stephen Ramseur's division north of the river that pinned down Federals around the junction, ammunition shortages (somewhat strange given the amount of supplies rescued the previous night from Frederick—perhaps no ammunition among them), and Ricketts' forced elongation of his line—such had occasioned the decisive moment in this battle.

As the Confederates undertook mopping up operations against isolated pockets of resistance, everyone on the Federal side sought but one thing—escape via the country lanes leading upstream to the highway to Baltimore. Henry's 10th Vermont, on Ricketts' far left, was nearly cut off when the rest of their brigade retired from the roadside ditch defenses along the Washington turnpike. Their colonel had to double-time his men over rough terrain, under heavy enemy fire, "parallel to our line of battle and across the enemy's front for some distance." He simply left his severely wounded to the enemy's mercy. Struggling over one of the ridges above Gambrill's Mill, both Vermont color bearers fell exhausted from their labors. Corporal Alexander Scott grabbed the two flags and bore them away safely, thus earning a Medal of Honor which was issued on September 28, 1897. Henry's command eventually made it to the Baltimore Road, and on to Monrovia, scarcely sixty-nine men and two officers. There, they discovered (like the rest of Wallace's beaten force), a locomotive and empty passenger cars waiting idly on the track where the National Road crossed the railroad not far from New Market.[40]

Ramseur Secures the Railroad Bridge

Other Vermonters out on the skirmish line north of the river also miraculously escaped. They had been there since early morning, with Marylanders and New Yorkers, "pop-popping" away at their Southern counterparts amidst the corn, wheat, and clover fields. Without any orders since an early visit by Ricketts himself, they had cheered when either Wiegel or one of Alexander's gunners had blasted the Best barn. They had managed to avoid being outflanked, much to Wallace's relief. "I remember of telling Gen. Ricketts that I feared you were so much absorbed in the contest that the enemy would have an opportunity to turn your position and cut you off," wrote Wallace to Captain George E. Davis a quarter-century after the battle. And, while the two senior officers were speaking, "I saw them send a strong detachment behind some trees which intercepted your view of their operation," he went on. Fortunately, Davis and company "discovered the movement in time and retired from the position," Wallace approvingly noted. Davis' "management was admirable," said the Hoosier warrior, and Ricketts, seeing Davis' adroitness apparently had cried out, "Good for Davis. By God, he's a trump," to which in 1899, Wallace added his "I am still of the same opinion."[41]

The Vermonters had shrugged resignedly when their nominal chieftain, Lieutenant Colonel C. G. Chandler, simply deserted them for safe haven back across the river. Lieutenant Davis claimed that few of the 100-days Marylanders suffered casualties, "unless by the weight of their heavy knapsacks, for most of them left us in season to have reached a place of safety," in point of fact the western blockhouse. There was little love lost between the veterans and those they considered home guards, although Davis and Brown got along well enough. Still, as the Vermonter claimed, "we knew not the plan or situation, only as apparent to the eye." And, the enemy had kept them busy all day.[42]

Caught unawares by the burning of the covered bridge (Davis always claimed it came at mid-morning or 10:30; others, including Wallace, stated half-past noon), the Vermonters, plus the two companies of New York "Heavies," and whatever residue of the 1st Maryland Potomac Home Brigade soldiers held fast, stayed tightly engaged with Ramseur's men. This handful (200 men at most) singularly held off the Confederates no matter that the thrust straight at the covered bridge soon became ancillary to Early's search for a flank approach. The Washington (or Georgetown, as contemporaries called it) pike *was* the avenue to Washington, and hence the focal point of the defense. So, Vermonters like Daniel B. Freeman, and his buddy, George Douse, both of Company G, took posts either on the bridge over the railroad (using sturdy timber stringers as makeshift breastworks), or in the adjacent hillock corn field (now the site of the 14th New Jersey monument) and continued to pick off rebels. Behind them lay other skirmishers covering the Frederick Junction complex, the western-most blockhouse, and, of course, John Garrett's iron railroad bridge. All day, these men provided a Thermopylaean effort—stretched thinly across a small triangle of ground beside the Monocacy. Perhaps, more than any others on the field that day, these two hundred determined soldiers truly disrupted Old Jube's timetable, and ultimately won the footrace to Washington. Of course, no one knew this at that moment.[43]

To these Federals then, the succession of covered bridge burning and isolation, the protection of the sole remaining escape route via the railroad bridge, and the continued brisk fire-fight "rendered our situation very exciting," concluded Davis. Hard pressed by Ramseur's men in their coordinated drive with Gordon's attack across the river by 3:30 P.M., and seeing Ricketts collapse behind them— the "division headquarters flag was crossing the track in our rear. We must leave now, or never"—Davis now guided the withdrawal of his little band. Brown and his Marylanders had already melted back to the rifle pits on the east side of the river. It remained for the Vermonters to extricate themselves. Stepping lightly across the railroad bridge's cross ties while ducking the whistling "minie balls," several of Davis' people were hit, falling into the river forty feet below, to end up later in the Andersonville prison camp. Fully one third of his 275-man detachment were killed, wounded or captured. Still, Davis too, won a postwar Medal of Honor (issued on May 27, 1892) because he "held the approach to two bridges against repeated assaults of superior numbers, thereby materially delaying Early's advance on Washington."[44]

Once across, Davis noticed the absence of Captain Brown and his men as they passed empty rifle pits at the east end of the bridge. But for the moment, and years thereafter, said Davis: "It has always been a mystery how any of us escaped the bullet or capture." Right on their heels, however, came screaming "Tarheels," led by Colonel Thomas F. Toon brandishing the battle flag of the 20th North Carolina. The Southerners had been frustrated for too long, particularly when the 23d North Carolina had been unable to take the blockhouse earlier in the afternoon, and Colonel W. S. Davis of the 12th North Carolina had been unable to effect a coordinated final assault on the Vermonters in the railroad cut with the rest of brigadier Robert D. Johnston's brigade until almost the end of the action. Now they were not to be denied elation in final victory as they merged with Gordon's jubilant men in overrunning the field hospital at Gambrill's Mill.

The elated rebels soon captured hundreds of additional hapless Union stragglers, lost in the melange of woods and hollows while trying to make their way to the Baltimore Road. These included about 300 bluecoats cornered about halfway up the reel's Mill Road toward Crum's Ford. Major Henry Kyd Douglas of Early's staff claimed to have taken a body of skirmishers over the railroad bridge too, and Sergeant John H. Worsham of the 21st Virginia recalled that when the enemy started running in all directions, "up went our old yell all along the line of [Gordon's] division, and it was answered" by

Ramseur's men across the river. By 5:00 P.M., maybe earlier, the main battleground at Monocacy had been cleared of organized resistance as Ramseur's men plus a section from Chapman's battery pursued the rapidly departing Federals northward to Bartonsville.[45]

Tyler Covers the Retreat

Brigadier General Erastus Tyler's role now became crucial if Wallace's battered survivors were to escape. Rodes' division also pressed forward late in the afternoon against the stone or jug bridge, just as Confederate victory seemed assured downstream. By 6:00 P.M., Colonel A. L. Brown's resolute Buckeyes on Reich's ridge astride the National Road west of the river came under heavy pressure and were in danger of being overrun. Virtually in charge of all the combat on the northern end of the line, Brown, like Davis in front of the covered bridge, had stood his ground all day. Captain Leib and McGinnis had "handsomely repulsed" what had appeared to be Major Harry Gilmor's effort to force Hughes Ford north of the ridge early in the day. Brown's men on the exposed ridgeline, however, were mainly responsible for blunting Rodes' thrust.

Brown's people had even stymied some sort of feint toward Reich's and Crum's ford area to the south, using men drawn from the 144th as well as the 149th Ohio National Guard. The 3d Maryland Regiment Potomac Home Brigade and three companies of the 1st Maryland Regiment Potomac Home Brigade had mainly held that sector. The see-saw skirmishing before the jug bridge, however, had lasted until late afternoon when Wallace ordered Brown personally (sometime between 4:00 and 5:00 P.M.) to hold his position "to the last extremity," and when "pressed so hard that nothing more could be done, to command my men to disperse and to take care of themselves," recalled the Buckeye colonel for the record.[46]

Tyler had just started his reserve 11th Maryland forward from the meadow below Bartonsville, east of the bridge, to help Brown when Wallace's orders arrived. He now rode forward with aides Captain F. I. D. Webb and Lieutenant E. Y. Goldsborough to personally command the bridge defense. He subsequently sent Goldsborough to tell Colonel William T. Landstreet to take his 11th Maryland back down the turnpike toward New Market. Thus, he had lost the services of his reserve for the bridge defense, just as Rodes' skirmishers assaulted Brown. While their sharpshooters pinned Brown's men down from sniping positions in J. Simpson's log house atop their own ridge to the west, the rebels slipped around the Federals' flanks. Then came word that Southerners were in the woods east of the Monocacy, and were closing in on the eastern approach to the jug bridge, while local citizens also informed Tyler and Brown that "the main body of the army had moved out two hours before." Abandoning their ridge position, the Ohioans retreated across the bridge under heavy rebel artillery fire, as Tyler rode off to see about the rumors of rebels at Bartonsville.[47]

Brown rallied some of his soldiers in an orchard on the ridge east of and commanding the jug bridge. There they delivered several volleys at the oncoming Confederates, both Rodes' men and those of Ramseur's division that were slipping upstream to cut off Wallace's retreat. Brown's men suddenly bolted, however, discarding guns and accoutrements in panic. A brief rally enabled the colonel to save some 300 survivors of the collapse. Leib, meanwhile, directed by Tyler to cover Brown's bridgehead withdrawal, was nearly cut off and had to escape northward toward Hughes' Ford. Thwarted there, he directed McGinnis and the detachment of the 149th Ohio as to the best route for them to retreat, and then took off in search of the rest of the army. He eventually fell in with Lieutenant Colonel David Clendenin's 8th Illinois survivors about midnight near New Market. McGinnis' Company C retreated up the Linganore Road to Mount Pleasant, also rejoining their parent unit eventually.[48]

Other Federals claimed to have given "the enemy a running fight all the way back to Ellicott's Mills." Still, all was confusion on the Baltimore Road, and even Tyler and his staff became temporarily separated from the rest of the army. Riding back to Bartonsville, they reached the entrance to the road leading to Hughes' Ford at the N. O. Cline house, and off to their right were Confederate horsemen in the orchard at Bartonsville. The greycoats opened fire and gave chase, causing Tyler and his staff to seek the line of escape taken similarly by Leib. Unable to shake their pursuers very easily, Tyler's group continued up the east bank of the Monocacy to the Liberty Road. Turning east onto this thoroughfare, they rode into the village of Mount Pleasant. Here they surprised a rebel patrol plundering a store. The Confederates opened fire, Tyler and company spurred their mounts with the Rebels in chase, and two Union orderlies were captured. Tyler, Webb, and Goldsborough finally sought refuge overnight with a local Unionist family, and the next day rejoined Federal contingents who reoccupied Frederick before following Wallace back to Baltimore.[49]

Baltimorean William H. James in Company A of the 11th Maryland argued disgustedly later that the charge that Wallace's men had run from the field, as "made by persons who were fifty miles off" was absurd. Whatever the truth, a hot, dirty, ragtag army welcomed citizens' buckets and pans of fresh water along their retreat through National Road towns like New Market that night. Still, in all, Tyler's brigade had accomplished its assignment. The rest of the army escaped as a result of their stopgap fight at the jug bridge. For example, Alexander's battery passed unscathed onto the turnpike from country lanes at Bartonsville even if nearly out of ammunition and almost useless. Alexander left two guns and the remaining ammo to help the rear guard. The gunners had sacrificed their battery wagon of tools and equipment so as to use their horses to draw off the large, spiked howitzer that Wallace and Ricketts both had prized so much. The small brass cannon that had done blockhouse duty elsewhere was similarly lifted into one of Alexander's remaining wagons, said unit historian Frederick W. Wild, and "we were proud of the fact that we went into the fight with six cannon and came out with eight." Little wonder that Wallace put a cheery face on the situation as he claimed in his initial after-action report to Washington from Ellicott's Mills on the B & O the next afternoon. "I do not now think myself seriously beaten," he reported even though the facts clearly indicated otherwise. Such optimism may seem unwarranted from the perspective of over a century. Yet, Federal pockets of resistance and success did attend the immediate post-battle period.[50]

* Clendenin's Final Shots *

For instance, at Urbana on the Washington turnpike, Clendenin's jaded troopers (actually, no more than 115 in number at most), pitched into a rebel flanking column that it surprised in the middle of the village. The Illini horsemen charged these riders from McCausland's force, and captured the "Night Hawk Rangers" flag of Company F, 17th Virginia Cavalry, while mortally wounding its latest chieftain, Major Frederick F. Smith (buried today nearby with one of his troopers). The Yanks were elated with the banner, saucily embossed with the motto "Liberty or Death," a small consolation for a week of hot, tiring, and frustrating labor. Ironically, the Virginians' commander, Lieutenant Colonel William Cabell Tavenner, had been cut down in one of McCausland's first assaults in the Araby fields, and had apparently been the one to inform Peter Robertson of the 106th New York that Early possessed overwhelming strength in numbers. Now, at the end of the day, a Unionist lady of Urbana expressed such delight at Smith's demise that she dispatched a letter to the wife of the Illinois corporal who had shot him, "complimenting him in the highest terms."[51]

Clendenin then withdrew, contesting his retirement all the way back to the railroad at Monrovia until pursuers broke off the action. The intensity of the cavalry's feuding with one another at Monocacy was attested by the unit adjutant's experience. "Run down" in a corn field by a rebel pursuer, with only a fence between them, the Federal chose to ignore his opponent's repeated enjoinder to "surrender, you son of a bitch." Instead, the Illinoisan fired several shots "for his mother," he claimed later, before finally being captured. Even then, when his captor seemed out of ammunition, the adjutant wrested the reins from the rebel's grasp and slipped away. Since the fence still separated the two antagonists, there was little that the unarmed Confederate could do but shake his fist angrily.[52]

* * * *

The battle of Monocacy was over. Wallace's first dispatch went to Halleck in Washington, from the "crossing of the Baltimore Pike and Railroad." "I am retreating with a footsore, battered, and half-demoralized column," he iterated. Having battled from 9 A.M. till 5 P.M. against an enemy numbering "at least 20,000," Wallace thought the VI Corps troops had "fought magnificently," and he noted "two fresh regiments of the Sixth Corps are covering my retreat." He had discovered them at the crossing, contentedly awaiting developments; their commander never truly able to explain his negligence in not pushing forward to the battlefield. To Halleck, Wallace simply enunciated: "You will have to use every exertion to save Baltimore and Washington." Wallace's fatigue and dejection shone through the telegram as it did also in a similar wire to Baltimore and Ohio president John Garrett from "Plane Number 1." "I did as I promised," he wrote the railroader, "held the bridge to the last." He had been overwhelmed; troops fought splendidly; losses fearful. Could a relief train meet his defeated force at Ellicott's Mills; please, "don't fail me," beseeched the Hoosier. Both communiques were on recipients' desks before midnight.[53]

Meanwhile, just as Ricketts had predicted, the Confederates back at the river were in no shape to move on toward Washington that evening. They simply flopped down in camp on the battlefield, among the dead and dying. The battery commander who had inadvertently opened fire on color bearer George Pile of the 37th Virginia appeared to tell him: "Boy, you had a narrow escape, I fired three shots at you and took deliberate aim as I ever did at anyone. My, but I'm glad to see you alive." Obviously, so was Pile. Major Jed Hotchkiss, Early's staff cartographer among other things, remembered that they crossed over the Monocacy, set up headquarters near the junction, and moved nearly everything across the stream while pursuing the enemy for two miles. "The day was intensely warm and very dusty," he remarked. "We had plenty of Uncle Sam's coffee, sugar, pickled pork, and beans and crackers to do us several days," reckoned Virginian James Hutcheson. Richard Wolfolk Waldrop of the 21st Virginia agreed, having breakfasted that morning coming out of town "at a house of a warm Secesh lady." John Worsham recalled that he and his comrades in the 21st Virginia bivouacked in an orchard with Yankee wounded, some of whom they provided with food and water. Worsham and his friends then bathed in the Gambrill Mill pond "which refreshed us very much."[54]

Captured Lieutenant M. J. Stearns of Company F, 106th New York, remembered the kindness of First Sergeant John Henry Johnson, Company H, 6th North Carolina, "who provided me with food and water and blankets to cover me." Roderick A. Clark of Company K, 14th New Jersey, had similar good fortune when one young rebel, who had earlier vowed he would rather put a bayonet in him than give him a drink, mentioned his parent unit, and his captor told him, "that was the regiment that guarded about 900 of us to Fort Delaware after the battle of Antietam, you used us well, and I will do the same for you." He came to him several times during the night with sustenance, and adjusted the wounded Federal's position periodically, "propping me up on knapsacks and blankets," and supplying him with water.[55]

Barns and houses in the neighborhood became temporary field hospitals. Many of the structures still stand today. In addition to a field hospital set up near Gambrill's mill, Thomas Claggett's "Arcadia" and George Markell's house across the Buckeystown Road, north of the river, are two such houses. Union surgeon Dr. David F. McKinney, a local man, took charge of the Federal wounded and was so captivated with "Arcadia" that he returned to purchase the property after the war. Glenn Worthington recalled years later how his father had aided the painfully wounded Lieutenant Colonel John Hodge of the 9th Louisiana with a shot of good whiskey from the family cellar. Hodge then went by ambulance to Frederick with the other more seriously injured, ostensibly numbering in the hundreds.[56]

The dead were eventually interred on the battlefield, although it took several days to complete the task. One Georgian remembered fifty years later: "We fought well, but we saw many of our companions fall. That night we dug a long ditch, wrapped their blankets around them carefully and laid them to rest to await the resurrection morn." Some Federals remembered passing by the field within a fortnight to find still unburied fallen lying about. Frederick W. Wild of Alexander's Battery recounted a visit to the ruins of the Best barn (the sharpshooters' sanctuary) about a week after the fighting "and counted six head boards stuck in the ground along the edge of a long trench, with name and regiment marked on it." After the war, the dead would be transferred to the Antietam National Cemetery, as well as Mount Olivet Cemetery on the southern edge of town. Some family members came to take loved ones home to North or South, much as they did all over the war-stricken land.[57]

Meanwhile, at the close of the battle, the Confederate leaders rode over the scene counting heads and congratulating one another upon their success. Artilleryman J. Floyd King estimated that 11,000 Confederates had "defeated and routed" the defenders, causing 1,600 Federal casualties at a cost of only 1,000 Southerners. Breckinridge emerged from chatting with John Worthington, who had come out of his cellar to greet the distinguished former vice president, and for a few moments shared the sound of whistling "Minies" until the Kentuckian reminded him that only he, the soldier, not Worthington, a civilian, had the duty to suffer such fire and suggested that he return to the safety of his cellar. Early's second-in-command told the elated Georgian: "Gordon, if you ever made a fight before, this ought to immortalize you." Even the normally dyspeptic Early sought out Zebulon York to raise his handling of his command, which had done its duty nobly. York chuckled to his Richmond friend later that this seemed a compliment, coming from one of the South's "most cross-grained and faultfinding" generals.[58]

As a blood red sun began to sink beyond distant Catoctin Mountain, the acrid battle smoke began to dissipate, and only cries of wounded men and horses, and sharply receding gunfire to the east marred the summer evening along the Monocacy. In the Thomas house cellar, the refugees were nursing their wounded rebel when he suddenly brightened, exclaiming "there's the cry of victory, raise me up." Just then the door to the outside was jerked open by another inquiring Confederate, seeking his wounded mate. "Imagine, if you can," recalled Mamie Tyler some fifty years later, "the sight that greeted the eye when released from our prison cell." She and her friend Alice Thomas, along with the others, saw "the soft carpet of grass" by the house had become the "resting place of dead and dying soldiers, a battlefield in verity and truth." One poor dying soldier asked for a pillow remarking, "I am the last of five brothers," all slain in battle. Among the first to greet them was General Gordon, with the exclamation: "What, women and children here?" Then he told them: "Girls, you must be brave, and do what you can for these poor men. We have not surgeons enough here." And, so they did, she said, and when night descended upon that camp, the scene was a novel one. Voices of dying men, some singing, others praying, and a few cursing in their delirium filled the night air. They were profoundly disturbed by a dead man lying outside their room upstairs, but, said the young woman, "that was a small matter at the close of so eventful a day," when " excitement and enthusiasm had filled every one with courage and a desire to help our cause."[59]

SIX

The Race for the Capital

In retrospect, everyone should have known that Washington, not Baltimore or points north, was Jubal Early's target by the evening of July 9. Perhaps it was less apparent to the people of the time. As General Robert E. Lee told President Jefferson Davis the next day (enclosing a New York *Herald*, dated the eighth): "You will see the people in the U.S. are mystified about our forces on the Potomac." That at least would "teach them they must keep some of their troops at home and that they cannot denude their frontier with impunity; but even he was unaware yet of the affair on the Monocacy. A New York *World* reporter had been cut off in Frederick by the Confederate advance, and New York *Times* correspondent George F. Williams had been prevented from reaching the battlefield by military closure of the Baltimore and Ohio Railroad for any but army traffic. Williams, the newspaper's Shenandoah Valley agent, ingeniously got to Relay House and climbed aboard a train of wounded. He recreated the order of battle for the units, and then interviewed a Monocacy farmer who had accompanied those wounded as ersatz corpsman. Equipped with information accurate enough to win subsequent plaudits even from Major General Lew Wallace, Williams rushed to the local telegraph office and wired New York before rebel raider Harry Gilmor closed the line north of Baltimore. Only the *Times* had news of Monocacy, but could not get it into print until the next day.[1]

So, on the night of July 9, even the retreating Wallace and his battered army could not be sure that Early wasn't following him towards Baltimore. In fact, the fog of war pervaded all of upper Maryland. A mysterious mounted force—Bradley Johnson's—ranging eastward and north of the retreat route seemed suspicious. Still, this late in the war, skeptics might be found on all sides. A thoroughly non-plussed Secretary of Navy Gideon Welles noted Grant's admission that rebels were out in force ("without, however, giving his reasons or the facts," he added), and that likely the general "has thought and is prepared for this." In Welles' view, however, Grant "displays little strategy or invention." "It is a scheme of Lee's strategy," claimed the bewhiskered New Englander, "but where is Grant's?"[2]

Then, by mid-evening, the word of Wallace's defeat on the Monocacy trickled into the War Department. At 7:35 P.M., Baltimore and Ohio president John W. Garrett wired that the army was "sadly defeated," and "things looked very badly, indeed." If thoroughly alarmed by such reports—confirmed by Wallace himself as the evening wore on—neither Stanton nor Halleck showed immediate signs of panic. The chief of staff passed the information on to Grant at 9:00 P.M., although casting some doubt upon the credence of the source of the reports. More importantly, he noted ignorance of the slow-moving West Virginia column under Major David Hunter, in whom so much faith was placed by so many. "I do not deem it safe to with-draw any forces from Harpers' Ferry till he forms a junction," said Halleck. So, there would be no mounting of any threat against the raiders' rear from that quarter.

Two hours later, Halleck wired Grant that he now thought it prudent to forward the rest of the VI Corps to Washington since the XIX Corps was coming too slowly from the Gulf. Grant had already surmised as much, although still unaware of Wallace's fate. In fact, at 6:00 P.M., he had even wired Washington: "If the President thinks it advisable that I should go to Washington in person I can start in an hour after receiving notice, leaving everything here on the defensive." The telegram would not reach Halleck before 1:05 P.M. the next afternoon![3]

Actually, while Wallace passed those anxious hours in delaying Early on the Monocacy, Grant and Meade had continued their intelligence game about Robert E. Lee's whereabouts. They wondered if he had sent additional reinforcements north under Lieutenant General James Longstreet. Rumors circulated to that effect, although in the capital itself, the day had passed innocently with more shuffling of fort garrisons and other administrative trivia, a continued impasse over mustering Pennsylvania militia, and discounting wild rumors about rebel scouts inside the District line.

Major D. W. C. Thompson of the 2d Massachusetts cavalry sent word from his camp on Muddy Branch, west of Rockville, that he would obstruct roads and do everything possible to hinder and ha-rass the enemy if he moved that way. Things were quiet enough with his commanding officer, Colonel Charles Russell Lowell, Jr., over at

Falls Church in northern Virginia. But Thompson noted ominous sounds of gunfire and smoke rising to his north beyond Sugar Loaf Mountain, "which might have been the bridge over the Monocacy at the Junction." Tension and inaction continued as handmaidens in the July heat. Telegraph keys clicked with news about rebel horse-stealing all over the Maryland-Pennsylvania border beyond Frederick, and ever-escalating Confederate strength figures of 40,000 to 50,000. There was very little hard data about Wallace's army.[4]

By late evening, however, such reports when coupled to the suddenly erupting news about Wallace's defeat sent the northeast into full-blown frenzy. The president of the Philadelphia, Wilmington, and Baltimore Railroad, who had importuned Welles the day before to send a gunboat to protect his line over Gunpowder Creek north of Baltimore, now wired that public excitement and uncertainty regarding affairs in Maryland and Virginia had reached such volcanic proportions. Only word from the War Department or its local officials could stem the panic. Close to midnight, Lincoln himself received a wire from Baltimore "first citizens," Thomas Swann, Evan T. Ellicott, William E. Hooper, Thomas S. Alexander, and Michael Warner stating that "Baltimore is in great peril," couldn't he please send reinforcements immediately to save the city. There was probably small comfort in Stanton's 8:20 A.M. dispatch to John Garrett the next morning that: "I think it will turn out that Wallace's troops are in better condition than he supposed last night."[5]

Wallace's Retreat and Consolidation

As Wallace's battered force left the Monocacy, Confederates like I. G. Bradwell of Company I, 31st Georgia, claimed to have fired the last shot in a bitterly contested action. Probably none of the defeated Federals was in any mood to recall the stirring Victory hymn of Eastertide—"the strife is o'er, the battle done, the victory of life is won; the song of triumph has begun, Alleluia." Theirs had not been victory, and their triumph was mere survival. But, they had stood and fought; they had done their duty. Some were resigned to defeat, few understood what the battle had been all about, in the first place, and most probably echoed Illinois cavalryman Silas Wesson's diary entry: "We got whipped, what did they send us out there for?" The Marylanders ran and the VI Corps boys had done "it all alone." His company lay scattered, "I don't know where half of them are," he concluded. Above all, Wesson and his compatriots were bone tired, dirty, thirsty, and grateful to see another sunrise.[6]

Confederate Cavalry Ransacking New Windsor, Maryland

Johnson's cavalry continued the foraging activities of Early's army thereby losing valuable time for his Point Lookout mission.

Motteley and Campbell-Copeland.
The Soldier in Our Civil War (1885), vol. II, p. 301.
After an artist's sketch.

Spires of Baltimore from Fort McHenry

While not Bradley Johnson's objective, his raid unnerved local citizens and Union authorities in this city. They hastily constructed fortifications to stop the raiders.

U.S. Army Military History Institute

Sketch of Early's Cavalry Driving Off Farmers' Cattle during the Invasion of Maryland

Such actions hampered accomplishment of Early's principal mission of taking Washington.

Motteley and Campbell-Copeland,
The Soldier in Our Civil War (1885), vol. II, pp. 302–303.
By noted artist Edwin Frobes.

President Abraham Lincoln at Fort Stevens to Witness an Evening Attack

Lincoln, his wife, and other members of his administration were present on both days of the battle.

Motteley and Campbell-Copeland.
The Soldier in Our Civil War (1885), vol. II, p. 297.
After a contemporary sketch.

President Abraham Lincoln under Confederate Fire at Fort Stevens, July 12, 1864
From bar-relief sketch, Schwizer artist, Lincoln Stone, Fort Stevens
Courtesy National Park Service

Battleground National Cemetery, on Seventh Street Road (modern Georgia Avenue) in the District of Columbia

This was the final resting place for forty-one Union participants in the battle of Fort Stevens.

U.S. Army Military History Institute

Screened by Lieutenant Colonel David R. Clendenin's Illinois horsemen as well as remnants of the 159th Ohio Mounted Infantry (and those fresh regiments of the VI Corps that had never gotten to the battle), Wallace retired back through New Market, Mount Airy, Lisbon, Cooksville, and other hamlets on the National Road. He was accompanied by at least some Frederick County African-Americans, seemingly in the Union army; men like Zack Robinson, Thomas D. Bond, and Will Schooly, who went all the way to Ellicott City and Baltimore. Buckets and tubs of water stood at curbside, especially in New Market, while the twenty-minute rest stops partly rejuvenated the soldiery. The unsullied 67th Pennsylvania, 5th Maryland, and remainder of the 122d Ohio—the fresh regiments—had alighted from their train and taken a blocking position squarely across the turnpike at New Market. That had helped, but an incensed Ricketts had been so irate about the gaff that he eventually brought charges against Colonel John F. Staunton, the brigade commander. Neither Wallace nor Ricketts was pleased at finding "the missing brigade" standing idle while the rest of the little army had suffered such a resounding defeat.

In fact, everyone was testy. Colonel William Truex "had a quarrel" with Ricketts. The division commander would not allow Truex "to put his horses on the cars," Major Peter Vredenburgh wrote his family in August. The general "had all of his old pack horses and mules on board, which made the colonel mad, so he "ripped out at him, and was put under arrest." Later in July when they returned to the Frederick area when Early threatened to recross the Potomac, Major General David Hunter dismissed him from the service for "disobedience of orders and insubordination." No matter by that point, Vredenburgh (himself to die the next month in the battle of Opequon) contended, "there is only a few of us left, and it don't take a very talented man to command the remnant of the old 14th [New Jersey]."[7]

For the moment, however, sore feet and fatigue proved more worrisome than either rebel pursuers or the "might-have-beens" of that battle by the evening of July 9. The 9th New York Heavy Artillery paid only passing salutation to St. Charles College (named for Charles Carroll of Carrollton, the last survivor of the signers of the Declaration of Independence), as it made its way to Ellicott's Mills, forty-three miles from the battlefield and fifteen from Baltimore proper. "Our boys are more interested in food and raiment than in mind and religion," recalled chronicler Alfred Seeyle Roe, years later.[8]

Thus, Wallace's men enthusiastically embraced the "enterprising village, loyal to our flag," as Vermont lieutenant George E. Davis described Ellicott's Mills. "Here our horses received their first drink of water for more than twenty-four hours," recounted Baltimore battery historian Frederick W. Wild, as they plunged into the cooling waters of the Patapsco River without waiting for removal of harnesses. Their equally fatigued groomsmen curried and fed them, before seeking their own succor. As it was the Sabbath, the populace were dressed in Sunday best, and serenaded the soldiery with "the Battle Cry of Freedom" before spreading a banquet before them. To the appreciative soldiers, many of them hungry from having little food since breakfast the day before, "it seemed almost like heaven to us."[9]

The proximity of the railroad to Wallace's retreat route greatly expedited the retirement. At least two hundred wounded had been removed from the battlefield and they were placed aboard the idling train at Monrovia, together with other stragglers from the fight. Back they went along the slow, winding B & O through the Patapsco River Valley that night. Reaching Baltimore at 5:00 A.M. the next day, they were living proof that railroad president John W. Garrett, as usual, had the situation well in hand. He had dispatched three additional locomotives and ninety empty cars to rendezvous with the marching troops at Ellicott's Mills. Later in the morning, Garrett's agent there wired that troops were slowly arriving, and were being loaded aboard the cars in the absence of army oversight. "There is now firing going on in the rear in two different directions," contended the railroader, for the "enemy was pushing the rear slowly," a fact found nowhere else in surviving records.[10]

Wallace arrived at the Ellicott's Mills about 2:00 in the afternoon. Within minutes, he had penned his initial after-action report, providing basic details to alert superiors about the hard-fought battle, the valor of the defense (particularly that of Ricketts and his division), and suggesting "my casualty list will be quite severe," without providing numbers. He did estimate that he had not lost over 200 prisoners, and thought his overall loss "cannot possibly equal that of the enemy." The general most wanted to focus matters that would be of highest interest to Washington officials facing the next stage of the rebel onslaught. For one thing, Wallace calculated that Early had deployed about 18,000 men for the various attacks on the Worthington-Thomas properties, while "at least 2,000 more" had skirmished and fought "in my front across the river." Each one of the enemy's four lines of attack had presented a front greater than Ricketts' men "all deployed," hence Wallace's estimate.[11]

Wallace quickly pointed to his three objectives at Monocacy and what they now meant to the Union high command. First, he had intended keeping open the rail communication with Harpers Ferry; second, to cover the roads to Washington and Baltimore; and third, to make the enemy develop his force, he said. He had failed in all but the latter, he claimed. He added, however, his estimate that "the enemy must have two corps north of the Potomac (crediting 'his column operating in the region of Hagerstown, that about Harper's Ferry, and the one which fought me yesterday')." He added that one dying rebel officer had told a VI Corps staffer that Robert E. Lee was personally managing the operation, and would shortly have "three corps about the Potomac for business against Washington and Baltimore." "This circumstance is true," he concluded, "give it what weight you please." A more thorough report would follow, Wallace promised, once he had Ricketts' account in hand.

The Hoosier citizen-soldier then turned to more immediate concerns in his district. In his August report, Wallace would claim that he had originally intended to march directly from the battlefield back to Baltimore, but had been stopped at the mills by Halleck's directive to "rally your forces and make every possible effort to retard the enemy's march on Baltimore." Frankly, he was just as happy to do so. His force needed rest, food, and ammunition, and Ellicott's Mills was the first possible point on the railroad for effecting such rehabilitation. Later that afternoon, he directed Ricketts to send two of his regiments to garrison Relay House (the 10th Vermont subsequently fulfilled the purpose), that pivotal junction where the Washington line branched from the main stem south of Baltimore. An incompleted blockhouse there provided only cursory protection against marauders. The rest of the Monocacy force would either return to the city, or, like Clendenin's four cavalry companies, and Alexander's guns, remain with Ricketts, taking post at "this village" to deter the enemy.[12]

Demoralization among Wallace's troops was especially apparent with the inexperienced Marylanders. Sergeant William H. James of the 11th Maryland recalled that on July 11, he proceeded home to Baltimore, "not having been able to ascertain where our regiment had been sent to," but satisfied that he had brought back everything that he had carried into battle. This included musket, accoutrements, rubber blanket, "and all the cartridges dealt out to me, except a few that had been fired off." Some of his comrades fared less well, he gloated, for their sore feet had caused them to jettison all such excess baggage. At home, he secured a bath, clean clothes, and after a few hours rest, "was all most myself again." Later, in the afternoon, he found his regiment encamped out at Greenwood on Gay Street; he set out to rejoin them that evening. "I was gladly welcomed back by Capt. Courtney and my comrades who had feared that I had been gobbled up by the rebels." Later in July, portions of his regiment returned to picket the vicinity of Monrovia, New Market, and Mount Airy. James and his company were not paid off and mustered out until October 6. Having risen to the rank of sergeant major by this time, James received the beneficent sum of $140.15 for one hundred days service in defense of his state.[13]

As it turned out, many of Wallace's VIII Corps survivors temporarily went home to catch a quick bath and meal before reporting back to duty. "Of course my parents and all were glad to see me," recalled Frederick Wild, "and to know I had come out of the battle." After the war, the Baltimore Battery historian recalled that they never received any additional ammunition at Ellicott's Mills. Rather they had transferred all remaining rounds to support one gun, which was then sent out the York Road toward Towson, where rebel raiders were rumored to be, while the rest of the battery went back to its old camp on North Avenue. That night they marched off to Fort McHenry to secure the much needed ammunition. Just how much shifting around took place remains unclear, but Vermont Lieutenant Lemuel Abbott was sure of one thing. He penned in his diary "Our regiment was never before in such disorder, i.e., so many stragglers," and both Wallace and Ricketts necessarily had to leave it to the soldiers themselves to mourn their fallen comrades, and get themselves back into shape for business.[14]

In some cases, Monocacy's impact was staggering. Of five hundred Green Mountain boys who had marched into Virginia's famed Wilderness in early May, said Lieutenant George E. Davis later, "we numbered about 175 men," after Monocacy, given stragglers. Similarly, of the 950 Jerseymen who had departed their state with the 14th Infantry, only 358 entered the battle on their old campgrounds beside the Monocacy, and "but ninety-five were left for duty on the night of July 9, without an officer to command them," suggested Sergeant J. Newton Terrill, years later. W. L. Gardner's Company K, 110th Ohio, took sixty-two men into action, and came out with thirty. The largest company in the 9th New York Heavy Artillery could muster only thirty-one men after Monocacy. Even the much-maligned 100-days 149th Ohio counted 130 men killed, wounded or prisoners—a performance that proved "a revelation to the old soldiers, and a surprise to the enemy," claimed one of their number. On the other hand, Clendenin's cavalry suffered only one killed and one wounded on July 9, the other four killed and nineteen wounded occurring in skirmishes and at Fort Stevens during other phases of the campaign.[15]

As the stragglers rejoined their commands over the next day or so, tales of narrow escapes and heroics enlivened campfire conversations. Brigadier General Erastus Tyler with personal staff members Captain Francis I. D. Webb and Lieutenant E. Y. Goldsborough, with several orderlies, became separated from the rest of their command in the melee that attended last ditch fighting at the stone bridge. They found a lane leading to the old Liberty Road, but soon saw clouds of dust to the northwest on the Woodsboro Road, and barely made it to Mount Pleasant before stumbling into a squad of rebel cavalry plundering a store. Their orderlies were either wounded or captured in the ensuing scrape, but the officers took to the woods where, for the next day, they hid out in the house of Unionist Ephraim Creager. Not until Monday, the eleventh, would they venture forth. Found by a squad of Federal cavalry that had driven the rear of the Confederate column out of Frederick, they were escorted back down the National Road to the Baltimore area where Tyler rejoined his men at the Relay House.[16]

First Sergeant Brooks Clark of Company K, 10th Vermont, and Clendenin's adjutant (by the name of Humphrey), both escaped capture by chance. Clark and a comrade took a prisoner whom they proceeded to shepherd toward Baltimore avoiding the well-traveled, and rebel-held roads, they claimed. Tired and disgusted with this hard going, Clark almost relinquished his pistol to their antagonist. Remembering that his fate then would be Andersonville prison camp, Clark shrank back at the last moment, and finally got his charge to the Baltimore provost marshal only to find himself subject to incarceration along with the rebel, for being a straggler. Incensed with this reward for both Monocacy service and taking a prisoner, Clark's tongue "was loosened and he exercised a Yankee's privilege of freeing his mind" to the astonished official. The latter's only reply was, "go back to your regiment," which Clark did quickly.

Humphrey, meanwhile, had engaged a grayclad rider in a corn field, sparring with him across a fence while both remained mounted. Firing a last shot "for his mother," and missing, Humphrey wrenched the reins from his captor's grasp when the latter, too, ran out of ammunition. Since the fence still separated the two men, there was little that the hapless rebel could now do but shake his fist in anger as Humphrey rode off into the sunset.[17]

More tragic were the injured. First Lieutenant Jefferson O. McMillen of Company K, 122d Ohio, had held that rank barely two weeks when he took a mortal wound through his right lung at Monocacy. He survived evacuation to the Camden hospital in Baltimore where he died on the seventeenth, only twenty-two years old. A brother George, three years older, had gone off to war in that same regiment, but was captured at the Wilderness. He was now held captive in Andersonville. Corporal Roderick A. Clark of the 14th New Jersey was also wounded, but captured on the field and taken by the rebels into a Frederick hospital. The nurses had been sent away before the battle to avoid capture, but citizens now stepped in to care for the injured from both sides. One young lady, Lizzie Ott, scrubbed Clark from head to toe for a full half-hour. She then bed-sat his recovery for twelve long weeks, aided by his visiting mother.[18]

Still another Frederick lady, widow Ruth Doffler, watched over dying Lieutenant John F. Spangler, Company A, 87th Pennsylvania. Spangler died within the week, and his grieving father came from York, Pennsylvania to retrieve the body for burial at home in Prospect Hill Cemetery. The elder Spangler soon returned, this time to marry the woman who had cared for his son unto death. Lieutenant Charles Haack of Company K of the same regiment was not so fortunate as to have someone care for him, dying at Ellicott's Mills following evacuation. Buried temporarily in the local Methodist church cemetery, his family, too, came to retrieve the body to take home for permanent burial. Indeed, a grieving York city sent delegations to both Frederick and Baltimore, and the city's severe loss in this one battle led to construction of a special commemorative flag pole on South Water Street and predictable patriotic oratory. Annie Zimmerman and other York ladies stitched a flag for the pole, emblazoned with the words, "The Union Forever."[19]

Wallace Defends Baltimore

Brigadier Generals William Walton Morris and John Reese Kenly, commanding the Second and Third Separate brigades at Baltimore, spent the ninth of July mustering their meager resources to protect the city (such citizens and militia as the German Rifles of Schuetzen Verein), and helped shuttle all possible aid forward to Wallace. Both brigadiers were combat veterans, although Morris, an aging West Pointer from New York City, had been in the army since the War of 1812, and last saw action in Florida in the 1830s. Widely respected as a regular major in the Fourth U.S. Artillery, he had helped save the Monument City from secessionist elements in 1861, and subsequently kept a lid on political prisoners at Fort McHenry as well as unrest in the streets while occasionally filling in for the assigned departmental commander. Late in the evening he did so once again, under direct orders from Secretary Stanton.

Kenly, by contrast, a native Baltimorean and local lawyer, had served in the Mexican War and local militia, then commanded the First Maryland (U.S.) Infantry as well as the so-called "Maryland Brigade" of the Army of the Potomac, as well as the third division, I Corps. The arrival of Grant saw him shunted back to his hometown and a local defense role. Together, the two brigadiers counted perhaps 871 men in regularly constituted contingents, 300 additional recruits, and whatever citizen corps might be mobilized by local Union League politicans. Halleck also instructed Morris "to stop and use all troops from New York; also two regiments expected via Harrisburg, from Johnson's Island [Ohio prison camp]."[20]

What Morris had to work with were largely organized companies from the 1st Eastern Shore Maryland Infantry, the 159th Ohio National Guard, and Battery H, 3d Pennsylvania Artillery, stationed ar various forts, hospitals, camps, railroad stations, and other administrative points around the city. Baltimore's fortifications were by no means either as extensive or as systematized as those at Washington, but like the latter were constantly undergoing maintenance and repair. They were more directed at crowd control of the inner city secessionists element than guarding against external threat. So Morris directed Colonel L. J. Jackson of the Buckeyes to push a company out to the first tollgate on the Reisterstown Road at or near the junction with the Druid Hill Park Road. He also sent word to Major H. B. Judd at Wilmington, Delaware to organize and arm citizens of the First State to protect railroad bridges on the Philadelphia, Wilmington, and Baltimore line. Even if Early's main army wasn't pursuing Wallace, it became obvious that some fairly large band of Confederates was bearing down on the city and its environs. With the rather fluid situation in the Middle Department they could cause mischief, especially north and west of town.[21]

Indeed, the portion of Early's raiders led by Brigadier General Bradley T. Johnson had been in the saddle pretty much since dawn on the day of the battle. Unenthusiastic about their apparently impossible mission of transiting three hundred miles in the process of threatening Baltimore, disrupting enemy communications, going to Point Lookout to free prisoners and then back up to a rendezvous with Early at Washington, Johnson had promised his chief only that "I would do what was possible for men to do." So, he had started out, ensuring that Major General Robert Rodes' left flank was secure in the early morning fighting in the Hughes Ford-stone bridge sector. Then it was off for a day of frolic, liberating stores and shops at Liberty and New Windsor, scavenging more horses, and greeting random friends and sympathizers (especially the young ladies), among the mostly shuttered and locked houses along the route, first to Westminster and then to Reisterstown. Some of his men, like Virginian J. Kelly Bennette, marveled at the affluent farms, and wished they, not the Yankees, owned them. "Heaven bless the Liberty girls," wrote Bennette after one comely young woman especially plied him with food and clothing. Meanwhile, the guns of Monocacy rumbled in the distance.[22]

Few of the possibly 1,500 men with Johnson knew about the ultimate target. Some soon discovered more immediate tasks at hand. Maryland Major Harry Gilmor, whose "Glen Ellen" country home lay not far from Baltimore, received the assignment to first devastate bridges, track and telegraph along the Northern Central Railroad at

Cockeysville. Then, ultimately, he and 150 men from the 1st and 2d Maryland battalions went off on a circuitous strike against the Philadelphia and Wilmington Railroad at the Gunpowder River crossing at Magnolia Station, north of Baltimore. Here, they captured trains and a Union general, Major General William B. Franklin, held off several gun boats, and escaped unscathed, returning literally through the disorganized and demoralized Baltimore defenders.

Meanwhile, Johnson and the main force cut a more leisurely pace, having burned Maryland Governor Augustus Bradford's country home outside Baltimore in retaliation for Hunter's deliberate destruction of Virginia Governor John Letcher's Lexington, Virginia house, and other valley depredations. They stopped on Sunday to enjoy "the charming society, the lovely girls, the balmy July air, and the luxuriant verdure of 'Maryfields'" near Cockeysville. Similarly unconcerned about making haste on Monday, Johnson's main force moved southward, ravaging an ice cream wagon near Owing's Mills, but alert to reports of Union waterborne reinforcements standing off Locust Point in the city, intent upon taking the train for Washington. Johnson sent word of this to Early and then moved on parallel to the railroad toward the capital. He carefully avoided the last "debris" of Lew Wallace's Monocacy army near Ellicott's Mills; "so unmercifully flogged by Early," J. Kelly Bennette noted in his diary. The weather was blisteringly hot, the pace slow, and like all during the campaign, men were strung out all over the region for various reasons. Telegraph wires became particular targets of the raiders in order to harass Yankee communications. Point Lookout was almost an afterthought.[23]

Meanwhile, everyone in Baltimore seemed more apprehensive than their counterparts over at Washington. Wallace wired the War Department on the morning of the eleventh, "the panic here is heavy and increasing." He asked for cavalry and help, but Washington officials replied negatively. Even the president told Baltimore resident Thomas Swann and his fellow citizens that their city was not the most threatened point and that he thought everyone should "be vigilant, but keep cool," as he hoped neither of their two cities would be taken. About all authorities could do in the Monument City then was to erect street barricades against raiders, impress horses and civilians, put more emergency police in the streets, and gossip on the corners about the mayhem caused by refugees from the country, Sigel's fleeing wagon train from the west, and the influx of the battered Monocacy survivors. Ricketts' division, numbering scarcely 2,488 men, remained mostly at Ellicott's Mills, while another small contingent protected the vital Relay House junction on the railroad with Washington and the west. Slowly, the summer soldiers and Army of the Potomac veterans alike recovered from their ordeal.[24]

Marylander William H. James was fortunate to get home to shave, bathe his blistered feet, put on clean clothes, "and after a few hours rest was all most myself again." He soon rejoined his reconstituted unit at Greenwood on Gay Street beyond the main part of town. Frederick W. Wild of the Baltimore artillery did the same thing. But, lack of cavalry prevented officials from any more active contest of the rebels' passage around the town. Lieutenant Colonel David Clendenin's tired survivors merely found livery stables and dropped off to much needed sleep. Eventually, they would be sent out to investigate matters at Cockeysville, where at least one of their number, a combative Irishman named Daniel "Coon Creek" O'Conner, got into a fight about running horses with his corporal and was shot dead for his trouble. Such re-energized combat troops should have been out "running" rebels, but for most of the immediate days following Monocacy, everyone was too tired and disorganized to do much. The 9th New York "Heavies" reported so many stragglers from their ranks that rations went begging when they finally left Ellicott's Mills for a new camp in Washington Park on the edge of the city. The boys gave a needy woman two-thirds of a barrel of pork that had been left over, "a larger supply than she had ever possessed at any one time before," said the unit's historian later.[25]

Notwithstanding Baltimore's well-earned reputation as a Secessionist city, as well as the fact that a concerted push by Bradley Johnson might well have taken the place, this was not his target. Not until the thirteenth was the region fairly clear of raiders, but by that time too, many of the Federals had left, including Ricketts' veterans, transferred to help out at Washington. Gone too, was Lew Wallace as operational commander of the Middle Department and VIII Corps troops. Supplanting him by General Orders number 228 from Washington on July 11 was Major General Edward O. C. Ord, one of Grant's preferred subordinates from the west. Veteran corps commander in Mississippi and Louisiana, who had graduated West Point the year that Grant had entered the academy, 1839, Ord was an old-line regular; Wallace yet another disgraced citizen soldier and politician in uniform who had been licked in battle, in the eyes of official Washington. Queried by Wallace as to his own status, Secretary of War Stanton replied bluntly that the Hoosier remained "in charge of the administration of the department," but "in respect to all military operations and movement, whether defensive or aggressive, [Ord] is by special assignment of the President the superior in command."[26]

Ord could reassure Halleck by nightfall on the twelfth that not only had Frederick been recovered, but telegraph service had been reopened both to the west as well as to City Point via the circuitous route down the eastern shore. The "whole country is panic-stricken," with rebels reported all over the place, he added. His available maneuver force of between 2,000 and 3,000 100-days men and armed citizens, 200 sailors, and 500 African-American recruits (plus Ricketts' 2,488 veterans) lacked the mobility of cavalry to chase the raiders. Scarcely 100 horsemen were available to him so he could do little more than send out reconnaissance, a chore that Wallace might have accomplished just as resolutely had he remained in operational command. Wallace contended later that if he had been allowed to march directly from the Monocacy to Baltimore his men would have reached the city on the evening of the tenth in time to have driven off the marauders who, under Johnson, had moved by the Liberty Road from Frederick City and had "taken post in the vicinity of Cockeysville." Such would have resulted in saving the bridges on the railroad to Philadelphia, he advanced.

In effect, however, neither Ricketts nor Tyler would have made any difference in countering Johnson's and Gilmor's mounted columns. They might have deterred a Confederate assault on Baltimore, but maybe not. It was all quite moot since "as soon as it was certainly known that the enemy had marched against Washington I ordered [Ricketts] to Baltimore," observed Wallace. The best the Hoosier could do was to write John Garrett on July 18, thanking the railroad president and his assistant, W. P. Smith, for "very great services rendered to me and my little army before and after" the battle. To sum up, said Wallace, without the railroad and Garrett's energetic and zealous management it would have been impossible "for me to have maintained my position five minutes" in the presence of Jubal Early's forces. Wallace was quite certain of one thing. "Monocacy on the flags of the defeated participants" like himself "cannot be a word of dishonor."[27]

Early Races Time and Temperature

It was still a race against time—and the temperature. Old Jube's troops spent Saturday night on the Monocacy battlefield. They ransacked John Lyeth's residence beside the railroad, burning his military papers, ostensibly (claimed the victim after the war), because both Wallace and Tyler had used the structure for their headquarters. Only miller James Gambrill's claim that the place belonged to him spared the building itself from torching. Lyeth had been captain of Company H, 1st Regiment Maryland Home Brigade, until May, a fact undoubtedly imparted to the rebels by some local secessionist for retaliation. Otherwise, on the field, everyone was too busy gathering booty and flotsam from the battle to worry much about the dead and apparent carnage. Riding over the field after the fight, Henry

Truehart of McNeill's Rangers (attached to Imboden's cavalry) wrote his brother that the Confederates buried only their own dead, and while gathering up both sides' wounded, he saw "wounded Yanks 26 hours after the fight lying in the broiling sun with no water & no attention & so concealed that they might never [be] found."[28]

Chief of Artillery J. Floyd King wrote his sister on July 15 that of 11,000 Confederates engaged, losses were 1,000 men. Early himself estimated losses around 700 killed and wounded, a figure substantiated the next day by returning Federal medical authorities in Frederick. Inasmuch as Gordon's division (which had borne the brunt of the heavy fighting) claimed 698 for its share of the losses, the army's total may have been higher. Terry's brigade alone suffered approximately 10 percent of the possible 1,000 men it carried on its rolls; Evans' brigade claimed 375 casualties out of 1,000. T. E. Morrow of the 8th Louisiana wrote his father in early August that "our regt. lost more men according to their number carried in than any other fight with the exception of Sharpsburg since the war began," with his company alone contributing two-thirds of the number shot down. In truth, Confederate losses only assume importance because they impaired the expedition's future fighting and marching capabilities for the test before Washington.[29]

The rebels were up and abroad by daylight the next morning. In fact, Lieutenant Colonel Amos M. Thayer, Brigadier General Albion Howe's signal officer from Harpers Ferry, reported at 5:30 on the tenth that the enemy's forces had left Frederick and "are now all across the Monocacy River, save a rear guard of 200 cavalry." Certainly Brigadier General John McCausland's battered rebel horsemen took the point early on the turnpike toward Washington. In fact, Early's battle-fatigued army was not ready for any rapid departure. Major General Stephen Ramseur's contingents lingered trying to protect wrecking parties at John Garrett's iron railroad bridge. Confederate staff officer Henry Kyd Douglas remembered that "for the want of sufficient powder the attempt was a failure," adding that he watched "a ludicrous attempt by one artillery battery to blow it to pieces with solid shot." The stone piers (apparently still underpining the modern steel railroad span across the Monocacy to this day), proved too sturdy, claimed one Federal later. So, the famous Baltimore and Ohio bridge, that had lured Lew Wallace and his Baltimore force out in the first place, and that had survived the human thunder and lightning that had raged around it the day before, endured the pounding on the tenth, also. Other property at the junction, however, went up in smoke.[30]

Major General John B. Gordon also took time, in the company of a chaplain and young Mamie Tyler and Alice Thomas, to bury two of his officers—Colonel J. H. Lamar and Lieutenant Colonel J. D. Van Valinburg of the 61st Georgia. The sun was rising in the east, "giving color to all imaginable objects," and the birds "seemed to be chanting a requiem in the grand old tree under which we stood," Mamie Tyler noted fifty years later. Lamar's faithful body servant stood "with the bullet torn hat of his master pressed to his heart, weeping bitterly," she remembered. She also recalled "the most gratifying memory" to the two girls was Gordon's approval of their conduct. "You have been brave girls," he told them alluding to their care of the wounded, "I will never forget you." Indeed, he did not. After the war he saw Miss Tyler in a throng at a New York hotel and called out to "Mamie Tyler, the little Rebel of Frederick City and one of the heroines of the Battle of Monocacy."[31]

Federal forces from Maryland Heights remained sluggish both in returning to Harpers Ferry as well as in pursuing Early's army as it moved south beyond Frederick. Local constabulary like Colonel Henry Cole's Maryland cavalry hesitantly picked up straggling rebels all over the rear of Early's army west of Frederick, but did little else. True, Lieutenant Colonel William Blakely and the 14th Pennsylvania Cavalry (he had succeeded Brigadier General Julius Stahel in charge of the cavalry, apparently) were among the first bluecoats to "liberate" Frederick. But Howe had generally clung back, fearing the strength of the Confederates, much to the chagrin of signaler Thayer who claimed that all along his corps had developed rebel movements and that the whole of Howe's force could have advanced with more alacrity against Early's rear.

Reoccupation of Harpers Ferry (where on the morning of the ninth they discovered a burning depot, quartermaster storehouses and bakery), and a half-hearted pursuit of Early's main body were all that Howe seemed ready to undertake. Blakely and Thayer, at least, got as far as Urbana behind Ramseur by late in the afternoon on the tenth. Some time was also spent in burying the Monocacy dead and assisting with the wounded in Frederick, left by the rebels. Frankly, Howe was no more tepid in his reaction than Major General Henry Halleck and the War Department in Washington. When at 8:30 P.M. that night Howe reported "no enemy on the Virginia side of the river between this place and Hancock," and that "the movements of the enemy this morning indicate a movement on the Frederick and Baltimore pike," all that the chief-of-staff could answer was that he had no instructions other than to "open communication with General Hunter and effect a junction with his army." There was no indication that Howe should become more active in Early's rear toward Washington.[32]

The forty-mile march to Washington on July 10 was a killer for Early's army. Temperature in the nineties, dust choking the marching ranks, a nine-mile-long wagon train plus livestock adding to the congestion, and the Monocacy prisoners tagging along disconsolately completed the picture. Outriders discovered Keefer Thomas' horses in the nooks and crannies of Sugarloaf (neighing horses always betrayed their presence to alert cavalrymen). Union horsemen, however, clung to the flanks of the marchers, and the vanguard of Hunter's own troops liberated Frederick by mid-day, pushing Early's rear guard off down the Georgetown turnpike. Buckner McGill Randolph of the 49th Virginia claimed that Union cavalry dashing into the city that morning were ambushed and badly cut up. Henry Truehart of McNeill's Rangers in Imboden's ranks wrote his brother about the nasty firefight in the dusty city streets where no one could determine friend or foe with a half-dozen or so rebels and 40–50 bluecoats as casualties. Staffer Henry Kyd Douglas remained with Ramseur's rear guard, admitting in turn that "we were annoyed somewhat by the enemy's cavalry."[33]

Colorful little hamlets like Urbana, Hyattstown, and Clarksburg turned out to succor blue and gray alike, with tubs of water and barrels of crackers laid out by Unionist Columbus Winsor at Urbana. The cheery greeting of an elderly Clarksburg woman: "Why, those are our men! Why, Union men, of course!" brought forth cheers from the dejected captives in the column. Still, Sergeant Major John G. Young of the 4th North Carolina recalled how pretty women rode horseback for miles just to catch glimpses of their heroes in gray, while "some few 'Marylanders'" joined ranks for the campaign, probably due to the recent conscription draft for the Union army in the local congressional district.[34]

When all was said and done, it was mostly officer cries to "close up, close up" and hard marching, with only occasional bantering between guards and prisoners, that enlivened the drudgery of the trek. By evening, roadsides were littered with thirsty, worn-out rebels, utterly incapable of marching further. Ramseur's men rejoined the main column about 1:00 A.M. They had been shadowed by Yankee cavalry probably either Wells's rump 8th Illinois or Blakeley's 14th Pennsylvania. They, too, dropped into makeshift bivouacs incapable of further movement. "The day was very hot and the roads exceedingly dusty," Early related to Lee on July 14, "but we marched thirty miles." He reduced that figure by ten miles in his postwar autobiography. Whichever, the fact was that Old Jube's army was strung out north and south of Gaithersburg, that night, and nowhere in sight of the capital.[35]

Cooking fires were soon lit, and the smell of coffee and fresh victuals wafted across the countryside. Again, the soldiery made quick work of local larders, icehouses, and available livestock. Farms like those of Ignatius Fulks and John T. De Sellum were ravaged in this manner. De Sellum hosted Early and his officers that night, and despite pro-Southern feelings and his ownership of slaves, incurred Confederate wrath by suggesting the seceded states should simply give up their cause and return to the Union under prewar conditions. The next morning when De Sellum implored Early to spare his own property, the crusty Virginian simply replied that "you can't expect favour or protection" since De Sellum did not seem sympathetic to the Confederacy. In any case, such continuing lack of discipline and indiscriminate thievery hardly won sympathy among borderland Marylanders. On the other hand, when twenty-one-year-old William D. Scott of the 14th Virginia Cavalry was shot while out foraging near Clopper's Mill, the miller's family took him in and nursed him, although a local doctor could not save his life. They saw to his burial in the local St. Rose of Lima Catholic church graveyard, located on the modern Clopper Road, west of Gaithersburg.[36]

By now, a scratch force of Yankee cavalry (organized from dismounted riders at the Giesboro depot in southeast Washington), had gone out to contest the Confederates' advance. Joined by Major Levi Wells' remnants of the 8th Illinois Cavalry that had escaped toward Washington from the Monocacy defeat, these troops led by Pennsylvania Major William H. Fry had also stopped briefly at De Sellum's "Summit Hill" farm on Sunday, after a little firefight with McCausland's advance at Gerrardsville. The skirmishing continued southward on Monday through Rockville where a number of fallen men and horses littered the village streets.

By 4:00 P.M., Fry had sent a dispatch to Major General Christopher C. Augur, commanding the Department of Washington (XXII Corps), telling them "that the forts in the vicinity of Tennallytown [on the Georgetown or Rockville pike inside the District] should be strongly guarded as the enemy's column is a mile long." Indeed, by nightfall, the city's safety seemed to hang in the balance. Few residents slept well; the clatter of orderlies, mustering units and shifting equipment kept the streets in a hubbub, and refugees from the North brought in wide-eyed tales of rebel depredations. Farmers living in the invaders' path sought refuge in the city, and as Frederick Seward, the secretary of state's son recalled: "By every northern road their wagons were coming in, loaded with their household goods, accompanied by cattle hastily gathered and drive before them." Early's ragtag force seemed only a hair's breadth from the most spectacular victory of the war. Everything depended upon the events of the morrow.[37]

Monday, the eleventh of July, dawned clear and continued hot. The thermometer rose quickly to the nineties once more, further debilitating Early's soldiers, still a good day's march from Washington City. Major John Mosby, whose partisans had disturbed Union picnickers across the river at Falls Church on Sunday, continued to harass Union outposts in the vicinity of Great Falls, upriver from the Chain Bridge near forts Marcy and Ethan Allen. He, at least, kept garrisons pinned in place south of the Potomac. At an early hour, McCausland resumed heavy skirmishing south of Rockville.

This time the antagonists were Colonel Charles Russell Lowell's makeshift Massachusetts-Illinois cavalry contingent that had relieved Fry's men when the latter had run short of ammunition. The fighting seesawed along the Georgetown or Rockville pike in areas now part of suburban Bethesda in northwest Washington. Finally, close to the well defended heights at Tennallytown (where massive Fort Reno sat atop a hillock 430 feet above sea level), McCausland was stopped by the long line of fortifications that marked the Northern defenses of Washington. "We sent them a few bombshells and they stopped firing and left," B. F. Marshall of the 1st New Hampshire Heavy Artillery wrote his mother later from nearby Fort Simmons. Over the previous war years, gangs of trainees, Freedmen or "contrabands," engineers, and hired laborers from the North had constructed an immense interconnected system of forts, batteries, rifle-trenches, abatis entanglements, and cleared fields of fire that presided over farmland and country lanes as well as the highways out of the city. The fortifications at Tennallytown would be a tough nut for Early to crack, thought McCausland.[38]

At least, this seemed to be what McCausland conveyed to Early during a mid-morning consultation in Rockville. Old Jube himself had been up early, conscious of making haste before the boiling sun reached its zenith. Marching orders had been carefully prepared by Colonel A. S. "Sandie" Pendleton the night before, and reputedly had Robert Rodes' division up and on the road by 3:30 A.M. That may or may not have happened, but the march plan left much to be desired. An artillery battalion would march between each infantry division, while the long wagon train preceded Echols' division in the rear. While Federal harassment of the rear and flanks had dropped off, this arrangement only ensured that the foot-sloggers would be eating an inordinate amount of dust from the heavy, wheeled vehicles. It was not one of Early's better ideas, as it turned out. Then, heeding McCausland, Early decided to turn eastward at Rockville, and strike for the next available highway into the city. The forts might be weaker on this Seventh Street Road, as it was called, even though this move added fully ten to twelve additional miles to the schedule. Early thought he might catch the Yankees by surprise with this maneuver, since McCausland would continue a heavy demonstration at Tennallytown to fool them into thinking his was the main avenue of attack.[39]

The march eastward to Leesborough (modern Wheaton), and then via the Seventh Street Road (or Washington-Brookville, or even Union turnpike) to Silver Spring and the District line proved exhausting. As Old Jube observed in reports and his autobiography, the heat, absence of rain for several weeks, and suffocating dust clouds—all took their toll on man and beast. He might have added the brutal fight at Monocacy, the previous day's arduous marching, and the oppressive, even sleepless night meant that "our progress was therefore very much impeded." Still, Early and his officers pushed the column relentlessly, and it seems doubtful that even the mighty Stonewall Jackson would have done any better had he been present. The thermometer registered 94 degrees at W. H. Farquehar's "Lonesome Hollow" farm at nearby Sandy Spring. On past Samual Vier's grist mill on upper Rock Creek marched the sweating men, horses, wagons, and artillery. Then turning to the right at Mitchell's Crossroads and Leesborough and onto the highway into Washington, they pushed in the unrelenting heat.

"This has been an awfully hot day," jotted Richard Woolfolk Waldrop of the 21st Virginia in his diary, "the road is lined with stragglers." Men dropped by the roadsides like flies. "Our division was stretched out almost like skirmishers," recalled John Worsham from Gordon's division. Onward they pressed, past an incomplete little country church, Grace Episcopal, in whose graveyard seventeen of their comrades would soon find ultimate peace after the battle that lay ahead. Sligo Post Office was reached, and more men dropped off looking for brooks and wells—and liquor supplies in the country store there—anything to slake their thirst. "I'll have you in Washington before nightfall," shouted Early, riding up and down the column trying to cajole his jaded men to make haste. This was impossible, however. They had to slacken the pace, he reported later, because of the heat and swirling dust. Off in the distance, Federal signal officers at Fort Reno, and farther east at Fort Totten, easily caught sight of this dusty spectacle and knew that the main threat to the city was now shifting eastward.[40]

Still more men slipped out of the ranks as the army reached the sylvan oasis of old Washington newsman and political figure Francis Preston Blair's "Silver Spring" farm at the District line. Discovered by Blair and his daughter while riding in the early 1840s, the bubbling spring had become a pool in a parklike setting with shade trees and comfortable country mansion nearby. The elder Blair's son, Montgomery (Lincoln's postmaster general), had a similar property adjacent, which he called "Falkland," and with both owners away, the weary Confederates were only too happy to call it quits by mid-day, and take refuge on these properties while awaiting developments. Early, however, had other ideas, and he spurred ahead with the cavalry advance to see what the situation was regarding the Union defenses in this area. He left it to his subordinates to continue the task of consolidating his army in preparation for taking Washington by nightfall.

By 11:00 A.M., the Confederates had begun to attack Union pickets on the Seventh Street Road. By noon, heavy skirmishing was in progress both here and on the Rockville pike to the west. Colonel George H. Smith's 62d Virginia Mounted Infantry took the lead into the District, steadily pushing back 100-days soldiers of the 150th Ohio National Guard Infantry, and the veteran 25th New York Cavalry. There in the distance, shimmered the main line of enemy entrenchments in the haze of early afternoon. Early rode forward, arriving "a short time after noon," before Fort Stevens, and finding the works "were but feebly manned." Less than twelve hundred yards of orchards and farmland, with an occasional house, and a broad, swale-like swath of terrain was all that separated Early from those fortifications. True, they appeared "to be very strong and constructed very scientifically," he claimed later, but as at Monocacy, initial reports indicated that the defenders were merely militiamen and other scratch contingents. One captured Yankee, attired in a long broadcloth coat, according to Thomas Toon of the 20th North Carolina, told them that defenders of the city "were counter jumpers, clerks in the War Office, hospital rats and stragglers." Early thought that he had won the race for the capital. He looked around for infantry to make the assault and quickly finish the task.[41]

While Early awaited the arrival of Rodes' foot soldiers, he counted the odds. Probably only one-third of his army was truly deplorable at this point, and timing was everything. Surely he could punch through the defenders and get into the city before dark, there to plunder government storehouses and await the arrival of Bradley Johnson and the liberated prisoners from Point Lookout. It was a long shot, but Early was not about to shirk the challenge. Just then, Old Jube began to chat with a local farmer about the character and strength of Washington's protection. "Nothing but earthworks," claimed the civilian, with maybe 20,000 men in them around the city. Early may have realized that earthworks "in the then state of the science of war" and defended even by 20,000 men presented a formidable undertaking. At the time he merely shrugged and told his informant that if that was all in the way of his army, "we would not mind that." Secretly, Old Jube must have paused. One may wonder if Early's heart was ever truly in a pitched battle against fixed fortifications after he gained this intelligence.

Nonetheless, the general directed deployment of a strengthened skirmish line (that was about all he could muster anyway), with the intention of preparing the assault on the defenses.[42]

At that moment, early on the afternoon of July 11, Early seemed ready; his army was not. As he informed Lee three days later: "When we reached the right of the enemy's fortifications, the men were almost completely exhausted and not in a condition to make an attack." No doubt many, if not most, were indeed capable only of dropping in the shade and resting. Yet, there was another side to the story, if Elizabeth Blair Lee, old Francis Preston Blair's daughter, heard the account correctly. A number of Early's soldiers found Silver Spring and its contents—including demijohns of naval whiskey acquired by Blair the year before—far too alluring. Ransacking the house, cavorting in the family's clothing, including those of the women of the household, "there was a perfect saturnalia in progress" when Early and Breckinridge rode back from the battle line to the mansion about five o'clock. Enraged with the officer responsible for the frolic, Early ostensibly yelled, "You have ruined our whole campaign," suggesting that if he had pushed to the forts that morning at eight o'clock, "we would have taken them." Now reinforcements from Grant had arrived and "we can't take them without immense loss perhaps 'tis impossible." Breckinridge also cursed the mischief and sent for another regiment to guard the house. Apparently, the troops were not too tired for looting.[43]

Whatever Early told the unknown officers and later Lee, he still was determined to try an attack. He had won the race, but miscalculated the time and temperature, as well as the lack of discipline in the old valley army. Then too, the Confederate skirmish line found a very combative foe, fully supported by fortress artillery, once the combat moved to within fifty to one hundred and fifty yards of the works. Moreover, just as the assault seemed to be getting into high gear, Early "saw a cloud of dust in the rear of the works towards Washington, and soon a column of the enemy filed into them on the right and left, and skirmishers were thrown out in front, while an artillery fire was opened on us from a number of batteries." The general subsequently thought these reinforcements indicated arrival of Ulysses S. Grant's relief force from Petersburg.

In reality, their 1:30 P.M. appearance was merely "the dismounted of the Second Division of the Cavalry Corps, Army of the Potomac, 600 strong, commanded by Major George G. Briggs, Seventh Michigan Cavalry," declared Union defense line commander Major General Alexander McCook later. Nevertheless, this added push (which restored the Union skirmish line to a more respectable 1,100 yards from the line of works), combined with Early's inability to get the major portion of his army into line at the moment of truth. Early's window of opportunity—that had been closing ever since Monocacy, if not before—was about to be slammed shut. Even Old Jube made a costly decision at this juncture. As he explained it later, he now went over to a mere reconnaissance, that "consumed the balance of the day."[44]

Many participants had fully expected a Confederate assault that afternoon. It never came. New York correspondent Sylvanus Cadwallader recounted how the rebels simply stacked arms up and down their line, built fires, and cooked their dinners before even beginning to skirmish with any resolution. A battery of artillery unlimbered in his brother-in-law's front yard, but most of the dirty, heat-jaded Confederates were too weary to begin a major fight. Cadwallader always wondered about Early's inaction, he said, for the Federal lines could have been carried at any point "with the loss of a few hundred men." A volley, one Rebel Yell, and a vigorous charge would have given them Washington, claimed Virginia cavalryman John Opie. Major General John B. Gordon boasted that he had personally ridden "to a point on those breastworks at which there was no force whatever," and that the unprotected space was "broad enough for the easy passage of Early's army without resistance." Color bearer George C. Pile of the fragmentary 37th Virginia claimed (perhaps rhetorically): "We got within sight of the dome of the capitol and I placed my flag on the outer breastworks of the enemy, remaining there several hours." Meanwhile, inaction prevailed, and the young Southerners wondered why their leader denied them a chance to capture enemy's works, plunder the city, and capture Old Abe.[45]

Still others, however, like Virginian John Worsham, took a more sober view, claiming that "the most formidable looking [line of fortifications] I ever saw" had been a blessing in disguise and gave thanks that the army had not been ordered to assault that position. Somehow, all that afternoon of July 11, the decision lay in the balance. Suddenly, at some point, with time slipping away, the army recovered its strength, yet Early seemed to lose his resolve. It was at that point about 4:10 P.M. that the general gave up the race for the capital. At the same time, Major General Horatio G. Wright, commanding the Union VI Corps telegraphed Augur from Fort Stevens: "The head of my column has nearly reached the front...." The Army of the Potomac had reached the fray.[46]

Grant Races Time and Tide

While Jubal Early frittered away the afternoon skirmishing against VI Corps ghosts, the real thing was not far away. Major

General Horatio G. Wright, the corps commander, had gotten a brigade from his first, and three brigades from his second division aboard five troop transports at City Point, Virginia the day before. They had departed at 11:00 A.M. on July 10, just about the time that Early finally got his own men moving down the hot highway to Washington. Another boat, the *Crescent*, similarly passed Fort Monroe, conveying a brigade of the XIX Corps, up by sea from New Orleans. By noon on the eleventh, Wright's men had begun landing at the Washington wharves. They were still several hours' march from the Northern defense line. For the next four hours, in fact, while Early's people lounged under shade trees out at Silver Spring, the VI Corps boys had marched and countermarched about the city, chafing under confusing orders and conflicting notions about their intended role in the unfolding drama.[47]

Wright's waterborne move resulted from Grant's somewhat tardy recognition of the seriousness of Early's threat. Even an unsubtle personal "suggestion" from the commander in chief at 2:30 P.M. on the tenth that the general should "provide to retain your hold where you are, ... and bring the rest with you personally, and make a vigorous effort to destroy the enemy's force in this vicinity," met with a rather torpid response. Lincoln echoed Halleck's words that there were no field forces available to maneuver against the rebels, that the 100-days men and invalids scarcely sufficed to defend Washington and Baltimore both, and that Wallace "was so badly beaten" at the Monocacy that he could little more than attempt to defend the latter city. Any aid from Pennsylvania and New York "will scarcely be worth counting," the president feared.

Grant replied at 10:30 P.M. that night (received in Washington at 7:00 A.M. on the eleventh) suggesting that he had sent a whole corps, "commanded by an excellent officer," besides 3,000 other troops, that a 6,000-man division of the XIX Corps was also en route, and that such would "be able to compete with Ewell [Grant persisted in erroneously identifying that general as the commander of the raiders]." Hunter's people would soon add 10,000 more to the game. "I think on reflection," he concluded, "it would have a bad effect for me to leave here," and with Ord at Baltimore, and Hunter and Wright with their forces following the enemy up, "could do no good." Entirely too flippantly, he closed: "I have great faith that the enemy will never be able to get back with much of his force."[48]

Grant never deviated from this position over the next several days, despite dire predictions from Halleck and Assistant Secretary of War Charles A. Dana. Lincoln, in an 8:00 A.M. reply on July 12, seemed to acquiesce, although he subtly pointed out that: "The enemy will learn of Wright's arrival, and then the difficulty will be to unite Wright and Hunter south of the enemy before he will cross the Potomac." Meanwhile, Grant and Meade preoccupied themselves worrying about reports that Confederate corps commanders James E. Longstreet or A. P. Hill, even Lee himself, had gone north to help in Maryland, and how Union cavalry commander, Major General Philip H. Sheridan might make a reconnaissance of the Weldon Railroad to determine what was going on at Petersburg. Grant had sent a trusted subordinate, Major General E. O. C. Ord to straighten matters out at Baltimore. "I would give more for him as a commander in the field than most of the generals in Maryland," he declared bluntly. As for the Monocacy debacle, in Grant's words to Meade on the tenth, "Wallace has been whipped at Monocacy bridge, and driven back in great confusion." It was as simple as that to the man whose previous opinions of the Hoosier were nebulous at best based on the Shiloh controversy.[49]

Most of all, Grant intended Wright to take the lead in cutting off Early's escape across the Potomac upstream from Washington. For that reason, Halleck had conveyed initial orders to the VI Corps to take position behind Fort Sumner, on the far left of the Northern defense line, above Chain Bridge. Here the veterans could best utilize the river and aqueduct roads out of the city to unite with Hunter coming from Harpers Ferry. Then, just as Wright's men began the hot trek out Pennsylvania Avenue on the early afternoon of the eleventh, Early had "opened the ball" (to quote the quaint phrase of the day connoting the onset of battle) before Fort Stevens. Seriously out of position, Wright had to retrace his steps to Seventh and Eleventh Streets when a courier redirected his route to the vicinity of the Military Asylum, not far from Fort Stevens. So, the Army of the Potomac arrivals—pawns in Grant's overall strategic plan—having won their own race against time and tide to relieve the city, momentarily became as irrelevant to the crisis unfolding out the Seventh Street Road as the fagged butternut host lounging about on the Francis Blair farm.[50]

Wright reported to McCook at Fort Stevens about 3 o'clock and to Augur about seventy minutes later (although he also sent a telegram announcing his arrival to the secretary of war from Fort Reno to the west about this same time). Since "General McCook's men are not as good as mine," he asked permission to send out a brigade to disperse the rather pesky enemy skirmish line. Headquarters, however, demurred, stating that the veterans should remain in the rear, guarding against an enemy breakthrough. Initial elements of the First Brigade, First Division, XIX Corps similarly arrived at the city wharves in this period and were shunted out the Old Bladensburg Road to the vicinity of Fort Saratoga—far to the

right and away from the fighting. Apparently reports of enemy cavalry activity caused this deployment, as well as dispatch of Federal
mounted reconnaissance into that area, too. At Fort Stevens, meanwhile, Lincoln, his wife, and other civilians appeared at different times,
anxious to view the unfolding spectacle in the suburbs. The president mounted the parapet—thus becoming the only president in the
nation's history to endure hostile fire while in office—and several
bystanders yelled at him to get down. Then, about 5:00 P.M., mounting Confederate pressure became too much for the ersatz force of
100-days men, convalescents, and dismounted cavalrymen manning
the Union skirmish line. Another moment of crisis had come in the
action.[51]

McCook's men had effectively neutralized Confederate ardor all
afternoon. Their breech-loading carbines had enabled them to maintain a level of fire that conveyed a false impression of a more aggressive and powerful defense, suggested one commentator when he heard
about the fight later. But, the heat and electricity of the experience
had worn them down by late afternoon, just as it had the Confederate
marchers earlier in the day. At least once, rebel sharpshooters made
servicing the heavy guns in Fort Stevens completely untenable.

So, Brigadier General Frank Wheaton's First Brigade, Second
Division, VI Corps, received the assignment of recovering the initiative on the skirmish line. It was an all-Pennsylvania affair at first,
with the 98th, 102d, and 139th Infantries accomplishing the task by
7:00 P.M. The 93d Pennsylvania and 62d New York joined the firefight, with support from the heavy artillery in the works. The VI Corps
boys had brought no artillery with them. Dark settled over the field
in an arena that now stretched from Battery Smeade and Fort De
Russy west of Rock Creek to Fort Slocum, the next major fortification east of Fort Stevens. It had been an anxious afternoon at many
points. Lieutenant Edgar S. Dudley, 2d U.S. Artillery, who helped
man Fort Marcy on the Virginia side of Chain Bridge during the raid,
contended later that a determined Confederate drive at this moment
could have taken the fort and then swept down the rifle pits on either side. "The line once broken, the work done, and the city would
be in their possession," was his feeling.[52]

As the guns thundered at Fort Stevens, one hundred miles to
the south, General Robert E. Lee penned a lengthy dispatch to Early.
Evidencing far better intelligence about his adversaries than Grant
and his generals apparently had gleaned about Confederate operations, Lee told Old Jube about Hunter's movements, the departure
of dismounted cavalry, Ricketts' division, and other reinforcements
for Washington. Even though his subordinate was learning these
things first hand at that moment, Lee wanted "to apprise you of this

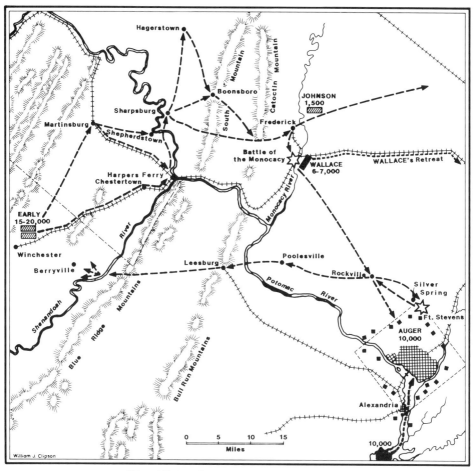

Map 15. Early's Raid Recapitulation

fact that you may be on your guard and take this force into consideration with others that may be brought to oppose you." Of course, Early "must be guided by the circumstances by which you are surrounded," information that he might collect on the spot, and should not feel committed to any particular line of conduct, "but be governed by your good judgement." If Federal pressure got too strong, then Early should retire south of the Potomac by the fords east of the Blue Ridge, said Lee. Provision-rich Loudoun County could replenish the expedition's supplies and forage, he thought, "giving you a strong country through which to pass," and enabling Early "to retire to the Valley and threaten and hang upon the enemy's flank should he push towards Richmond." Finally, suggested the ever-aggressive commander of the Army of Northern Virginia: "I need not state to you the advantage of striking at the bodies of troops that may be collected to oppose you in detail before they are able to unite." When, and if, this dispatch ever got through to Early, on the night of July 11, he was already thinking about his options.[53]

Washington City passed another restless night amid all kinds of rumors and disquieting sounds of the military activity in the suburbs. The Lincolns presumably returned to the White House, while additional armed citizens, and newly arriving Union reinforcements took their places in the Northern trenches. In fact, they would continue to arrive all the second day of the fighting. Dr. Daniel M. Holt of the 121st New York in Colonel Emory Upton's brigade noted debarking about 2:00 P.M. in a rainstorm and finding the city in a state of excitement. "The inhabitants appear to believe we have saved them from certain death," he jotted in his diary, adding "for *once* we are appreciated." "If ever the old Sixth Corps was appreciated and looked up to it was then," he wrote his wife the next day.[54]

Dawn of the twelfth brought no release from the tension, the heat, and the constant "pop-popping" of the musketry. Moreover, now was the moment of truth for Old Jube and his army. Would they or would they not assault Washington's fortifications? Early and his generals had laid out the stakes over wine and cigars in Blair's country mansion the night before. They had talked about the danger of remaining where they were; the necessity of doing something, lest the passes of South Mountain and the fords of the upper Potomac be closed to their retreat. Yet, Early himself "being very reluctant to abandon the project of capturing Washington," determined to make an assault on the enemy works at daylight, "unless some information should be received before that time showing its impracticality," and thus informed his commanders. That information proved to be a dispatch from Bradley Johnson, stating that reliable sources suggested "that two corps had arrived from General Grant's army, and that his whole army was probably in motion." This delayed Early's planned attack "until I could examine the works again."[55]

Indeed, Early rode down the Seventh Street Road at first light on July 12 to examine the enemy works. He found "the parapets lined with troops," he said in his memoirs, but did not elaborate upon that finding. Frankly, Union authorities had simply thrown everything they had a hand in to the lines, with quartermaster clerks, more veteran reservists and convalescents, D.C. militiamen and even sailors from the navy yard joining with new arrivals like Brigadier General Emory Upton's Second, and Colonel Oliver Edwards' Third brigades of the First Division of the VI Corps. Captain Andrew Cowan's 1st New York Battery and Lieutenant Jacob Lamb's Battery C, 1st Rhode Island Light Artillery, added mobile firepower to the defenders' arsenal. Many of these soldiers were returning to familiar scenes, having encamped in the area and constructed some of the forts earlier in the war. A plethora of general officers and much confusion attended the Union side. But, there could be no mistake they had manned the works in depth, and this was what Old Jube saw through his binoculars in dawn's early light.[56]

Captain A. B. Beamish, 98th Pennsylvania, recalled that when one of Early's commissary sergeants had stumbled into Union lines by mistake about 10:00 P.M. the night before, he had spotted the unmistakable VI Corps troops with their Greek cross cap badges. The rebel intruder had exclaimed: "If the Holy Cross of Christ Fellows are here, Gen. Early had better give up the idea of taking Washington." That was precisely the general's conclusion the next morning. As he informed Lee two days later, an assault, even if successful "would be attended with such great sacrifice as would insure the destruction of my whole force before the victory could have been made available." If unsuccessful, he added, it would "necessarily have resulted in the loss of the whole force." Perhaps unduly pessimistic, perhaps merely iterating what he had known to be true all along, it is idle speculation—at a distance of one hundred thirty years—to conjecture that Stonewall Jackson might have thought any differently. At any rate, having "reluctantly determined to retire," Early proceeded to threaten the city all day on the twelfth in order to retreat under cover of darkness. So, skirmishing resumed in earnest, but little more.[57]

At that very moment, in fact, Washington stood cut off from the North by Bradley Johnson's raiders severing rail and telegraph lines north of Baltimore. As his band clattered southward toward the Washington branch of the Baltimore and Ohio and the highway toward Washington (ostensibly still bent upon getting to the Point Lookout rendezvous), Northern financial markets teetered as "greenback" currency (legal tender and lifeblood of wartime business) cascaded in value to thirty-five cents on the dollar. Monied classes worried that the government had only one chance in three of saving itself from the rebel threat. Near Beltsville, however, a courier from Early caught up with Johnson and told him the Point Lookout operation was off. He and his men should rejoin the main army to the west at Silver Spring. So, after ripping up more railroad and telegraph property and skirmishing as they rode across country through the Maryland Agricultural College (a few score of their outriders may have penetrated to the edges of the Northern fortification line west of Bladensburg Road on the northeastern side of the city), Johnson's column reached Silver Spring that evening.[58]

At the same time, indecision continued to cloud the Washington battlefront. Grant's emissary at the capital, Assistant Secretary of War Charles A. Dana, wired that nobody seemed able or willing to make decisions about an offensive to entrap Early. Halleck "will not give orders except as he receives them; the President will give none, and until you direct positively and explicitly what is to be done, everything will go on in the deplorable and fatal way in which it has gone on for the past week," noted the civilian official. The president held his customary noon cabinet meeting, and then, as on the day before, rode out to see how things were going at Fort Stevens.[59]

Lincoln once again took his place atop the parapet—to inspire the defenders as well as satiate his almost adolescent curiosity about the fighting. "*Father Abraham*, wife and son" had followed Upton's reinforcements out to the fort that afternoon in their carriage, Dr. Daniel Holt of the 121st New York wrote his wife. Then, once again, the president came under sharpshooter fire. A surgeon was cut down by a bullet as he stood beside the tall figure, garbed in black with his tall hat. Repeated enjoinders and oaths to get him down met with little response. Finally, General Wright had to tell him point-blank that he could not guarantee his commander in chief's safety, and Lincoln reluctantly obliged. Maybe it was young Captain Oliver Wendell Holmes, perhaps Aunt Betty Thomas (the free black woman whose property had been confiscated to enlarge Fort Stevens two years before and who, unaccountably, seemed to be in the fort that day)—or a half-dozen others who later claimed the honor of dramatically telling the president to get off the Fort Stevens' parapet. In any event, this action undoubtedly gave the president nine more months of life and added yet another tale to the Lincoln legend.[60]

Lincoln's exposure that afternoon unfortunately cost the lives of scores of boys in blue, in addition to the wounding of many others. Anxiety over his presence on the parapet caused Wright and McCook to launch a sortie, designed to push back the troublesome rebel sharpshooters. Under a thunderous artillery barrage that tore apart several houses sheltering the snipers, Wheaton's command again led the assault. Acting under a personally signed order of the president, the heavy guns blasted Confederate lines, and then two brigades from the division, which Wheaton temporarily commanded, swept forward. Notwithstanding Confederate soldier observations that "we lay around all day [the twelfth] and skirmished, and pretended like we would charge the enemy's works till night," or that they simply "lay in line during the whole day—nothing of importance transpired," a nasty little battle swirled about the area for several hours. Gordon's division had to prove that it still had some fight left after Monocacy, in order to thwart the Yankee drive. When it ended, some 250 to 375 bluecoats had been killed or wounded from commands barely total-ing 1,000 men going into the action. Yet, they had erased the threat to the president's life. Then, like all good veterans by this stage of the war, they were content not to push their luck. When Old Jube's army began to fade northward from Silver Spring in the lengthening twilight, Wheaton's people made no move to follow them. The Union had won the race to save Washington.[61]

Fort Stevens' Afterglow

Neither Early nor his principal commanders said anything much about this little fight. Nor did he or John C. Breckinridge evidence awareness that they might be staring across the intervening battle lines at the president of the United States that day. By evening, and overnight, the Confederate troops themselves slipped out of make-shift bivouacs and force-marched for the upper Potomac crossings. Early was now in a much greater hurry to get away than he had been to reach Washington, it seemed. Staff major Henry Kyd Douglas may have captured the subtle nuance when he recounted the after-dark meeting between Early, Breckinridge, and Gordon as they prepared to leave Silver Spring. Whether in "a droll humor, perhaps one of relief," noted Douglas, Early quipped in his falsetto drawl: "Major, we haven't taken Washington, but we've scared Abe Lincoln like hell!" Douglas incautiously replied: "Yes, General, but this afternoon when that Yankee line moved out against us, I think some other people were scared blue as hell's brimstone!" Was that true, asked Breckinridge softly. "That's true," muttered Old Jube, "but it won't appear in history!"[62]

A brightly burning Falkland mansion marked the passage of Early's men from the scene, sparking future controversy as to just who torched Montgomery Blair's house. Old Preston Blair's Silver Spring home was spared, ostensibly through intercession of cousin John Breckinridge, who had enjoyed the family's hospitality on nu-merous occasions. Federal activity left the area in a shambles too, and seventeen dead comrades and ninety wounded left to tender mercies of Federal surgeons also testified to the war's touch. A new Battleground National Cemetery soon marked the final resting place for some forty-one Union participants in the battle, notwithstanding the landowner's displeasure at having his property used for such purpose. Elsewhere seventeen dead Confederates were gathered from various farms and placed in the Grace Episcopal graveyard, near the structure that ironically served as the Blairs' parish church.

Throughout an area now occupied by suburban neighborhoods and the Walter Reed Army Medical Center, property owners and soldiers, at the time, moved about gathering arms and refuse from the battle. Sightseers couldn't wait to view the damage and the carnage, and in the following month, Elizabeth Blair Lee noted greater irritation with those voyeurs than with the enemy's destruction, admitting that if the Union troops had occupied the place, the damage would have been similar. That evening, however, nobody thought much beyond the banner headline of *The Evening Star*: "The Rebels Have Disappeared from Our Front." Most of Washington simply breathed a sigh of relief.[63]

Still, people naturally had hoped for something more on the Union side. Assistant Secretary of War Dana exclaimed that with Grant's reinforcements, "there was force enough to save the capital; but I soon saw that nothing could possibly be done toward pursuing or cutting off the enemy for want of a commander." Frankly, he noted, matters would go on "in the deplorable and fatal way in which they had been going for a week," for "want of a head" unless Grant acted. Then word surfaced that Halleck had tattled about Montgomery Blair's reference to army officers as "poltroons" and the "disgraceful affair" at Fort Stevens. Lew Wallace, by comparison, "would at least fight," had muttered the postmaster general. Old Preston Blair proceeded to show the president and other cabinet officials the extent of the Confederate encampments, and even Lincoln and Secretary of the Navy Gideon Welles (among others) were forced to admit that: "Our city was saved by stupidity and slowness of the Rebs."[64]

Welles exclaimed that they could have taken the capital on Monday without the loss of a hundred men. That thought had not prevented this curmudgeon from censuring Montgomery Blair's brother-in-law, Rear Admiral Samuel F. Lee, about leaving his Hampton Roads station in his flagship USS *Malvern* and coming to Washington thereby "yielding to the panic that was created." In the end, however, the notion that "'God was on our side, and dealt in mercy,'" pervaded feeling among Lincoln and his friends. But, there were many like convalescent Sergeant J. D. Bloodgood of the 141st Pennsylvania who had been in charge of a forty-man detail at the Central Guard House during the whole affair. He decided later that, "I haven't any doubt that Early could have captured and burned the whole city if he had made an energetic assault when he first came before it."[65]

Early drove his army to the Potomac after Fort Stevens as mercilessly as he had from Rockville to Silver Spring three days before. This time, however, he enjoyed a day's head start in the race for the river fords. Wright and Quincy Gillmore, temporarily commanding the XIX Corps troops, never got their pursuit column in motion before the mid-day heat of the thirteenth. New York regimental surgeon Daniel Holt wrote his wife disgustedly that they had waited all day merely "for the rebels to *get out of the way*." Early's men recounted suffering equaled only by that of the march southward after Monocacy. One North Carolinian noted marching all night with nothing to eat along the way except dewberries. Another claimed to have secured nothing for twenty-four hours except discarded scraps from other people's mess pans. Color bearer George C. Pile of the 37th Virginia recalled that a doctor, seeing he was sick and worn out, had told him to get in an ambulance "and stay there until we crossed the Potomac, which I did." Virginia artillerist Henry Robinson Berkeley thought it was the toughest march he had ever made, and everyone sought stray horses to ease their sore feet. Guards carelessly let their Yankee prisoners slip away, and Louisiana chaplain, Father James B. Sheeran, thought the whole army looked more like demoralized cavalry as it neared the Potomac. "We had marched four hundred miles in about a month's time" was the way George Pile saw it.[66]

* * * *

Frankly, the character of the Federal pursuit was wretched. "An egregious blunder," Dana styled it, the upshot of which was that "Early escaped with the whole of his plunder." The Army of the Potomac veterans had won their race to the capital via the luxury of steamboats. But not having marched or fought any major battle in weeks, they lost the subsequent footrace to bag the raiders. Joining other defenders, similarly lacking the toughening of hard-marching in the July heat (Hunter's people had come east by rail, for example), the bluecoats might have been more refreshed than their opponents, and certainly less burdened with plunder. Additionally, Wright and Gillmore had originally a shorter axis to the interception point at the upper fords from their position in the Washington defense via River Road. Yet, they allowed Early and easily 10,000 to 12,000 weary men, in excess of 1,000 captured horses plus 2,000 other livestock, and wagon loads of booty—plus over $200,000 or so in cash—to exit Maryland unscathed by mid-day of July 14. As Dana caustically suggested, their pursuers under Wright accomplished nothing, and drew back as soon as the latter "got where he might have done something worthwhile."[67]

The battered and decimated 14th New Jersey like other of Ricketts' surviving units from the Monocacy joined in the post-raid chase that Wright's column conducted all over northwestern Virginia and upper Maryland. In only sixteen days since leaving Petersburg, they had traveled 300 miles by water, 116 by rail, and 175 on foot, for a total of 400 miles! Recrossing the Potomac at Chain Bridge on July 23 after pursuing Early toward Winchester, they received four months' back pay two days later. The next day they started upriver again on foot for Harpers Ferry. They marched ten miles that afternoon to Rockville through Tennallytown, D.C. The next day it was eighteen more miles through Gaithersburg and Clarksburg, halting in the afternoon near Hyattstown "with sore and blistered feet." Actually, recalled a veteran later, they now hoped to go into battle "rather than be marched to death."

Nevertheless, another ten-mile march on July 28 through Hyattstown and Urbana brought them to the Monocacy battlefield. "The ground was broken and traces of the conflict could be seen on all sides, remnants of shells, cannon, horses, unburied corpses lay strewn about," Terrill remembered. Moreover, while the rebels had failed to blow up the railroad bridge, they had burned the hotel and water tank at the depot, as well as the "bridge crossing at the main road." The Jerseymen found the 3d Maryland Potomac Home Brigade guarding the bridge, so the footsore veterans marched on through Jefferson, Petersville, Knoxville, and Sandy Hook before crossing the Potomac at Harpers Ferry and continuing to Halltown. They made twenty-five miles in all on July 29, claimed Terrill.[68]

Little wonder that an irritated President Lincoln confided to his personal secretary, John Hay, late in the day that Wright had telegraphed him about Early's escape and how he had halted his own column in order to send out an infantry reconnaissance. The commander in chief sarcastically explained this lapse as Wright's "fear that he might come across the rebels and catch some of them." Here was Grant's own chosen instrument of pursuit unwilling to close with the enemy. "The Chief is evidently disgusted," was Hay's way of understating Lincoln's view of the end of Jubal Early's frolic in Maryland. Lost in the frustration was the role Monocacy had played in the whole affair. That could come later, however, when the dust had settled.[69]

SEVEN

The Legacy—1864

Old Jube's army briefly recuperated near Leesburg, Virginia after returning from Maryland. The army's commander penned his obligatory report to General Robert E. Lee and then returned to a threatening position in the lower Shenandoah Valley. Jubal Early's role in fixing Union forces in place in the region and threatening the enemy capital remained unchanged. The Army of the Valley District, however, would not advance north of the Potomac again. Still, its mere presence continued to cause uneasiness for weeks thereafter. Union forces maneuvered back and forth in the drought and heat to thwart any further Confederate incursions against railroad, canal, or even Washington. There seemed to be little time to analyze the "might-have-beens" of the recent campaign except in the newspapers.

Most Confederate editors naturally declared success. The Richmond *Examiner* proclaimed accurately that Maryland and Pennsylvania were wild with excitement as "the consternation and alarm are greater than ever before." It praised Early and his men for carrying destruction and harsh war to the North (a contention hotly debated by the rival Richmond *Enquirer*), and was sure that such operations intensified Northern desires for peace. The Augusta, Georgia *Constitution* took up the same theme—that Early's raid would increase the peace party's chances of victory in the autumn elections. However, there were naysayers from the rump of old western block editors and politicians who felt Early's corps should have been applied to the war elsewhere—namely in Georgia against William T. Sherman before Atlanta. Even the Richmond *Dispatch* summarized a New York paper which advanced that the invasion had forced President Abraham Lincoln's opponents to stand with Washington in defense of the country. President

Maryland Citizens Succored Federal Soldiers Pursuing Confederates during All Three Invasions—1862, 1863, 1864

Frank Leslie's Illustrated History of the Civil War (1895), p. 458.

Early Escapes to Virginia

By July 14, 1864, Early's force with booty, stolen livestock, and minor casualties returned to Virginia leaving Washington officials perplexed as to how to end his threat.

Harper's History of the Great Rebellion (1866) vol. II, p. 708.

After an artist's sketch.

Ruins of Chambersburg, Pennsylvania

McCausland's raid was the event which finally caused Washington authorities and Grant to seek a consolidated command to find and annihilate Early's valley army.

Courtesy Library of Congress

Major General Philip Henry Sheridan, U.S.A.

Chosen by Grant (with Lincoln's approval) to destroy Early, it took "Little Phil" September and most of October to accomplish the feat. The threat posed by the Army of the Valley to Washington, and the Union occupation of the Shenandoah Valley did not completely end until the late winter of 1864–65.

Jefferson Davis adamantly contended that Early's success "gave us an opportunity to assume the offensive with no unreasonable hope of capturing" Washington instead of losing the Confederate capital.[1]

Certainly the *Enquirer* took especial exception to the Confederates' heavy hand of plunder and confiscation during the late invasion. "We hesitate to believe that any Confederate officer would take upon himself to fix the status of Maryland against the Confederacy," it intoned, and thus treat her as an enemy "to be preyed upon and plundered as though she had exhibited no sympathy for our cause, and had been actively our foe." The editor wanted the ransom money returned to the plundered towns of Hagerstown, Middletown, and Frederick. As for Maryland harboring any lingering yearning to go with the Confederacy, the chances were now slim as Early's men sensed best. Apparently, they failed to communicate this fact of 1864 to the public press of the South.[2]

It was obviously far too early to tell the impact of Early's campaign on Lincoln's chances of reelection. But, things boded well for the South at that moment. Moreover, the activity of Confederate agents operating from Canada and a visit by unofficial peace commissioners from the North also indicated a weakening in Yankee war resolve. Still, the elections remained two to three months away. Meanwhile, Southern battle commanders on the Virginia front had little time to perform post-operational analyses of events like Monocacy—history even then.

* Contemporary Perspective *

Early, in fact, glossed over the Monocacy affair simply as Gordon's "rout" of Ricketts and Wallace, causing them to leave the field "in great disorder" and retreat "in haste" to Baltimore. He drew no link between that day's events and those of July 10 and 11 when heat, dust, and fatigue following the battle had wreaked havoc with his marching column toward Washington. Rather, Early pointed only to the temperature and dust as part of a continuum whereby the formidable Washington forts and the arrival of Lieutenant General Ulysses S. Grant's veterans from Petersburg had caused him to pull back from an assault on the Northern capital.

In the end, said Early, his ultimate determination to retire came principally from "the conviction that the loss of my force would have had such a depressing effect upon the country, and would so encourage the enemy as to amount to a very serious, if not fatal, disaster to our cause." He regretted that, "I did not succeed in capturing

Washington and releasing our prisoners at Point Lookout," a statement that should have put to rest posterity's uncertainty about Early's ultimate goals. He alluded to having caused "intense excitement and alarm" both in Washington and Baltimore, as well as all over the North, mostly by exaggerated estimates of his strength and rumors that Lee himself commanded the expedition. Early advised, however, that Washington could never be taken "unless surprised when without a force to defend it." Once again, however, he failed to admit that the day's delay, occasioned by the battle of Monocacy, had directly affected that element of surprise.[3]

Major General John B. Gordon alone of Old Jube's principal subordinates gave much space to the Monocacy battle in his July 22 after-action report. Even then, most of his focus lay with the sanguinary nature of the action, not with its overall implication for the invasion. Others like Major General Stephen Ramseur viewed the larger picture. He wrote to his wife on July 15, 1864, that natural obstacles alone had prevented the taking of Washington. "The heat and dust was so great that our men could not possibly march further," he commented. Thus, time was given to the Federals to reinforce the fortifications. Still, he concluded, they had accomplished a good deal, "and I hope we still do good work for our cause." Even the men in the ranks viewed the matter more broadly. Caleb Linker wrote home that while he and his comrades had come within sight of Washington, and had spent two days there, they had not really "accomplished anything." Sergeant Major Joseph McMurran of the 4th Virginia was more perceptive, noting: "It was thought that if we could have reached Washington about six hours earlier it could have been taken with comparatively small loss." Lieutenant Leonidas Lafayette Polk of the 43d North Carolina declared to his father on July 17: "Without doubt, we caught the Yankee nation napping and there never has been such confusion, alarm and consternation on the continent. If our General has not the very best of reasons, history will rob him of all his bright laurels for failing to embrace this golden moment. This army has certainly been nearer his Capital than Grant has or probably ever will be to ours."[4]

Interestingly, none of these Confederates connected the Monocacy victory adversely with what transpired subsequently before the capital. McMurran, in fact, enthusiastically compared Early's success with Lee's defeated invasion of the previous year. He rattled off in his diary the succession of defeating the VI Corps at Monocacy, marching on Washington and driving Grant's army from Richmond, and the new likelihood that "the prospect of peace encourages all and even the people of Maryland say that Lincoln will now have to make a proposition for an 'armistice.'" Appreciating that once they had encountered veteran Federals in Washington's forts, "the game was not worth the sacrifice of life." He still gloated that "we are now victorious over our enemies by virtue of 'the boldest march of the war.'"

Henry Truehart, serving with McNeill's Partisan Rangers under Imboden's general supervision, declared that "the battle of Monocacy Station" was a "desperate one and a complete triumph of our arms." Indeed, he told his brother "everywhere that we met them we crushed them or drove them before us," and no wonder, "for never was a nation so surprised at the appearance of an invading army." The Federals could not recover "till we knocked at the gate of Washington and then they were terror stricken throughout the land." An invasion from the land of the dead could not have surprised them more, he claimed. Why Early did not take Washington bothered him greatly for, "it could have been done easily the first day [11th] and at small sacrifice." Report has it, Truehart said, that Early was "ordered by Genl Lee not to enter the city but simply to make demonstrations." There was certainly something "other than the opposing forces which prevented his doing it," this ranker concluded irately.[5]

In Richmond, of course, at first, they had heard nothing about Grant being forced back from that city, much less anything about a successful battle at some little place called Monocacy in Maryland. Only when Yankee newspapers trickled in from across the battle lines would Lee learn of Early's victory over Wallace. He passed the news to President Jefferson Davis at 9:30 P.M. on the twelfth. Still, other War Department bureaucrats like Robert H. Kean felt Early's activities excited the public far more than the dreary accounts of Joe Johnston's steady retreat in north Georgia. Secretary of War James Seddon halfway expected Early to take Washington, Kean noted in his journal, but the clerk doubted it. Of course, he declared: "Early, Rodes, Gordon, and Ramseur are men to dare and do almost anything." Nowhere did Kean mention Monocacy, although fellow clerk John B. Jones did in his diary.[6]

Jones, in fact, waxed quite eloquently about Early's victory over Lew Wallace near Frederick, Maryland. He claimed that reports had Erastus Tyler and William H. Seward both captured, besides many other prisoners, and that "the slaughter was great and the pursuit of the routed army was toward Baltimore." It was his feeling that the excited public believed "that great results will grow out of the invasion of the country held by the enemy." Twice before there had been little result from such invasions. This time it would be different. In fact, two days later, on the fifteenth, said Jones, an officer just in from Petersburg had conveyed news of Baltimore's capture, gleaned from a Washington newspaper. The Monument City's inhabitants had cooperated whole-heartedly with the captors, he said. "Our people are in ecstasies," he beamed, the realization of the grand conception of a great general, the immortalized Lee, "if it only be true." Alas, he moaned the next day, it had all been a hoax for neither Baltimore nor Washington had been captured, and receipt of the *Chronicle* newspaper from the Northern capital, dated July 14, confirmed that Early was "recrossing the Potomac [but] with an immense amount of stores levied in the enemy's country, including thousands of horses, etc." Such gains were bittersweet sounds to Richmonders who had hoped for something far more satisfying.

As for Lee himself, there was little in his pronouncements other than strategic implications as to what Early was doing. He did not want to publicize too strongly the new activities of the valley army, because such publicity might compromise its effectiveness. "I may say that so far as the movement was intended to relieve our territory in that section of the enemy," Lee wrote Davis, "it has up to the present time been successful." Absence of specific reference to the Monocacy victory suggested that battles were only important if they produced ultimate success. Lee still believed strongly, even after Early's failure to take Washington, that a mounted raid might penetrate the city's defenses of the Potomac River, "and excite the alarms of the authorities at Washington."[7]

Additional weeks would pass before Lee realized the impossibility of accomplishing even that more modest undertaking. Grant and the Union soon showed that they simply had too many men with which to press the Gray Fox before Richmond and Petersburg and still neutralize Early in the Valley. Lee tried to maintain his own pressure in turn all summer—sending another separate force under Lieutenant General Richard Anderson and Major General Wade Hampton to Culpeper, east of the Blue Ridge and within striking distance of Washington as well as supporting distance of the Shenandoah. Never again, however, could he spare a full field army to operate across the Potomac. Brigadier General John McCausland's controversial raid on Chambersburg, Pennsylvania and into western Maryland at the end of July was something different—more an indication of the twisted path of angry retaliation and retribution to which both sides had now descended after four summers of conflict. Monocacy and the July success in Maryland were a fast fading chimera of the Army of Northern Virginia's past glories, not a prelude to the future. Singular Union victories over Early at Winchester, Fisher's Hill, and Cedar Creek in the autumn all underscored that conclusion.[8]

Monocacy proved no less enigmatic for the Union at first. After all, it was another defeat, and Generals Halleck and Grant, even the president, used words like "badly beaten," "serious defeat," "defeated and badly cut up," and "whipped" in reference to Wallace's experience. Of course, all of that was said in the spirit of the moment—a moment of crisis—which none of the senior leadership cared to admit. For Northerners in the capital, news of the Monocacy defeat only meant even greater threat to their city. There was little thought beyond the fact that Wallace and his little army had been brushed aside with impunity by the enemy. Public buildings commissioner Benjamin Brown French jotted in his diary on July 10, "The news this morning give rather a squally aspect to affairs up about Frederick," although he admitted that nobody really knew what the result would be ultimately. After Lee's defeat in Pennsylvania the previous year, "I did think they would never be permitted to return," but now they were back, and Lee lived to lead his armies, "and defy ours!" Congressman Albert Gallatin Riddle of Ohio later remembered that Wallace's defeat "disturbed us at the Capital a good deal, though we were hardened beyond a panic." Nonetheless, there was uproar in Washington for a few days. Then, Monocacy, too, was swept away in the swirl of events whereby Early stumbled before Fort Stevens, yet managed to escape to Virginia with booty, prisoners, and fame intact.[9]

Lincoln said little about Monocacy directly, but the anxiety provided by Wallace's defeat could be sensed in the pivotal dispatch he sent to Grant at 2:30 P.M. the day after the battle. Therein, the president came closest ever to ordering his senior commander "to retain your hold where you are [at Petersburg], certainly, and bring the rest with you personally, and make a vigorous effort to destroy the enemy's force in this vicinity." Lincoln called it "suggestion," and "not an order," and thought Grant could accomplish the task if he moved promptly. Grant demurred; Lincoln acquiesced and the VI Corps reinforcements plus Early's missteps let the chance to take Washington pass as Monocacy slipped by in another averted crisis.[10]

At the same time, Lincoln and his cabinet family were more personally concerned how that battle had affected Secretary of State William Henry Seward. Seward's son, commander of the 9th New York Heavy Artillery, had been rumored among the fallen or captured. Then, even that personal crisis passed as he surfaced just about the time Army of the Potomac veterans extinguished Early's chance to breach the city's defenses in the suburbs. Ironically, the president may have actually had the legacy of Monocacy more strikingly conveyed to him by an incident involving a visit to the 9th "Heavies" camp shortly thereafter. A young soldier from Company D stepped impetuously to the chief executive's carriage and proudly displayed a memento of that battle to his commander in chief. There, in an eagle crossbelt plate lay embedded a rebel bullet. Half spent, it had merely stunned the soldier at Monocacy and now provided a souvenir. Old Abe looked at the little relic and then in his inimitable fashion told the lad: "Young man, keep that for your children and grandchildren, for future generations will prize that as the greatest heirloom you could possibly leave them."[11]

Of the veteran soldiers of the Army of the Potomac, only those who participated with Ricketts probably took special heed of Monocacy. For their comrades, left back at Petersburg, like Edward Schilling of the 4th Maryland, the events of Early's raid blurred together in letters home. Nonetheless, credit for finally thwarting the Confederates before the capital distinctly belonged to their own VI Corps men and nobody else, in their view. Lew Wallace probably placed the battle of Monocacy into the war's larger meaning more quickly than anyone. By August, when he submitted a final, more formal report (supported by a detailed battle map by Charles F. Von Lindenberg), the Hoosier warrior fully understood the battle's meaning. Noting the need to collect Union dead in one burial plot on the field itself, the defeated yet defiant general proposed an epitaph for a monument to preside over that grave. Wallace suggested the words: "These men died to save the National Capital, and they did save it." With that simple dedication (hidden in a dispatch of the time), the battle of Monocacy slipped into the mists of national memory.[12]

The Northern press proved more vociferous in its criticism of Early's invasion as "a distressing and desolating event." Scoring the administration for lack of military preparation, Harper's Weekly, for one, urged that every state "should be virtually under arms until this rebellion is conquered." Frank Leslie's Illustrated Newspaper joined in, sarcastically suggesting that had the rebels "come up out of the ground, or dropped from the clouds," it would have scarcely created "more astonishment, confusion and alarm." The War Department and mere "corps of observation scattered along the upper Potomac" came in for castigation since it was impossible to ascertain whether the enemy numbered 1,500 or "exceeded twice 15,000." Of one thing, the Leslie's editor could proclaim, however, Lew Wallace had rendered "incalculable service to the country." He had delayed the enemy's advance upon Washington "a whole day," and gained "such conclusive information of the enemy's strength and designees," as to give the War Department "explicit warning of the impending danger."[13]

* Ransom and Retribution *

Monocacy and Early's visit was never forgotten by citizens of Frederick and environs. Ironically, the battle's most immediate legacy fell upon them—the famous ransoming of the city, the requisition and thievery, the dislocation of their lives. Prosperous upper Maryland had fallen victim to Jubal Early's vendetta to make the North pay for the heartaches and destruction visited upon his own Virginia countrymen. Since the intent of his invasion had been at least in part that of gathering supplies and booty, vengeance easily slipped into the equation when discipline and rules against plunder sagged badly with each Confederate footstep on Maryland soil. Whatever the motives, part of the story of July 9 and the Monocacy battle was played out in town on the community by soldiers of the Confederacy. Over the next few months and several years, Monocacy and Early's passage became inextricably linked with the overall dislocation of the final summer and autumn of the war whereby guerillas, marauders, McCausland's cavalry, and even Union pursuers crisscrossed the area causing further damage and ill-feeling with the citizenry.

In February 1865, Frederick's mayor and Board of Aldermen called for reimbursement of the ransom paid to Early the previous summer, claiming their right that the Federal government remunerate the local banks. By summer, the frustrated farmers of Middletown valley claimed similar reimbursement for loss of animals, not merely from the rebels, but from U.S. government agents who subsequently appeared and spirited away said animals "without allowing the farmers a single cent for their expenditure of time, trouble and food," according to the *Maryland Union*. And, only later would the Maryland legislature authorize Hagerstown to issue bonds to redeem the bank note drafted at the time of McCausland's visit.[14]

Early abused Maryland "without stint," Middletown burgess William J. Irving claimed, and said he "had come here to give us a taste of what they had suffered [and] as a retaliation for what Hunter had done on his raid." Just who eventually reimbursed whom in this neighborhood remains unclear. The scavaging rebels, however, made up for it among the farms along their route of march to Frederick, obviously. The situation naturally festered until the good years after the war eventually made up the difference.[15]

Perhaps Frederick residents themselves were too relieved at being spared Southern torches in 1864. While individual groups of Confederate cavalrymen apparently walked into Frederick stores, as they had done at Hagerstown and elsewhere, and liberated what they found (leaving worthless Confederate scrip in payment), Frederickans became too preoccupied with survival immediately after the event. "These are awful times," observed local businessman Jacob Engelbrecht in his diary, "one day we are as usual and the next day in the hands of the enemy." Whatever the final outcome of the war, he decided, "come weal or woe—come life or death, we go for the

Union of the States forever,—one and Inseparable." Over time, however, that $200,000 became a festering memory. Edward
Goldsborough, local state's attorney and himself a veteran of the
Monocacy fight, later prepared an affidavit on behalf of the city and
its residents which pointed out: "We believe that the circumstances
under which this money was paid, if not sufficient to establish a legal
claim, certainly do impose upon the government a moral obligation
to repay to Frederick City this money, that was demanded, as we
shall show because of the assistance rendered by the loyal citizens
in the removal and protection from capture, by the Confederate army
under General Early on July 9, 1864, of immense quantities of government stores and supplies that had been brought to Frederick City,
for the use of the Union Army." Further, the plaintiffs wryly noted: "It
is apparent that the Government of the United States received the
benefit of this ransom in the saving of its stores." Frederick, they
said, was the only town in the nation in which United States government property was saved by payment of such a ransom.[16]

Goldsborough went on to iterate the array of Federal facilities in
Frederick that had been protected, in essence, by the ransoming
transaction. These included two quartermaster warehouses having a
capacity of 400,000 and 600,000 pounds respectively, a commissary
store for 500,000 pounds, bakeries capable of producing 10,000 loaves
of bread daily, a forage house with a capacity of 8,000 barrels of corn,
transportation stables for 250 horses, quartermaster stables for an
additional 28 mounts, as well as ambulance stables for 56 more
horses, and miscellaneous corral and stables for 160 horses. He also
noted a General Hospital and field hospitals for 10,000 patients (and
furnished with the finest and best hospital appliances and medical
stores, and workshops such as blacksmith shops, wagon makers
shops, repair shops, paint shops, "and in fact everything needed for
the use of a well equipped army—amounting in value at a fair estimate from $1,000,000 to $1,500,000," in 1902 dollars. So,
Goldsborough had little compunction in claiming that the $200,000
ransom payment shielded or secured "immunity from search and
the protection of property, in which large quantities of valuable and
expensive supplies belonging to the Government were stores, and
that said goods were saved from capture and subsequently upon the
reoccupation of the city by the Union troops, restored to the Government." Not only were these goods "very necessary to the Government
at that time, but their value fare exceeded the amount of the ransom,
to-wit $200,000."[17]

The former soldier and state's attorney suggested that the
$200,000 tribute "has largely increased our municipal taxes, and
has been a drawback to the city's progress and improvement ever

since the war, and will continue to be so." Thirty-eight years of sub-sequent peace had seemingly dulled unstinting sacrifice and loyalty to the Union of the Engelbrecht ilk. Local townsmen sought reimbursement for the ransom-saved Federal property, but only silence attended post-Civil War petitions to Washington. It was never definitively calculated how much interest Frederick actually paid on this debt to local banks—$200,000 to $600,000 has been suggested. The city repaid half of the total principal debt in 1868 through the issuance of bonds, with further reimbursement made through slight reduction of city taxes, which continued through 1896. The final maturity, however, was retired only on September 29, 1951, more than eighty-seven years after Allan's group exacted Jubal Early's money from Frederick at the height of the nearby battle of Monocacy. In ceremonies at City Hall and at Citizens National Bank (where city officials accompanied by the presidents of all the local banks carried the check in an old basket similar to that used in 1864) the liquidation of the old debt was finally consummated. Nevertheless, despite repeated enjoiners from local representatives and senators in Congress, the Federal government to this day has deftly avoided any involvement in the debt settlement. Ironically, the bittersweet joke may have been ultimately on Early's soldiers. Buckner McGill Randolph of Company C, 49th Virginia, ruefully wrote in his diary on July 9: "Got nothing in Frederick. All appropriated by Staff off. & QM "& A.C.S."[18]

* Monocacy, Early, and Upper Maryland *

In the end then, the battle's direct legacy affected the people of upper Maryland less than Early's general transit of their region. Several years would pass before commerce actually returned to prewar levels around Hagerstown, local historian S. Roger Keller has suggested. He recounts how that part of the state west of South Mountain remained in ferment all summer and into the autumn, beleaguered by random groups from both armies and always by irregulars of some stripe. McCausland's Chambersburg raid at the end of the month was only the most infamous occurrence because its impact extended west to Hancock and Cumberland. Sharpsburg, Keedysville, and the neighborhood of St. James College experienced almost constant pilfering and other travesties to civilians.[19]

Establishment of a large horse corral at Hagerstown to resupply mounts for the Union Army of the Shenandoah signaled the autumn's activity south of the Potomac. Ultimately, refugees from the Shenandoah Valley would report the Union army's widespread

destruction of civilian farm property as proof that the national government had turned from conciliatory to harsh war practices to bring
the rebellion to conclusion. Ranger John Mosby raided north of the
Potomac in retaliation, and the Federals maintained river surveil-
lance via Signal Corps stations and military patrols up and down the
Potomac. But, Monocacy had all but been forgotten.

Restoring the Thomas, Worthington, Gambrill and other properties, mending shattered fences, and suffering somewhat the loss of
cropland for the rest of the season seem to have been the most direct
impact that Monocacy had on the battlefield neighborhood itself. The
fighting ended too quickly for anything more. True, railroad facilities
at the junction were burned, as was the wooden bridge on the Washington or Georgetown pike. But, the Baltimore and Ohio Railroad
quickly resumed east-west operations, at least to Harpers Ferry, and
the junction became a staging area for continued combat against
Jubal Early in the Valley. Thomas Claggett's "Acadia" and George
Markell's home across the Buckeystown pike north of the Monocacy
were cleansed of the marks of the wounded and dying (although
Araby's porch pillars still showed signs of the struggle thirty years
later when Vermonter George E. Davis and comrades visited the battle
site). Beyond that, most Marylanders in Frederick County simply
blended the memories of the little battle with general passage of the
rebels through their neighborhood.

Still, many people complained. The good people of Frederick,
wrote local tailor and shopkeeper Jacob Engelbrecht in his diary on
July 14, had been without communication with the outside world for
a week. No newspapers had been received since July 7, the first arriving finally on the sixteenth. Even local Frederick newspapers mostly
prattled on merely about what seemed to be the customary summer
rebel visitation. Locals spent much time trying to calculate and re-
fute claims of casualties by both participants with the Frederick *Examiner* excoriating its pro-Confederate competitor, the *Republican
Citizen*, for spreading "a Rebel lie" that Lew Wallace and Erastus Tyler
"were repulsed and routed," suffering 2,000 casualties to scarcely a
quarter of that number on the Southern side. The *Examiner* claimed
to have tallied 551 Confederate wounded in local hospitals, while
"droves were seen by gentlemen on the battlefield with their arms,
hands, and heads tied up, making their way as rapidly as possible
towards the Potomac." A large number of dead buried on the field,
and prisoners "we saw arrive at Baltimore" fleshed out the portrayal.
In fact, chided the Unionist editor, his rival's staff should visit the
hospital "where they can procure a tolerable correct idea of the loss
sustained by their friends, the thieving Rebel army" (the term "thieving" constantly used by the loyal press). Still, as late as July 27, at

least fifty seriously wounded Confederates remained in care of ministering Frederick citizens (Southern sympathizer, Fannie Ebert, told her aunt, May Baughman, sister of the *Citizen's* embattled editor, John Baughman.[20]

Engelbrecht substantiated the number of wounded in his diary, but generally, the rest of the story was palpable Yankee propaganda kept up for at least another month by papers all over the region. More important than the battle and its human toll, it seemed, were statistics of property loss attributable to the raid, no doubt intended to "increase their stock of horses, cattle, money, and provisions" (since they stole all such supplies as they could get their hands on), noted Engelbrecht. He calculated Frederick County's loss at $2,000,000 or $3,000,000. The Middletown *Valley Register* thought it was more like about $1,000,000 for the whole area west to Hagerstown, Boonsboro, and Sharpsburg. Businessman Thomas Gorsuch wrote to his brother Robert in neighboring Carroll County that while the city had escaped destruction by paying ransom, "the community surrounding it [was] pretty well stripped of everything; stock, money, clothing, and everything [the rebels] could use or get away."[21]

At least one other Frederick County resident was even more graphic. Elihu Rockwell wrote Mrs. E. R. Coleman in Canandaigua, New York, deploring the acts of people "raised among us." He cited Bradley T. Johnson and James Smith, son of a local minister, in particular. They had enjoyed the "immunities" of citizens but now stood as traitors. These "Southern chivalry" had caused Rockwell and his Unionist brethren to "hide papers and other valuables in some nook or corner or secret place," and while fighting at the edge of town, "they murdered the wounded and helpless as they lay weltering in their blood." "Pirates," "bandetti" were terms Rockwell applied to the invaders "bearing devastation, destruction, and death in their pathway." Personally, he admitted that he and his family (although badly shaken and already in poor health) had not suffered as much as they had feared, remaining undisturbed in their own house largely by paying the contribution "levied upon us by the 'freebooters,' a sum of about $541.00." Urged by his family to leave Frederick, Rockwell sighed, "Where can I go to be certain that the evil may not be there too?" pointing out that even in upstate New York, Copperheads and raids from Canada constituted a danger.[22]

Citizens and the newspaper editors both echoed one theme. Early's raid plus the continuing drought made for a bad year in upper Maryland. The appearance of Major General David Hunter's army back in the area permitted hard-bitten Unionists to make good on their threats of retaliation against secessionist neighbors. As Rockwell had declared: "And yet, we have among us persons who still continue to justify all this and by all the means that they dare use, continue to aid and abet the rebellion." The Frederick *Examiner* enjoined citizens to petition military authority for recompense and relief. This would be assessed against property "of all known disloyalists" in their neighborhoods for the total amount of damages sustained in the raid. Indeed, this was precisely what Lew Wallace did once he returned to full charge of his Middle Department on July 14.

All across upper Maryland, Unionists were encouraged to single out collaborators so that enforcers such as Major Jonathan I. Yellott of the 1st Maryland Potomac Home Brigade could carry out Hunter's directive to arrest pro-secessionists like Frederick *Republican Citizen* editor John Baughman and his wife. For a time, soldiers occupied the newspaper's premises. Lawson Norris and family (also associated with that newspaper), Frank Heuser (telegraph operator at Monocacy Junction), John Reich and son (who lived about a mile and one-half east of town and had been charged with firing on Union soldiers during the battle), Harriet Pettit Floyd, and the Ebert family all numbered among those taken into custody (although released shortly thereafter). A number of ladies reputedly left Frederick for parts unknown with the advent of Hunter's dragnet, reported the *Valley Register*. Floyd and her two sisters hurried off to Baltimore and took the first train on the Northern Central Railroad to Bellefonte in the Pennsylvania mountains.[23]

On August 1, according to Engelbrecht, Hunter's presence occasioned more arrests by the local provost guard, comprising the 161st Ohio Infantry, Ohio National Guard. Taking the names from the *Examiner*, he enumerated twenty-two more citizens and their families due to be sent south. Heuser and Norris gained their release by mid-month, either by taking the oath of allegiance to the Union or proving their innocence. The rebels, proclaimed the *Valley Register*, had refused them entry to their lines, giving them a rough time in return. Nevertheless, the heavy-handed tactics of Union authorities and a wave of terror swept across upper Maryland in the wake of Monocacy and Early's appearance.[24]

That summer was "one of fear, dread, and discouragement to all lovers of the South," penned Harriet Petitt Floyd in her memoirs. Frederick was under martial law and "crowded with Goths and Vandals of Hunter's army." Exile and confiscation of property awaited citizens "not for anything they had *done*," but only because of their sympathies, she said. Enforcement of the Union oath of allegiance became as onerous in parts of the Free State as it was in occupied Tennessee and Kentucky. Feelings ran so strongly in the newspapers that it is as difficult now as then, perhaps, to separate fact from fiction. Baughman and Norris protested that there was no truth in the *Examiner*'s claim that Confederates stole watches, hats, money, combs, and other personal property directly off citizens during their visit. *Examiner* editors countered by naming the victims of "the low rascality," including tobacconist Henry Miller, Harrison Connely, Nicholas Hauser, Jacob Leilieb of Frederick and William Baker and Alex McKinistry of Buckeystown. They also suggested that their competitors should visit "the widows' home any where in the mountains to the west where they would find that their rebel friends had robbed these women of their horse, cow, clothing, flour and even their last dollar."[25]

The *Examiner* also discussed the heavy damage to the Chesapeake and Ohio Canal—"the special object of their fury and wantonness." Incalculable damage to locks and culverts, as well as destruction of over one hundred canal boats meant that trade "will be diminished at least one-fourth, for years to come." This meant inconvenience to "hundreds of loyal citizens who gain their livelihood solely by means of boating." Fortunately, said the paper, damage had been less severe to John Garrett's iron railroad bridge, which it took great pains to point out had only been "recently constructed" in place "of the one destroyed in the first raid about two years ago." Even in picturesque Middletown Valley, the recounting of destruction was designed to inflame the senses of all loyal men, causing them to rally for self-defense, it was hoped. And, the *Valley Register* specifically mentioned storeowners Culler and Levy, Wright and Hyatt, Rudy, Wingler, Herring and Crouse as well as Adam Miller, Frederick Stone, and Samuel Ahalt, as singled out by the rebels for theft of money and watches.[26]

The *Examiner* was sure of one thing. A local defense force (raised from victimized citizens regardless of political persuasion) was needed to counter such raids in the future. So much for confidence in the regular soldiers, and indeed, all summer those raids seemed threatening to upper Marylanders. "Scares," and "Stampedes" pervaded the hot, drought-stricken months, despite the constant passage of Union troops and their stop-overs beside the sylvan Monocacy to catch their breath and refresh bodies and spirits. In late July, McCausland's audacious foray that burned Chambersburg, Pennsylvania again illustrated the region's vulnerability. Then, even the Union's top general had settled on his own solution to the Early problem. Determined that his inept subordinates on the upper Potomac were not the answer, Grant chose Major General Philip H. Sheridan, one of his bright young stars from the western theater, to take charge. Old Jube's threat to Washington and the region was over. Little Phil's campaign to eliminate the Confederates in the Shenandoah was about to begin.[27]

Ironically, where it had taken months to brew, the whole issue was resolved by several hours' conference on the very ground where Early and Wallace had dueled on July 9. Journeying to Monocacy Junction on August 6, Grant discovered upwards of 16,000 Federals lounging along the banks of the river. Summoning David Hunter to Keefer Thomas's battle-scarred "Araby" house for a senior conference, they met in a second floor room over the library. Hunter admitted to having "lost" track of Early and his army as he tried to build a strike force from the VI and XIX Corps as well as his own Army of West Virginia. A displeased Grant explained how Sheridan would take command of the field force while Hunter could remain titular head of the department, if he desired. But, he was out of operational command. Grant also explained that he wanted the rebel logistical base destroyed—not houses and buildings, mind you, but anything else of value to the enemy. Inform the people, dictated Grant, "that so long as an Army can subsist among them, recurrences of these raids must be expected, and we are determined to stop them at all hazards." This was certainly appealing to "Black Dave" Hunter, but being shelved for Sheridan was not. He requested relief from his position, Grant happily concurred and immediately sent for Sheridan.[28]

Grant remained overnight at the junction in order to meet the new field general the next day. The clatter of trains and locomotive whistles announced the forward movement of the new "Army of the Shenandoah." A cordial breakfast with the Thomas family the next morning brought out light-hearted banter as five- or six-year-old Virginia Thomas told the amused general that her mother was decidedly pro-Southern, but that her father was "a Rebel when the Rebels are here and a Yankee when the Yankees are here." Her father squirmed uncomfortably, but Grant merely laughed and then rode back to the railroad station to await Sheridan. Their meeting was brief—a salute, a handshake, and a simple verbal passing of confidence and direction. Sheridan boarded a westbound train for his appointment with destiny in the Valley. Grant returned eastward en route back to City Point, Virginia. One young Union signal man at Harpers Ferry, David Seibert, wrote his father that day: "We expect some hard work is on hand and I expect something will be done now." When Sheridan and Grant parted ways that hot August day on the banks of the Monocacy, the undeviating path had begun toward a meeting with Lee at the McLean house in Appomattox the next April.[29]

As of August 1864, however, it was not yet over. As men from the 161st Ohio posted the town of Frederick, one of their lieutenants drowned while bathing in the Monocacy. A drunken private, Alonzo Earl, murdered a local North Market Street butcher in an altercation.

Jacob Engelbrecht kept track of "war prices" in his diary as coffee at sixty cents a pound, brown sugar at twenty-five cents per pound, salt at forty cents a peck, and ham at thirty cents a pound told house-wives that wartime inflation still prevailed. He also described the public hanging on July 21 of Granville Smeltzer for murdering Mary Nussbaum and her son the previous January. Out in the country people worried about Sheridan and Early.

The *Valley Register* told its readers as late as September 9 that Early appeared ready to once more carry the war across the Potomac. He had even issued an order according to deserters and prisoners, said the paper, that once across the river, his men were "to destroy every hay and wheat stalk, and such other property found in the line of march." Still, "he has failed to cross the river as yet and our farmers will not take the precaution to 'bag' their crops." Indeed, Early did not cross, the farmers gathered their crops unmolested before going to the polls later in the autumn. Sherman's victories in Georgia, and Sheridan's in the Shenandoah aided the Union cause more singularly than anything else on the battlefield. The Democratic party's trea-sonous platform, the soldier vote, and Unionists' determination to finish the war, however, all turned the tide. Lincoln and his adminis-tration survived by the narrowest of margins even in border state Maryland. Where the Old Line state had rejected the president in 1860, it now voted his reelection by 40,153 to 32,730. Soon the snows of winter covered the scars from that strife-torn period. Along the Monocacy, they particularly blanketed the scene where, in mid-sum-mer, blue and gray had battled each other so desperately for the road to the White House in Washington.[30]

* Maryland's Season of Bitterness *

Upper Maryland as a whole passed through a summer of bitter-ness in the wake of Early's raid. Millions of dollars in property lost ($80,000 alone, for example, in the Hagerstown section), lives dis-rupted, additional property damaged, political intimidation and bit-ter hatreds had been aroused once more. Turmoil from July to the middle of August in the western part of the state led to a petition addressed to the Union secretary of war and the provost marshal of the state asking for a postponement of military conscription in the district. Business upheaval and refugeeism due to Early's raid made it impossible to properly carry out this national policy, and the ex-emption was granted. Writing in 1868, Lew Wallace's friend, histo-rian Benson J. Lossing, estimated that railroad, telegraph, and canal damages due to Early's rampage had amounted to an estimated

$600,000. The Baltimore and Ohio Railroad had sustained $400,000 of damage; damages to private fencing and barns contributed another $250,000. Unabashedly, Lossing declared that "the invasion cost Maryland, according to the report of the committee of the state legislature, $2,030,000." Little wonder that ill feelings pervaded Maryland during the final summer of the war and would continue into the period of national reconstruction.[31]

The pain and anguish went beyond economic matters, however. Once the panic attending Early's passage had subsided, recrimination and hostility set in among Unionists against their Southern-sympathizing neighbors. From Baltimore and Annapolis, west to the Maryland panhandle at Cumberland, not only were military authorities anxious to clamp a lid of intimidation upon the populace, but members of the citizenry themselves clamored for revenge and restitution. It was not merely a matter of increased militia calls by Governor August Bradford to bolster the thin border guard protecting Maryland. It was more too than Major Generals David Hunter and Lew Wallace and their henchmen in provost offices suppressing dissidence, arresting known collaborators, and exiling or imprisoning would-be friends of the men in gray. Rather, newspapers across the state, together with legislators at the state house vociferously demanded punishment for Marylanders who had paved the way for rebel invasion and singled out their Unionist neighbors for rebel depredations. The Baltimore *American and Commercial Advertiser*, Baltimore *Clipper, Baltimore County Advocate*, Cumberland *Civilian and Telegraph*, and the Frederick *Examiner* all stirred the flames of hatred against those they termed traitors in their midst. The standard recommendation was that Unionists should be reimbursed for losses from the "pockets of Secessionists."[32]

A Maryland constitutional convention, whose meetings in Annapolis had been temporarily interrupted by the presence of Early's legions, passed a resolution calling for assessments against Confederate sympathizers and collaborators. Cries of inexpediency and military arbitrariness mixed with immediate lust for vengeance. As opposition leader Ezekiel F. Chambers perceptively noted, however, provisions allowing military department commanders in the state to assess known sympathizers for the damage sustained by loyal citizens during Early's raid violated the fundamental principles of government already set forth by the convention. Just what were they doing? he asked, for despite claiming to be a civil power, the body was proposing "to confer upon the military power a jurisdiction and exercise of a power which we do not ourselves possess." The convention eventually passed the assessment resolution, strengthened by further refinements to excoriate anyone who refused to sign a loyalty oath or persisted in openly supporting the Confederate cause by banishment or imprisonment.[33]

Still, the Unionist wrath fell heaviest on upper Maryland—the traditional invasion and burnt-over rural part closest to border fighting on the upper Potomac. Here Hunter took direct action, even without civil sanction from Annapolis. When Major Jonathan I. Yellott, Frederick provost marshal, asked for guidance on July 18, Black Dave shot back that immediate arrest of all persons and families known to have aided Early's invaders was the policy. The men would go to a military prison at Wheeling, West Virginia; their families would be sent beyond Federal lines. Their houses would be seized and used for offices, hospitals, or warehouses, while their furniture would be auctioned off to benefit Unionist citizens who had suffered losses from the raiders. In Cumberland, Hunter also singled out sympathizers with sons in Confederate service or who had aided the South. Yellott tempered the instructions to allow first for all males to appear and take the oath, although, as we have seen, he did enforce deportation of two newspaper editors of the *Republican Citizen* who had published a disloyal article. When Hunter tried to apply his Special Orders 141 in which he ordered the arrest and expulsion of sympathizers in Frederick on August 1, he ran afoul of even President Abraham Lincoln's weariness of the tactics of this controversial general. The president ordered Secretary of War Stanton to suspend the order.[34]

Lincoln's action, in turn, prompted renewed criticism from Unionist newspapers which strongly supported the general's attempt to put out the "fire in his rear." Sporadic intimidation by local officials like Yellott continued even after Hunter had been relieved of responsibilities by Grant and replaced by Sheridan. As late as December, twenty-four Liberty area residents were assessed $7,000.05 for damages done to a Unionist. Nothing ever came of the affair, however. Tempers had now cooled and intervention of John W. Garrett, president of the Baltimore and Ohio Railroad and friend of James Pearre (one of those assessed), went to Stanton who quashed the whole matter. In the end, actual retaliation by Maryland Unionists against their Secessionist brethren proved limited. National officials reined in overly zealous military commanders. Political rhetoric aside, bitterness may have pervaded the border state, but apparently not widespread reprisals.[35]

Monocacy contributed to an anxious summer and fall for the embattled Lincoln administration. Buffeted by criticism of prolongation of the war, national economic bankruptcy because of the continuing struggle, extension of abolition of slavery to the border states like Maryland, and the heavy presence of martial law and military oppression, that administration nevertheless survived, largely due to Union battlefield victories in Georgia and the Shenandoah Valley long after Monocacy had been forgotten. By September Maryland

citizens voted narrowly (30,274 to 29,699) to adopt a new state constitution that abolished slavery. Over eleven hundred Frederickans
approved by a margin of two to one; those in the county similarly
disposed. Later, memories of the disastrous summer helped Marylanders return Lincoln to the White House and prosecute the war to
the finish. In Federick City, the president won by a margin of 452
votes, out in the county, his margin stood at 1,256. Remembrance of
Early's invasion, the nasty clash at Monocacy, Washington's successful defense but escape of the raiders back to Virginia, and
McCausland's final incursion into the state's western panhandle, all
contributed to citizens' desire to put an end to further bloodshed and
damage to their lives and region.[36]

* The Return of Peace *

"How changed is everything around us from what it was in July
1864," Elihu Rockwell wrote to Mrs. E. R. Coleman on July 10, 1866.
Two years before, he claimed, citizens had had "to steal away" from
their homes in the "dead and silent hour of night and bury in the
earth our treasure, not knowing but the next hour may lay our home
in ashes." Armed men, "with murder in their hearts," rushed to and
fro through the streets of Frederick "in pursuit of whom they might
destroy." That awful time has passed, he trusted, but there were still
among the populace (even in New York state, he supposed) those
"who would not hesitate to involve us in all the horrors of the past
years, if they might obtain office." He singled out the new president,
Andrew Johnson, and new Maryland governor (and former Confederate), Thomas Swann. "My heart sickens at the thought that so few
men can be trusted," he sighed. Indeed, Maryland's wounds were
deep and slow to heal. In the aftermath of the bloody war, as authors
Robert I. Cottom, Jr. and Mary Ellen Hayward have observed: "Massachusetts would reconcile with South Carolina before Marylanders
would forgive one another."[37]

Such feelings made it virtually impossible for Maryland Confederates to return immediately to their native soil. Tempers were
high at that moment due to fellow Marylander John Wilkes Booth's
assassination of Abraham Lincoln. Ironically, Monocacy veterans
Lew Wallace and Lieutenant Colonel David R. Clendenin of the 8th
Illinois Cavalry would serve on the commission that tried the Lincoln conspirators. Clendenin would remain in the regular army,
serve in the West, and rise to command of the 2d United States
Cavalry before retirement in 1891. Wallace went on to become ter-
ritorial governor of New Mexico and minister to Turkey. A prolific

writer and lecturer, he became better known as author of *Ben Hur* than as a Civil War Horatius at Monocacy bridge.[38]

In the climate of hate after Lincoln's death, Edward Y. Goldsborough and eighteen other Frederick County Unionists petitioned President Johnson on April 24, to prevent Maryland Confederates from returning home. The supposed transgressions of these traitors were varied. They had voluntarily abandoned their state and borne arms against it for four years, claimed Goldsborough's group. The Maryland rebels had invaded their own state three times and "have crimsoned its soil with the life blood of thousands of our friends and brothers." They had stolen livestock, wasted fields and crops, burned dwellings and barns, "and reduced hundreds of our loyal people to poverty and want." Moreover, these outcasts "have burdened us and our children with an almost crushing public debt," said the Unionist petitioners, "thereby perpetuating the memory of their treason." Lastly, said Goldsborough and friends, their crimes culminated in "parricide, the horrible murder of the second Father of his Country, the great, the good, the generous hearted and lamented Abraham Lincoln."[39]

For such reasons, these Frederick Unionists could not tolerate "unrepentant traitors in our midst," and suggested banning them to avoid public disorder, breaches of the peace, and worse. That same day, the Baltimore city council also protested, and the state attorney general, James Speed, at the request of the War Department, delivered an opinion that parole terms as agreed upon at Appomattox would not apply north of the limits of the former Confederacy. Returning soldiers would not be guaranteed freedom from molestation. Therefore, Wallace, still commanding the Middle Department, promptly arrested and imprisoned paroled Confederate Maryland soldiers and further declared that disloyal citizens would be also subject to such treatment. Like other border states, only the passage of time would soften the hatred engendered by the late unpleasantness. Frederick County remained so prejudiced that its own native son, Bradley Johnson, found it more attrative to set up law practice in Richmond, where he served four years in the Virginia state senate. He returned to Maryland by 1879, but resided in Baltimore, not Frederick.[40]

For Monocacy Union veteran doctor David Ferguson McKinney, the ties to his battlefield experience were enough to cause him to settle quite near the scene. Raised in Pennsylvania and educated at Washington and Jefferson College and the Pennsylvania Medical College, McKinney had also witnessed the prewar bloodshed in Kansas. His acquaintance with Frederick County as a result of the battle at Monocacy led to his return and settlement there at the end of the war. He purchased Arcadia and three hundred and ten acres of prime agricultural limestone land from Robert McGill in August. Having tended to the wounded in the yard of this 1780 house of Arthur Schaef, McKinney made it his postwar home.[41]

McKinney's neighbors generally sought to recover damages resulting from the war's touch. In many cases, the Federal government may not have responded as they desired. Farmer John T. Worthington sent a claim to the United States Army Quartermaster Department for damages suffered at the hands of Hunter's men in September 1864. These soldiers had camped near his sixty-acre corn field, had marched through that field, and "fed a portion of the corn to their horses," while trampling down and destroying so much that it was "impossible to determine how much was actually fed," said the claimant. Thirty bushels of oats had been taken for the army's horses, while sixty panels of post-and-rail fencing (six rails high) had been likewise appropriated and promptly used for firewood by the voracious Yankee soldiers. Major General George Crook had headquartered in Worthington's house, swore its owner, and his neighbors, C. Keefer Thomas and J. H. Gambrill, attested to the validity of the claim, as did Worthington's summer helper, Thomas Palm, who remembered the incidents very well. Worthington's prominence on the Confederate side of the battle line during the Monocacy fighting may well have led to this travesty, although no specific mention was made of that fact.[42]

Elsewhere, James H. Gambrill apparently recovered nicely during Reconstruction. He may have lost his little mill house to natural causes at the end of the war for he apparently lived with his family in Baltimore for a year. Still, he retained the valuable Araby Mills and one hundred ten acres of land valued at $18,000 with the mill containing $5,000 worth of "wheat, corn, flour, and contents." All together, counting livestock, furniture, silver plate, gold and silver watches, and a residence, Gambrill held taxable property worth $24,000 in the postwar years. By the mid-1870s, he was able to build an elaborate mansard-roofed dwelling called "Boscobel" in the best French Second Empire style of the times. Perhaps Gambrill sought to compete with Thomas's restored Araby, or Worthington's Riverside Farm as symbols of postwar comfort and prosperity on the former battlefield. Even the Baltimore and Ohio rebuilt Monocacy Junction facilities and a sturdier railroad bridge in the early 1870s to handle the heavier equipment now traveling that line. Contemporary photographs as well as postwar sketches of combat artist James Taylor captured those structures for posterity. Naturally, too, the Washington turnpike boasted a new covered bridge to replace the structure burned by Wallace's men during the battle.[43]

EIGHT

Preservation and Monuments

For Americans so inclined to revisit the war, Monocacy began to enter the history books in the immediate postwar period. Virginian Edward A. Pollard discussed the "battle of Monocacy Bridge" as well as Early's invasion in his 1867 apologia, *The Lost Cause*. Yet, his half-page coverage was strewn with errors (miscasting Clement Evans for John B. Gordon as leading the decisive attack, and decided that Wallace's army "broke in shameful confusion, leaving the railroad and national pike, and retreating in the direction of Gettysburg." He also contended that Union losses amounted to more than a thousand killed and wounded, with another seven hundred as prisoners. Benson Lossing did far better in his popularized three-volume *Pictorial History of the Civil War*, having the careful coaching of his friend Lew Wallace as well as the general's wife. Still, he concluded: "But for that check of full thirty hours (for Early was so smitten that he could not move until noon the next day), the Capital would doubtless have been his prize, and a heap of black ruins its possible fate. In view of all the circumstances, the battle of the Monocacy appears as one of the most important and brilliant of the war."[1]

* Remembrance *

Such certainty appealed to General John B. Gordon, by now an aspiring political figure and ardent home rule exponent back in Georgia. Writing to Robert E. Lee on February 6, 1868, he declared that the battle of Monocacy "was one of the severest ever fought by my troops." He claimed one-third of his command had fallen dead or wounded, and, except for McCausland's cavalry "which had been driven off and did not again come into the fight," he had had no assistance from the rest of Early's army. He did admit to the long-range artillery fire from across the river and the fact that Robert Rodes' division "crossed the stream after the general retreat of the enemy began." The old soldiers were now beginning to justify their wartime deeds; Monocacy was no exception although relatively few of the participating generals wrote about it.[2]

By this point, the irascible Jubal Early had also taken pen in hand to rejoin the fight for self-vindication if nothing more. Explaining Monocacy in his memoirs, Old Jube was straight forward. His greater concern lay with rebutting critics about delays in the lower Shenandoah Valley during the approach march to Washington. He claimed: "Not one moment was spent in idleness, but that everyone was employed in making some arrangement, or removing some difficulty in my way, which it was necessary to make or remove so as to enable me to advance with a prospect of success." Similarly, he contended: "Some of the northern papers stated that, between Saturday and Monday, I could have entered [Washington]; but on Saturday I was fighting at Monocacy, thirty-five miles from Washington, a force which I could not leave in my rear; and, after disposing of that force and moving as rapidly as it was possible for me to move, I did not arrive in front of the fortifications until afternoon on Monday, and then my troops were exhausted, and it required time to bring them up into line."[3]

Early argued that he had just completed a march all the way from Lynchburg, which, "for its length and rapidity I believe, without a parallel in this and any other modern war," William T. Sherman's "marauding excursion not excepted." No, Jube would never admit that either his explicable, yet questionable delays in the lower Shenandoah or the day's loss of time eliminating Wallace at the Monocacy had undermined his ability to move quickly to Washington. Perhaps only Early knew what sort of timetable that he and Lee had developed for the operation. If not in 1864, then surely three years later, Early should have understood time's impact upon the late campaign. Even ten years after the battle, when he wrote the editor of the Baltimore *Gazette*, Old Jube still would not recognize the pivotal role of Monocacy. All that he would admit then was that "General Lee did not expect that I would be able to capture Washington with my small force; his orders were simply to threaten that city, and my only chances of capturing it depended upon its being found without any garrison." His chief, Early decided, undoubtedly "would have been gratified if I could have taken Washington, but when I suggested to him I would take it if I could, he remarked that it would hardly be possible to do so." By this time in his life, Early was fast

**Frederick or Monocacy Junction, circa 1873
Looking toward Washington Highway**

Courtesy Baltimore and Ohio Railroad Museum, Baltimore, Maryland

Postwar Railroad Bridge Crossing Monocacy, circa 1873

Lew Wallace's headquarters on right; site of capture of Union troops in left center distance. Photograph taken from Washington highway. Monocacy junction to left not in photograph.

Courtesy Baltimore and Ohio Railroad Museum,
Baltimore, Maryland

**14th New Jersey Monument,
Erected 1907**

*Photograph by David Roth,
Blue and Gray Magazine*

**Confederate Monument,
Mt. Olivet Cemetery,
Frederick, Maryland,
Dedicated 1881**

*Marken and Bielfeld
Souvenir of Historic Frederick
(1925), p. 31.*

**Modern View of Gambrill's Mill, Present Visitors' Center,
Monocacy National Battlefield, Photograph 1994**

Courtesy David Roth, <u>Blue and Gray Magazine</u>

**Modern View of Unrestored Worthington House,
Monocacy National Battlefield**

*Photograph by David Roth in 1994
Courtesy <u>Blue and Gray Magazine</u>*

joining other Confederate leaders who would spend the rest of their time rationalizing their own failed actions and other myths of the Lost Cause.[4]

As for the aging enlisted men who had suffered the thirsty and dusty race for Washington, many of them had long since lost their admiration for Jubal Early. They too, however, looked past Monocacy as the cause of their woes. Georgian I. G. Bradwell called it simply "this unimportant engagement" where his veteran brigade that had displayed splendid courage in all the great battles of the war was "decimated" by Lew Wallace's men. He debunked the whole notion that the battle had saved Washington since only a part of Early's army had been engaged, and losses had been mainly in Evans' brigade. Most of the survivors by then had had time to ponder the essential question posed by one of Carpenter's artillerymen. C. A. Fonerden soothingly observed, "It has been wondered why General Early at that time did not undertake the capture of Washington," but ducked rendering an answer. He merely declared that "our march then was continued to within sight of Washington where we went into camp and enjoyed our captured provender in a most comforting respite from active duty for a short period." Cavalryman John N. Opie who was less charitable, however, stated: "The fact is, that a volley, a Rebel yell, and a vigorous charge, would have given us Washington." Having taken the city, they could have simply marched across the bridges to Alexandria and back to Virginia. But, said Opie, like so many Confederate generals, Early had "sowed the seed but failed to reap the harvest." While his undisciplined army did little in the suburbs but commit depredations, this Virginian thought it best that they had not captured the city. Temptation to plunder would have reduced the place to a scene of ruin. Still, "Early lost the golden opportunity afforded him of immortalizing himself by capturing the capital of the nation." To Opie, Early himself "was about the only man in the army who believed it impossible of accomplishment."[5]

To Brigadier General Armistead Long, Early's artillery chief, there had been a false note all along. Writing in 1886, he declared that the campaign was remarkable "for having accomplished more in proportion to the force employed, and for having given less public satisfaction, than any other campaign of the war." This he attributed "to the erroneous opinion that the city of Washington should have been taken," a thought that "may be passed over as one of absurdities of public criticism on the war." Of course, there were other commentators, veterans who survived the subsequent humiliations of the autumn campaign in the Valley and the disasters at Opequon, Fishers Hill and Cedar Creek. Alexander Hunter of the 17th Virginia was one whose venomous criticism of Old Jube derived more from the events than the missed opportunities of the early summer.[6]

When Hunter decided in 1905 that the last chance the South had possessed of winning her independence "was deliberately thrown away by General Jubal Early," he was surely alluding to Cedar Creek and the events of October. Yet, he echoed Gordon's contention that the downward spiral had begun earlier in the heat and dust of the forced march after Monocacy. Hunter believed that from that day "the grim veterans fought well, but never with dash, and firm determination to do or die, the spirit which had heretofore made them victorious on many a bloody field." Certainly that elan had been evident that afternoon on the banks of the Monocacy when Gordon's people had smashed Ricketts! Hunter, however, quoted Gordon as stating that "the rank and file of the army were bitterly resentful that they were not permitted to enter [Washington]; they never forgave Early." The implication was that Old Jube had simply squandered Stonewall Jackson's fine old fighting corps. Monocacy was part of that process.

The victorious Union obviously spent less time rationalizing past mistakes or carping upon miscues. George Pond, associate editor of the *Army and Navy Journal*, penned the pivotal study of the Shenandoah Valley campaign of 1864 for Charles Scribner's Campaigns of the Civil War series in 1883 and stated about Monocacy: "Hours counted in the rescue of the national capital; and apart from the delay caused to the invading army, Wallace's merit is that he went to the right place at the right time, and did the best he could with such force as he had, not seeking to postpone the task of planting an obstacle in the enemy's path." Indeed, even the dying Ulysses S. Grant admitted in 1885 that "there is no telling how much" Early's failure before Washington "was contributed to by General Lew Wallace's leading what might well be considered almost a forlorn hope." If the Confederate host had been but one day earlier, said the old warrior, they might have entered the capital before the arrival of reinforcements which he had sent from Petersburg. Whether the delay caused by Monocacy amounted to a day or not, he concluded, Wallace contributed on this occasion, "by the defeat of the troops under him a greater benefit to the cause than often falls to the lot of a commander of an equal force to render by means of a victory." Surely Wallace and his army could not have hoped for a more singularly salutary comment on the matter.[7]

* Commemoration *

Perhaps the earliest soldier remembrance could be found simply in the word "Monocacy" emblazoned upon national banners such as that of the 9th New York Heavy Artillery (now preserved in the William Henry Seward house museum in Auburn, New York). Then too, an anonymous poem surfaced shortly after the close of the war, written by "Juvenis" and published in a Fredericksburg, Virginia newspaper. The author was obviously a Georgian, and his poem was more notable for pathos and maudlin spirit about death than the graphic details of the battle. So, remembrance awaited the postwar rise of the veterans' movement, the aging nostalgia of the veterans themselves, and North and South's desire to perpetuate the meaning of their sacrifices.[8]

Growth of the Grand Army of the Republic, a Union veterans organization, proved steady after its founding in Pittsburgh, Pennsylvania in September 1866. Despite Maryland's divisions, and postwar political climate that rejected ratification of the Fifteenth Amendment granting former slaves the right to vote, no less than thirteen GAR posts could be found in the state by 1878. In 1871, Confederate veterans organized the Society of the Army and Navy of the Confederate States in Maryland and sought to return the remains of Maryland Confederates from scattered battlefields. Organizations of the Maryland Line (Confederate) in 1880 further enhanced the picture of steadily more influential veterans groups interested in ensuring the care of ill or destitute companions or widows, and perpetuation of memories of their heroic deeds. By the twenty-fifth anniversary of the war, veterans on both sides were more than ready to recapture their youthful battlefield experiences through reunions and commemorations. From group publications such as *The National Tribune* (with soldier reminiscences) to actual visitation of their earlier fields of strife, veterans took renewed interest in even small battles like Monocacy.[9]

The sensitivity of the war in places like Frederick and upper Maryland may have dampened some of the early Confederate ardor. Yet, Frederick Unionists organized the Reynolds Post Number 2 of the GAR to honor Memorial Day. Removal of the dead from the fields and along the streams out on the Worthington and Thomas farms resulted in Union dead being sent to Antietam National Cemetery at Sharpsburg, while the Confederate fallen initially remained in burial trenches and isolated plots on the ground. Then, their remains, too, were taken up and placed in the Mt. Olivet Cemetery on the southern edge of Frederick (past which they had marched to their deaths in 1864). They were "buried in a mound at the end of the line." For years, their only marker was a Southern cross of pansies on Decoration Day, and then a simple marker labeled "Unknown." Finally, the Ladies Monumental Association and Confederate Memorial Society in Frederick raised $1,500, and a monument to the "Unknown Dead" rose over the gravesite. Brigadier General Bradley Johnson returned to preside over the June 2, 1881, unveiling. It poured rain, however, and exercises had to be held in the Opera House. Still, four hundred and eight Confederates had received their due at last.[10]

A meeting of Union participants in the battle on Inauguration Day, March 4, 1889, in Washington, decided to celebrate the anniversary of Monocacy, and at that celebration to organize a national association. Early in the summer, the Monocacy Monument Association was organized at Knapp's Hall, Baltimore, with Frederick W. Wild of Alexander's Baltimore Battery (the unit historian) as president. The organization planned to recognize the importance of the battle, and to erect a commemorative monument on the field. An executive committee drafted plans which resulted in a celebration on July 9, 1885—the battle's twenty-fifth anniversary—at Frederick. The Reynolds post of the G.A.R. hosted the event, along with local members of the Monument Association, a group styled "the Charleville band" in blue uniforms and gold trim, and the mayor and former Major E. Y. Goldsborough delivered brief remarks. Lew Wallace sent regrets that he could not attend (as did Colonel, later Brigadier General William W. Henry of the 10th Vermont), but $5,000 was raised for the Association. The meeting adjourned to the battlefield after C. A. Lovejoy of Baltimore showed his comrades a haversack that he had carried in the battle. "It is said," noted a newsman covering the event, "that some of the boys carried a rather strong article of benzine in their canteens."[11]

Monocacy's memorialization languished over the subsequent quarter century. Still, as surviving veterans grew older, they occasionally "held a camp fire" or visited scenes of youthful wartime fervor. On March 10, 1900, for instance, the York, Pennsylvania *Dispatch* reported a reunion held the previous evening in the Knights of St. Paul Hall where survivors of the 87th Pennsylvania heard Goldsborough expound on the battle of Monocacy. It helped that the speaker was first cousin to the Spanish-American war hero from Frederick, Rear Admiral Winfield Scott Schley (whose own forbear, B. H. Schley, like Goldsborough, had been a volunteer aide in the battle). Supposedly one hundred of the old 87th's survivors plus other veterans listened raptly, for as the reporter covering the event suggested, the city could remember the battle "whose guns were plain heard here"; a conflict that had "cast a gloom over York when the citizens heard that the Eighty-Seventh had lost seventy-four men in that terrible fight." The survivors, however, probably better

appreciated the adjoining festal board, laid out with compliments of
yet another Monocacy survivor, Captain W. H. Lanius, who had been
wounded there.[12]

Suddenly it was a new century, and the realization of their mor-
tality bore down upon Monocacy veterans. A sense of urgency pervaded their fiftieth reunion especially when their erstwhile leader,
Lew Wallace, wired from Cincinnati: "Have gone thus far on the road
to Frederick but find the cars so hot and exhausting I ought not to
proceed." Other worthies did, however, including brigadiers William
Henry Seward, Jr. from New York, Warren Keifer from Ohio, W. H.
Henry and Captain George F. Davis from Vermont, as well as Massachusetts state senator Alfred S. Roe. They were charged with raising
$10,000 for the Monocacy monument. One theme stood out from
their speeches at the City Opera House as well as from Wallace's
wire—Monocacy survivors to a man believed that they had indeed
been "the saviors of Washington" that hot July Saturday, fifty years
before.[13]

No national Monocacy monument ever rose over the battlefield,
although individual state memorials soon did. The Jerseymen were
the first to erect theirs, unveiling it beside the tracks of the Baltimore
and Ohio and close to the highway bridge crossing the river. Major
John O. Patterson recounted the unit's deeds in a ceremony on July
9, 1907, as an assemblage of over one hundred and eighty veterans
and friends (an astonishing turnout considering only ninety-five men
of the 14th New Jersey had emerged unscathed from the battle) swel-
tered in the heat. The monument, a handsome granite shaft of seven
sections (partly dressed and partly rough stone), was surmounted by
an infantryman, reaching for a cartridge as he gazed toward the distant foe. Tablets described the regiment's role in the action. That
night, a reunion was held in Junior's Fire Hall in Frederick, and the
participants learned that sister state Pennsylvania planned to ex-
pend $10,000 for her monument, which as it turned out was dedi-
cated the following year.[14]

The monument to the three Pennsylvania regiments at Monocacy
was unveiled before some two hundred and fifty survivors at 12:30
P.M. on November 24, 1908. The crowd was kept waiting by the lieutenant governor's luncheon in his private rail car at the junction, but
he emerged eventually to deliver an impassioned patriotic speech
about saving the republic as a beacon of liberty for the rest of the
world. Other speakers including Captain Robert T. Cornwall (formerly
of Brigadier General James B. Ricketts' staff during the battle), the
ubiquitous E. Y. Goldsborough and W. H. Lanius also made remarks.
Then, the thirty-five-foot shaft of Blue Westerly granite was unveiled.
It bore customary battle information about 67th, 87th, and 138th

regiments, and a curbing of granite surrounded the plot, located beside the old Washington turnpike nearly opposite the intersection of Baker Valley Road and Araby church. Then, the veterans straggled off to hunt relics from the battle.[15]

Southerners finally received their share of Monocacy memorialization when, on the fiftieth anniversary of the battle in 1914, the Fitzhugh Lee Chapter of the United Daughters of the Confederacy in Frederick erected a simple marker beside the Washington turnpike at the Best farm north of the river and railroad (claimed as Robert E. Lee's headquarters before Antietam). The project had been initiated by the chapter four years before with the first contributions coming from Georgia U.D.C. chapters. A unpretentious Maryland granite marker, about twelve feet high, held a bronze tablet in memory of the Southern soldiers who fell in the battle. Colonel Robert E. Lee, Jr., grandson of the Confederate chieftain, delivered the keynote speech, suggesting that, "The Confederate soldier needs no monument; his deeds are his monuments." Certainly many if not most of the 1,000 spectators agreed. The Reverend Doctor Randolph H. McKim, Confederate veteran and rector of the Epiphany Episcopal Church in Washington, delivered the invocation while "Maryland, My Maryland," "America" and "The Star Spangled Banner" were sung, and soldier stories were swapped liberally among those present like ex-Confederates Randolph Barton and Alfred Wheeler, and former Federal J. J. Kahler, all from Baltimore.[16]

Newsmen ballyhooed Wheeler as well as Early's old artillerist, Brigadier General John Floyd King, and Mrs. Ellicott Fisher as having the most fascinating tales. Wheeler recounted how all his comrades had been barefoot, in much need of food and clothing, but had found little among Wallace's supplies. The refuse of "Yankee Feats" provided old bacon rinds, "which they devoured with great relish," was his story, at least. Wheeler also remembered that his artillery unit had had no luck in battering down the wooden highway bridge because the cannon balls simply went through the structure and it refused to fall. Equally enthralling for the spectators in 1914 were King and Fisher (nee Mamie Tyler), who had not seen one another since 1865, and immediately repeated the story of his visiting "Araby" house seeking food at the close of the battle, and then ducking the need to identify himself as commanding the artillery that had made life so miserable that afternoon for young Mamie and other refugees cowering in the cellar. Tyler excused him, fifty years later, for that lapse of Southern chivalry.

Vermont completed the trend of erecting veterans' monuments at Monocacy in 1915. A small granite marker bearing the distinctive Greek Cross of the VI Corps was sited on the northwest corner of the old turnpike and Baker's Valley Road across from Araby church and the Pennsylvania monument on land purchased from William G. Baker. Designating the position of the 10th Vermont in the pivotal afternoon fighting at Araby, it bore Wallace's immortal comment about the battle to save Washington, "and we saved it." Missing from the roster of monuments, however, were memorials to the men from New York and Ohio, or even those Virginia loyalists of the hated Loudoun Rangers who had fought at Monocacy. No former Confederate state monument ever appeared, although on the one hundredth anniversary of the battle, July 9, 1964, Maryland finally erected a modest marker adjacent to the Confederate stone that read "to honor the Maryland soldiers who fought for Union and Confederacy."[17]

As the years passed and the veterans died off, interest waned. The turnpike to Washington was relocated to the present Maryland Route 355 configuration, and the *Confederate Veteran* reported in February 1928 that the Vermont and Pennsylvania monuments (perhaps even the New Jersey stone as well) "are very much neglected and some of them almost hidden from view by bushes and briars growing up around them." The absence of veterans' interest and visits, and America's preoccupation with other concerns in the 1920s and 1930s only exacerbated the forgotten nature of battle sites like Monocacy. On the eve of World War II, the seventy-fifth anniversary was marked in the summer of 1939 with a full recounting of the battle and its meaning in the local Frederick newspapers. To all but the most ardent student of the Civil War, however, Monocacy had become merely a small, localized historical shrine.[18]

* Modern Preservation and Interpretation *

Other forces were at work by the 1930s to save Monocacy. In fact, mention of the site as a national park had occurred at the time of the Vermont monument's unveiling. The movement gathered momentum over the next decade, but at the local level. A Monocacy Battle Field Memorial Association reflected the interest of Frederick countians Colonel D. John Markey, Charles McC. Mathias, Robert E. Delaplaine, John S. Hersey, W. Harry Haller, James H. Gambrill, Jr., Charles F. Kreh, and Judge Glenn H. Worthington (the child witness to the battle and author of what was then the most comprehensive account of the battle, published in 1932). Glenn O. Garber of the local Chamber of Commerce, and even the sole surviving Union general from the war, former Speaker of the House of Representatives, Major General J. Warren Keifer of Ohio, were brought in for support. Keifer had actually missed the battle due to a wound suffered in the Wilderness, but his brigade had been at Monocacy, and he lent his support to a bill introduced in Congress in 1928 to make Monocacy a national park. The greatest concern at that point was about land donation by private owners, not government purchase, and the impact of government tour roads upon the integrity of working farms. Everyone embraced the Antietam model whereby such roads would permit landowners to still derive the economic benefit of the fields at Monocacy.[19]

Congress finally passed an act six years later, authorizing $50,000 to implement the national park. Signed by President Franklin D. Roosevelt, "Monocacy National Park" came into being under the assumption that the actual land would be donated at no cost to the taxpayer. Of course, the nation lay in the grip of a depression and so the situation languished for decades. The National Park Service, as custodial successor to the War Department for historic battlefields like Monocacy, conducted several field investigations and preliminary studies prior to the Second World War. Other priorities obtained, however, and with the exception of Worthington, few if any other historians even spotlighted the forgotten battle. The legendary Douglas Southall Freeman naturally proved an exception. In his masterful study of Confederate command in Virginia, Freeman advanced that Jubal Early's conduct of Monocacy suggested weaknesses. The battle had been fought largely by one division—that of John B. Gordon—although he admitted that might have been due to circumstances. Yet, "if it became a habit for Early to conduct his battles in this fashion, it might imply that he still was, in spirit and in strategical conceptions, a division and not a corps or army commander." Of course, Freeman was essentially setting Early up for later critique of his disastrous operations in the Shenandoah in the autumn. At least, Freeman had drawn national, even international, attention to Monocacy through his writing.[20]

Meanwhile, back at the battlefield, no land donations were forthcoming through the years, and no federal development took place. The eventual commercial value spiral of the farmland mitigated against owner beneficence, and Monocacy's centenary passed with only minor commemoration (erection of the very modest Maryland monument), and reenactment or scholarly analysis of the affair. Civil War "buffs" largely had more interest in Monocacy than even the local populace as the hundredth anniversary came and went in 1964 with modest commemoration. Only with the rise of environmentalist and preservationist concern about endangered historic sites would there be a new backdrop for action. In the process, Monocacy acquired status on the National Register of Historic Places on February 4, 1975, and later that year, Representative Goodloe Byron guided amendment to the original 1934 act that permitted federal land acquisition

and definite development of a park. A name change to "Monocacy
National Battlefield" followed in 1976, with further amendment of
the law two years later that increased authorized park acreage. The
government was now a serious land owner, and the community generally seemed amenable to park development.[21]

What followed were the mandatory series of master planning,
land protection planning, environmental assessments, structure
analysis, and general management planning for a park that was expected to attract 350,000 visitors annually by 1979. Although recommended for inclusion in a park by Park Service historians before
World War II, later planners rejected the stone or jug bridge sector of
the fighting from acquisition plans as "basically peripheral to the
battle." Therefore, like so many other sites in their charge, the National Park Service remained one-dimensional in its approach to site
preservation and interpretation. It considered Monocacy to be a short,
straightforward battle worth of attention only in the sector that essentially embraced the railroad junction and axis of the highway to
Washington (including the Worthington and Thomas farms), but little
else. Even then, the Park Service faced an expensive acquisition program due to escalating land values as Frederick became a bedroom
community to the nation's capital by the 1980s.[22]

Some things seemed evident as Monocacy celebrated its 125th
anniversary in July 1989 with a major off-site reenactment and attendant publicity. With major core sections of the historic battlefield
still not under federal protection, and thus subject to commercial
exploitation, Monocacy National Battlefield needed public help. Local tourism still focused largely upon Frederick itself and its proximity to the more renowned Antietam and Gettysburg battlefields. Glim-
mers of hope that Monocacy might piggy-back onto Frederick's own
resurgence in interest and local pride seemed reassuring to students
of the Civil War who recognized particular value in preserving this
piece of the four-year struggle.

Land acquisition over the next six years added significant battlefield property north of the river on the Best farm and around the junction. The Worthington farm joined the Gambrill property as major hold-
ings south of the river. Residential areas along the old Washington
turnpike and Maryland Route 355 would not be disturbed, and the
government planned to employ Gambrill's "Boscobel" house as a national training center for craftsmen working in historic preservation.
Still, most glaringly, "Araby" or the C. Keefer Thomas place that formed
the centerpiece of the battle, remained on the endangered land status
list. The stone or jug bridge sector was completely neglected, bisected
by rerouted roads and housing developments. Even then, two hundred and eighty-five absolutely key acres at the main battle site posed

a major problem in terms of Monocacy's preservation and government interpretation programs. Not unlike the infamous Frederick debt incurred through Early's requisition (a debt paid off by bond issue but never redeemed from the federal government), redemption of Monocacy for posterity remained incomplete.

In addition to local citizen interest and help, a support group styled "Friends of Monocacy Battlefield" spearheaded the drive for increased public awareness and interest in Monocacy. Not only did this body aid in hands-on volunteer work at the park, they assisted in Best farm acquisition efforts, stabilization and interpretation of the Worthington house and property, and educational forums. Lacking, of course, were field interpretive devices, a self-guided auto tour route, even the ability to visit many points associated with the battle itself. A major tourist announcement of the site's existence remained absent from nearby Interstate 270. That artery itself constituted a travesty since its construction carried the four-lane expressway directly across the Worthington-Thomas properties, thereby destroying forever any visual integrity for visitors seeking to imagine wheat shock-studded fields across which the two armies contended in July 1864. At least a superb overlook on the interstate—thanks to Congressman Goodloe Byron, enabled northbound travelers to savor the overall landscape of Monocacy Valley as well as small interpretive markers about Frederick and the battle.

More fortuitously, the Park Service took what remained of the old Gambrill mill and converted it into a visitor's center. Wayfarers, determined enough to seek out the almost hidden park entrance off busy Maryland Route 355 south of Frederick, could now appreciate a superb electric map depicting the battle. In July 1991—more than one hundred twenty-seven years after the battle and fifty-seven years after legislation created the national park, the United States government finally dedicated Monocacy National Battlefield. "This battlefield will now be properly protected as a cherished historic legacy," intoned Interior Secretary Manuel Lujan, Jr. to an audience of some two hundred fifty people on a hot July morning, quite reminiscent of the day of the battle. Maryland governor William Donald Schaefer waxed more enthusiastically—"at last we're here, at last we're here," he pronounced.[23]

In point of fact, however, had preservationists yet succeeded? While Maryland state senator Howard A. Denis of adjacent Montgomery County could write the editor of the Washington *Post* several days later how "the recognition finally given the Civil War Battle of Monocacy in Frederick County, Md., is long overdue," even he knew that public recognition could prove fickle. By 1994, when a special commission report on the state of the nation's Civil War battlefields

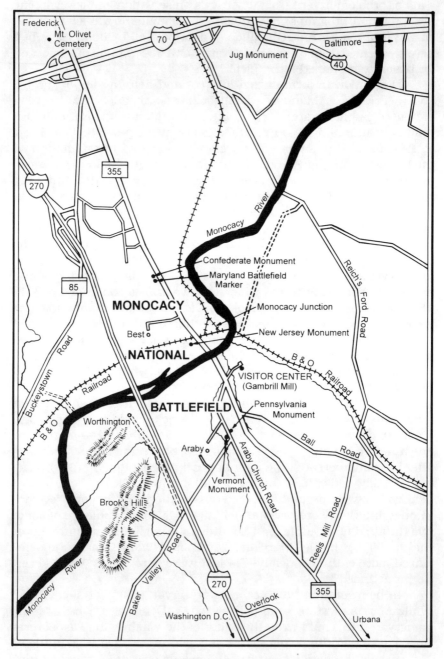

Map 16. Monocacy Battlefield Today

was publicly released, the authors suggested that Monocacy had good integrity for 1,014 managed acres of the authorized site. They also noted, however, that the threat was high to preservation of unacquired land deemed essential to the battle's interpretation. Morover, these same authors betrayed the continuing equivocation as to Monocacy's real meaning. They ranked the battle only as Category B or "having a direct and decisive influence on their campaign," rather than Category A, "having a decisive influence on a campaign and a direct impact on the course of the war." One hundred thirty years after the battle, historians nationally still would not admit to Monocacy's more substantial meaning for the final and crucial year of the Civil War.[24]

* * * *

National Park Service managers, interpreters, planners, and acquisition lawyers will continue their diligent task of quietly ensuring land preservation and development of interpretive tools for visitor understanding of Monocacy. Local civic groups, national organizations like the Friends of Monocacy Battlefield, and students of the Civil War generally will continue to help the effort and raise public awareness as park development itself goes forward. "You can go drive the public roads and see the monuments, but that's about all you can do right now," suggested one Park Service spokesman at the time of the one hundred thirtieth anniversary in July 1994. The park probably would not be fully developed with trails and wayside stations for another five to ten years. Once that happens, said the spokesperson, Monocacy "will outdraw Antietam," since this site would be the "first battlefield" tourists from Baltimore and Washington would visit upon leaving those cities.[25]

Whether or not such goals will be met remains as much a budgetary as publicity question. Surely, even now, the ghosts of blue and gray who fought and died at Monocacy can rest assured that their sacrifice finally has been properly sanctified and commemorated. While neither burial ground nor single monument over that ground fulfills Lew Wallace's personal dream for Monocacy, the park's existence, preservation, and future development reflect modern America's recognition of his immortal thought that his men had fought there "to save the National Capital, and they did save it." As for their noble opponents at Monocacy, perhaps the words of Lee's grandson and namesake spoken at the fiftieth anniversary only need obtain: "The Confederate soldier needs no monument; his deeds are his monuments."

APPENDIX 1

Army of the Valley District

(Second Army Corps; Army of Northern Virginia)

Lieutenant General Jubal A. Early
commanding

Brigadier General A. L. Long
Chief of Artillery

Rodes' Division (Major General Robert E. Rodes)

Battle's Brigade (Brigadier General Cullen A. Battle)

3d Alabama Infantry
5th Alabama Infantry
6th Alabama Infantry
12th Alabama Infantry
61st Alabama Infantry

Grimes' Brigade (Brigadier General Bryan Grimes)

    32d North Carolina Infantry
    43d North Carolina Infantry
    45th North Carolina Infantry
    53d North Carolina Infantry
    2d North Carolina (Battalion) Infantry

Cook's Brigade (Colonel Philip Cook)

    4th Georgia Infantry
    12th Georgia Infantry
    21st Georgia Infantry
    44th Georgia Infantry

Cox's Brigade (Brigadier General William R. Cox)

    1st North Carolina (State Troops) Infantry
    2d North Carolina (State Troops) Infantry
    3d North Carolina (State Troops) Infantry
    4th North Carolina (State Troops) Infantry
    14th North Carolina Infantry
    30th North Carolina Infantry

Ramseur's Division (Major General Stephen D. Ramseur)

Lilley's Brigade (Brigadier General Robert Lilley)

    13th Virginia Infantry
    31st Virginia Infantry
    49th Virginia Infantry
    52d Virginia Infantry
    58th Virginia Infantry

Johnston's Brigade (Brigadier General Robert D. Johnston)

    5th North Carolina (State Troops) Infantry
    12th North Carolina Infantry
    20th North Carolina Infantry
    23d North Carolina Infantry
    1st North Carolina Battalion Sharpshooters

Lewis' Brigade (Brigadier General William Lewis)
    6th North Carolina Infantry
    21st North Carolina Infantry
    54th North Carolina Infantry
    57th North Carolina Infantry

Breckinridge's Corps (Major General John C. Breckinridge)

Lieutenant Colonel J. Floyd King
Chief of Artillery

Gordon's Division (Major General John B. Gordon)

Evans' Brigade (Brigadier General Clement A. Evans/Colonel E. N. Atkinson)

    13th Georgia Infantry
    26th Georgia Infantry
    31st Georgia Infantry
    38th Georgia Infantry
    60th Georgia Infantry
    61st Georgia Infantry
    12th Georgia (Battalion) (Light artillery serving as infantry)

York's Brigade (Brigadier General Zebulon York) (consolidated)

Hays' old Brigade (Louisiana Tigers) (Colonel W. R. Peck)

    5th Louisiana Infantry
    6th Louisiana Infantry
    7th Louisiana Infantry
    8th Louisiana Infantry (all fragmentary regiments)
    9th Louisiana Infantry

Stafford's old Brigade (Colonel E. Waggaman)

    1st Louisiana Infantry
    2d Louisiana Infantry
    10th Louisiana Infantry (all fragmentary regiments)
    14th Louisiana Infantry
    15th Louisiana Infantry

Terry's Brigade (Brigadier General William Terry) (consolidated)

Jackson's old 1st or "Stonewall" Brigade (Colonel J. H. S. Funk)

    2d Virginia Infantry
    4th Virginia Infantry (all fragmentary regiments)
    5th Virginia Infantry
    27th Virginia Infantry
    33d Virginia Infantry

Jones' old 2d Brigade (Colonel R. H. Dungan)

    21st Virginia Infantry
    25th Virginia Infantry
    42d Virginia Infantry (all fragmentary regiments)
    44th Virginia Infantry
    48th Virginia Infantry
    50th Virginia Infantry

Stuart's old 3d Brigade (Lieutenant Colonel S. H. Saunders)

    10th Virginia Infantry
    23d Virginia Infantry (all fragmentary regiments)
    37th Virginia Infantry

Echols' Division (Brigadier General John Echols)
(formerly Breckinridge's and Elzey's divisions)

Wharton's Brigade (Brigadier General Gabriel C. Wharton)

    30th Virginia Infantry Battalion Sharpshooters
    45th Virginia Infantry
    51st Virginia Infantry

Echols' Brigade (Colonel George S. Patton)

    22d Virginia Infantry
    23d Virginia Infantry Battalion
    26th Virginia Infantry Battalion

*Vaughn's Brigade (Brigadier General Thomas Smith)

      36th Virginia Infantry
      45th Virginia Infantry Battalion
      60th Virginia Infantry

Thomas' Legion (North Carolina) (dismounted)
      43d   Tennessee Mounted Infantry (dismounted)
      59th Tennessee Mounted Infantry

Ransom's Cavalry Division (Major General Robert Ransom)

Imboden's Brigade (Brigadier General John Imboden/ Colonel George
    Smith)

      18th Virginia Cavalry
      23d   Virginia Cavalry
      62d   Virginia Mounted Infantry
      ** Contingents of McNeill's Partisan Rangers

McCausland's Brigade (Brigadier General John McCausland)

      14th Virginia Cavalry
      16th Virginia Cavalry
      17th Virginia Cavalry

---

* F. Ray Sibley suggests a different configuration for Vaughn and Smith during June
and July 1864 although it is unclear that all these units accompanied Early north of
the Potomac:

    Vaughn's Brigade (Brigadier General John C. Vaughn)
        3d   Tennessee Provisional Army Mounted Infantry
        39th   Tennessee Mounted Infantry
        43d   Tennessee Mounted Infantry
        59th   Tennessee Mounted Infantry
        1st   Tennessee Cavalry
        12th   Tennessee Cavalry Battalion
        16th   Tennessee Cavalry Battalion
        16th   Georgia Cavalry Battalion
        Portions of 60th, 61st, 62d Tennessee

    Smith's Brigade (Colonel Thomas Smith)
      Thomas (North Carolina) Legion Infantry Regiment + McKamy's Battalion
        36th   Virginia Infantry
        60th   Virginia Infantry
        45th   Virginia Infantry Battalion

** Sibley also notes other unattached cavalry including McNeill's Company of Partisan
Rangers and Company A, 1st Missouri Cavalry.

25th Virginia Cavalry
27th Virginia Cavalry Battalion
37th Virginia Cavalry Battalion

Johnson's Brigade (Brigadier General Bradley T. Johnson)

1st Maryland Cavalry Battalion
2d Maryland Cavalry Battalion
8th Virginia Cavalry
21st Virginia Cavalry
22d Virginia Cavalry
34th Virginia Cavalry Battalion
36th Virginia Cavalry

Jackson's Brigade (Brigadier General W. L. Jackson)

19th Virginia Cavalry
20th Virginia Cavalry
46th Virginia Cavalry Battalion
47th Virginia Cavalry Battalion

Horse Artillery (approx. 12–16 guns)

Jackson's Company (Charlottesville) Virginia Horse Artillery (T. E. Jackson) with McCausland's Brigade
McClanahan's Company (Staunton) Virginia Horse Artillery with Imboden's Brigade
Baltimore Light Artillery (2d Maryland) (Griffin) with Johnson's Brigade
Lurty's Virginia Battery (Lurty) with Jackson's Brigade

Artillery (Brigadier General Armistead L. Long)
(approximately 36–40 guns)

Braxton's Battalion (Major Carter M. Braxton)

Allegheny Artillery (Virginia)
Lee Artillery (Virginia) (Hardwicke)
Stafford Artillery (Virginia) (Cooper)

McLaughlin's Battalion (Major William McLaughlin)

Wise Legion Artillery (Virginia) (Company C, Lowry)
Lewisburg Artillery (Virginia)
Monroe Battery (Virginia) (Chapman)

Nelson's Battalion (Major William Nelson)

Amherst Artillery (Virginia) (Kirkpatrick)
Fluvanna Artillery (Virginia) (Massie)
Milledge Artillery (Georgia) (Milledge)

Recapitulation

Early's forces included sixty-seven infantry regiments, six battalions of infantry (or fragments), plus eleven regiments and nine battalions of cavalry, as well as three battalions (nine batteries) of field artillery, and four batteries of horse artillery. The force may have numbered as many as 20,000 men at some point, but more likely 14,000 or 15,000 at Monocacy. Losses in this campaign probably ranged from 1,500 to 2,000 with perhaps 1,050 to 1,150 suffered at Monocacy.

Sources

Brad Coker, *The Battle of Monocacy* (Baltimore, 1982), p. 44.

Albert E. Conradis, "The Battle of Monocacy," in Frederick Civil War Centennial Inc. *To Commemorate the One Hundredth Anniversary of the Battle of Monocacy* (Frederick, 1964), appendix II, p. 35.

George E. Pond, *The Shenandoah Valley in 1864* (New York, 1883).

F. Ray Sibley, Jr., *The Confederate Order of Battle; Volume I; The Army of Northern Virginia* (Shippensburg, 1996), pp. 86–88.

Tennessee Civil War Centennial Commission, *Tennesseeans in the Civil War, Part I* (Nashville: The Commission, 1964), pp. 268–270.

U.S. War Department, *The War of the Rebellion: The Official Records of Union and Confederate Armies* (Washington, 1880–1901), series I, volume 43, part 1, pp. 1002–1004, 1011–1013.

Jeffry D. Wert, *From Winchester to Cedar Creek: The Shenandoah Campaign of 1864* (Carlisle, 1987), pp. 316–317.

Federal Forces at Monocacy

Major General Lew Wallace
commanding

Middle Department (VIII Corps)
(Wallace)

First Separate Brigade (Brigadier General Erastus Tyler)

1st	Regiment Potomac Home Brigade Infantry (5 companies)
3d	Regiment Potomac Home Brigade Infantry
11th	Maryland Volunteer Infantry
144th	Ohio Volunteer Infantry (3 companies) (National Guard)
149th	Ohio Volunteer Infantry (7 companies) (National Guard)

Baltimore Independent Battery (Alexander) 6 guns
Blockhouse howitzer (Wiegel) 24-pounder howitzer
Small Mountain howitzer

Cavalry (Clendenin)

8th	Illinois Volunteer Cavalry (5 companies)
	Loudoun (Virginia) Rangers (Companies A, B)
159th	Ohio Volunteer Infantry (Detachment of 100 Mounted Infantry)

Wells' Mixed Cavalry Detachment

Third Division (VI Corps)
(Brigadier General James Ricketts)

First Brigade (Colonel William Truex)

14th	New Jersey Volunteer Infantry
106th	New York Volunteer Infantry
151st	New York Volunteer Infantry
87th	Pennsylvania Volunteer Infantry
10th	Vermont Volunteer Infantry

Second Brigade (Colonel Matthew McClennan)

> 9th New York Heavy Artillery (two battalions)
> 110th Ohio Volunteer Infantry
> 122d Ohio Volunteer Infantry (5 companies)
> 126th Ohio Volunteer Infantry
> 138th Pennsylvania Volunteer Infantry

VI Corps units at Monrovia, Maryland (Colonel John F. Staunton)

> 6th Maryland Volunteer Infantry
> 122d Ohio Volunteer Infantry (Detachment)
> 67th Pennsylvania Volunteer Infantry

Recapitulation

Wallace's forces included all or portions of seventeen infantry regiments, four cavalry units, one field gun battery, plus two unattached blockhouse howitzers. His strength approximated 2,500 VIII Corps, plus approximately 650 cavalry and perhaps 3,500 VI Corps veterans. His losses approximated 1,294–1,968 killed, wounded, and missing.

Sources

Brad Coker, *The Battle of Monocacy* (Baltimore, 1982), pp. 31, 49.

Frank Moore, editor. *Rebellion Record* (New York, 1868), volume 11, pp. 624–626.

Everad Hall Smith, "The General and the Valley: Union Leadership During The Threat to Washington in 1864," Ph.D. dissertation 1977 (Ann Arbor, University Microfilms, 1977), pp. 239–240, 247, appendices 5 and 6.

U.S. War Department, *War of the Rebellion: a Compilation of the Union and Confederate Armies* (Washington: 1880–1901), series I, volume 37, part 1, pp. 199–202.

Glenn H. Worthington, *Fighting for Time* (Frederick, 1932), pp. 259–260.

APPENDIX 2

Ohio One Hundred Days' Soldiers in 1864

By
Thomas A. Ware

Soldiers! I understand you have just come from Ohio—come to help us in this, the nation's day of trial, and also of its hope. I thank you for your promptness in responding to the call for troops. Your services were never needed more than now....

President Abraham Lincoln, June 11, 1864 [1]

This essay examines a little noted nor long remembered chapter in the sensitive wartime negotiations between Lincoln and his Civil War governors over policy and strategy. The issue then at stake was how to meet the seemingly insatiable federal demands for manpower while maintaining adequate security in those states exposed to both internal and external threats. Central to the resolution of that dilemma was the oft (and usually justly) maligned militia. The surprise offer of 85,000 of them for 100 days; active service during the critical spring and summer months of 1864 was, in effect, the "last hurrah" of the beleaguered (Old North) Western governors. On balance, the mixed results benefitted both donors and recipients about equally, which made the "deal" a fair and wise one.

To the extent possible, the contemporary political-military situation facing key decision makers will be reconstructed, but summarized. For reasons which become apparent, the twin foci of this

253

mini-drama are centered, alternately on Washington, D.C. and Columbus, Ohio; brief excursions are taken to camp and field to add essential perspective.

Background

Confederate defeats at Gettysburg and Vicksburg in July 1863 *should* have enabled the Union to win the war that year. But, people and events often confound latter day critics by failing to draw "obvious and rational conclusions." The Gray Fox—Southern General Robert E. Lee—had escaped to fight again, which depressed Northern president Abraham Lincoln, among others. Additionally, the North faced a number of serious problems. So did the South, but many of their vulnerabilities were less conspicuous.

At the beginning of the war, Great Britain and France recognized the "belligerent rights" of the Confederate States of America. There was a possibility that one or both would enter the war on her side, but the chances became dim after the Union's tactical draw but strategic victory at Antietam in September 1862 and virtually nil as a result of Gettysburg and Vicksburg. The South's "King Cotton" had been trumped by Northern wheat and strong public aversion to slavery in Great Britain. Still, the faint flame of a reversal in this situation continued into 1864. Louis Napoleon, King of the French, particularly remained a major irritant, especially with his ill-conceived attempt to create a rival power center in Mexico. Indeed, such hemispheric intervention via Napoleon's establishment of Austrian Archduke Maximilian as Emperor of Mexico, caused an ill-timed dispersion of Union military forces during the crucial spring campaign of 1864.[2]

On the national scene, millions of Northerners were discouraged and war weary by this stage of the conflict. This was especially so among so-called "Peace Democrats" who devised a plan for "Peace Without Victory," based on the belief that the war was unwinnable. Given the prevailing passions, such a peace would have led to *de facto* recognition of an independent Confederacy. Other splits in the Union might follow therefrom.

There were also sinister rumors—not unfounded—of an active and widespread conspiracy afoot to establish a Northwest Confederacy which would withdraw states like Ohio, Indiana, and Illinois from the Union. Although it is now clear that contemporary fears were exaggerated, they did have a significant impact on the loyal governors in the Old Northwest, and, to a lesser extent, on the Lincoln administration.[3]

Then too, the demands of the military draft, which had become increasingly onerous and unpopular, led to draft riots in New York and to armed resistance elsewhere. The able, but often obstructive governor of New York, Horatio Seymour, openly attacked the draft as unconstitutional. He thus became states' rights champion in the North. Coupled with serious rifts in the president's cabinet, and his party in trouble because of the war, even in his home congressional district, the Union faced a tough election year in 1864, and even Lincoln entertained doubts that he could win a second term.

Besides the ever-escalating costs of the war in blood and national treasure, there was yet another cost factor. A strong belief spread across party lines that the chief executive was unduly and illegally tampering with such basic rights as *habeas corpus*, freedom of the press, and protection from arbitrary arrest. Indeed, well he might have been—in order to win the war! But, politicians like Senator Benjamin Wade of Ohio was one of the leaders of an unofficial drive to unseat Lincoln as the Union Party's candidate for president, even though the bald facts of war and politics eventually dissipated that movement. Still, another major victory by Lee or Confederate forces in Georgia might have provided the deeper despair and loss of hope required to unseat the incumbent president and elect a peace candidate.[4]

Statistically, the North still enjoyed a huge advantage in money, materiel, and manpower. The inevitable attrition of total war had hurt the South more deeply, and Confederate forces were everywhere on the defensive. Yet, in the vital eastern theater, the North had no general who could approach the charismatic leadership, the cool nerve, and the operational skill of Robert E. Lee. Lincoln, however, thought that he had found the antidote in western general Ulysses S. Grant. The president, who had learned a great deal about strategy through bitter experience and uncommon sense, recognized Grant as a fighter who won, and so brought him east to counter Lee. It remained to be seen if Lincoln's confidence was well placed in a man judged to be a failure and a drunkard before the war.

National Policy and Strategy

The gloomy situation did not cause Lincoln to change policies, but rather to change the command structure, commanders, and strategy. His policy remained simple and straightforward: win the war as soon as possible, and preserve the Union by any and all means necessary. Everything else, including his own reelection, was secondary. With congressional support, he established a modern, centralized command system with the resurrected rank of Lieutenant General to head the military side. Grant was promoted to that rank and given the title of General in Chief, while Major General William Tecumseh Sherman was named to head the other major operation in the west. The agreed-upon strategy was also simple and direct: concentrate all possible power and then use it simultaneously and continuously against the main Confederate forces. Defeat and destruction of those forces took precedence over terrain objectives. The abiding question remained: how did that policy and strategy merge with the political situation in such sensitive areas as the Old Northwest?[5]

Out in Ohio

In January 1864, stout and feisty John Brough became Ohio's third war governor. The previous July, this ex-Democrat had made a powerful speech in Cleveland in which he announced his view of the major issue at stake in the war. In the speech he roared: "Either slavery must be torn out root and branch, or our Government will exist no longer." No room for compromise in those words, and similar tough statements helped him win an unexpected but decisive guber-natorial victory over the brilliant, unbending Clement Vallandigham, the intellectual and political leader of dissident "Copperheads," mainly midwestern Peace Democrats who were avid States Righters and thus often sympathetic to the Confederacy. After a nervous election night vigil, Lincoln's fears turned to joy and he wired Brough: "Glory to God in the Highest, Ohio has saved the nation."[6]

Neither Ohio nor the Union was yet saved. Brough had to keep his own state loyal and mobilized for victory—no mean task. He soon found himself "in the swirl of problems and pressures that had faced his predecessors." He had to continue raising troops, cope with the federal draft, provide for Ohio's soldiers already in the field, and "stand guard against secret societies, and protect his own political inter-ests." Reports of armed secret societies were everywhere. The Order of American Knights (Sons of Liberty) was rumored to be planning attacks to seize arsenals, free and arm Confederate prisoners of war, resist the draft, and initiate a full scale rebellion. Brough's opposi-tion was only fanned further by the fiery Sam Medary's incendiary newspaper, the *Crisis*.[7]

The overt military threat to Ohio's peace and tranquility was an-other worry. There were leaks of a plan to transport Southern sympa-thizers across Lake Erie from Canada, to seize the prisoner-of-war camp on Johnson's Island near Sandusky. The possibility that Confederate cavalry wizard John Morgan would try to repeat his daring feat of July 1863 when he rode across all of southern Ohio was also voiced.

Morgan had been captured and incarcerated in the Ohio state penitentiary at Columbus, only to escape near the end of the year. Brough had a legal and moral obligation to deter or defeat any attack on his state from without or within, and he was not the person to shirk responsibility or to fret unduly about alternatives or "petty legalities." He had appointed the able and energetic B. R. Cowen as his Adjutant General, and Cowen was prepared to brighten the previous administration's plan for a slimmer, tougher, organized militia.

The Role of War Governors

The governors were the linchpins of the Civil War military personnel system. Without them neither Union nor Confederacy could have raised and sustained their armies. Attempts to expand the regular United States Army had not proven effective, and over time, even the notion of volunteerism lost its appeal. By law, the governors were commanders-in-chief of their various state militia until accepted into federal service. The states raised companies, organized regiments, and commissioned the elected officers. In fact, military draft quotas that succeeded volunteerism, while administered locally by federal Assistant Provost Marshals, were established primarily to force the governors to recruit better and faster.

Governors also had to prove that they were "the soldiers' friends" in order to get elected or re-elected. So they visited the sick and wounded, and cared for needy dependents. They were also responsible for administering the state militia. All together, they fought hard with the secretary of war, and periodically with the president, over their share of the increasingly painful manpower quotas (there were four such calls for manpower made in 1864), and over federal infringement on their prerogatives as chief executives of their states. The western governors, although solidly loyal, believed that their strategic problems were neglected in Washington. They met several times to put pressure on Lincoln. Over time, however, his power expanded, while theirs steadily declined.[8]

Ohio's Militia in Review

In 1861, Ohio's militia system, as in all the states, was in tatters, except for some fancy drill companies. Lincoln's call for 75,000 volunteers from the militia for a period of ninety days service produced 22,000 accepted by the state, but only thirteen regiments (of 1,000 men each) were actually mustered into federal service. Then governor,

William Dennison and his adjutant general were both inexperienced and generally inept in military matters, but they knew that Ohio's 436 miles of border with slave states had to be defended beyond the Ohio River. Dennison and fellow eastern governors persuaded Lincoln that their residual mobilized militia should be employed to support the Unionist movement in the western counties of Virginia and to keep Kentucky in the Union. Both objectives were achieved at low cost, although three months' service proved insufficient for long-term suppression of the rebellion. The next call was for three years.[9]

Other crisis calls for short term militia, and continued formation of new regiments throughout the war (a total of two hundred and thirty had been raised by 1865) frustrated whatever efforts Ohio made to create an effective militia which could protect her territory and people. In the autumn of 1862, the invasion of Kentucky by Confederate forces under Braxton Bragg and Edward Kirby Smith threatened Ohio, and then governor David Tod appealed to his militia to equip *themselves*, organize companies and regiments, and march to the relief of Cincinnati. Over 15,000 so-called "Squirrel Hunters" did so, and aided Major General Lew Wallace in defense of that "Queen City."

Tod recognized the futility of trying to defend his state on such a basis. So he asked his Adjutant General to establish a much smaller and more select body of "organized volunteer militia" as opposed to the more than 4,000 separate companies (about 300,000 men) then carried on the rolls. Some progress was made, but Morgan's raid occurred too soon, and as Adjutant General Cowen reflected later:

> The inefficiency of the militia, as it then was, had been demonstrated in the Kirby Smith raid in 1862, in which 'from fifty thousand to seventy-five thousand'...were called out. This was emphasized in the following year in the Morgan raid in which fifty thousand were again called out, only to be scattered like sheep without a shepherd whenever the bold raiders came in sight.[10]

Ohio's Policy and Strategy

Brough and Cowen made a good political and military team. Together they read the state's internal and external threats clearly (if a bit luridly at times), and neither was loath to devise radical and politically risky counters to such threats. In effect, the governor's policy was to do all possible to help the Lincoln administration "win the war in '64," while concurrently protecting their state. Their strategy therefore was to combine their own reserve strength (nearly ten percent of Ohio's manpower was already in service), with that of their neighbors in the Midwest to reinforce Grant and Sherman by guarding their lines of communication thus freeing manpower to fill the ranks of the fighting armies. At the same time, such a strategy would provide for their own defense in depth from marauders and any chance rebel invasion.

The "organized militia" program initiated by Governor Tod consisted of ninety-nine regiments and battalions with a nominal strength of 44,000 men. Although considerable progress had been made, they were still far from being ready for active service. Cowen, immediately after assuming office in January 1864, moved with speed and administrative skill to improve and accelerate the reorganization. He had a bill drafted by veteran officers which easily gained passage in the March legislature. Key provisions of the bill were that the organized militia was to consist only of volunteers, and those males of military age (18 to 45) who did not volunteer would have to pay a $4.00 per year "commutation" fee to support a newly designated National Guard. There was nothing that Cowen could do about the statutory requirement for electing officers, but he and his staff did recommend strongly that experienced, discharged veterans be chosen for command positions. The later success of this National Guard was due largely to the discipline and leadership provided by those veterans, as it turned out. Further, he had instructed the county military committees to advise local Guard commanders "...to prune out all men who are unfit for active duty in the field."[11]

Cowen had the idea of offering certain of these units to the national government for special purposes. Therefore, Brough's first move was to request from Washington that he be permitted to call up several organized militia regiments for defense of his state's southern border. To achieve that end, he asked ex-governor Dennison to go to the nation's capital to gain approval from Secretary of War Edwin M. Stanton. This official, however, doubted the necessity for such a move, and disapproved the request, fearing the "jealousy of other states" if Ohio had its own army. The pugnacious Brough had only begun to fight on this issue. When, on April 16, Cowen told him that he felt their National Guard was ready for active duty, Brough caught an early train for Washington to argue his case in person before the president.[12]

Western Governors Invade the Capital

Lincoln listened carefully to Brough's plan for turning his National Guard over to the central government. They could be employed to protect lines of communication, supply depots, prison camps, and key cities, and the idea intrigued the president. Still, he declined the offer because of its high potential for casting doubt on the ability of the national government to raise troops in the normal fashion, and for creating envy among the other states. Still, he had no wish to lose the help of so large a force in the existing emergency. He therefore suggested that Brough convene a meeting of the western governors, unbeknownst to Lincoln, and have them offer 100,000 men for 100 days, without revealing the fact that Brough had already offered nearly half that number. Therefore, governors from Indiana, Illinois, and Iowa soon joined Brough in Washington. James Lewis of Wisconsin could not join them, but agreed to the proposal. Michigan's governor did not attend the meeting nor did his state provide any of the planned troop quota. But, the others presented Lincoln and his cabinet with the jointly agreed upon plan. They also concurred on waiting two days until Grant and other commanders could be polled on the idea.[13]

The essential parts of the proposal were as follows. Five states would offer 85,000 troops for 100 days (Ohio to furnish 30,000 of them). The troops would be mustered in by regiment within twenty days of the plan's acceptance. The United States government would clothe, arm, equip, transport and pay them. They would serve in fortifications or *wherever needed*. The men would receive no bounty, nor would they be credited against the draft quota, and while the draft would continue, individual Guardsmen would be "credited for the service rendered." Grant acceded to the scheme on April 21, declaring that as a rule he would oppose short term men, but 100,000 men in a time of crisis might be of "vast importance." Stanton went along (his staff estimated that the cost to the government would approach $25,000,000) and on April 22, 1864, Lincoln formally accepted the plan. The burden now rested on his secretary of war and the governors to implement the scheme promptly and efficiently.[14]

Back in Columbus

Immediately following Lincoln's approval, Brough wired Cowen with the gist of the agreement and instruction to "Set the machinery at work immediately." Mobilization orders were issued to the Guard's unit commanders on Monday, April 25. General Orders Number 12 set the rendezvous for Monday, May 2d, with a telegraphic strength report due at Columbus by 4:00 P.M. The state of Ohio was electrified by this development.[15]

Brough, wisely or not, remained in Washington for several more days. The week between the call and the actual rendezvous was filled with complaints and pleas of all sorts. Even ex-governor Dennison personally led a hastily organized committee to protest to Cowen that the call would be economically and politically disastrous and was unauthorized. Others "proved" that it was unconstitutional, illegal, and void. The adjutant general knew it was a large gamble. He later wrote:

> I knew that there was no authority to compel the Guard to muster into the United States Service. We were preparing it for muster, and intended to introduce it to the mustering officer. There our office would terminate. The muster was to be their voluntary act.[16]

Cowen remained calm and even kept his sense of humor beneath the intense pressure, and continued to work effectively at a frenetic pace. When Brough belatedly returned, he naturally drew off much of the lightning. The loyalists finally accepted the *fait accompli*, and later, many including Dennison, enthusiastically supported the call-up. The Peace Democrats, Copperheads, and others urged defiance of the call-up and continued to exploit the National Guard issue as an explosive one up to and through the November election. But, few of the strident protests came from members of the Guard who, almost to a man, were staunch Union men and the cream of the residual military-aged manpower. Many of them, in fact, were actually above or below the draft age.

The Guard Musters and Marches

Anxiety in Columbus and Washington increased as the appointed mobilization day approached. How many men would report for duty? By 7:30 P.M. on May 2d, Cowen proudly wired Stanton: "Thirty-eight thousand (38,000) are in camp and ready for muster." That was 8,000 men over the quota, although almost 2,000 of them were culled out before actual muster. The day after the rendezvous, the editor of the pro-Union Chilliocothe *Scioto Gazette* explained that:

> The order calling out the National Guard for one hundred days' service, took our citizens generally by surprise, and found most but poorly prepared to respond to the call. The season has been backward, and owing to the scarcity of help, farmers are behind with their work, so that the call was a severe

test of their patriotism, but to their honor we can say they met it in an excellent spirit....[17]

The hard work of equipping, reorganizing into minimum strength companies and regiments, and mustering them into federal service was conducted at Camps Chase (Columbus) and Dennison (Cincinnati). As an example, the eight understrength companies of the 27th Ohio National Guard from Ross County were reorganized into seven and then consolidated with three (reduced from four) of the 55th Ohio National Guard Battalion from Clinton County. The amalgamated unit became the 149th Ohio Volunteer Infantry, and was led by Colonel A. L. Brown of the 27th Regiment. The Lieutenant Colonel and Adjutant from that regiment were sent home and replaced by their counterparts from the 55th Battalion. There were many hurt feelings in the process.[18]

Major Ebenezer Roselle remembered the day of muster: "...in our blue uniforms, and arms glistening in the sun, keeping step to the music—listened to a short speech from the Governor—then heard the words 'All who will volunteer in US service for one hundred days step four paces to the front.' [as] every man in the regiment stepped proudly to the front and was mustered in as [a member of the] 149th OVI." Ironically, in all the proceedings, only one company (about eighty men) in the entire Guard refused to muster and it was immediately dismissed, dishonorably, *en masse* from Ohio's service. None of the men was permitted to reenlist in the Guard, as it was later surmised that the company's officers were at fault.[19]

The telegraph wires between Columbus and Washington were alive with questions and answers as to reporting dates and places for the new regiments. Brough also requested that the War Department accept the five or six regiments raised over his quota. Stanton responded quickly that: "I will accept all of the troops you can raise. The other states will be deficient and behind time. *We want every man now...they may decide the war.*" And, indeed, the other states had neither the counterpart structure to Ohio's National Guard by which they could be mustered quickly, nor such an energetic governor. In the end, the statistics stood as follows:[20]

State	Promised	Mustered	% of Quota
Ohio	30,000	36,254	120.8
Indiana	20,000	7,197	36.0
Illinois	20,000	11,328	56.6
Wisconsin	5,000	2,134	42.7
Iowa	10,000	3,901	39.0
TOTAL	**85,000**	**60,814**	**71.5**

Within two hectic weeks, practically all of Ohio's Guardsmen deployed to garrisons along the long line of the Baltimore and Ohio Railroad or specific places such as Harpers Ferry, Baltimore, or Washington. Only five of the forty-one regiments (plus a single battalion) as mustered, stayed in Ohio. The other states sent their units to support Sherman. Veteran infantry and large heavy artillery (converted to infantry) regiments were released to reinforce advancing Union armies in the field. Both Lincoln and Stanton expressed their gratitude to Brough, and exploiting his initiative, they later asked several other governors to raise 100 Days' soldiers. About 20,000 were eventually mustered from New York, Pennsylvania and Massachusetts, and Maryland, New Jersey and Kansas voluntarily furnished a total of some 2,500 men.[21]

In Forts and Field

The anticipated function for these temporary soldiers was to hold fortifications and guard lines of communication. But, "other duties as assigned" (to use a modern phrase) also obtained. Once the men were in uniform and away from home, large numbers of them actually requested frontline duty. Nine Ohio regiments went to the Army of the James (one member of the 133d Ohio National Guard, Joseph Gregg, won a Medal of Honor there). Many of the other regiments also experienced combat, while protecting the Baltimore and Ohio and its vulnerable bridges. Out west, other 100 Days troops battled Nathan Bedford Forrest's horsemen as well as countless irregulars.[22]

The most extensive and consequential combat involving these men resulted from Lieutenant General Jubal Anderson Early's July raid on Washington. Several Ohio regiments held Maryland Heights across from Harpers Ferry and dominated the road to the capital from that point. Possibly the greatest single service came from those "Century Plants" (as some veterans called them) who served with the ubiquitous Lew Wallace at the battle of Monocacy on July 9. The most deployable of his Middle Department contingents consisted of the Ohio units, and they provided Wallace with the initial means for holding the bridges over the Monocacy River near Frederick, Maryland. This defense forced Early to stop, and show his strength to Wallace. Luckily for the Union, the bulk of Major General James B. Ricketts' division from the Army of the Potomac arrived in time to conduct the heaviest fighting in this pivotal battle.

Right Flank Action at Monocacy

The 11th Maryland (a 100 days outfit) supported part of the Union artillery and covered a crucial ford, but it was the combined companies of the 149th (seven) and the 144th (three), plus one hundred mounted infantry of the 159th Ohio Volunteer Infantry, all under Colonel Brown, who engaged in some of the sharpest skirmishing of the Monocacy affair. Positioned at the important Stone or Jug Bridge which carried the National Road to Baltimore across the Monocacy, as well as a small ford farther upstream, they spent twelve hot and trying hours containing the Sharpshooter Corps and later the Georgia brigade of Major General Robert Rodes' Confederate division.

Suffering heavy losses in proportion to their numbers, Brown's men kept about three hundred of his men in hand as the rest of Wallace's army disintegrated and retired from the field. His action permitted the majority of this force to escape to Baltimore. Afterward, authorities generally agreed that Wallace's bold decision to fight Early cost the Confederates a day's march time, and thus any chance to capture Washington. The Ohio National Guardsmen had contributed to this result.[23]

Lincoln and Guardsmen Under Fire

When Early reached the northern defenses of Washington on July 11, 1864, the forts were held largely by thinly stretched Ohio National Guardsmen. Although determined to fight, they were ill-trained on the heavy artillery and inexperienced as infantry. Before the hot, tired, and dusty Confederate marchers had closed completely on the fortification line in preparation for an assault, veteran VI Corps troops had filed into the trenches, fresh from a waterborne trip from Petersburg to save the capital. When President Lincoln underwent Confederate sniper fire during the battle at Fort Stevens on July 11 and 12, he was observed closely by men of the 150th Ohio Veteran Infantry. Some believed that he unduly exposed himself in order to encourage these young, raw soldiers. Other 100-days soldiers participated in stopping Early's attack on Washington including the 147th and 151st Ohio Volunteer Infantry regiments. Later, the 144th and 149th Ohio Volunteer Infantry marched up and down the Shenandoah Valley in pursuit of Early. Several of their companies were battered in fights with partisans led by the famous John Mosby. Between Monocacy and Mosby, two hundred prisoners from the Guard regiments ended their service in Southern prison pens, scores of whom died before the war ended.

Because of their perceived worth, and the insatiable require-
ments of the war that bloody summer, the 149th Ohio Volunteer
Infantry was not mustered out until the end of August. They had
served faithfully for one hundred twenty-one days! Of the 83,612
One Hundred Days men from eleven states, 1,753 died in service or
in rebel prisons (only about 100 were killed in battle, while hundreds
were wounded). As with all Civil War units, sickness took the heaviest toll with most of these deaths coming before the soldiers had
acquired natural immunity and knowledge of life in camp and field.[24]

Muster Out

Back home, the Ohio National Guardsmen reverted to their militia role and organization. They were not mustered out of state service until March 1866. Fears of, and prospects for, a Northwest Confederacy or a Morgan-style raid vanished. The attempted raid on
Johnson's Island was compromised and bungled. Ohio was safe for
the remainder of the war, and many of the Younger Guardsmen volunteered for active service.

A Brief Evaluation

The human cost was high, as was the political and economic
toll. The war was not won in 1864, and the disruption to political
amity and home front production was important. Politically, the
scheme hurt Governor Brough rather by the blunt, insensitive manner that he suppressed opposition rather than the cost of "illegality"
of the call-up. Astutely, he decided not to seek renomination. He
died in office from overweight, overwork, and ultimately gangrene.
Yet, Brough's idea of a special service created a burst of rejuvenated
patriotism among the Guardsmen, their families and friends, which
ultimately balanced the inconvenience and personal costs of the duty.
Brough's bold, but not altogether altruistic offer of "free" troops
gave Lincoln and the national government a badly needed psychologi-
cal boost, in what everyone considered the darkest time of the war.
Whether or not the issue of the 100 Days men helped or hindered
Lincoln's reelection in the fall, the president was grateful for their summer contribution. The opening quotation of this essay notes his welcome to an arriving Guard regiment; in late August, he personally
thanked the 148th, 164th, and 166th Ohio Volunteers before they
returned home. The soldier vote was critical to Lincoln's reelection; he
had sensed this fact, and sued these men to carry his message back
to the homefront. In turn, the president always enjoyed his personal

encounters with his boys in blue and learned much about patriotism from them.[25]

Militarily, the issue was more clear cut. When the 155th Ohio Volunteer Infantry returned to Circleville and again became the 92d Ohio National Guard regiment, the governor personally welcomed them, declaring: "I know positively now, that but for the response of those National Guards upon that occasion, the cause of the Union would have been lost." Indeed, the Guardsmen had contributed to the wearing down of Confederate foemen. They offset the heavy Union losses in battles from the Wilderness to the James. As Grant told Halleck on May 26: "I may be mistaken, but I feel that our success over Lee's army is already assured. The promptness and rapidity with which you have forwarded reinforcements has contributed largely to the feeling of confidence inspired in our men, and to break down that of the enemy." Of course, Appomattox lay nearly a year in the future, and many equally bloody days and months lay in-between.[26]

What was the net worth of these "summer soldiers"? Previous short-term militia calls had been inconclusive in monies expended, morale, and lost labor, and the results had been inconclusive at best. Naturally, short-term militia received ridicule from long-term, battle-hardened veterans, both then and after the war. Yet, the 100-days initiative helped produce a significant outcome on the national level. Ohio's organization of a select volunteer militia, led by a cadre of capable and experienced leaders, established a standard and set an example for the future. The National Guard, composed of such citizen-soldiers, remains to this day part of the nation's defense establishment. Despite substantial shortcomings, they were in 1864, and remain so today, "cost effective" as a supplement to veteran or regular troops.

The One Hundred Days Men Memorial

President Lincoln, in order to show his deep appreciation to those Buckeyes who had responded so quickly and enthusiastically in May 1864, directed that a special Certificate of Honorable Service be issued to each of them. As his Special Executive Order of September 19, 1864 read: "In the Valley of the Shenandoah, on the Peninsula, in the operations on the James River around Petersburg and Richmond, in the battle of Monocacy, and in the entrenchments of Washington, and in other important service, the National Guard of Ohio performed with alacrity the duty of patriotic volunteers, for which they are entitled to, and are hereby tendered through the Governor of their State, the national thanks." Three weeks later, a similar executive order thanked the One Hundred Days soldiers from Indiana, Illinois, Iowa, and Wisconsin for their contributions to victory in the west. Years later, George Perkins, member and historian of the 149th Ohio Volunteer Infantry, wrote about his memories and relics of that special service. "But the most prized," he declared, was "the engraved and engrossed card of thanks given by the president of the United States, under seal of the Government, and signed by the martyred friend of every Union soldier, Abraham Lincoln."[27]

APPENDIX 3

Monocacy Self-Guided Motor Tour

The following self-guided tour (full or abbreviated and designed for motor vehicles) will help visitors understand the scope and extent of the battle of the Monocacy. Four to five hours should be allowed for the full tour due to traffic, road arrangement, and stopping time. The tour exceeds the limits of the Monocacy National Battlefield. As in any historical site visit, one should always allow maximum time not only for understanding the story but appreciating the scenery and topography.

STOP 1 - I-270 SCENIC VIEW OVERLOOK

DIRECTIONS - Take Interstate 270 north from Washington using any modern roadmap. Approximately thirty-five miles from the city, you will find the *SCENIC VIEW* overlook on right (open until dark under suitable weather conditions). The tour starts here (0 mile mark).

FACILITIES - Here is the best place to begin your Monocacy tour, thanks to longtime Congressman Goodloe Byron who represented the area. Visitors can learn briefly from interpretive markers about the history of the Monocacy River valley, the clustered spires of Frederick, and Monocacy—the battle that saved Washington from capture during the Civil War. Moreover, general appreciation of the scenic panorama of Frederick, the Monocacy valley, and Catoctin Mountain as well as terrain features can be obtained by walking to the edge of the field in front of the markers.

STOP 2 - PRELUDE ACTION AT MIDDLETOWN

DIRECTIONS: Return to I-270 North, proceed approximately three miles to I-70 West and then to Exit 49, Alternate US 40 West (8.0 mile

268

mark) turning left at stoplight to Braddock Heights and Middletown. Proceeding a total of approximately 11.1 miles (from Scenic Overlook) to eastern edge of Middletown (Town Center Plaza shopping mall and Coblentz Road).

HISTORIC SITES: Once on Alternate US 40 West, you will be traveling a historic highway in the footsteps of the men of both armies. Modern Braddock Heights was Solomon's Gap in the Catoctin Mountain during the Civil War. At approximately 10.4 mile mark you will pass Motter's Tavern on your left (just before crossing Hollow Creek) and at 10.8 mile mark, the Town Center Plaza will appear on your right. In this vicinity occurred the Middletown cavalry action between Bradley Johnson, Harry Gilmor, and David Clendenin on July 7, 1864. It marked the prelude action to the battle of Monocacy. The Daniel Kefauver farmstead to your left and the Charles Coblentz farmstead to your right provide the approximate parameters of the battle site. By turning right onto Coblentz Road at the 11.1 mile mark and proceeding .4 of a mile, you will see the Coblentz farm on right. Jubal Early headquartered here on the night of July 8, while his army encamped in the area on both sides of Alternate US 40.

Retrace your route eastward on Alternate US Route 40, again passing through the Middletown battlefield (including Motter's tavern at creek). Climbing Catoctin Mountain once more, pause at small scenic overlook—the approximate area of Clendenin's rear-guard action by Alexander's Baltimore Battery on July 7. Descending the mountain on the east side, you will pass a historical marker on your right denoting the site of Braddock's Spring from French and Indian War campaigns of British Major General Edward Braddock (which undoubtedly quenched the thirst of Early's parched soldiery in 1864), and in the "S" curve thereafter, Hagen's Tavern on left was Bradley Johnson's command post and the site of further skirmishing as prelude to Monocacy.

STOP 3 - BATTLE OF FREDERICK SITES

DIRECTIONS: Continue east on Alternate US 40 to Mount Phillip Road at 15.8 mile mark, turn right to Butterfly Lane at 16.3 mile mark, turn left, continuing to traffic light at St. Johns Literary Institution at Prospect Hall (located on Monocacy-era Prospect Hill)—at 18.2 mile mark —and turn left as if to enter US 15 South (*do not, however, make that entry!*). At bottom of hill, you will see marker denoting Major General George Gordon Meade's assumption of command of the Army of the Potomac in this vicinity in June 1863 (18.3 mile mark). The Civil War-era highways from Harpers Ferry and Jefferson converged at Prospect Hill in 1864 (now obscured by modern highway system). Keep left (*not entering US 15*) and proceed via Himes Avenue to Seneca Drive at the 19.0 mile mark.

HISTORIC SITES: In the fields stretching toward Frederick stood the right of the Confederate skirmish line for fighting on July 7 and 8 between Johnson, Clendenin and Gilpin's troops for control of Harpers Ferry road access into the city. The Rizer and Zimmerman farms that covered the ground (now occupied by roads, suburbs and shopping malls between this area and downtown Frederick), witnessed sharp fighting preparatory to the battle of July 9 at Monocacy Junction.

DIRECTIONS: Turn right on Seneca Drive to Hillcrest Drive (19.1 mile mark), right onto Maryland Route 144 (19.7 mile mark), getting immediately in left lane for left turn onto Baughman's Lane (just beyond State Police Station)—20.1 mile mark.

HISTORIC SITES: This area constituted the middle and left of the Confederate skirmish position on July 8 along what was known as Burnt Mill Road. It also constituted contested ground between Clendenin and Johnson the day before. Across from Police Station (behind Midas Muffler) on the south side lies Hagen's Hill from which the Confederate Baltimore Light Battery dueled with Alexander's Union Baltimore Artillery at the junction of the Hagerstown and Harpers Ferry roads at the western edge of Frederick.

DIRECTIONS: Continue on Baughman's Lane to Shookstown Road stop light (20.8 mile mark), turn right, crossing one-lane bridge, to Rosemont Avenue (21.1 mile mark), right on Rosemont (historic Almshouse Road) to West Second Street (21.5 mile mark), again turning right at historic Schifferstadt house and proceed on West Second Street.

HISTORIC SITES: You have now passed from the left flank anchor of Johnson's Confederate battle line at the Shookstown Road/ Baughman's Lane intersection to the right flank skirmish line of Tyler, Gilpin, and Clendenin near the historic German-American Schifferstadt house (the oldest house in Frederick, still standing, and possibly America's finest example of German colonial architecture). The Federal battle line of July 8 faced Carroll Creek and wound southward to the high ground intersection of the Hagerstown turnpike and Harpers Ferry road.

DIRECTIONS: Proceed on West Second Street to College Terrace Avenue (22.0 mile mark) and turn right; proceed to major intersection and stop light at West Patrick Street (Maryland Route 144) (22.3 mile mark), follow one way signs left onto West South Street—Maryland Route 144 headed intown.

HISTORIC SITES: You are now at the junction of the Hagerstown and Harpers Ferry roads where Union forces under Tyler, Gilpin and Clendenin contested entry into Frederick on July 8, 1864. From this high ground on the western edge of the city, they skirmished with Bradley Johnson's cavalry descending from Catoctin Mountain. Alexander's battery dueled with their Confederate counterparts from Baltimore from this vicinity.

STOP 4 - DOWNTOWN FREDERICK

DIRECTIONS: Continue east on South Street (Maryland Route 144) to South Market Street (Maryland Route 355) traffic light (23.1 mile mark). Turn left into heart of Frederick, noting period architecture, streets and other sites.

HISTORIC SITES: Proceed northward on South Market Street noting the Civil War-era Baltimore and Ohio passenger station on the southeast corner of Market and All Saints Street (23. 2 mile mark) where Wallace, the 10th Vermont, and other reinforcements coming from Monocacy Junction alighted on July 8 for the fighting west of town. On the northwest corner of Market and West Second Street, Jubal Early briefly maintained a command post early on the morning of July 9 while enjoying the hospitality of Dr. Richard Hammond. You may choose to tour Old Courthouse Square (the heart of Civil War Frederick), two blocks west at this point by turning left at Second Street one or two blocks. Similarly, other fine old houses line the streets of this western Maryland town, many dating to its earliest days on the colonial frontier. (Note: A visitor's center and the Frederick Historical Society, Inc. are both located on East Church Street and warrant a side visit.)

STOP 5 - STONE (JUG) BRIDGE COMBAT SECTOR

DIRECTIONS: Drive east on either Church or East Third Street to East Street then right to rejoin Maryland Route 144 (Old National Road). Turn left on Maryland 144 or East Patrick Street to the new location of the Jug Bridge Monument on Bowman's Road to your left (25.5 mile mark).

HISTORIC SITE: Here in a small park, the historic and famous Jug monument has been relocated from the old bridge crossing farther east.

The history of the Jug and bridge, and the Marquis de Lafayette's 1824 visit to Frederick can be appreciated by appropriate historical markers.

DIRECTIONS: Continue on Bowman's Road past Motor Vehicle Administration (MVA) facility to "dead end" (26.3 mile mark) for overview of Stone Bridge sector of Monocacy battlefield from the Confederate perspective. Retrace steps to Maryland Route 144 East, turning left, and proceed to Quinn Orchard Road (27.5 mile mark)—approximate site of Rodes' Confederate battleline on July 9. Continue on Maryland Route 144 to sign East Patrick Street Extended on left or "Park and Ride" on right. Turn left into parking area on north or left side of highway. Tyler's Ohio troops occupied this general vicinity for the heavy skirmishing with Rodes' men.

HISTORIC SITES: You will note historic houses in the area including Hargett house on north side of the original Old National Pike. While private property and not accessible, continuation by foot toward river on roadway leads to the Stone Bridge toll house (ca. 1807) and remains of the stone bridge abutments. This general floodplain area witnessed heavy fighting late in the day on July 9 as did the higher ground from Quinn Orchard Road to ridgeline where you parked.

STOP 6 - FREDERICK WAREHOUSES/HOSPITALS

DIRECTIONS: Return to downtown Frederick via Maryland Route 144 East, turning left at South Carroll Street (30.4 mile mark).

HISTORIC SITES: East All Saints Street (at 30.5 mile mark) was the area of warehouses and the Baltimore and Ohio freight station facilities providing a supply base for Federal operations in the Frederick vicinity.

DIRECTIONS: Continuing on South Carroll Street, you will see the stone back of the old Hessian Barracks (now on grounds of the Maryland School for the Deaf) that served as site of a U.S. General Hospital during the war (30.8 mile mark). Proceed to dead end and turn right into alley, the John Loats farmstead to your left (31.0 mile mark) was the ostensible location of Early's command post for the later stages of the Monocacy battle on July 9. Continue to Maryland Route 355 (South Market Street) turning left.

STOP 7 - BEST FARM/CONFEDERATE POSITION

DIRECTIONS: Drive south on Maryland Route 355, staying in left lane so that you can bear left at third traffic light (Buckeystown Road confluence)—31.7 mile mark. The abrupt narrowing of Route 355 (after passing Francis Scott Key Shopping Mall on right), marks the northern boundary of the Monocacy National battlefield (33.4 mile mark). Stop at Confederate and Maryland commemorative markers on right side of road for orientation but—*Please Note—Maryland Route 355 is a heavily trafficked highway. BE CAREFUL!*

HISTORIC SITES: You are now standing where Stephen Ramseur's Confederates would have viewed the battle with the Best farm to your right and front, Monocacy Junction beyond the fields to your left front, and the covered bridge across the Monocacy on the turnpike to Washington—straight ahead. Heavy skirmishing in this sector plus numerous Confederate artillery positions on both sides of the highway are of interest. Proceed south on highway ahead noting period Best farm buildings on right and fields on both sides of Route 355 that witnessed the sharp skirmishing by Vermont and Maryland Federals with Ramseur's men, before the highway overpass of Baltimore and Ohio Railroad (33.7 mile mark).

STOP 8 - NEW JERSEY MONUMENT/MONOCACY JUNCTION

DIRECTIONS: Slow down as you cross railroad overpass (33.8 mile mark) to turn right abruptly into lane leading to 14th New Jersey monument parking.

HISTORIC SITES: Here lay the 14th New Jersey campgrounds from 1862–63 as well as further scenes of heavy skirmishing and fighting north of river on July 9, 1864. The "triangle" of Monocacy Junction, western blockhouse and railroad bridge sites may be reachable on foot from this point. The railroad right-of-way was the original Baltimore and Ohio main line between the Chesapeake Bay and the west constructed years before the Civil War.

STOP 9 - COVERED BRIDGE CROSSING/GAMBRILL'S MILL

DIRECTIONS: Continue south on Maryland Route 355, crossing river at covered bridge crossing site. Union earthwork remains may be seen by parking on left at top of hill. Proceed to National Battlefield entrance (34.3 mile mark) and *yielding to oncoming traffic*, turn left abruptly into Gambrill's Mill lane. Park car and go to National Park Service Visitors Center in restored remnant of Gambrill's mill for electric map orientation, exhibits, and information.

HISTORIC SITES: After visitor orientation, query NPS staff as to what sites may be reached by foot in immediate vicinity of Gambrill's Mill. Gambrill's postwar mansion, the immediate final scenes of combat during the Federal retirement from battle, site of Wallace's headquarters, and bivouac and hospital area are in this vicinity. Due to the incipient development of the park, however, it is best to be guided by National Park Service personnel as to appropriate visitation sites. It is of particular importance to ask about accessibility to Worthington farm for subsequent visitation on tour.

STOP 10 - ARABY/WORTHINGTON FARMS COMBAT AREA

DIRECTIONS: Depart Gambrill's Mill Visitor Center, continue directly across Maryland Route 355 onto Araby Church Road (Civil War-era Washington turnpike), proceeding to entrance to Araby farm lane (34.7 mile mark). On your right you will pass en route the high hill field and site of final resistance by Ricketts' veterans. Araby lane (private) leads to the restored Thomas mansion. Proceed to Araby Church and Baker Valley Road intersection (34.8 mile mark).

HISTORIC SITES: You are now in the most important part of the combat area of the battle of Monocacy, July 9, 1864, with the Pennsylvania and Vermont monuments attesting to the significance. Note the original road embankment beside Araby farm that served as a strong defensive position for Truex's brigade. The Vermont monument site provides a good view of Araby and its surrounding fields of combat.

DIRECTIONS: Proceed slowly west on Baker Valley Road, for a better view of Araby house (35.1 mile mark). A panoramic view of the fields where McCausland battled Ricketts and the swirl of fighting around the Thomas house and barn can be gained before view is obscured when passing under I-270. Immediately thereafter (35.5 mile mark) will be found the gate and Worthington lane which may or may not be accessible on a given day. The unrestored structure is well worth a visit although the interstate now obscures the vista seen by Confederates from Worthington house to Araby. However, a good view of the Baker farmstead and Brooks Hill can be secured from the Baker Valley Road at this point.

STOP 11 - BUCKEYSTOWN ROAD HOSPITALS

DIRECTIONS: Continue on Baker Valley Road to Maryland Route 80 (Buckeystown-Urbana road) (37.1 mile mark). Turn right and go to Michael's Mill Road (37.8 mile mark) immediately after crossing Monocacy River. Here Early's army might have crossed and gained the Washington turnpike at Urbana without a battle. Turn right on Michael's Mill Road (Maryland Route 880), passing Michael's Mill (1739) into the picturesque hamlet of Buckeystown. Turn right again on Maryland Route 85 to Frederick (39.0 mile mark).

HISTORIC SITES: At the 40.2 mile mark, a left turn onto Lime Kiln Road will take you past the M. J. Grove house, across the railroad to one of lime kiln ruins from which Confederate cavalry scouts reconnoitered the battle transpiring beyond the Monocacy (40.5 mile mark). Returning to Route 85 and turning left, will carry you past the Arcadia mansion hospital site (41.7 mile mark) on left, and the Markell house hospital site on right shortly thereafter (42.0 mile mark). Just after crossing Ballenger Creek between these sites, Marcies Choice Lane to the right approximates the farm lane that Confederates used to reach the McKinney-Worthington farm ford to outflank Wallace and Ricketts. Today it is inaccessible due to county government facilities in the vicinity. Joseph Hooker ostensibly received the order relieving him of command of the Army of the Potomac and replacing him with George G. Meade for the Gettysburg campaign in the dooryard of Arcadia.

STOP 12 - MOUNT OLIVET CEMETERY

DIRECTIONS: Continue on Maryland Route 85 (Buckeystown Road) to merge with Maryland Route 355 just south of Frederick (44.3 mile mark). Left onto Route 355 will bring you to the gate of Mt. Olivet Cemetery on left (44.9 mile mark). Turn into cemetery and proceed straight to back fence of cemetery.

HISTORIC SITES: Note the line of 87 identified Confederate graves. A mass gravesite of 408 Confederates killed in the Monocacy fighting may be found at the Confederate monument nearby (32.7 mile marker). Monuments to Monocacy unknown, Confederate unknown, Frederick Confederates, as well as burial sites for local notables Francis Scott Key, Thomas Johnson, and Barbara Fritchie are located in this cemetery.

STOP 13 - URBANA CAVALRY ACTION

DIRECTIONS: Retrace your route south on Maryland Route 355, through the battlefield some 6.5 miles to Urbana Church Road (52.1 mile mark). Turn right to Urbana Methodist Church and Cemetery (52.2 mile mark). Continue on Urbana Church Road to intersection with Maryland Route 80, left to Urbana crossroads and Maryland Route 355.

HISTORIC SITES: Here Confederate Lieutenant Colonel William C. Tavenner and Major Frederick F. Smith, both of the 17th Virginia cavalry are buried next to the church ruins. The cavalry action between Clendenin and Johnson took place in the center of town along Maryland Route 355 between present day intersections of Maryland Route 80 west to Buckeystown, and east to Centreville. Historical properties Tucker's Place and Cockey's House and Store provide the historical parameters for the fighting which ensured protection to Wallace's retreating Federals to the north.

STOP 14 - WALLACE'S RETREAT ROUTE

DIRECTIONS: Return north on Maryland Route 355 to Reel's Mill Road (55 mile mark), turn sharply right to Ball Road (56 mile mark), right again to bottom of hill and Reel's Mill Road (57.7 mile mark). Turn left to follow Union retreat route from Monocacy battle.

HISTORIC SITES: Off to your left at the 57.7 mile mark (Double Tree Court), lies the site where 300 Federals were captured by Ramseur's men during the retreat. Continue on Reel's Mill Road (as Wallace's retreating army did) to Reich's Ford Road intersection (58.1 mile mark). To your left lies the Monocacy bridge crossing at Crum's Ford. Here on high ground, Landstreet's 11th Maryland deterred passage until late in the afternoon on July 9. The Crum-Reich house lies approximately one mile further toward Frederick on this road. Reich's Ford can be reached upstream via Pine Cliff Park Road just before crossing the Monocacy. Wallace's army turned right at the Reel's Mill/Reich's Ford Road intersection, veering north to Bartonsville via country lanes shortly thereafter.

STOP 15 - TYLER'S FINAL STAND

DIRECTIONS: From the Reich's Ford Road and Reel's Mill Road intersection, the tour route continues to Hines Road (59.6 mile mark), then left to intersection with Bartonsville Road (61.2 mile mark). Turn left and follow this road to Maryland Route 144. A short zigzag to left and onto Linganore Road will lead past Dr. Baxter Road on left (leading down to Stone [Jug] bridge abutments) on east bank of Monocacy (62.9 mile mark).

HISTORIC SITES: This line of high ground north and south of the turnpike from Baltimore into Frederick constituted the right flank Ohio National Guard positions of Wallace's six-mile defense line. In this general vicinity, Tyler's command made its final defensive stand as pursuing Confederates appeared in the vicinity of Bartonsville. Tyler and party escaped capture by following the Linganore Road northward, past where Buckeye contingents earlier in the day had contested passage of Hughes Ford about one mile upstream. The road eventually intersects with the Liberty Road—artery used by Johnson's expedition to Baltimore and Point Lookout. Wallace's defeated army marched eastward on the turnpike to New Market and the railroad at Monrovia.

END OF TOUR

This ends the suggested Monocacy battle tour. You may either return to Frederick westward via Maryland Route 144 (joining interstate 70 en route) or follow Wallace's line of retreat eastward on Route 144 to New Market and Monrovia and on to Baltimore. Similarly, you may wish to follow Early's route to Washington following the battle of Monocacy via Maryland Route 355 through Hyattstown, Clarksburg, Gaithersburg, to Rockville and thence to Bethesda and the District of Columbia via Wisconsin Avenue NW, or through Silver Spring to the District of Columbia and Fort Stevens via Georgia Avenue NW.

ABBREVIATIONS TO ENDNOTES

AAH	Alabama Department of Archives and History
CHS	Chicago Historical Society
DUL	Duke University Library
FC	Filson Club
FCHS	Frederick County Historical Society
FWM	Fort Ward Museum and Historical Library
HL	Huntington Library
ISHL	Illinois State Historical Library
LC	Library of Congress
MAHS	Massachusetts Historical Society
MCHS	Montgomery County Historical Society
MDHS	Maryland Historical Society
NARA	National Archives and Records Administration
NCHA	North Carolina Department of History and Archives
NLHA	North Louisiana Historical Association
NYHS	New York Historical Society
ORA	*Official Records of Union and Confederate Armies*
SHC/UNC	Southern Historical Collection, University of North Carolina, Chapel Hill
TLA	Tennessee State Library and Archives
TUL	Tulane University Library
UGL	University of Georgia Library
UNCL	University of North Carolina Library
USAMHI	United States Army Military History Institute
VAHS	Virginia Historical Society
VSLA	Virginia State Library and Archives
VTHS	Vermont Historical Society
WRHS	Western Reserve Historical Society

ENDNOTES

PREFACE

1. Lucius E. Chittenden, *Recollections of President Lincoln and His Administration* (New York and London, 1891), p. 390; John B. Gordon, *Reminiscences of the Civil War* (New York, 1904), pp. 311–313.
2. John W. Schildt, *Drums Along the Monocacy*, Chewsville, Md., 1992, pp. 5-26.
3. William Jarboe Grove, *History of Carrollton Manor, Frederick County, Maryland* (Frederick, 1928), pp. 192–193.
4. Gary W. Gallagher, *Fighting For the Confederacy: The Personal Recollections of General Edward Porter Alexander* (Chapel Hill, 1989), pp. 339–340.
5. See for example, James M. McPherson, *Battle Cry of Freedom: The Civil War Era* (New York, 1988), p. 756; Peter J. Parish, *The American Civil War* (New York, 1975), p. 466; Allan Nevins, *The War for the Union: The Organized War to Victory 1864–1865* (New York, 1971), p. 88; contrasted with Gary W. Gallagher, "Monocacy," in Francis H. Kennedy, editor, *The Civil War Battlefield Guide* (Boston, 1990), p. 238; B. F. Cooling, *Jubal Early's Raid on Washington, 1864* (Baltimore, 1989), pp. 80–81 and chaps. 4 and 5; and Frank Vandiver, *Jubal's Raid* (New York, 1960), chaps. 4, 5, 6.
6. See Jeffry D. Wert, *From Winchester to Cedar Creek* (Carlisle, 1987); Thomas A. Lewis, *The Shenandoah in Flames* (Alexandria, 1987); Edward J. Stackpole, *Sheridan in the Shenandoah* (Harrisburg, 1961); for general accounts, while Cooling, *Jubal Early's Raid*, chaps. 7, 8, develops the continuing threat to Washington.
7. See McPherson, *Battle Cry of Freedom*, pp. 757–758; Albert Castel, *Decision in the West: The Atlanta Campaign of 1864* (Lawrence, Kans., 1992), pp. 288, 345, 446, 475, 547; Bruce Catton, *The Civil War* (Boston, 1960), p. 198.
8. Quoted in Worthington, *Fighting for Time*, p. 244.
9. Ronald Reagan, "Why We Should Always Remember," *The Washington Post*, June 5, 1994, Outlook Section, p. C-1.

CHAPTER ONE

1. The Second Corps' experience can be followed in the classic Douglas Southall Freeman, *Lee's Lieutenants* (New York, 1942–1944), vol. 3, also, Noah Andre Trudeau, *Bloody Roads South: the Wilderness to Cold Harbor* (Boston, 1989); Gary W. Gallagher, editor, *Fighting for the Confederacy: the Personal Recollections of General Edward Porter Alexander* (Chapel Hill, 1989).

2. Joseph T. Durkin, editor, *Confederate Chaplain: War Journal of Reverend James B. Sheeran* (Milwaukee, 1960), p. 93.
3. Bell I. Wiley, editor, George Dallas Musgrove, *Kentucky Cavaliers in Dixie: Reminiscences of a Confederate Cavalryman* (Jackson, Tenn, 1957), p. 61; Edward A. Pollard, *The Lost Cause* (New York, 1867), p. 532; U.S. War Department, *The War of the Rebellion: the Official Records of Union and Confederate Armies* (Washington, 1880–1901), ser. I, vol. 37, pt. 1, pp. 439–440, 709, 760–762, hereafter cited *ORA* with appropriate series, volume part, and page.
4. Lee A. Wallace, *Fifth Virginia Infantry* (Lynchburg, 1988), p. 60; Charles G. Osborne, *Jubal: The Life and Times of Jubal A. Early, C.S.A.* (Chapel Hill, 1992), pt. 1.
5. Ezra Warner, *Generals in Gray* (Baton Rouge, 1959), pp. 34–35, 79–80, 111, 191–192, 197–198, 251–252, 253–254, 263.
6. E. B. Long, *The Civil War Day by Day: an Almanac, 1861–1865* (Garden City, N.Y., 1971), p. 529; *ORA*, I, 37, pt. 1, pp. 703–704, 766.
7. Background for the campaign may be followed in Frank E. Vandiver, *Jubal's Raid: General Early's Famous Attack on Washington* (New York, 1960), chap. 1; Benjamin Franklin Cooling, *Jubal Early's Raid, July 1864* (Baltimore, 1989), chap. 1; Alexander, *Recollections*, pp. 438–439.
8. On Lee's thinking at the time, see Clifford Dowdey and Louis Manarin, editors, *The Wartime Papers of Robert E. Lee* (New York, 1971), pp. 774–775, 807.
9. *ORA*, I, 37, pt. 1, p. 346; Jubal A. Early, *War Memoirs* (Baltimore, 1989 edition), p. 371; Letter Michael Andrus – B. F. Cooling, June 2, 1993, author's files.
10. Osborne, *Jubal*, pp. 242–243; Freeman, *Lee's Lieutenants*, III, pp. xv, 510, 524; Samuel J. Martin, *The Road to Glory: Confederate General Richard S. Ewell* (Indianapolis, 1991), pp. 320–321, citing Campbell Brown–Richard Ewell, June 5, and Jubal Early–Ewell, June 13, both 1864, both Polk, Brown, and Ewell family papers (SHC/UNC).
11. Dowdey and Manarin, *Lee Papers*, pp. 782, 807, 811; also Edward S. Wilson, "The Lynchburg Campaign," in W. H. Chamberlin, editor, Ohio Commandery, Loyal Legion of the United States, *Sketches of War History, 1861–1865* (Cincinnati, 1896), IV, pp. 133–147; Don P. Halsey, *Historic and Heroic Lynchburg* (Lynchburg, 1935), chaps. 3 and 5; Robert Grier Stephens, Jr. compiler/editor, *Intrepid Warrior: Clement Anselm Evans, Confederate General from Georgia* (Dayton, 1992), pp. 419–420.
12. Thomas A. Lewis, *The Shenandoah in Flames* (Alexandria, Va, 1987), pp. 56–58, 68; J. Kelly Bennette diary, July 1, 1864 (SHC/UNC).
13. *ORA*, I, 51, pt. 2, pp. 175–176; Zebulon York, "Official Report," July 22, 1864, Eldridge collection, Huntington Library; Leonidus L. Polk to wife, June 16, 1864 (SHC/UNC).
14. Early, *Memoirs*, pp. 382–383; Laura Virginia Hale, *Four Valiant Years in the Shenandoah Valley* (Strasburg, Va., 1968), pp. 378–380.
15. Virgil Carrington Jones, *Ranger Mosby* (Chapel Hill, 1944), pp. 185–186; Jeffry D. Wert, *Mosby's Rangers* (New York, 1990), p. 170.
16. *ORA*, I, 37, pt. 1, pp. 174–176; T. A. Meysenburg, "Notes," July 3, 1864 (DUL); Samuel Clarke Farrar, *The Twenty–Second Pennsylvania Cavalry* (Pittsburgh, 1911), pp. 257–263.
17. R. G. Coleman to wife, July 6, 1864, Mary E. Schooler papers, J. Stoddard Johnston, "Notes," July 3, 1864 (both DUL); *ORA*, I, 37, pt. 2, p. 591; Hale, *Four Valiant Years*, pp. 380–381.
18. Early, *Memoirs*, p. 394.

19. *ORA*, I, 37, pt. 2, p. 15; also useful is Everard Hall Smith, "The General and the Valley; Union Leadership During the Threat to Washington in 1864," Unpublished doctoral dissertation, University of North Carolina at Chapel Hill, 1977; George E. Pond, *The Shenandoah Valley in 1864* (New York, 1833), chaps. 2–4.

20. Useful perspective on the Union position includes: Trudeau, *Bloody Roads South* (Boston, 1989), and *The Last Citadel: Petersburg, Virginia, June 1864– April 1865* (Boston, 1991); William D. Matter, *If It Takes All Summer: the Battle of Spotsylvania* (Chapel Hill, 1988).

21. On the issue of defending Washington, see Benjamin Franklin Cooling, *Symbol, Sword, and Shield: Defending Washington During the Civil War* (Hamden, Conn., 1975; reprint, Shippensburg, Pa.), especially chaps. 2, 5, 7.

22. On unified command, see Bruce Catton, *Grant Takes Command* (Boston, 1968), chaps. 6–8; Ulysses S. Grant, *Personal Memoirs* (New York, 1885), vol. 2, chap. 46; T. Harry Williams, *Lincoln and His Generals* (New York, 1952), chap. 12; Russell F. Weigley, *The American Way of War: a History of United States Military Strategy and Policy* (New York, 1973), chap. 7.

23. *ORA*, I, 33, pp. 383–384, 472; 36, pt. 3, pp. 665–666; 37, pt. 1, pp. 602, 611–612.

24. Smith, "The General and the Valley," pp. 142–153, also chaps. 2, 3.

25. Sigel and Weber, see Ezra Werner, *Generals in Blue* (Baton Rouge, 1964), pp. 447–448, 545–546; for an analysis of Union intelligence problems at this time, see William B. Feis, "A Union Military Intelligence Failure: Jubal Early's Raid, July 13–July 14, 1864," *Civil War History*, 36 (September 1990), pp. 209–225.

26. Patricia L. Faust, editor, *Historical Times Illustrated Encyclopedia of the Civil War* (New York, 1986), p. 376.

27. Charles A. Dana, *Recollections of the Civil War* (New York, 1898), p. 22; *ORA*, I, 37, pt. 1, pp. 680–682; pt. 2, p. 15; Smith, *General and the Valley*, pp. 138– 142, 167.

28. *ORA*, I, 37, pt. 1, pp. 694–695.

29. Ibid., pt.1, pp. 174–175; pt. 2, pp. 3, 4; Howard K. Beale, editor, *The Diary of Edward Bates, 1859–1866* (New York, 1971), p. 382.

30. *ORA*, I, 37, pp. 33, 38; and pt. 1, pp. 176, 184–185.

31. Lee C. Drickamer and Karen D. Drickamer, compilers and editors. *Fort Lyon to Harper's Ferry* (Shippensburg, Pa., 1987), pp. 192–195.

32. *ORA*, I, 37, pt. 2, pp. 33, 38; and pt. 1, pp. 176, 184–185; on Stahel, see, Warner, *Generals in Blue*, pp. 469–470; Lewis, *The Shenandoah in Flames*, pp. 31, 33, 34, 36, 41, 43, 48–49, 51, 58.

33. *ORA*, I, 37, pt. 2, 33.

34. Ibid., pt. 2, p. 58; Baltimore *Sun*, July 4, 1864.

35. *ORA*, I, 37, pp. 59, 60, 79, 80.

36. Margaret Leech, *Reveille in Washington; 1860–1865* (New York, 1941), pp. 329–330; Tyler Dennett, *Lincoln and the Civil War in the Diaries and Letters of John Hay* (New York, 1939), p. 207.

37. Long, *Civil War Day by Day*, pp. 531–533; Virginia Jeans Laas, *Wartime Washington: the Civil War Letters of Elizabeth Blair Lee* (Urbana, 1991), pp. 397–400; Leech, *Reveille*, pp. 329–330.

38. Donald B. Cole and John J. McDonough, editors, Benjamin Brown French, *Witness to the Young Republic: a Yankee's Journal, 1828–1870* (Hanover, N.H., 1989), pp. 452; David Donald, editor, *Inside Lincoln's Cabinet: the Civil War Diaries of Salmon P. Chase* (New York, 1954), pp. 212–235.

39. Howard K. Beale, editor, *Diary of Gideon Welles* (New York, 1960), vol. 2, p. 68; Dowdey and Manarin, *Wartime Papers*, pp. 8–11; Long, *Civil War Day by Day*, p. 534.

CHAPTER TWO

1. Clement A. Evans, editor, *Confederate Military History* (New York, 1962, ed.), vol. 2, pp. 90, 91; John E. Worsham, *One of Jackson's Foot Cavalry* (Jackson, Tenn., 1964 ed.), pp. 233–234; Henry Kyd Douglas, *I Rode With Stonewall* (Chapel Hill, 1940), p. 293; Robert Park, "Diary," *Southern Historical Society Papers* I (1876), p. 378; W. H. Runge, editor, *Four Years in the Confederate Artillery: Diary of Private Henry Robinson Berkeley* (Chapel Hill, 1961), p. 85; John N. Opie, *A Rebel Cavalryman with Lee, Stuart, and Jackson* (Chicago, 1899) pp. 244–245; John G. Young diary, July 6, 1864 (NCHA); Wilmington, N.C., *Daily Journal*, July 27, 1864.

2. George H. Lester, "War Record of the Tom Cobb Infantry," in UDC Georgia Division, *This They Remembered* (Washington, Ga., 1965), p. 106; Manly Wade Wellman, *Rebel Boast: First at Bethel – Last at Appomattox* (New York, 1956), p. 169; John O. Casler, *Four Years in the Stonewall Brigade* (Dayton, 1971 ed.), p. 227.

3. Jubal Anderson Early, *Jubal Early's Memoirs* (Baltimore, 1989 ed.), pp. 385–386; Edward J. Stackpole, *Sheridan in the Shenandoah* (Harrisburg, 1961), p. 53; Douglas Southall Freeman, editor, *Lee's Dispatches* (New York, 1965), pp. 269–271; Clifford Dowdey and Louis Manarin, editors, *The Wartime Papers of R. E. Lee* (New York, 1961), pp. 807–808; U.S. War Department, *The War of the Rebellion: A Compilation of the Official Records of the Union and Confederate Armies* (Washington, 1880–1901), ser. 1, vol. 37, pt. 1, pp. 766–768, 769–770, hereinafter cited ORA; R. G. Coleman to wife, July 6, 1864, Mary E. Schooler papers, Perkins Library (DUL).

4. Millard Bushong, *Old Jube* (Boyce, Va., 1955), p. 197; Coleman to wife, July 6, 1864 (DUL); ORA, I, 37, pt. 2, p. 592; Park, "Diary," p. 377; Young diary, July 4, 1864 (NCHA); William Beavens diary, July 4, 5, 1864 (SHC/UNC); Wellman, *Rebel Boast*, pp. 166–167.

5. S. Roger Keller, *Events of the Civil War in Washington County, Maryland* (Shippensburg, Pa., 1995), pp. 333–335; J. Thomas Scharf, *History of Western Maryland* (Baltimore, 1968 ed.), pp. 285–286; Early *Memoirs*, pp. 384–386; Festus P. Summers, *The Baltimore and Ohio in the Civil War* (Gettysburg, 1993, ed.), pp. 123–124; Ezra Warner, *Generals in Gray* (Baton Rouge, 1959), p. 147.

6. Keller, *Events*, pp. 339–342.

7. Richard R. Duncan, "Maryland's Reaction to Early's Raid in 1864: A Summer of Bitterness," *Maryland Historical Magazine* (Fall 1976), pp. 250–251.

8. Scharf, *History*, pp. 286–287; E. Y. Goldsborough, *Early's Great Raid: Battle of Monocacy* (n.p., 1898; Frederick, Md., 1989 reprint), p. 6.

9. Stackpole, *Sheridan in the Shenandoah*, pp. 54–55; Frank Vandiver, *Jubal's Raid* (New York, 1960), pp. 89–93; Benjamin Franklin Cooling, *Jubal Early's Raid, 1864* (Baltimore, 1989), pp. 41–42; "Report of General Terry, July 22, 1864" (CHS), Chicago, Illinois.

10. Recounted in Paul and Rita Gordon, *A Playground of the Civil War* (Frederick, 1994), pp. 176–179.

11. Scharf, *Western Maryland*, p. 287; Middletown *Valley Register*, July 22, 1864; J. Kelly Bennette diary, July 1–6, 1864 (SHC/UNC); "A Brief Sketch of Cole's Independent Maryland Volunteer Cavalry," n.d., pp. 7, 8 (MDHS).

12. Summers, *The Baltimore and Ohio in the Civil War*, chaps. 2 and 8; for more on Garrett, see, William Bruce Catton, "John W. Garrett of the Baltimore and Ohio: A Study in Seaport and Railroad Competition, 1820–1874," Ph.D. dissertation, 1959; Paul Winchester, *The Baltimore and*

Ohio Railroad (Baltimore, 1927); William R. Quinn, editor, *The Diary of Jacob Engelbrecht* (Frederick, 1976), vol. 3, September 7, 1862 entry.

13. Lewis Wallace: *Lew Wallace: An Autobiography* (New York, 1906), vol. 2, pp. 698–700.

14. Ibid., pp. 701–704; *ORA*, I, 37, pt. 2, p. 17, also pp. 16, 18.

15. Wallace, *Autobiography*, II, p. 705; *ORA*, I, 37, pt. 1, pp. 573–574, also pp. 193–194.

16. Frederick H. Dyer, compiler, *A Compendium of the War of the Rebellion* (New York, 1959, edition), vol. 3, pp. 1231, 1233, 1234, 1237, 1550–1551.

17. Wallace, *Autobiography*, II, pp. 704–707; Ezra Warner, *Generals in Blue* (Baton Rouge, 1964), p. 515.

18. Warner, *Generals*, pp. 707–711.

19. In addition to Wallace's autobiography, especially II, pp. 577–580; see Irving McKee, "*Ben Hur Wallace*": *The Life of General Lew Wallace* (Berkeley and Los Angeles, 1944), pp. 52–57, 64–65, 70.

20. McKee, *Ben Hur Wallace*, pp. 66–70.

21. *ORA*, I, 37, pt. 2, p. 53; the message traffic for this period can be followed pp. 17–78; also Wallace, *Autobiography*, II, chap. 71, especially pp. 712–713; on the cannon see Francis W. Wild, *Memoirs and History of Capt. F. W. Alexander's Baltimore Battery* (Baltimore, 1912), p. 131.

22. *ORA*, I, 37, pt. 2, p. 33.

23. Ibid., pt. 2, pp. 34–35; also pt. 1, p. 219.

24. Ibid., pt. 2, pp. 36–38, 54.

25. Ibid., pt. 2, p. 55.

26. Ibid., pt. 1, p. 4; Jeffry D. Wert, *Mosby's Rangers* (New York, 1990), pp. 171–173; also Briscoe Goodhart, *History of the Independent Loudoun Virginia Rangers* (Washington, 1896), pp. 132–133; John H. Alexander, *Mosby's Men* (New York, 1907), pp. 76–84; W. H. Engler, "After Horses," *The National Tribune*, October 28, 1909; Virgil Carrington Jones, *Ranger Mosby* (Chapel Hill, 1944), p. 186.

27. William Jabor Grove, *History of Carrollton Manor, Frederick County, Maryland* (Frederick, 1928), p. 398; Wert, *Mosby's Rangers*, pp. 172–173.

28. Wert, *Mosby's Rangers*, p. 173; for a slightly different view of Mosby's contribution, see Carl Brent Beamer, "Gray Ghostbusters: Eastern Theatre Union Counterguerrilla Operations in the Civil War, 1861–1865," Ph.D. dissertation, Ohio State University, 1988, pp. 98–99.

29. Wallace, *Autobiography*, II, pp. 714–717; *ORA*, I, 37, pt. 2, pp. 54–56, 72–73; George W. Prowell, *History of the Eighty–Seventh Pennsylvania* (York, 1901), p. 179.

30. *ORA*, I, 37, pt. 2, pp. 6, 12, 25–29, 42–48, 74–78, 91.

31. Ibid., I, 37, pt. 2, pp. 70–71, 77–78.

32. Ibid., pp. 62–63.

33. Ibid., p. 59.

34. Ibid., pp. 61–62; 51, pt. 1, pp. 1169–1170.

35. Ibid., pp. 68–70.

36. Ibid., pp. 64–65, also pp. 16–18, 21–23, 36–38, 39, 40, 42–43.

37. David Donald, editor. *Inside Lincoln's Cabinet: The Civil War Diaries of Salmon P. Chase* (New York, 1954), pp. 231–232.

38. Virginia Jeans Laas, editor, *Wartime Washington: The Civil War Letters of Elizabeth Blair Lee* (Urbana and Chicago, 1991), p. 400.

CHAPTER THREE

1. Clifford Dowdey and Louis H. Manarin, editors, *The Wartime Papers of R. E. Lee* (New York, 1961), pp. 814–816; Dan Oates, editor, *Hanging Rock Rebel:*

Lieutenant John Blue's War in West Virginia and the Shenandoah Valley (Shippensburg, Pa., 1994), p. 302.

2. Jeffry D. Wert, *Mosby's Rangers* (New York, 1990), pp. 178–179, citing Mosby to F. F. Bowen, June 12, 1895 [?], Bowen papers (VAHS).

3. Jubal Early, *War Memoirs* (Baltimore, 1989 edition), pp. 385, 386; Robert E. Lee, *Recollections and Letters of General Robert E. Lee* (Garden City, 1904), pp. 131–132; George Wilson Booth, *Personal Reminiscences of a Maryland Soldier* (Baltimore, 1907), pp. 126–127; Douglas Southall Freeman, editor, *Lee's Dispatches* (New York, 1915), pp. 269–271; Dowdey and Maranin, *Lee's Papers*, pp. 766–768; R. G. Coleman to wife, July 6, 1864, Mary Schooler papers, Duke University (DUL); Earl Schenck Meirs, editor, *A Rebel War Clerk's Diary by John B. Jones* (New York, 1958), p. 400.

4. U.S. War Department, *War of the Rebellion: Official Records of Union and Confederate Armies* (Washington, 1880–1901), ser. I, vol. 37, pt. 2, pp. 83–85, hereinafter cited *ORA*; Lewis Wallace, *An Autobiography* (New York, 1906), vol. 2, pp. 717–718; E. B. Long, *The Civil War Day by Day: an Almanac, 1861–1865*, (Garden City, 1971), p. 534; The Frederick (Md.) *Examiner*, July 6, 1864; Charles A. Dana, *Recollections of the Civil War* (New York, 1898), p. 229.

5. *ORA*, I, 37, pt. 2, pp. 79, 80.

6. Ibid., 80–81; J. Newton Terrill, *Campaign of the Fourteenth Regiment New Jersey Volunteers* (New Brunswick, 1884), p. 72; Lemuel A. Abbott, *Personal Recollections and Civil War Diary 1864* (Burlington, 1908), p. 94.

7. *ORA*, I, 37, pp. 80–81.

8. Ibid., pp. 80–85.

9. Ibid., pp. 87–91.

10. Ibid., pp. 95–97; also S. Roger Keller, *Events of the Civil War in Washington County, Maryland* (Shippensburg, Pa. 1995), pp. 340–341.

11. Wallace, *Autobiography*, II, p. 717; *ORA*, I, 37, pt. 2, pp. 86, 87, 91, also 51, pt. 1, pp. 1170–1171; Robert G. Stephens, *Intrepid Warrior, Clement Anselm Evans* (Dayton, 1992), p. 424.

12. Wallace, *Autobiography*, II, p. 721; William H. James, "A Baltimore Volunteer of 1864," *Maryland Historical Magazine* (March 1941), p. 23; Frederick W. Wild, *Memoirs and History of Capt. F. W. Alexander's Baltimore Battery* (Baltimore, 1912), pp. 118–119; *ORA*, I, 51, pt. 1, pp. 1170–1171.

13. Silas D. Wesson diary, July 1, 4, 5, 6, 1864, *Civil War Times Illustrated Collection* (USAMHI), Carlisle Barracks, Pa.

14. *ORA*, I, 37, pt. 1, p. 219; pt. 2, pp. 34, 91; Abner Hard, *History of the Eighth Illinois Cavalry* (Aurora, Ill, 1868), pp. 294–295; John H. Alexander, *Mosby's Men* (New York, 1907), chap. 8; Wert, *Mosby's Rangers*, pp. 173–177.

15. Wallace, *Autobiography*, II, pp. 718–720; Frederick W. Wild, *Memoirs and History of Capt. F. W. Alexander's Baltimore Battery* (Baltimore, 1912), p. 119; *ORA*, I, 37, pt. 1, p. 219.

16. *ORA*, I, 37, pp. 92–94.

17. Wallace, *Autobiography*, II, pp. 720–721; *ORA*, I, 51, pt. 1, p. 1173.

18. *ORA*, I, 37, pt. 1, pp. 219–220; 51, pt. 1, pp. 1172–1173; Wallace, *Autobiography*, II, pp. 722–724; Hard, *Eighth Illinois Cavalry*, p. 296; Goodhart, *Independent Loudoun Virginia Rangers*, p. 134; Scharf, *History of Western Maryland*, p. 287.

19. Harry Gilmor, *Four Years in the Saddle* (New York, 1866), pp. 188–189; J. Kelly Bennette diary, July 7, 1864 (SHC/UNC).

20. *ORA*, I, 51, pt. 1, p. 1172; Wallace, *Autobiography*, II, pp. 724–725.

21. Wallace, *Autobiography*, II, pp. 724–725; Samuel Clarke Ferrar, *The Twenty-Second Pennsylvania Cavalry and the Ringgold Battalion* (Pittsburgh, 1911), p. 269.

22. Wallace, *Autobiography*, II, pp. 727–729; *ORA*, I, 37, pt. 1, pp. 195, 214, 219–223; also 51, pt. 1, 1174–1175; Bradley T. Johnson, "My Ride Around Baltimore in 1864," *Journal of the United States Cavalry Association* (September 1889), p. 252; Gilmor, *Four Years in the Saddle*, pp. 189–190; Wild, *Alexander's Baltimore Battery*, p. 120; William R. Quinn, editor, *The Diary of Jacob Engelbrecht* (Frederick, 1976), pp. 271–272; Letter, Elihu H. Rockwell to Mrs. E. R. Coleman, July 25, 1864 (FCHS).

23. *ORA*, I, 37, pt. 2, p. 110; also 51, pt. 1, pp. 1172, 1173; E. Y. Goldsborough, *Early's Great Raid . . . Battle of Monocacy* (Frederick, 1989 reprint), pp. 8–11; Quinn, *Engelbrecht*, typescript, p. 273.

24. Wild, *Alexander's Baltimore Battery*, pp. 119–120; Quinn, *Engelbrecht*, p. 274.

25. *ORA*, I, 37, pt. 2, pp. 101, 108, 110; T. J. C. Williams and Folger McKinsey, *History of Frederick County, Maryland* (Baltimore, 1967 reprint), I, p. 386; Scharf, *History of Western Maryland*, p. 288; Gilmor, *Four Years in the Saddle*, p. 189; Bradley T. Johnson, "My Ride Around Baltimore", p. 252.

26. *ORA*, I, 37, pt. 2, pp. 99, 100, 108, 116–118.

27. Ibid., pt. 2, pp. 98–101, 104–108, 115–117.

28. Ibid., pp. 100–101, 110–115; pt. 1, pp. 194, 204; George R. Prowell, *History of the Eighty-Seventh Pennsylvania* (York, 1901), p. 175; Lemuel A. Abbott, *Personal Recollections and Civil War Diary* (Burlington, 1908), p. 94.

29. Wallace, *Autobiography*, II, pp. 733–734; *ORA*, I, 37, pt. 1, pp. 113–114; 51, pt. 1, p. 1172; Goldsborough, *Early's Great Raid*, pp. 12–13.

30. *ORA*, I, 37, pt. 2, pp. 593–594.

31. Ibid., pt. 1, pp. 120–121, 128; Wallace, *Autobiography*, II, pp. 735–736.

32. Wallace, *Autobiography*, II, pp. 736–738; *ORA*, I, 51, pt. 1, pp. 1174–1175.

33. Wallace, *Autobiography*, II, pp. 736–738; James Taylor "Sketchbook," Western Reserve Historical Society, Cleveland, Ohio; Goldsborough, *Early's Great Raid*, pp. 12–13; *ORA*, 51, pt. 1, p. 1174; as shown in Festus P. Summers, *The Baltimore and Ohio in the Civil War* (Gettysburg, 1993 edition), picture 29.

34. Unidentified 1932 clipping (FCHS); George E. Davis, "Washington's Peril," *The National Tribune*, August 21, 1884; G. G. Benedict, *Vermont in the Civil War*, (Burlington, 1888), II, pp. 20–21; Hard, *Eighth Illinois Cavalry*, pp. 297–298; Wild, *Alexander's Baltimore Battery*, p. 120; James, "Baltimore Volunteer," pp. 23–24; Paul and Rita Gordon, *A Playground of the Civil War* (Frederick, 1894), p. 163.

35. *ORA*, I, 37, pt. 2, p. 124; also Glenn H. Worthington, *Fighting for Time* (Frederick, 1932), pp. 81–84; Hard, *Eighth Illinois Cavalry*, pp. 297–298; Gilmor, *Four Years in the Saddle*, pp. 189–190; J. Kelly Bennett diary, July 8, 1864 (SHC/UNC); George R. Prowell, *History of the Eighty-Seven Pennsylvania* (York, 1907), 179.

36. Joseph Urner, "Life in Frederick During the Civil War," typescript no date, p. 3 (FCHS).

37. Wallace, *Autobiography*, II, pp. 741–742; Early, *Autobiography*, pp. 385–386.

38. Young diary, July 7, 8, 9, 1864 and Thomas F. Toon, "Draft Report on Twentieth [N.C.] Regiment, July 7, 8, 9, 1864 (both NCHA), Raleigh; Rufus Woolwine diary (VSLA); Buckner McGill Randolph diary (SHC/UNC); I. G. Bradwell, "Early's March to Washington in 1864," *Confederate Veteran*, XVII (May 1920), p. 176; and unpublished typescript of same, chap. 3, (MDHS); Thomas S. Kenan, compiler, *Sketch of Forty-Third North Carolina* (Raleigh, 1895); Archie P. MacDonald, editor, *Make Me a Map of the Valley:*

the Civil War Journal of Stonewall Jackson's Topographer (Dallas, 1973), p. 214.

39. Urner, "Life in Frederick," pp. 4–6.

40. *ORA*, I, 51, pt. 2, p. 1175, also 37, pt. 1, 195; Wallace, *Autobiography*, II, pp. 743–745.

41. Wild, *Alexander's Baltimore Battery*, pp. 121–122; Prowell, *Eighty–Seventh Regiment, Pennsylvania*, pp. 177–178.

42. Wallace, *Autobiography*, II, pp. 746–747; J. Thomas Scharf, *History of Western Maryland* (Baltimore, 1968 edition), p. 288; Frederick *News*, November 28, 1908; Terrill, *Fourteenth New Jersey*, p. 73; J. C. Patterson, "The Battle of Monocacy," *The National Tribune*, October 27, 1898; Hard, *Eighth Illinois Cavalry*, p. 298; Prowell, *Eighty–Seventh Pennsylvania*, pp. 178–179.

43. *ORA*, I, 37, pt. 2, p. 127; Wallace, *Autobiography*, II, pp. 743–747, 750–751.

44. *ORA*, I, 37, pp. 120–121, 127–128.

45. *ORA*, I, 37, pt. 2, pp. 120–127, 130–133.

46. Ibid., pp. 119–120.

47. Virginia Jean Laas, *Wartime Washington: the Civil War Letters of Elizabeth Blair Lee* (Urbana, 1991), pp. 401–402; Silas D. Wesson diary, July 8, 1864; Silas D. Wesson papers, Civil War Times Illustrated Collection (USAMHI).

48. Johnson, "My Ride Around Baltimore," p. 252; Hotchkiss journal, July 8, 1864, Library of Congress (Washington, D.C.) (LC); Frank Vandiver, *Jubal's Raid* (New York, 1960), p. 101; E. B. Lont, *The Civil War Day by Day* (Garden City, 1971), p. 535; Alexander, *Mosby's Men*, pp. 86–87; Virgil Carrington Jones, *Ranger Mosby* (Chapel Hill, 1944), p. 186; also *Gray Ghosts and Rebel Raiders* (New York, 1956), p. 402; Middletown, *The Valley Register*, July 22, 1864.

CHAPTER FOUR

1. Bradley T. Johnson, "My Ride Around Baltimore," *Journal of the United States Cavalry Association* (September 1889), p. 252; Clifford Dowdey and Louis H. Manarin, editors, *The Wartime Papers of R. E. Lee* (New York, 1971), pp. 807, 811; Harry L. Decker, "Bradley Tyler Johnson," clipping (FCHS); Edward B. Williams, editor, *Rebel Brothers* (College Station, 1995), pp. 198, 201.

2. J. Kelly Bennett diary, July 8, 1864 (SHC/UNC); John G. Young diary, July 8, 1864 (NCHA).

3. Thomas J. Scharf, *History of Western Maryland* (Philadelphia, 1881), pp. 298–299; Robert E. Park, "Diary," *Southern Historical Society Papers*, I (1876), p. 378; Joseph T. Durkin, editor, *Confederate Chaplain* (Milwaukee, 1968), p. 94; Henry Kyd Douglas, *I Rode with Stonewall* (Chapel Hill, 1940), p. 293.

4. Glenn H. Worthington, *Fighting For Time* (Baltimore, 1930), pp. 282–283; Marken and Bielfeld, *Souvenir of Historic Frederick* (Frederick, 1925), pp. 1–3; Jarboe Grove, *History of Carrollton Manor* (Frederick, 1928), p. 315.

5. Worthington, *Fighting*, pp. 282–289; William R. Quinn, editor, *The Diary of Jacob Engelbrecht*, (Frederick, 1976), pp. 271–272; Paul and Rita Gordon, *A Playground of the Civil War* (Frederick, 1994).

6. Grove, *History*, p. 172.

7. Charles C. Osborne, *Jubal: The Life and Times of General Jubal A. Early, CSA* (Chapel Hill, 1992), p. 118; Alfred Seelye Roe, *History of the Ninth New York Heavy Artillery* (Worcester, 1899), p. 425n; Festus P. Summers, *The Baltimore and Ohio in the Civil War* (Gettysburg, 1992 edition), chaps. 1 and 2;

George Rogers Taylor, *The Transportation Revolution* (New York, 1951), pp. 17, 19, 22, 23, 29, 30, 77, 367; Hilde Kagan, editor, *The American Heritage Pictorial Atlas of United States History* (New York, 1966), pp. 80, 151; Gordon, *A Playground of the Civil War*, chaps. "A House Divided," "Politics," "The Care and Wounded," and "The Sisters of Charity."

8. Scharf, *Western Maryland*, pp. 288–289; Edward Delaplaine, "General Early's Levy on Frederick," in Frederick County Civil War Centennial, *To Commemorate the Battle of Monocacy* (Frederick, 1964), pp. 48–54; Quinn, *Engelbrecht*, pp. 271–274.

9. William Allan journal, pp. 29–30 (SHC/UNC).

10. Delaplaine, "Early's Levy," pp. 45–53, with photocopies of original ransom documents included.

11. Gordon, *A Playground of the Civil War*, pp. 168–174; facsimiles of Frederick corporation replies and tally sheet in Whitmore and Cannon, Ibid., pp. 56–57; also Scharf, *Western Maryland*, p. 289; Millard Bushong, *Old Jube: A Biography of General Jubal A. Early* (Boyce, Va., 1955), p. 197; Delaplaine, "General Early's Levy," pp. 50–54.

12. Quinn, *Engelbrecht*, p. 275; Allan journal, pp. 29–30 (SHC/UNC); Archie P. McDonald, editor, *Make Me a Map of the Valley* (Dallas, 1973), p. 215; Young diary, p. 28 (NCHA).

13. Edward Y. Goldsborough, preparer, *The Appeal of Frederick City, Maryland, to the Congress of the United States, for the Payment of its claim of $200,000* (circa 1902), pp. 3, 6.

14. David J. Lewis, *Frederick War Claim: Evidence and Argument in Support of Bill to Refund Ransom Paid By the Town of Frederick . . . 1912*, copy, Frederick Historical Society, pp. 3, 4, 18, 19, 20.

15. W. T. McDougle, "An Indiana Soldier at the Battle of Monocacy," *The National Tribune*, February 21, 1884.

16. Abner Hard, *History of the Eighth Cavalry Regiment, Illinois Volunteers* (Aurora, 1868), pp. 298–299; Silas D. Wesson diary, July 9, 1864, Carlisle Barracks, Pa. (USAMHI); U.S. War Department, *War of the Rebellion: the Official Records of Union and Confederate Armies* (Washington, 1880–1901), ser. I, vol. 7, pt. 1, p. 220.

17. Grove, *Carrollton Manor*, p. 239.

18. Bernard A. Olsen, editor, *Upon The Tented Field* (Red Bank, N.J., 1993), pp. 31–118 *inter alia*.

19. Ibid., pp. 51, 80.

20. Ibid., pp. 252–253; J. Newton Terrill, *Campaign of the Fourteenth New Jersey Volunteers* (New Brunswick, 1884), p. 73, and "Shenandoah Valley . . . Battle of Monocacy," *The National Tribune*, October 8, 1891; J. C. Patterson, "The Battle of Monocacy," *The National Tribune*, October 27, 1898.

21. Alfred Seelye Roe, *History of the Ninth New York Heavy Artillery* (Worchester, 1899), pp. 124–125; William H. James, "A Baltimore Volunteer of 1864," *Maryland Historical Magazine*, XXXVL (March, 1941), pp. 24–25; Frederick W. Wild, *Memoirs and History of Captain F. W. Alexander's Baltimore Battery* (Baltimore, 1912), p. 123; Hard, *Eighth Illinois Cavalry*, p. 298; George R. Prowell, *History of the Eighty-Seventh Pennsylvania Volunteers* (York, 1901), pp. 178–180.

22. Lewis Wallace, *Lew Wallace: an Autobiography* (New York, 1906), vol. 2, pp. 748–752.

23. Ibid., pp. 752–754.

24. Ibid., pp. 754–755.

25. Grove, *Carrollton Manor*, pp. 245–246; Worthington, *Fighting for Time*, pp. 169, 172.

26. T. J. C. Williams, *History and Biographical Record of Frederick County, Maryland* (Baltimore, 1910), p. 332; George F. Davis, "Washington in Peril," *The National Tribune*, August 21, 1884; Ronald W. Johnson, "Gambrill Mill Evaluation and Brief Special History Study," Monocacy National Battlefield, typescript, December 1984, pp. 1–4, copy Defending Washington files, Fort Ward Museum and Historical Site, Alexandria, Va.

27. Worthington, *Fighting for Time*, pp. 235–236; Roe, *Ninth New York Heavy Artillery*, pp. 126, 301–302.

28. *ORA*, I, 37, pt. 1, pp. 196, 214, 217, 220–222; Hard, *Eighth Illinois Cavalry*, pp. 298–299.

29. *ORA*, I, 37, pp. 216–217, 221–222.

30. William H. James, "A Baltimore Volunteer" (1941), pp. 25–26; Wild, *Alexander's Baltimore Battery*, p. 123; G. C. Benedict, *Vermont in the Civil War* (Burlington, 1888), vol. 2, p. 309.

31. W. W. Old, diary, July 9, 1864, and Jedediah Hotchkiss, journal, July 9–10, 1864 (both LC), Washington D.C.; *ORA*, I, 37, pt. 1, pp. 214, 217; Wallace, *Autobiography*, II, pp. 756–757.

32. W. W. Lyle, *Lights and Shadows of Army Life* (Cincinnati, 1865), pp. 119–121.

33. James, "A Baltimore Volunteer," pp. 26–27; Grove, *Carrollton Manor*, p. 315; Worthington, *Fighting for Time*, pp. 107–111; Wallace, *Autobiography*, II, pp. 758–764; Terrill, *Fourteenth New Jersey*, p. 74; Prowell, *Eighty-Seventh Pennsylvania*, pp. 179–180.

34. E. Y. Goldsborough, *The Battle of Monocacy*, (n.p., 1898), pp. 17, 19; Wild, *Alexander's Baltimore Battery*, pp. 124–125.

35. *ORA*, I, 37, pt. 1, pp. 96, 223.

36. Wild, *Alexander's Baltimore Battery*, pp. 123–124, 126; James, "A Baltimore Volunteer," p. 26; Prowell, *Eighty-Seventh Pennsylvania*, p. 180; Patterson, "The Battle of Monocacy," *The National Tribune*, October 27, 1898; W. L. Gardner, "The Battle of Monocacy," *The National Tribune*, December 6, 1888; Lew Wallace to George E. Davis, March 29, 1889, George E. Davis Pension File, National Archives and Records Administration, Washington, D.C.

37. *ORA*, I, 37, pt., pp. 96, 223; Roe, *Ninth New York*, pp. 192–230; Wallace, Ibid., pp. 760–762; Lemuel A. Abbott, *Personal Recollections and Civil War Diary* (Burlington, 1908), pp. 98–99; Wild, *Alexander's Baltimore Battery*, p. 125; George C. Davis, "Washington in Peril," *The National Tribune*, April 21, 1884.

38. Roe, *Ninth New York Heavy Artillery*, p. 307; Early, *Memoirs*, p. 387; Walter C. Strickler, "How a Lie Saved the Capital," *The National Tribune*, April 30, 1903.

39. *ORA*, I, 37, pt. 1, pp. 217, 222; Thomas A. Ware telephone interview with Edwin C. Bearss, September 13, 1978, in Bearss, "Documentation Troop Movement Maps, Battle of Monocacy, July 9, 1864," typescript, Monocacy National Battlefield, 1979, p. 6.

40. Early, *War Memoirs*, pp. 386–387.

41. *ORA*, I, 37, pt. 1, p. 220; Grove, *Carrollton Manor*, pp. 67, 70, 81, 88, 246–247, 370.

42. Abbott, *Recollection and Diary*, p. 100; Hard, *Eighth Illinois Cavalry*, pp. 298–299; Worthington, *Fighting for Time*, p. 118; *ORA*, I, 37, pt. 1, p. 220; Grove, *Carrollton Manor*, p. 245.

43. George F. Davis, "Washington in Peril," *The National Tribune*, August 21, 1964, pp. 403–404, 634.

44. Robert T. Cornwell - wife, August 1, 1864, quoted in Edward S. Delaplaine, "Today is 133th Anniversary of Battle of Monocacy," *The Frederick Post*,

July 9, 1977; Wallace, *Autobiography*, II, pp. 757–770; Early, *War Memoirs*, p. 387; *ORA*, I, 51, pt. 1, pp. 1175–1176, also 37, pt. 1, pp. 196, 205, 211; Goldsborough, *Battle of Monocacy*, p. 19; Haynes, *Tenth Vermont Infantry*, p. 193; Peter Vredenburgh – Mother, July 12, 1864, in Peter Vredenburgh, *Letters of Major Peter Vredenburgh*, (n.p., n.d.); Abbott, *Recollections and Diary*, pp. 99–100; Roe, *Ninth New York*; p. 126.

45. Goldsborough, *Battle of Monocacy*, p. 19; Wild, *Alexander's Baltimore Battery*, pp. 124–125; Briscoe Goodhart, *History of the Independent Loudoun Rangers*, (Washington, 1896), p. 137; Frederick *Daily News*, July 9, 1914.

46. Worthington, *Fighting for Time*, chap. 14; Early, *War Memoirs*, p. 387; Wallace, *Autobiography*, II, p. 770, fn.1; Peter Robertson, "Monocacy," *The National Tribune*, January 24, 1884; Roderick A. Clark, "Monocacy," *The National Tribune*, April 15, 1886.

47. Wallace, *Autobiography*, II, pp. 774–775; *ORA*, I, 37, pt. 1, pp. 214, 217.

48. Albert E. Conradis, "The Battle of Monocacy," in Frederick County Civil War Centennial, Inc., *To Commemorate the One Hundredth Anniversary of the Battle of Monocacy* (Frederick, 1964), p. 21; *ORA*, I, 37, pt. 1, pp. 213–219; Goldsborough, *Monocacy*, p. 18.

49. W. H. Engler, "The Brave Act of a Comrade," *The National Tribune*, September 9, 1909.

50. G. G. Benedict, *Vermont in the Civil War* (Burlington, 1888), II, pp. 196–199; Abbott, *Recollections*, pp. 100–101; Worthington, *Fighting for Time*, p. 113, Goldsborough, *Monocacy*, p. 19; Wild, *Alexander's Baltimore Battery*, pp. 123–125; Edwin M. Haynes, *History of the Tenth Vermont* (Rutland, 1894), pp. 192–193.

51. *ORA*, I, 37, pt. 1, pp. 197–198; 51, pt. 1, p. 1177; Wallace, *Autobiography*, II, pp. 773–777; Wild, *Alexander's Baltimore Battery*, pp. 126–127.

52. Wallace, *Autobiography*, p. 775; Worthington, *Fighting for Time*, pp. 113–114; Roe, *Ninth New York Heavy Artillery*, p. 128.

53. *ORA*, I, 37, pt. 2, pp. 133, 143; Charles A. Dana, *Recollections of the Civil War* (New York, 1898), p. 229.

54. Dana, *Recollections*, pp. 139–140, 145–146.

55. Ibid., pp. 144, 149–155, esp. 154.

56. Wallace, *Autobiography*, II, p. 773; *ORA*, I, 37, pt. 2, pp. 150, 152.

CHAPTER FIVE

1. U.S. War Department, *War of the Rebellion: the Official Records of Union and Confederate Armies* (Washington, 1884–1901), ser. I, vol. 37, pt. 2, pp. 133, 143, 150.

2. Ibid., pp. 141–155.

3. Ibid., pp. 137–139.

4. Ibid., pt. 1, pp. 196–197; Lew Wallace, *Autobiography* (New York, 1906), vol. 2, pp. 773–774.

5. *ORA*, I, 37, p. 197; Wallace, *Autobiography*, II, pp. 774–775.

6. Jubal Anderson Early, *Autobiographical Sketch and Narrative* (Baltimore, 1989 reprint), p. 387; Wallace, *Autobiography*, II, pp. 775–776.

7. Wallace, *Autobiography*, II, p. 776; *ORA*, I, 51, pt. 1, p. 1176; Warren Ripley, *Artillery and Ammunition of the Civil War* (New York, 1970), p. 367; George R. Prowell, *History of the Eighty-Seventh Pennsylvania* (York, 1901), p. 183.

8. Glenn H. Worthington, *Fighting for Time* (Frederick, 1932), pp. 123–125; Wallace, *Autobiography*, II, pp. 777, 781; *ORA*, I, 37, pt. 1, pp. 205, 224; Lemuel A. Abbott, *Personal Recollections* (Burlington, 1908), pp. 100–101; also Peter Vredenburgh, *Letters of Peter Vredenburgh* (n.p.).

9. Frederick W. Wild, *Memoirs and History of Capt. F. W. Alexander's Baltimore Battery* (Baltimore, 1912), p. 127; Frederick H. Dyer, compiler, *A Compendium of the War of the Rebellion* (New York, 1959 edition), vol. 3, p. 1231.

10. Wallace, *Autobiography*, II, p. 780; Nathaniel E. Harris, *Autobiography: the Story of an Old Man's Life with Reminiscences of Seventy-Five Years* (Macon, 1925), pp. 86–87.

11. Prowell, *Eighty-Seventh Pennsylvania*, pp. 181,182, 186; *ORA*, I, 37, pt. 1, p. 205.

12. Worthington, *Fighting for Time*, p. 126; Wallace, *Autobiography*, II, p. 781; Arner Hard, *History of the Eighty Cavalry Regiment Illinois Volunteers* (Aurora, 1868), pp. 300–301; Edward C. Bearss, "Documentation Troop Movement Maps, Battle of the Monocacy" (October 1878), p. 53; *ORA*, I, 37, pt. 1, p. 220.

13. Osceola Lewis, *History of the One Hundred and Thirty-Eighth Pennsylvania* (Norristown, 1866), pp. 116–117; Wild, *Alexander's Battery*, pp. 126–127; *ORA*, I, 37, pt. 1, pp. 197–198, 205, 220; J. C. Patterson, "Battle of Monocacy," *The National Tribune*, October 27, 1898.

14. *ORA*, *Atlas*, Plates 83/9, and 94/3; William H. Runge, editor, *Four Years in the Confederate Artillery* (Chapel Hill, 1961), pp. 86–87.

15. William C. Davis, *Breckinridge* (Baton Rouge, 1974), p. 445; John H. Worsham, *One of Jackson's Foot Cavalry* (Jackson, Tenn., 1964 edition), p. 103; Worthington, *Fighting for Time*, p. 129; "Report of General Terry," July 22, 1864, Chicago Historical Society (648), Chicago, Illinois.

16. John B. Gordon, *Reminiscences* (New York, 1904), pp. 310–311; *ORA*, I, 37, pt. 1, pp. 350–351; Ralph L. Eckert, *John Brown Gordon* (Ann Arbor, 1984), vol. I, p. 106; Wallace, *Autobiography*, II, pp. 775–776; I. G. Bradwell, "The Shenandoah Valley Campaign of 1864," typescript (MDHS), and published versions, "Early's Demonstration Against Washington in 1864," XXII (October, 1914), p. 439; "Early's March to Washington in 1864," XXVIII (May, 1920), p. 177, and "In the Battle of Monocacy, Md.," XXXVI (February, 1923), pp. 56–57, all *Confederate Veteran*.

17. Wallace, *Autobiography*, II, pp. 777–778.

18. Alfred Seeyle Roe, *History of the Ninth New York Heavy Artillery* (Worchester, 1899), p. 128; "Biographical Information on Alfred Nelson Sova (1847–1935)," Defending Washington files (FWM).

19. Wallace, *Autobiography*, II, p. 781; Early, *Autobiography*, p. 390; Worthington, *Fighting for Time*, p. 159; *ORA*, I, 51, pt. 1, p. 1177; 37, pt. 2, pp. 137–139; also pt. 1, p. 197.

20. Wallace, *Autobiography*, II, pp. 782–784; for the apparently only surviving dispatch from Wallace to either Grant or Halleck, see Wallace's post battle dispatch received in Washington at 11:42 P.M., *ORA*, I, 37, pt. 2, p. 145.

21. Wallace, *Autobiography*, II, pp. 784–786.

22. Worthington, *Fighting for Time*, p. 154; Wallace, *Autobiography*, II, pp. 790–793; Gordon, *Reminiscences*, p. 313.

23. Early, *Autobiography*, p. 388; Gordon, *Reminiscences*, p. 311; *ORA*, I, 37, pt. 1, pp. 350–351.

24. Wallace, *Autobiography*, II, p. 793; *ORA*, I, 37, pt. 1, pp. 207–212, inter alia; Robert G. Stephens, *Intrepid Warrior: Clement Anselm Evans* (Dayton, 1992), pp. 425–426.

25. Harris, *Autobiography*, pp. 89–90; "Meet for the First Time," Frederick *Post*, July 9, 1914; Prowell, *Eighty-Seventh Pennsylvania*, pp. 182–183; James Stahle memoirs (USAMHI).

26. Nichols, *A Soldier's Story*, (n.p., 1898), pp. 170–171.

27. Worthington, *Fighting for Time*, pp. 154–155; Bradwell "Shenandoah Valley," 3, (MDHS) and published versions; T. E. Morrow to father, August 2,

1864, Special Collections (TUL), copy in Defending Washington files (FWM).

28. Edwin M. Haynes, *History of the Tenth Vermont* (Rutland, 1894), pp. 193–194; *ORA*, I, 37, pt. 1, pp. 205, 208–209, 212–213; Lewis, *One Hundred and Thirty-Eighth Pennsylvania*, pp. 114–116; Alfred S. Roe, *Ninth New York Heavy Artillery* (Worcester, 1899), pp. 131–132; Prowell, *Eighty-Seventh Pennsylvania*, p. 186; Nichols, *A Soldier's Story*, pp. 170–171; Bradwell, "Shenandoah Valley".

29. James Durkin, editor, *Confederate Chaplain: a War Journal of Rev. James B. Sheeran* (Milwaukee, 1960), p. 984; Bradwell, "Shenandoah Valley," 6; Terry L. Jones, *Lee's Tigers* (Baton Rouge, 1987), pp. 211–212; *ORA*, I, 37, pt. 1, pp. 211–212, 351; Zebulon York to B. B. Wellford, July 18, 1864, Reel One, White-Wellford, Taliaferro-Marshall family papers, Chapel Hill (SHC/UNC).

30. "Meet for the First Time," Frederick *Post*, July 9, 1914; Peter Vredenburgh to mother, July 12, 1864, Vredenburgh, *Letters*; Bernard A. Olsen, *Upon The Tented Field* (Red Bank, N.J., 1993), p. 253.

31. Compare Worthington, *Fighting for Time*, pp. 155–156 with Barton's postwar account in Margaretta Barton Colt, *Defend the Valley: a Shenandoah Family in the Civil War* (New York, 1994), pp. 331–332; J. Floyd King - J. Stoddard Johnston, July 27, 1864, Thomas Butler King papers (SHC/UNC).

32. Worsham, *One of Jackson's Foot Cavalry*, pp. 238–239; Gordon, *Reminiscences*, p. 312; Bradwell, "Shenandoah Valley," pp. 4, 5; Worthington, *Fighting for Time*, pp. 135–138; Hutcheson, "Saved the Day," p. 77; Worsham, *One of Jackson's Foot Cavalry*, pp. 235–239.

33. Helen E. Howell, editor, *Chronicles of the One Hundred and Fifty-First Regiment, New York* (Albion, 1911), pp. 86–87; Worsham, *One of Jackson's Foot Cavalry*, pp. 235–239; "Report of General Terry, July 22, 1864; (CHS); Roe, *Ninth New York*, pp. 121–132; Lewis H. Clark, *Military History of Wayne County, New York* (Sodus, N.Y., 1881), p. 601.

34. George C. Pile memoir, Confederate Collection (TLA); Early, "Early's March to Washington in 1864," *Battles and Leaders*, IV, pp. 496–497; *ORA, Atlas*, Plates 83/9 and 94/3; Worthington, *Fighting For Time*, p. 137.

35. Worsham, *One of Jackson's Foot Cavalry*, pp. 237–238; Hutcheson, "Saved the Day," p. 77.

36. Wild, *Alexander's Baltimore Battery*, p. 127; Lewis, *One Hundred and Thirty-Eighth Pennsylvania*, pp. 116–117; Patterson, "Battle of Monocacy," Bradwell, "Battle of the Monocacy, Md.", p. 57; Gordon, *Reminiscences*, pp. 312–313; Roe, *Ninth New York Heavy Artillery*, pp. 131–132; Stahle, "Memoirs" (USAMHI); *ORA*, I, 37, pt. 1, pp. 209, 213.

37. Gordon, *Reminiscences*, p. 312; Bradwell, "Shenandoah Valley," p. 7; Roe, *Ninth New York*, p. 133; Clark, *Military History of Wayne County*, p. 601; Frederick W. Seward, *Reminiscences of A War-Time Diplomat and Statesman* (New York, 1916), p. 245.

38. *ORA*, I, 37, pt. 1, p. 224.

39. Hutcheson, "Saved the Day," p. 77; Bradwell, "Shenandoah Valley," p. 7; Patterson, "The Battle of Monocacy," *The National Tribune*, October 27, 1898; Wild, *Alexander's Baltimore Battery*, p. 129; Zebulon York - B. R. Welford, July 18, 1864 (SHC/UNC).

40. G. C. Benedict, *Vermont in the Civil War* (Burlington, 1888), vol. 2, pp. 315–316; Haynes, *Tenth Vermont*, pp. 195, 202; U.S. Department of the Army, *The Medal of Honor* (Washington, 1948), p. 164.

41. Letter, Lew Wallace - George E. Davis, March 29, 1889, Davis pension file (NARA), copy, Defending Washington files (FWM).

42. Benedict, *Vermont in the Civil War*, II, pp. 314–315; Haynes, *Tenth Vermont*, pp. 197–199; Roe, *Ninth New York*, pp. 128–129; *ORA*, I, 37, pt. 1, p. 215.

43. Daniel B. Freeman, "Fighting Them Again," *The National Tribune*, March 18, 1897, which includes a hand–drawn sketch of Freeman's view of the action at this point.

44. U.S. Department of the Army, *Medal of Honor*, p. 164; Benedict, *Vermont in the Civil War*, pp. 314–315; Haynes, *Tenth Vermont*, pp. 197–199; Davis, "Medal of Honor Certificate," May 23, 1892, Davis pension file (NARA, copy FWM).

45. Thomas F. Toon, "Draft Report on the Twentieth Regiment, North Carolina State Volunteers, CSA," August 1, 1864 (NCHA); V. E. Turner and H. C. Wall, "Twenty-Third Regiment," in Walter E. Clark, editor, *Histories of Several Regiments and Battalions from North Carolina* (Raleigh, 1901), vol. 2, pp. 245–246; Richard W. Iobst, *The Bloody Sixth North Carolina Regiment* (Gaithersburg, 1987), p. 215; Haynes, *Tenth Vermont*, pp. 196–204; U.S. Department of the Army, *The Medal of Honor*, p. 164; George F. Davis, "Washington in Peril," *The National Tribune*, August 21, 1884; Worsham, *One of Jackson's Foot Cavalry*, pp. 238–239; Richard C. Iobst and Louis H. Manarin, *The Bloody Sixth North Carolina* (Raleigh, 1965), p. 215; Diary of William W. Old, entry July 9, 1864 (LC); Henry K. Douglas, *I Rode With Stonewall* (Chapel Hill, 1940), p. 293; King - Johnston, July 27, 1864 (SHC/UNC).

46. *ORA*, I, 37, pt. 1, pp. 217, 222; Samuel Clarke Ferrar, *The Twenty-Second Pennsylvania Cavalry* (Pittsburgh, 1911), p. 269; George Perkins, *A Summer in Maryland and Virginia* (Chillicothe, 1911), pp. 20–21; E. Y.. Goldsborough, *Early's Great Raid . . . Battle of Monocacy* (n.p., 1898), pp. 18, 25–26; unidentified clipping, Baltimore *Sun*, ca. July 15, 1864 (MDHS).

47. William H. James, "A Baltimore Volunteer of 1864," *Maryland Historical Magazine* (March, 1941), pp. 28, 29; C. R. Van Tress, "Saved the Day at Monocacy," *The National Tribune*, October 22, 1903.

48. *ORA*, I, 37, pt. 1, p. 222; Edwin C. Bearss-Thomas Ware telephone interview, September 14, 1978, cited in Bearss, "Documentation Troop Movement Maps Monocacy," p. 70.

49. Goldsborough, *Early's Great Raid*, pp. 26–27; *ORA*, I, 37, pt. 1, p. 215.

50. *ORA*, I, 37, pt. 1, pp. 192, 224; Wild, *Alexander's Baltimore Battery*, pp. 130–131; James, "Baltimore Volunteer," p. 29.

51. Hard, *Eighth Illinois Cavalry*, p. 300; *ORA*, I, 37, pp. 220–221; Wallace, *Autobiography*, II, pp. 807–808, describes the banner; Silas D. Wesson diary, July 10, 1864, entry, Wesson papers, Civil War Times Illustrated Collection (USAMHI).

52. Hard, *Eighth Illinois Cavalry*, p. 301; *ORA*, I, 37, p. 221.

53. *ORA*, I, 37, pt. 2, pp. 139, 145.

54. Worsham, *One of Jackson's Foot Cavalry*, pp. 239–240; James Hutcheson, "Saved the Day at Monocacy," *Confederate Veteran* (February, 1915), p. 77; "Terry's Report" (CHS); Jedediah Hotchkiss journal, July 9–10, 1864 (LC); W. H. Runge, editor, *Four Years in the Confederate Artillery* (Chapel Hill, 1961), p. 86; Richard Woolfolk Waldrop diary, July 9, 1864 (SHC/UNC); George C. Pile memoir (TLA).

55. M. J. Stearns, "Monocacy," *The National Tribune*, July 1, 1891; Roderick A. Clark, "Monocacy," *The National Tribune*, April 15, 1886.

56. William Jarboe Grove, *History of Carrollton Manor* (Frederick, 1928), pp. 65–67; Worthington, *Fighting for Time*, pp. 158–159, 161–162.

57. Wild, *Alexander's Baltimore Battery*, p. 125; Frederick *Daily News*, July 9, 1914.

58. York to Wellford, July 18, 1864, and J. Floyd King to sister July 15, 1864 (both SHC/UNC); William C. Davis, *Breckinridge: Statesman, Soldier, Symbol* (Baton Rouge, 1974), pp. 445–446; Worthington, *Fighting*, pp.166–167.

59. "Meet for First Time Since Fight," Frederick *Post*, July 9, 1914.

CHAPTER SIX

1. J. Cutler Andrews, *The North Reports the Civil War* (Pittsburgh, 1955), pp. 590–591.

2. Gideon Welles, *Diary* (Boston, 1909), vol. 2, pp. 68–70.

3. U.S. War Department, *The War of the Rebellion: Official Records of Union and Confederate Armies (ORA)*, (Washington, 1884–1901), ser. I, vol. 37, pt. 2, pp. 134–136, 139, 145.

4. Ibid., pp. 135–137, 142–143, 150–152.

5. Ibid., pp. 160, see also pp. 140, 154.

6. Silas D. Wesson diary, July 10, 1864, Civil War Times Illustrated Collection (USAMHI) Carlisle Barracks, Pa.; "Victory" anonymous Latin, Translated by Francis Pott, 1861, *Hymnal of the Protestant Episcopal Church* (New York, 1933 edition), p. 223; Glenn T. Worthington, *Fighting for Time* (Baltimore, 1932), photograph facing p. 266.

7. Bernard A. Olsen, editor, *Upon The Tented Field* (Red Bank, N.J., 1993), pp. 258, 259, 270–274.

8. Alfred Seelye Roe, *History of the Ninth New York Heavy Artillery* (Worcester, 1899), p. 135; *ORA*, I, 37, pt. 1, pp. 208, 218, 222, 224; William Jarboe Grove, *History of Carrollton Manor* (Frederick, 1928), p. 390.

9. George E. Davis, "Washington in Peril," *The National Tribune*, August 21, 1884; Frederick W. Wild, *Memoirs and History of Capt. F. W. Alexander's Baltimore Battery* (Baltimore, 1912), p. 132; Abner Hard, *History of the Eighth Illinois Cavalry* (Aurora, 1868), p. 301; William H. James, "A Baltimore Volunteer of 1864," *Maryland Historical Magazine* (March 1941), pp. 29–31; J. Newton Terrill, *Campaign of the Fourteenth New Jersey* (New Brunswick, 1884), p. 75; George R. Prowell, *History of the Eighty-Seventh Pennsylvania* (York, 1901), p.188; *ORA*, I, 37, pt. 1, pp. 208, 218, 222, 224.

10. *ORA*, I, 37, pt. 2, pp. 145, 160–161.

11. Ibid., pt. 1, pp. 191–192.

12. Ibid., p. 198; also I, 51, pt. 1, p. 1177; Captain M. P. Craighill, "Report of Operations upon Field Works in Middle Department, May 1864," Case 5390, Record Group 77, Records Corps of Engineers (NARA), Washington, D.C.

13. James, "A Baltimore Volunteer of 1864," pp. 31–33.

14. Lemuel A. Abbott, *Personal Recollections and Civil War Diary* (Burlington, 1908), p. 119; Prowell, *Eighty-Seventh Pennsylvania*, p. 189; G. G. Benedict, *Vermont in the Civil War* (Burlington, 1888), vol. 7, pp. 315–316; *ORA*, I, 37, pt. 1, p. 198; Wild, *Alexander's Baltimore Battery*, p. 133.

15. Abner Hard, *History of the Eighth Illinois Cavalry Regiment* (Aurora, Ill., 1868), pp. 302–303; George Perkins, *A Summer in Maryland and Virginia* (Chillicothe, 1911), p. 25; Roe, *Ninth New York*, p. 135; Benedict, *Vermont in the Civil War*, p. 317; W. L. Gardner, "The Battle of Monocacy," December 2, 1888; J. C. Patterson, "The Battle of the Monocacy," October 27, 1898; J. Newton Terrill, "The Shenandoah Valley," October 8, 1891, all *The National Tribune*, and Terrill, *Fourteenth New Jersey*, p. 75.

16. E. Y. G. Goldsborough, *Early's Great Raid* (Frederick, 1898), p. 27; *ORA*, I, 37, pt. 1, p. 215.

17. George E. Davis, "Captor or Prisoner," *The National Tribune*, August 14, 1884; Hard, *Eighth Illinois Cavalry*, p. 301.

18. Roderick W. Clark, "Monocacy," *The National Tribune*, April 15, 1886; Wilfred W. Black, "Civil War Letters of George Washington McMillen and Jefferson O. McMillen, 122nd Regiment, O.V.I.," *West Virginia History* (April 1971), pp. 185–187.

19. Prowell, *Eighty-Seventh Pennsylvania*, pp. 185–187; Roderick W. Clark, "Monocacy," *The National Tribune*, April 15, 1886; Worthington, *Fighting for Time*, p. 163.

20. *ORA*, I, 37, pt. 2, pp. 113–114, 146–147, also pp. 552–553; for Morris in Baltimore see II, 1–8 *inter alia*; Ezra Warner, *Generals in Blue* (Baton Rouge, 1964), pp. 261–262; Francis B. Heitman, *Historical Register and Dictionary of the United States Army* (Washington, 1903), vol. 7, pp. 292–293.

21. *ORA*, I, 37, pp. 147–149; Craighill, "Report of Operations Upon Field Works in Middle Department," RG 77, NARA.

22. J. Kelly Bennette diary, July 9, 1864 (SHC/UNC); Bradley T. Johnson, "My Ride Around Baltimore in Eighteen Hundred Sixty-Four," *Journal of the United States Cavalry Association* (September 1889), pp. 251–253; Harry Gilmor, *Four Years in the Saddle* (New York, 1866), pp. 190–191; Carroll County *Record*, July 1895, quoted in Frederick Shriver Klein, editor, *Just South of Gettysburg* (Westminster, 1973), pp. 216–217.

23. See Johnson, "My Ride," pp. 254–257; Bennette diary, July 11, 1864; also Robert E. Michel, *Colonel Harry Gilmor's Raid Around Baltimore* (Baltimore, 1976), pp. 13–26; for fuller account see, Benjamin Franklin Cooling, *Jubal Early's Raid on Washington: 1864* (Baltimore, 1989), chap. 6; for retribution aspects, see Ted Alexander, "McCausland's Raid and the Burning of Chambersburg," *Blue and Gray Magazine* (August 1994), pp. 11–12, 60.

24. *ORA*, I, 37, pt. 2, pp. 173–185, 212–213; C. J. McGwinn to John Garrett, July 12, 1864, Robert Garrett Family Papers (LL).

25. Roe, *Ninth New York Heavy Artillery*, pp. 135–136; Wesson diary, July 11, 17, 1864 (USAMHI); Hard, *Eighth Illinois Cavalry*, pp. 301–302; Wild, *Baltimore Battery*, pp. 133–134; James, "A Baltimore Volunteer," pp. 31–32.

26. *ORA*, I, 37, pt. 2, pp. 214–215, 247–248; Edwin M. Stanton to John Garrett, July 12, 1864, Robert Garrett Family Papers (LC); Warner, *Generals in Blue*, pp. 349–350.

27. *ORA*, I, 37, pt. 1, p. 198; pt. 2, pp. 247–249; Lew Wallace to John Garrett, July 18, 1864; Stanton to E.O.C. Ord, July 12, 1864, Garrett Family Papers (LC).

28. John Lyeth pension claim, 1879 (NARA); Edward B. Williams, editor, *Rebel Brothers* (College Station, 1995), p. 201.

29. *ORA*, I, 37, pt. 1, pp. 204, 342, 352; Henry Kyd Douglas, *I Rode With Stonewall* (Chapel Hill, 1940), p. 294; J. Stoddard Johnston, "Notes of March of Breckinridge's Corps," July 10, 1864 (NYHS); E. N. Atkinson, "Report of Evans' Brigade," July 22, 1864, Eldridge Collection (HL); J. Floyd King - sister, July 15, 1864, Thomas Butler King collection, and W. H. Aycock - W. R. Redding, July 23, 1864, Redding papers (both SHC/UNC); T. E. Morrow - father, August 2, 1864, Special Collections (TUL).

30. J. Newton Terrill, "Shenandoah Valley," *The National Tribune*, October 8, 1891; *ORA*, I, 37, pt. 1, p. 183; Douglas, *I Rode with Stonewall*, p. 294.

31. "Meet for the First Time Since Fight," Frederick *Post*, July 9, 1914.

32. *ORA*, I, 37, pt. 1, pp. 170, 179–183; pt. 2, p. 172; Lee C. and Karen D. Drickamer, compilers/editors, *Fort Lyon to Harper's Ferry* (Shippensburg, Pa. 1987), pp. 193–194; C. Armour Newcomer, *Cole's Cavalry or Three Years in the Saddle* (Baltimore, 1895), chap. 14.

33. Buckner McGill Randolph diary, July 10, 1864 (VAHS); Douglas, *I Rode With Stonewall*, p. 294; Williams, *Rebel Brothers*, pp. 198, 201.

34. George Perkins, *A Summer in Maryland and Virginia* (Chillicothe, 1911), p. 52; J. Cutler Andrews, *The South Reports the Civil War* (Princeton, 1970), pp. 408–409; Sergeant Major John G. Young, diary, pp. 39–40 (NCHA); W. W. Scott, editor, "Diary of Captain H. W. Wingfield," *Bulletin of the Virginia State Library*, XVI (July 1929), p. 43; Baltimore *Sun*, July 9, 1874; *ORA*, I, 37, pt. 1, pp. 203–204; Douglas, *I Rode With Stonewall*, p. 294.

35. *ORA*, I, 37, pt. 1, p. 348, also pp. 203–204; Jubal Anderson Early, *Autobiographical Sketch and Narrative of the War Between the States* (Baltimore, 1989, edition), p. 389.

36. Clay Hamilton and Charles T. Jacobs, "Greenbrier Civil War Soldier Buried in Maryland," Lewisburg, West Virginia, *Daily News*, October 11, 1983; John T. De Sellum, reminiscence, copy, n.d. pp. 46–52; "Farm Family in County had 1,800 troops as 'Guests,'" undated clipping (both MCHS); Alexander Hunter, *Johnny Reb and Billy Yank* (New York, 1905), p. 650; Perkins, *A Summer*, pp. 52–53.

37. *ORA*, I, 37, pt. 2, pp. 155–157, 166–167, 170–190 *inter alia*, 248, 249; Virginia Campbell Moore, "Reminiscences of Life Along the Rockville Pike During the Civil War," *The Montgomery County Story* (November 1984), p. 137; Frederick W. Seward, *Reminiscences of A War-Time Statesman and Diplomat* (New York, 1916), p. 245.

38. B. F. Marshall to Mother, July 17, 1864, copy, Defending Washington Files (FWM); On the defenses, see John Gross Barnard, *A Report on the Defenses of Washington* (Washington, 1871), plate 30; Benjamin Franklin Cooling and Walton B. Owen, *Mr. Lincoln's Forts: a Guide to the Civil War Defenses of Washington*, (Shippensburg, Pa., 1989), pp. 137–148, appendix D; *ORA* I, 37, pt. 2, pp. 199–209 *inter alia*.

39. *ORA*, I, 37, pt. 1, pp. 348, also p. 247; Early, *Autobiography*, p. 389; Frank Vandiver, *Jubal's Raid* (New York, 1960), pp. 149–151.

40. *ORA*, I, 37, pt. 1, pp. 240, 348; W. H. Farquhar, *Annals of Sandy Spring or Twenty Years of History in a Rural County in Maryland* (Baltimore, 1884), p. 13; Mildred Newbold Getty, "The Silver Spring Area," *The Montgomery County Story* (November 1963), pp. 3–4; John Worsham, *One of Jackson's Foot Cavalry* (Jackson, Tenn., 1964), pp. 241–242; G. W. Nichols, *A Soldier's Story of His Regiment* (Jessup, Ga.), p. 173; John G. Young, diary (NCHA), pp. 39–40; K. Willard Brown, *The Signal Corps, U.S.A. in the Rebellion* (Boston, 1896), Department of Washington chapter.

41. *ORA*, I, 37, pt. 1, p. 348, also pp. 231, 243, 244–245, 255; Early, *Autobiographical Sketch*, pp. 389–390; Vandiver, *Jubal's Raid*, pp. 151–152; Thomas Toon, "Twentieth Regiment" in Walter E. Clark, editor, *Histories of Several Regiments and Battalions from North Carolina* (Raleigh, 1901), vol. 2, p. 123.

42. Early, "The Advance on Washington in 1864," *Southern Historical Society Papers* (July, August, 1881), p. 306; also *Autobiographical Sketch*, p. 390; *ORA*, I, 37, pt. 1, pp. 245, 246.

43. Virginia Jeans Laas, editor, *Wartime Washington: the Civil War Letters of Elizabeth Blair Lee* (Urbana, 1991), p. 413.

44. Early, *Autobiographical Sketch*, p. 390; *ORA*, I, 37, pt. 1, pp. 231, 240, 241, 244.

45. George C. Pile memoir (TLA); John B. Gordon, *Reminiscences of the Civil War* (New York, 1904), p. 314; Sylvanus Cadwallader [Benjamin P. Thomas editor], *Three Years with Grant* (New York, 1955); John Opie, *A Rebel Cavalryman with Lee, Stuart, and Jackson* (Chicago, 1899), p. 246.

46. *ORA*, I, 37, pt. 1, p. 265; Worsham, *One of Jackson's Foot Cavalry*, p. 242.

47. *ORA*, I, 37, pt. 1, pp. 265, 270–273, 275.

48. Ibid., pp. 155–156.

49. Ibid., pt. 2, pp. 156–159.

50. Ibid., pt. 2, pp. 156–159, 191–194, 207, 209.
51. Ibid., pt. 1, pp. 265, 275; pt. 2, pp. 199, 205, 207, 209; on Lincoln at Fort Stevens, see Cooling, *Jubal Early's Raid*, pp. 125–136; John H. Cramer, *Lincoln Under Enemy Fire* (Baton Rouge, 1948), chaps. 2 and 3 especially.
52. Edgar S. Dudley, "Reminiscence of Washington and Early's Attack in 1864," Military Order of the Loyal Legion, Ohio Commandery, *Sketches of War History* (Cincinnati, 1888), I, pp. 122–123; *ORA*, I, 37, pt. 1, pp. 275–276; George Haven Putnam, *Memories of My Youth, 1844–1865* (New York, 1914), p. 340; S. J. Weiler, "Cavalry at Fort Stevens," *The National Tribune*, April 5, 1900; Robert Connelly, "At Fort Stevens," *The National Tribune*, July 19, 1900.
53. Clifford Dowdey and Louis Manarin, editors, *The Wartime Papers of R. E. Lee* (New York, 1971), pp. 819–820.
54. James M. Greiner, Janet L. Coryell and James R. Smither, editors, *A Surgeon's Civil War* (Kent, Ohio, 1994), pp. 219–220.
55. Early, *Autobiographical Sketch*, p. 392; *ORA*, I, 37, pt. 1, p. 348.
56. *ORA*, I, 37, pt. 1, pp. 271, 280–281; pt. 2, pp. 225–246, inter alia; while the action is more fully covered in Cooling, *Jubal Early's Raid*, chap. 5.
57. *ORA*, I, 37, pt. 1, pp. 13, 170–172, 232, 259; A. B. Beamish, "Battle at Fort Stephens [*sic*] Near Washington, DC, July 12, 1864, a Little Different Version," *Grand Army Scout and Soldiers Mail*, July 10, 1886.
58. On Johnson, see Cooling, *Jubal Early's Raid*, chap. 6; and Morgan Royce, "Reminiscence of Fred W. Royce," n.d. The Filson Club, Louisville, Ky.
59. *ORA*, I, 37, pt. 2, p. 223; Charles A. Dana, *Recollections of the Civil War* (New York, 1898), pp. 230–232.
60. Cooling, *Jubal Early's Raid*, pp. 140–145 covers the second time Lincoln was under Confederate fire; also Greiner, et al., *A Surgeon in the Civil War*, p. 220.
61. E. N. Atkinson, "Report of Evans Brigade," July 22, 1864, Eldridge collections (HL); G. W. Nichols, *A Soldier's Story of His Regiment* (Jessup, Ga., 1890), p. 172; *ORA*, I, 37, pt. 1, pp. 232, 246–248, 276–277.
62. Henry Kyd Douglas, *I Rode with Stonewall* (Chapel Hill, 1940), pp. 295–296.
63. *The Washington Evening Star*, July 13, 1864; New York *Times*, July 14, 1864; Laas, *Wartime Washington*, pp. 413, 420, 421; Cooling, *Jubal Early's Raid*, chap. 7.
64. Dana, *Recollections*, pp. 232–233; Laas, *Wartime*, p. 422; also *ORA*, I, 37, pt. 2, pp. 260–261.
65. J. D. Bloodgood, *Personal Reminiscences* (New York, 1893), pp. 186–187; Robert M. Browning, *From Cape Charles to Cape Fear: the North Atlantic Blockading Squadron During the Civil War* (Tuscaloosa, 1993), pp. 77–78.
66. Greiner, Coryell, and Smither, *A Surgeon's Civil War*, p. 221. George C. Pile memoir (TLA); Joseph T. Durkin, editor, *Confederate Chaplain, War Journal of Rev. James B. Sheeran* (Milwaukee, 1960), p. 381; William H. Runge, editor, *Four Years in the Confederate Artillery: Diary of Private Henry Robinson Berkeley* (Chapel Hill, 1961), p. 88; Roe, *Ninth New York Heavy Artillery*, p. 136; J. Kelly Bennette diary, entry July 13, 1864, and William Beavens, diary, entries July 13, 14, 1864, pp. 78–79 (both SHC/UNC); Robert Park, "Diary," *Southern Historical Society Papers I* (1876), p. 381.
67. Dana, *Recollections*, pp. 232–233.
68. J. Newton Terrill, "Shenandoah Valley," *The National Tribune*, October 8, 1891.
69. Tyler Dennett, *Lincoln and the Civil War in the Diaries and Letters of John Hay* (New York, 1939), p. 210, also pp. 208–209; Cooling, *Jubal Early's Raid*, pp. 186–194.

CHAPTER SEVEN

1. The immediate impact in Confederate circles can be followed in Larry E. Nelson, *Bullets, Ballots, and Rhetoric: Confederate Policy for the United States Presidential Contest of 1864* (University, Ala, 1980), pp. 58–61; David E. Long, *The Jewel of Liberty: Abraham Lincoln's Re-Election and the End of Slavery* (Mechanicsburg, Pa., 1994), pp. 207–208 provides the Union perspective.

2. Paul and Rita Gordon, *A Playground of the Civil War* (Frederick, 1994), pp. 197–198.

3. U.S. War Department, *War of the Rebellion: The Official Records of Union and Confederate Armies* (Washington, 1880–1901), ser. I, vol. 37, pt. 1, pp. 348–349.

4. Joseph McMurran diary, July 13, 14, 1864 (VSLA), Richmond; B. F. Cooling, *Jubal Early's Raid on Washington, 1864* (Baltimore, 1989), chap. 7; Leonidus Lafayette Polk - father, July 17, 1864, and Stephen Ramseur - wife July 15, 1864 (both SHC/UNC); Caleb Linker - Daniel Linker and family, July 17, 1864, CSA Archives, Miscellaneous Officer and Soldiers Letters, (DUL); Gordon's report is in *ORA*, I, 37, pt. 1, pp. 350–352.

5. Edward B. Williams, editor, Rebel Brothers (College Station, 1995), pp. 198–199, 201.

6. John B. Jones [Earl Schenck Miers, editor], *A Rebel War Clerk's Diary* (New York, 1958), pp. 401–403; Edward Younger, editor, *Inside the Confederate Government: the Diary of Robert Garlick Hill Kean, Head of the Bureau of War* (New York, 1957), pp. 162–164; Clifford Dowdey and Louis H. Manarin, editors, *The Wartime Papers of R. E. Lee* (New York, 1971), pp. 821–822.

7. Dowdey and Manarin, *Wartime Papers*, pp. 822–824.

8. For Lee's communiques in this period, see Ibid., pp. 825–831, 832–833, 834, 835, 845–846, 852–853, 856–857, 862–863, 864–865, 879; for a provocative essay on the Chambersburg episode, see Everard H. Smith, "Chambersburg: Anatomy of A Confederate Reprisal," *The American Historical Review* (April 1991), pp. 432–455.

9. Albert Gallatin Riddle, *Recollections of War Times* (New York, 1895), p. 286; Benjamin Brown French [Donald B. Cole and J. McDonough, editors], *Witness to the Young Republic: A Yankee's Journal* (Hanover, N.H. and London, 1989), p. 452; *ORA*, I, 37, pt. 2, pp. 155–158.

10. *ORA*, I, 37, pp. 155–156.

11. Glenn H. Worthington, *Fighting for Time* (Baltimore, 1932), p. 157; Gideon Welles, *Diary* (Boston, 1901), vol. 2, p. 71; Frederick W. Seward, *Reminiscences of a War-Time Statesman and Diplomat* (New York, 1916), pp. 246–247.

12. *ORA*, I, 37, pt. 1, pp. 198, 200, 347–348, 351–352, and Atlas Plate 94/3; Edward Schilling, [Barbara Schilling Everstine], *My Three Years in the Volunteer Army of the United States of America* (n.p., 1985), p. 75.

13. *Frank Leslie's Newspaper*, July 23, 30; *Harper's Weekly*, July 23; all 1864; Gordon, *A Playground of the Civil War*, pp. 197–198.

14. Richard R. Duncan, "Maryland's Reaction to Early's Raid in 1864: A Summer of Bitterness," *Maryland Historical Magazine* (Fall 1969), p. 251; J. Thomas Scharf, *History of Western Maryland* (Pittsburgh, 1882), vol. 7, pp. 285–286; Gordon, *A Playground of the Civil War*, pp. 222–223.

15. Middletown *Valley Register*, July 22, 1864.

16. Goldsborough, *Early's Great Raid*, p. 3; William R. Quinn, editor, *The Diary of Jacob Engelbrecht* (Frederick, 1976), p. 275; Allan journal, pp. 29–30 (SHC/UNC); John Young diary, p. 38, Raleigh (NCHA); Archie P. MacDonald, editor, *Make Me a Map of the Valley* (Dallas, 1973), p. 215; David J. Lewis, *Frederick War Claims: Evidence and Argument in Support*

of Bill to Refund Ransom Paid by the Town of Frederick, 1912, (copy FCHS), pp. 3, 4, 18, 19, 20; Edward Y. Goldsborough, preparer, *The Appeal of Frederick City, Maryland, to the Congress of the United States, for the Payment of its claim of $200,000*, ca. 1902.

17. Goldsborough, *Early's Great Raid*, pp. 3, 6.
18. Buckner McGill Randolph, diary, July 9, 1864 (VAHS); Delaplaine, "Early's Levy," p. 54; Pamphlet, "'Frederick Under Two Flags 1861–1865, The Ransom of Frederick City," no date; John W. Schildt, *Drums Along the Antietam* (Chewsville, Md., n.d.), p. 61.
19. S. Roger Keller, *Events of the Civil War in Washington County, Maryland* (Shippensburg, Pa., 1995), pp. 342–358.
20. Frederick *Examiner*, July 27, 1864; "Old Diary Tells of Early's Raid," Frederick *Daily News*, July 9, 1914.
21. Frederick *Examiner*, July 20, 27; Frederick *Maryland Union*, July 21, 28; Middletown *Valley Register*, July 21, all 1864; Thomas Gorsuch to Robert Gorsuch, July 19, 1864 (FCHS).
22. Elihu Rockwell to Mrs. E. R. Coleman, July 25, 1864 (FCHS).
23. Middletown *Valley Register*, August 12; Frederick *Maryland Union*, August 18; Frederick *Examiner*, July 27, all 1864, Transcripts of letters regarding Baughman and Ebert families of Southern Sympathies; Order of Arrest and Release, Issac Reich and family, 1864, August 1, 3, 1864; Harriet P. Floyd, "Civil War Memoirs," typescript, no date; Robert Cornwell to wife, August 3, 1864, all Edward S. Delaplaine collection; Elihu H. Rockwell to Mrs. E. R. Coleman, July 25, 1864, Fannie Ebert to Mary Baughman, July 27, 1864, August 2, 1864 (all FCHS).
24. Middletown *Valley Register*, Ibid.; Quinn, *Engelbrecht*, pp. 279–280, entry August 3, 1864.
25. Frederick *Examiner*, July 27, 1864; Floyd memoir (FCHS).
26. Middletown *Valley Register*, July 22; Frederick *Examiner*, July 20, both 1864; Carey scrapbook (MDHS), Baltimore.
27. On McCausland's raid, see Theodore Alexander et al., editors, *Southern Revenge: Civil War History of Chambersburg, Pennsylvania* (Shippensburg, Pa. 1989); Ted Alexander, "McCausland's Raid and the Burning of Chambersburg," *Blue and Gray Magazine* (August 1994), pp. 11–18, 46–64; Smith, "Chambersburg: Anatomy of A Confederate Reprisal," pp. 432–455; B. F. Cooling, *Jubal Early's Raid, 1864* (Baltimore, 1989), chap. 8; Frederick *Examiner*, July 27; Frederick *Maryland Union*, July 28; Middletown *Valley Register*, August 12, all 1864; Quinn, *Engelbrecht*, pp. 276–279, entries July 29, 30, August 1, 2, 3, all 1864.
28. Crucial communiques from this time-frame can be found in John Y. Simon, editor, *The Papers of Ulysses S. Grant* (Carbondale and Edwardsville, 1967–1991), vol. 11, pp. 376–383.
29. Worthington, *Fighting for Time*, pp. 205–207; Ulysses S. Grant, *Personal Memoirs* (New York, 1886), II, pp. 319–320; David Seibert to father, August 7, 1864, Seibert family papers, Harrisburg Civil War Round Table Collection, Carlisle Barracks, Pennsylvania (USAMHI).
30. Middletown *Valley Register*, September 9, 1864; Quinn, *Engelbrecht*, pp. 277, 279, entries July 22, August 2, both 1864; on the election, see Long, *The Jewel of Liberty*, pp. 217–259, 265–271, 285.
31. Benson J. Lossing, *The Civil War in America* (Hartford, 1868), vol. 3, p. 347, fn. 3.
32. Duncan, "Maryland's Reaction to Early's Raid in 1864," pp. 271–273.
33. Ibid., pp. 274–277.
34. *ORA*, I, 37, pt. 2, pp. 315–316, 339–341, 365, 366, 378, 390, 583–584; vol. 53, pt. 1, pp. 726, 823, 960, 962.

35. Duncan, "Maryland's Reaction to Early's Raid," pp. 278–279.
36. Gordon, *A Playground of the Civil War*, pp. 221–232.
37. Robert I. Cottom, Jr. and Mary Ellen Hayward, *Maryland in the Civil War: a House Divided* (Baltimore, 1994), p. 114; also Rockwell to Coleman, July 10, 1866 (FCHS).
38. Ezra J. Warner, *Generals in Blue* (Baton Rouge, 1964), pp. 535–536; William H. Powell and Edward Shippen, *Officers of the Army and Navy (Regular) Who Served in the Civil War* (Philadelphia, 1892), p. 88.
39. Frederick, Maryland Citizen Petition to President Johnson, April 24, 1865, in Leroy P. Graf, editor, *The Papers of Andrew Johnson* (Knoxville, 1986), vol. 7, pp. 626–627.
40. Ezra J. Warner, *Generals in Gray* (Baton Rouge, 1949), p. 157; Frederick Citizen Petition, April 24, 1865.
41. T. J. C. Williams, *History of Frederick County* (Baltimore, 1967 reprint), vol. 2, p. 1552.
42. Case of John T. Worthington of Frederick County, Md., June 28, 1873, File G-2129, Records of the Quartermaster General, Record Group 92 (NARA), cited in Edwin C. Bearss, "Documentation, Troop Movement Maps, Battle of the Monocacy" (Washington, 1979), pp. 110–111.
43. Festus P. Summers, *The Baltimore and Ohio in the Civil War* (Gettysburg, 1992 reprint), illustrations, pp. 22–27; Ronald W. Johnson, "Gambrill Mill Site Evaluation and Brief Special History Study, Monocacy National Battlefield" (Denver Service Center, December 1984); Susan Shufelt, "Historical Architecture Survey of Boscobel House, Monocacy National Battlefield" (Denver Service center, May 1984).

CHAPTER EIGHT

1. Lossing, *Civil War in America*, III, pp. 344–346; Edward A. Pollard, *The Lost Cause: a New Southern History of the War of the Confederates* (New York, 1867), pp. 535–536; Irving McKee, *Ben Hur Wallace* (Berkeley, 1947), pp. 45–46, 69–70, 74.
2. John B. Gordon - Robert E. Lee, February 6, 1868 (VAHS).
3. Jubal A. Early, *A Memoir of the Last Year of the War for Independence* (Lynchburg, 1867), pp. 54–56, 60.
4. Printed in Richmond *Sentinel*, [June, 1875].
5. John N. Opie, *A Rebel Cavalryman with Stuart and Jackson* (Chicago, 1899), pp. 246–247; C. A. Fondern, *A Brief History of the Military Career of Carpenter's Battery* (New Market, Va.: 1911), p. 48; I. G. Bradwell, "Early's Demonstration Against Washington in 1864," *Confederate Veteran* (October 1914), p. 438.
6. Alexander Hunter, *Johnny Reb and Billy Yank* (New York, 1905), pp. 651–652; quoting John B. Gordon, *Reminiscences of the Civil War* (New York, 1903), pp. 314–316; Armistead Long, *Memoirs of Robert E. Lee* (New York, 1886), pp. 359–360.
7. Grant, *Memoirs*, II, p. 306; George E. Pond, *The Shenandoah Valley in 1864* (New York, 1883), p. 59.
8. "Juvenis," "Battle of Monocacy," reprinted in Frederick *Daily News*, July 9, 1864; on postwar memorialization and remembrance see Kirk Savage, "The Politics of Memory: Black Emancipation and the Civil War Monument," in John R. Gillis, editor, *Commemorations: the Politics of National Identity* (Princeton, 1994), chap. 7.
9. Cottom and Hayward, *Maryland in the Civil War*, pp. 114–118; for *National Tribune*, reminiscences, see our bibliography attached.

10. William Jaboe Grove, *History of Carrollton Manor* (Frederick, 1928), p. 338; Frederick *Daily News*, July 9, 1914; "End of Civil War Brought Reconstruction Problems Here," 1945, E. P. Goldsborough, vertical files (FCHS).
11. Frederick *Daily News*, July 9, 1889.
12. York, Pennsylvania *Dispatch*, March 10, 1900.
13. Frederick *Daily News*, July 9, 10, 1904.
14. Ibid., July 9, 1907; Worthington, *Fighting for Time*, pp. 222–226.
15. Frederick *Daily News*, November 24, 1908.
16. Frederick *Daily News*, Frederick *Post*, both July 9, 1914.
17. Frederick *Daily News*, June 24, 1915.
18. Ibid., July 6, 7, 1939; "Memorial Park on Monocacy Battle Field," *Confederate Veteran* (February 1928), p. 44.
19. U.S. Congress, 70th, First Session, House Committee on Military Affairs, *Hearings on National Military Park at Monocacy, Md., April 13, 1928* (Washington, 1928), pp. 7–14; Worthington, *Fighting for Time*, pp. 275–276; "Memorial Park," p. 44.
20. Douglas Southall Freeman, *Lee's Lieutenants: a Study in Command* (New York, 1944), vol. 3, pp. 560–568, especially 568; Charles W. Porter, Harry Langley, W. E. Little, "Report of Field Investigations Relating to the Monocacy National Military Pt.," 1940; Oscar S. Bray and Charles W. Porter, "A Report on a Proposed Road on the Monocacy Battlefield," 1940; Ruth Graham, "Battle of the Monocacy," ca. 1935, and "Field Investigation, Monocacy National Battlefield," 1935; Howard Smith, "Battle of Monocacy," January 1934; Alvin P. Stauffer, "Monocacy Battlefield Site," 1936; and Harry T. Thompson, "A Report on the Monocacy Battlefield," 1937, all National Park Service, all Harpers Ferry Center Library, Harpers Ferry, West Virginia.
21. Land Protection Plan, Monocacy National Battlefield, 1983, p. 3.
22. Compare Ibid., with Porter, Langley, Little, "Report of Field Investigations," on the Stone/Jug bridge sector issue.
23. Frederick *News*, July 15, 1991; Washington *Post*, July 4, and December 14, 1989; Miscellaneous 125th anniversary commemorative brochures, announcements, Monocacy Preservation folder, Defending Washington files, Alexandria, Va. (FWM); see also John W. Schildt, *Drums Along the Moncacy* (Chewsville, Md., n.d.), chap. 7.
24. Civil War Sites Advisory Commission, *Report on the National Civil War Battlefields* (Washington, 1993), pp. 3, 30; Howard A. Denis, "How Washington Was Saved," Washington *Post*, August 3, 1991.
25. "Civil War Battlefield Is Faithful to the Past," Montgomery County *Journal*, July 5, 1994.

APPENDIX 2

1. J. G. Nicolay and J. Hay, editors, *Complete Works of Abraham Lincoln* (New York, 1894), vol. 10, pp. 123–124.
2. Allan Nevins, *The War for the Union: the Organized War to Victory, 1864–1865* (New York, 1971), vol. 4, pp. 3, 33, 144–146.
3. E. J. Benton, *The Movement for Peace Without a Victory During the Civil War* (Cleveland, 1918), inter alia.; H. H. Wubben, Civil War Iowa and the Copperhead Movement (Ames, 1980), chap. 8, State of Ohio, *Annual Report of the Adjutant General*, 1864 (Columbus, 1865), inter alia.
4. W. B. Hesseltine, *Lincoln and the War Governors* (New York, 1948), p. 297; Carl Sandburg, *Abraham Lincoln: The War Years* (New York, 1939), vol. 3, pp. 136–137; E. H. Roseboom, *A History of Ohio: The Civil War Era, 1850–1873* (Columbus, 1944), pp. 430–432.

5. T. Harry Williams, *Lincoln and His Generals* (New York, 1952), chap. 12; Nevins, *War for the Union*, vol. 4, chap. 1; Ulysses S. Grant, *Personal Memoirs* (New York, 1885), vol. 2, chaps. 46 and 47.

6. R. H. Abbott, *Ohio's Civil War Governors* (Columbus, 1962), p. 39.

7. Ibid., pp. 40–41; Roseboom, *Ohio: the Civil War Era*, p. 427; Whitelaw Reid, *Ohio in the War: Her Statesmen, Her Generals and Soldiers* (New York, 1868), vol. 1, pp. 202–204.

8. Hesseltine, *Lincoln and the War Governors*, inter alia.

9. Ohio *Adjutant General Reports*, 1862, 1863, 1864, inter alia.

10. B. R. Cowen, "The One Hundred Days Men of Ohio," in Military Order of the Loyal Legion of the United States, Ohio Commandery, *Sketches of War History*, 1861–1865, vol. 5 (Cincinnati, 1903), p. 365.

11. Ibid., pp. 365–367; Ohio *Adjutant General Report*, 1864, pp. 12–13.

12. Reid, *Ohio in the War*, vol. 1, p. 208.

13. U.S. War Department, *War of the Rebellion: the Official Records of the Union and Confederate Armies* (Washington, 1880–1901), ser. I, vol. 37, and ser. 3, vol. 4, inter alia; Ohio *Adjutant General Report*, 1864, inter alia; Cowen, "Hundred Days Men," pp. 367–368.

14. *ORA*, ser. III, vol. 4, pp. 237–239.

15. Ohio *Adjutant General Report*, 1864, pp. 18–20.

16. Cowen, "Hundred Days Men," pp. 370–371, 374.

17. Chillicothe, *Scioto Gazette*, May 3, 1864.

18. G. Perkins, *A Summer in Maryland and Virginia, or Campaigning with the One Hundred and Forty-Ninth Ohio Volunteer Infantry* (Chillicothe, 1911), pp. 14–15.

19. Ibid., pp. 46–47; *Ohio Adjutant General Report*, 1864, pp. 30–32.

20. *ORA*, ser. III, vol. 4, pp. 1266–1267.

21. Ibid.

22. Ibid., ser. I, vol. 37, pt. 2, inter alia; vol. 43, pt. 1, inter alia; Lew Wallace, *An Autobiography* (New York, 1907), vol. 2, 72–75; Perkins, *One Hundred and Forty-Ninth Ohio*, inter alia; J. C. Cannon, *Memorial: One Hundred and Fiftieth Ohio, Company K* (Lakewood, Ohio, 1907), p. 6.

23. *ORA*, ser. I, vol. 37, pt. 1, pp. 213–215, 216–219, 221–223.

24. W. F. Fox, *Regimental Losses in the American Civil War* (Albany, 1895), inter alia.

25. Nicolay and Hay, *Complete Works of Abraham Lincoln*, vol. 10, pp. 199–200, 202–203, 208–209.

26. Grant, *Personal Memoirs*, vol. 2, pp. 253–254, 556–557; John Brough, "The Defenders of the Country and Its Enemies: the Chicago Platform Dissected," speech delivered on September 3, 1864, Circleville, Cincinnati, 1903.

27. Perkins, *One Hundred and Forty-Ninth Ohio*, p. 64; *ORA*, ser. III, vol. 4, pp. 707, 708, 755, 756.

BIBLIOGRAPHY

Primary Sources—Archives

Alabama Department of Archives and History, Montgomery, Alabama (AAH)

Cullen Andrews Battle papers

Chicago Historical Society, Chicago, Illinois (CHS)

William Terry papers

Duke University Library, Durham, North Carolina (DUL)

Confederate States of America, Archives, Army, Miscellaneous Officers and Soldiers Letters

Edwin Hardin papers

Journal of Anonymous Crewman, Steamer *George Leary*

Edmund Jennings Lee papers

T. A. Meysenburg Notes on Battles around Martinsburg, Virginia.

Robert Smith Rodgers papers, History of Second Eastern Shore Regiment, Maryland Infantry

Mary Eliza (Fleming) Schooler papers

The Filson Club, Louisville, Kentucky (FC)

Morgan Royce papers

Fort Ward Museum and Historic Site, Alexandria, Virginia (FWM)

Defending Washington collection (includes Monocacy)

Frederick County Historical Society, Frederick, Maryland (FCHS)

Elbert Baughman family papers

Robert Cornwell papers

Edward S. Delaplaine collection

Thomas Gorsuch papers

Battle of Monocacy files

Rich family papers

Elihu Rockwell papers

Joseph Urner reminiscence

Huntington Library, San Marino, California (HL)

James W. Eldridge collection

John Page Nicholson collection

Illinois State Historical Library, Springfield, Illinois (ISHL)

Reuben T. Prentice papers

William R. Rowley papers

Library of Congress, Washington, D.C. (LC)

Thomas L. Feamster diary

Samuel P. Heintzelman papers

Jedediah Hotchkiss journal

Montgomery C. Meigs papers

William W. Old diary

Maryland Historical Society, Baltimore, Maryland (MDHS)

Augustus Bradford papers

I. G. Bradwell papers

Carey scrapbook

Civil War Miscellaneous collection

Rebecca Davis diary

Harry Gilmor papers

Rinehart diary

Richard P. Thomas papers

Massachusetts Historical Society, Boston, Massachusetts (MAHS)

F. C. Morse papers

Montgomery County Historical Society, Rockville, Maryland (MCHS)

John T. De Sellum letters

National Archives and Records Administration, Washington, D.C.

John McF. Lyeth pension file

Record Group 77, Records of the Corps of Engineers

Record Group 92, Records of the Quartermaster General

New York Historical Society, New York, New York (NYHS)

John Fleming recollections

J. Stoddard Johnston notes

Naval History Society collection

James H. Rochelle

Southard Family papers

North Carolina Department of History and Archives, Raleigh, North Carolina (NCHA)

Augustus Clewell papers

Thomas F. Toon papers

John G. Young diary

North Louisiana Historical Association Archives, Centenary College of Louisiana, Shreveport, Louisiana (NLHA)

Richard Colbert letter

Tennessee State Library and Archives, Nashville, Tennessee (TLA)

George C. Pile memoirs

Tulane University Library, New Orleans, Louisiana (TUL)

Association of the Army of Northern Virginia papers

T. E. Morrow papers

U.S. Army Military History Institute, Carlisle Barracks, Pennsylvania (USAMHI)

Civil War Miscellaneous collection

Richard Castle papers

James M. Gasper papers

Henry Ivins papers

George E. Kimball papers

Paul Lounsberry papers

Jacob A. Schmid papers

Anson B. Shuey papers

Civil War Times *Illustrated* collection

David B. Lang papers

Silas D. Wesson papers

Harrisburg Civil War Round Table collection

Seibert Family papers

Lewis Leigh collection

Eugene Blackford papers

Sondus W. Haskell papers

Overton Steger papers

James Sheeran diary

James A. Strahle memoirs

University of Georgia Library, Athens, Georgia (UGL)
    John B. Gordon family papers
University of North Carolina Library, Chapel Hill, North Carolina (UNCL)
    Southern Historical Collection
        William Allan collection
        William Beavans collection
        J. Kelly Bennett diary
        Carrie E. Clack papers
        James E. Green diary
        William R. Gwaltney papers
        Thomas Butler King papers
        John Paris papers
        Leonidus Lafayette Polk papers
        Stephen D. Ramseur papers
        W. R. Redding papers
        Richard Woolfork Waldrop papers
        William Henry Wills papers
Vermont Historical Society, Montpelier, Vermont (VTHS)
        Aldace F. Walker letters
Virginia Historical Society, Richmond, Virginia (VAHS)
        Millard Bushong/Jubal A. Early papers
        District of Columbia Supreme Court, Davis and Breckinridge indictments
        Robert E. Lee Headquarters papers
        Buckner McGill Randolph diary
            Rufus Woolwine diary
Virginia State Library and Archives, Richmond, Virginia (VSLA)
        Joseph McMurran diary
Western Reserve Historical Society, Cleveland, Ohio (WRHS)
        W. H. Hayward papers
        James Taylor sketchbook

Primary Sources—Printed
Newspapers and Periodicals

Army and Navy Journal
Baltimore *Sun*

Chillicothe, *Scioto Gazette*

Frank Leslie's Illustrated Newspaper

Frederick *Examiner*

Frederick *Maryland Union*

Frederick *News*

Frederick *Post*

Harpers Weekly

Middletown *Valley Register*

Montgomery County *Sentinel*

Richmond *Sentinel*

Washington *Post*

Washington *Star*

Washington *Times Herald*

The National Tribune

Roderick A. Clark (14th New Jersey), "Monocacy," April 15, 1886

Robert Connelly, "At Fort Stevens," July 19, 1900

George E. Davis (10th Vermont), "Captor or Prisoner," August 14, 1884

George E. Davis (10th Vermont), "Washington in Peril," August 21, 1884

W. H. Engler (3d Maryland, Potomac Home Brigade), "The Brave Act of a Comrade," September 9, 1909

Daniel B. Freeman (10th Vermont), "Washington in Peril," April 21, 1884

W. L. Garnder (110th Ohio), "The Battle of Monocacy," December 6, 1888

W. T. McDougle (126th Ohio), "An Indiana Soldier at the Battle of Monocacy," February 21, 1884

J. H. McKinnon (110th Ohio), "The 110th Ohio at Monocacy," July 26, 1888

————. (126th Ohio), "Monocacy," March 11, 1886

J. C. Patterson (14th New Jersey), "The Battle of Monocacy," October 27, 1898

Peter Robertson (106th New York), "Monocacy," July 2, 1891

M. J. Stearns (106th New York), "Monocacy," July 2, 1891

Walter Strickler (Philadelphia, Pa.), "How a Lie Saved the Capital," April 30, 1903

J. Newton Terrill (14th New Jersey), "Shenandoah Valley - Monocacy," October 8, 1891

C. R. Van Tress (149th Ohio National Guard), "Saved the Day at Monocacy," October 22, 1903

S. J. Weiler (Cavalry), "Cavalry at Fort Stevens," April 5, 1900

Documents—Government

Ohio, State of. Adjutant General Report, 1862–1864. Columbus, State Printer, 1863–1865.

Tennessee, State of. Tennessee Civil War Commission, *Tennesseans in the Civil War*. Nashville: Tennessee Civil War Commission, 1864.

U.S. Civil War Sites Advisory Commission. *Report on the Nation's Civil War Battlefields*. Washington: National Park Service, 1993.

U.S. Congress, Seventieth, First Session, House of Representatives. Hearings before the Committee on Military Affairs, *To Establish a National Military Park at Battlefield of Monocacy, Maryland*, April 13, 1928. Washington: Government Printing Office, 1928.

U.S. Navy Department. *Official Records of the Union and Confederate Navies in the War of the Rebellion*. Washington: Government Printing Office, 1894–1927, 30 volumes.

U.S. War Department. *War of the Rebellion: A Compilation of the Official Records of the Union and Confederate Armies*. Washington: Government Printing Office. 128 volumes and atlas.

Documents—Other

Basler, Roy P. *The Collected Works of Abraham Lincoln*. New Brunswick: Rutgers University Press, 1953. 8 volumes.

Dowdey, Clifford, and Louis H. Manarin, editors. *The Wartime Papers of R. E. Lee*. New York: Bramhall House for Virginia Civil War Commission, 1961.

Dyer, Frederick H. *A Compendium of the War of the Rebellion*. New York: Thomas Yoseloff, 1959 edition. 3 volumes.

Dyer, Gustavus W., and John Trotwood Moore, compilers. *The Tennessee Civil War Veterans Questionnaires*. Easley, S.C.: Southern Historical Press, 1985. 5 volumes.

Freeman, Douglas Southall. *Lee's Dispatches: Unpublished Letters of General Robert E. Lee to Jefferson Davis and the War Department of the Confederate States of America, 1862–1865*. New York: G. P. Putnam's Sons, 1957.

Graf, Leroy P., Ralph W. Haskins, et al., editors. *The Papers of Andrew Johnson*. Knoxville: University of Tennessee Press, 1986–.

Moore, Frank, editor. *Rebellion Record: A Diary of American Events*. New York: D. Van Nostrand, 1868. 11 volumes.

Nicolay, John G., and J. Hay, editors. *Complete Works of Abraham Lincoln*. New York: Francis D. Tandy Company, 1905. 12 volumes.

Simon, John Y., editor. *The Papers of Ulysses S. Grant.* Carbondale, Ill.: Southern Illinois University Press, 1967–1991. 16 volumes.

Memoirs, Diaries, Reminiscences—Civilian

Bates, David Homer. *Lincoln in the Telegraph Office: Recollections of the United States Military Telegraph Corps During the Civil War.* New York: Century Company, 1907.

Beale, Howard K., editor. *The Diary of Edward Bates, 1859–1866.* New York: De Capo Press, 1971 edition.

Beauchamp, Virginia Walcott, editor. *A Private War: Letters and Diaries of Madge Preston, 1862–1867.* New Brunswick: Rutgers University Press, 1987.

Brooks, Noah (Herbert Mitgang, editor). *Washington D.C. in Lincoln's Time.* Chicago: Quandrangle, 1971 edition.

Carpenter, F. B. *Six Months at the White House with Abraham Lincoln: the Story of a Picture.* New York: Hurd and Houghton, 1867.

Chittenden, Lucius E. *Recollections of President Lincoln and His Administration.* New York: Harper and Brother, 1891.

Cole, Donald B., and John J. McDonough, editors. *Witness to the Young Republic: A Yankee's Journal, 1828–1870, Benjamin Brown French.* Hanover, N.H.: University Press of New England, 1989.

Dana, Charles A. *Recollection of the Civil War: With the Leaders at Washington and in the Field in the Sixties.* New York: D. Appleton and Company, 1898.

Dennett, Tyler. *Lincoln and the Civil War in the Diaries and Letters of John Hay.* New York: Dodd, Meade and Company, 1939.

Doster, William E. *Lincoln and Episodes of the Civil War.* New York: G. P. Putnam's Sons, 1915.

Emerson, Edward W. *Life and Letters of Charles Russell Lowell.* Boston: Houghton Mifflin and Company, 1907.

Laas, Virginia Neans, editor. *Wartime Washington: the Civil War Letters of Elizabeth Blair Lee.* Urbana: University of Illinois Press, 1991.

Marks, Bayly Ellen, and Mark Norten Schatz, editors. *Between North and South: a Maryland Journalist Views the Civil War: the Narrative of William Kilkens Glenn, 1861–1869.* Rutherford, N.J.: Fairleigh Dickinson University Press, 1976.

Miers, Earl Schenck, editor. *A Rebel War Clerk's Diary by John B. Jones.* New York: Sagamore Press, 1958.

Olsen, Bernard A., editor. *Upon the Tented Field* [Fourteenth New Jersey]. Red Bank, N.J., 1993.

Quinn, William R., editor. *The Diary of Jacob Engelbrecht.* Frederick, Md.: Frederick County Historical Society, 1976.

Riddle, Albert Gallatin. *Recollections of War Time: Reminiscences of Men and Events in Washington, 1860–1865*, New York: G. P. Putnam's Sons, 1895.

Seward, Frederick W. *Reminiscences of a War-time Statesman and Diplomat, 1830–1915*, New York: G. P. Putnam's Sons, 1916.

Staudenraus, P. J., editor. *Mr. Lincoln's Washington: Selections from the Writings of Noah Brooks, Civil War Correspondent.* South Brunswick: Thomas Yoseloff, 1967.

Tuckerman, Charles K. *Personal Recollections of Notable People.* New York: Dodd Mead and Company, 1895. 2 volumes.

Welles, Gideon. *Diary.* Boston: Houghton Mifflin, 1909. 3 volumes.

Younger, Edebard, editor. *Inside the Confederate Government: The Diary of Robert Garlick Hill Kean.* New York: Oxford University Press, 1957.

Memoirs, Diaries, Reminiscences—Confederate Military

Alexander, John H. *Mosby's Men.* New York: Neale, 1907.

"An Old Comrade," *A Sketch of the Life and Services of Major John A. Harman, Chief Quartermaster.* Staunton, Va.: Spectator Job Print, March 1876.

Barnett, Hoyt. "Recalls Gen. Early's Raid." *Washington Post,* July 14, 1935.

Booth, George Wilson. *Personal Reminiscences of a Maryland Soldier in the War Between the States.* Baltimore: By Private Subscription, 1898.

Bradwell, I. G. "Early's Demonstration Against Washington in 1864." *Confederate Veteran,* XXII, Number 10 (October 1914), 438–439.

———. "Early's March to Washington in 1864." *Confederate Veteran,* XXVIII, Number 5 (May 1920), 176–177.

———. "In the Battle of Monocacy, Md." *Confederate Veteran,* XXXVI, Number 2 (February 1928), 55–57.

———. "On to Washington." *Confederate Veteran,* XXXVI, Number 3 (March 1928), 95–96.

———. "The Battle of Monocacy, Md." *Confederate Veteran,* XXXVII, Number 10 (October 1929), 382–383.

Casler, John O. *Four Years in the Stonewall Brigade.* Girard, Kans.: Appeal Publishing Company, 1906, and Dayton, Ohio: Morningside Bookshop, 1971 edition.

Clark, Willene B., editor. *Valleys of the Shadow: The Memoir of Confederate Captain Reuben G. Clark, Company I, 59th Tennessee Mounted Infantry.* Knoxville: University of Tennessee Press, 1994.

Coffman, J. W. "Burning of the Blair House." *Confederate Veteran,* XIV, Number 7 (July 1911), 336.

Crenshaw, Edward. "Diary of Captain Edward Crenshaw." *Alabama Historical Quarterly* (1930), 449–450.

Daniel, John W. "General Jubal A. Early." *Southern Historical Society papers*, XXII (1894), 281–340.

Douglas, Henry Kyd. *I Rode With Stonewall: Being Chiefly the War Experiences of the Youngest Member of Jackson's Staff*. Chapel Hill: University of North Carolina, 1940.

Durkin, Joseph T., editor. *Confederate Chaplain: A War Journal of Rev. James B. Sheeran, c.ss.r., Fourteenth Louisiana, C.S.A*. Milwaukee: Bruce Publishing Company, 1960.

Early, Jubal A. "The Advance on Washington 1864." *Southern Historical Society Papers*, 9, Numbers 7 and 8 (July/August 1881).

———. *Autobiographical Sketch and Narrative of the War Between the States*. Philadelphia: J. B. Lippincott, 1912 and Baltimore, Md.: Nautical and Aviation Publishing Co., 1989.

———. "Early's March to Washington in 1864" in Robert Underwood Johnson and Clarence Clough Buel, editors. *Battles and Leaders of the Civil War*. New York: Century Company, 1884. 4 volumes (vol. 4).

———. *A Memoir of the Last Year of the War for Independence, in the Confederate States of America, Containing an Account of His Commands in the Years 1864 and 1865*. Lynchburg, Va.: C. W. Button, 1867.

———. (Frank Vandiver, editor). *War Memoirs*. Bloomington: Indiana University Press, 1960.

Gallagher, Gary W., editor. *Fighting for the Confederacy: the Personal Recollections of General Edward Porter Alexander*. Chapel Hill: University of North Carolina Press, 1989.

Gilmor, Harry. *Four Years in the Saddle*. New York: Harper and Brothers, 1866.

Gipson, Moses. "Valley Campaign of General Early." *Southern Historical Society Papers*, 34 (1906), 212–217.

Gordon, John B. *Reminiscences of the Civil War*. New York: Charles Scribners, 1904.

Hunter, Alexander. *Johnny Reb and Billy Yank*. New York: Neale, 1905.

Hutcheson, James A. "Saved the Day at Monocacy." *Confederate Veteran*, XXIII, Number 2 (February 1915), 77.

Johnson, Bradley T. "My Ride Around Baltimore in 1864." *Journal of the United States Cavalry Association*, II, Number 6 (September 1889), 250–260.

Long, Armistead Lindsay. *Memoirs of Robert E. Lee*. New York: J. M. Stoddart and Company, 1886.

McDonald, Archie P., editor. *Make Me a Map of the Valley: The Civil War Journal of Stonewall Jackson's Topographer.* Dallas: Southern Methodist University Press, 1973.

Mettam, Henry C. "Civil War Memoirs: First Maryland Cavalry, C.S.A." *Maryland Historical Magazine*, 58, Number 2 (June 1963), 139–170.

Musgrove, George Dallas (Bell Wiley, editor). *Kentucky Cavaliers in Dixie: Reminiscences of a Confederate Cavalryman.* Jackson, Tenn.: McCowat-Mercer Press, 1957.

Oates, Dan, editor. *Hanging Rock Rebel: Lt. John Blue's War in West Virginia and the Shenandoah Valley.* Shippensburg, Pa.: White Mane Publishing Company, 1994.

Opie, John N. *A Rebel Cavalryman with Lee, Stuart and Jackson.* Chicago: W. B. Conkey, 1899.

Park, Robert E. "Diary." *Southern Historical Society Papers*, I (1876), 370–386.

Rich, Edward R. *Comrades Four.* New York: Neale, 1907.

Runge, William H., editor. *Four Years in the Confederate Artillery: The Diary of Private Henry Robinson Berkeley.* Chapel Hill: University of North Carolina Press, 1961.

Scott, W. W., editor. "Diary of Captain H. W. Wingfield." *Bulletin of the Virginia State Library*, XVI, Numbers 2 and 3 (July 1927).

Taylor, Walter H. *Four Years With General Lee.* New York: D. Appleton, 1878.

Williams, Edward B., editor. *Rebel Brothers; The Civil War Letters of the Truehearts.* College Station: Texas A&M Press, 1995.

Worsham, John H. *One of Jackson's Foot Cavalry: His Experience and What He Saw During the War 1861–1865*, New York: Neale, 1912, and Jackson, Tenn.: McCowat-Mercer Press, 1964.

Memoirs, Diaries, Letters, Reminiscences—Union Military

Abbott, Samuel A. *Personal Recollections and Civil War Diary, 1864.* Burlington, Vt.: Free Press, 1908.

Beamish, A. B. "Battle at Fort Stephens [*sic*] Near Washington, D.C. July 12, 1864, A Little Different Version." *Grand Army Scout and Soldiers Mail* (Philadelphia), Saturday, July 10, 1886.

Black, Wilfred, editor. "Civil War Letters of George Washington McMillen and Jefferson O. McMillen, 122d Regiment, O.V.I." *West Virginia History*, 32 (April 1971), 171–193.

Bloodgood, J. D. *Personal Reminiscences of the War.* New York, 1893.

Cadwallader, Sylvanus (Benjamin P. Thomas, editor). *Three Years With Grant.* New York: Alfred A. Knopf, 1955 edition.

Drickamer, Lee C. and Karen D., compilers and editors. *Fort Lyon to Harper's Ferry: On the Border of North and South with "Rambling Jour": The Civil War Letters and Newspaper Dispatches of Charles H. Moulton (34th Mass. Vol. Inf.)*. Shippensburg, Pa.: White Mane Publishing Company, 1987.

Dudley, Edgar S. "A Reminiscence of Washington and Early's Attack in 1874" in Military Order of the Loyal Legion of the United States, Ohio Commandery, *Sketches of War History 1861–1865*, Cincinnati: Robert Clarke and Company, 1888, vol. 1, 107–127.

Grant, Ulysses S. *Personal Memoirs*. New York: Charles L. Webster, 1885. 2 volumes.

Gray, Richard A. Jr., editor. *1864 Pocket Diary of Pvt. George R. Imler, Co. E, 138th Regiment, Pennsylvania Volunteers: Personal Account of the Campaign of the Army of the Potomac from the Wilderness to Petersburg*. n.p., 1963.

Greiner, James M., Janet L. Coryell, and James R. Smither, editors. *A Surgeon's Civil War: The Letters and Diary of Daniel M. Holt, M.D.* Kent: Kent State University Press, 1994.

Hyde, Thomas W. *Following the Greek Cross*. Boston: Houghton Mifflin, 1895.

James, William H. "Blue and Gray I; A Baltimore Volunteer of 1864." *Maryland Historical Magazine*, XXXVI, Number 1 (March 1941), 22–23.

Lyle, W. W. *Lights and Shadows of Army Life*. Cincinnati: R. W. Carroll and Company, 1865.

Newcomer, C. Armour. *Cole's Cavalry or Three Years in the Saddle in the Shenandoah Valley*. Baltimore: Cushing and Company, 1895.

Olsen, Bernard, A. *Upon The Tented Field*. Red Bank, N.J., Historic Projects, Inc., 1993.

O'Ferrall, Charles T. *Forty Years of Active Service*. New York: Neale, 1904.

Perkins, George. *A Summer in Maryland and Virginia or Campaigning with the One Hundred and Forty-Ninth Ohio Volunteer Infantry*. Chillicothe: School Printing Company, 1911.

Porter, Horace. *Campaigning with Grant*. New York: Century Company, 1906.

Putnam, George Haven. *Memories of My Youth, 1844–1865*. New York: G. P. Putnam's Sons, 1914.

Quint, Alonzo H. *The Potomac and the Rapidan: Army Notes*. Boston: Crosby and Nichols, 1864.

Roe, Alfred S. "From Monocacy to Danville, A Trip with the Confederates." Rhode Island Soldiers and Sailors Historical Society, *Personal Narratives of events in the War of the Rebellion*. Providence: The Society, 4th series, Number 1, 1889.

————. *Monocacy*. Introduction and Notes by Jerry L. Harlowe. Baltimore: Toomey Press, 1996.

Schilling, Edward (Barbara Schilling Everstine, editor). *My Three Years in the Volunteer Army of the United States of America. From August 12th 1862 to June 10th 1865*. n.p., 1985 reprint.

Shaw, William H. *A Diary as Kept by William H. Shaw during the Great Civil War from April 1861 to July 1865*. n.p., n.d.

Stevens, George T. *Three Years in the Sixth Corps: A Concise Narrative of Events in the Army of the Potomac from 1861 to the Close of the Rebellion, April, 1865*. New York: D. Van Nostrand, 1870.

Stewart, Alexander Morrison. *Camp, March and Battle-field or Three Years and a Half with the Army of the Potomac*. Philadelphia: James B. Rodgers, 1865.

Vredenburgh, Peter. *Letters of Major Peter Vredenburgh...of the Battles and Marches of the Old Fourteenth Regiment N.J.* Vols. n.p. 187?

Wallace, Lew. *Lew Wallace: An Autobiography*. New York: Harper and Brothers, 1906. 2 volumes.

Unit Histories—Confederate

Barlett, Napier. *Military Record of Louisiana*. New Orleans, Graham and Company 1875 and Baton Rouge: Louisiana State University Press, 1964 edition.

Clark, Walter E., editor. *Histories of the Several Regiments and Battalions from North Carolina in the Great War 1861–1865*. Raleigh: E. M. Uzell, 1901. 5 volumes.

Delauter, Roger V., Jr. *Sixty-Second Virginia Infantry*. [Virginia Regimental Series]. Lynchburg: M. E. Howard, Inc. 1988.

Fondern, C. A. *A Brief History of the Military Career of Carpenter's Battery*. New Market, Va.: Henkel and Company, 1911.

Goldsborough, W. W. *The Maryland Line in the Confederate Army, 1861–1865*. Baltimore: Kelly, Piet and Company, 1869 and Guggenheimer, Weil and Company, 1900.

Iobst, Richard W., and Louis H. Manarin. *The Bloody Sixth: The Sixth North Carolina Regiment's Confederate States of America*. Raleigh: North Carolina Confederate Centennial Commission, 1965.

Jones, Terry L. *Lee's Tigers: The Louisiana Infantry in the Army of Northern Virginia*. Baton Rouge: Louisiana State University Press, 1987.

Kenan, Thomas S., compiler. *Sketch of the Forty-Third Regiment North Carolina Troops (Infantry)*. Raleigh: n.p., 1895.

Murray, Allan J. *South Georgia Rebels: the True Wartime Experiences of the Twenty-Sixth Regiment Georgia Volunteer Infantry, Lawton-Gordon-Evans Brigade, Confederate States Army, 1861–1865*. St. Mary's, Ga.: By Author, 1976.

Nichols, G.W. *A Soldier's Story of His Regiment (Sixty-First Georgia) and Incidentally of the Lawton-Gordon-Evans Brigade Army of Northern Virginia*. n.p., 1898 and Kennesay, Ga.: Continental Book Company, 1961, edition.

Park, Robert E. "The Twelfth Alabama Infantry, Confederate States Army." *Southern Historical Society Papers*, 33 (1905), 193–296.

Robertson, James I. *The Stonewall Brigade*. Baton Rouge: Louisiana State University Press, 1963.

Smith, W. A. *The Anson Guards: Company C, Fourteenth Regiment North Carolina Volunteers 1861–1865*. Charlotte: Stone Publishing Company, 1914.

Stegeman, John F. *These Men She Gave: Civil War Diary of Athens, Georgia*. Athens: University of Georgia Press, 1964.

United Daughters of the Confederacy, Georgia Division, Oglethorpe County Chapter 1292, Lexington. *This They Remembered: the History of the Four Companies...Who Went from Oglethorpe County to Serve in the War Between the States*. Washington: Washington Publishing Company, 1965.

Wallace, Lee A., Jr. *Fifth Virginia Infantry*. [Virginia Regimental Series]. Lynchburg: H. E. Howard, Inc., 1988.

Wellman, Manly Wade. *Rebel Boast: First at Bethel—Last at Appomattox*. New York: Henry Holt, 1956.

Unit Histories—Union

Benedict, George Grenville. *Vermont in the Civil War*. Burlington: Free Press Association, 1888. 2 volumes.

Brown, J. Willard. *The Signal Corps, U.S.A. in the War of the Rebellion*. Boston: U.S. Veteran Signal Corps Association, 1896.

———. *Record of Service of Company K, One Hundred and Fiftieth Ohio O.V.I., 1864*. n.p., 1903.

Cannon, James. *Memorial, One Hundred Fiftieth Ohio, Company K*. n.p., 1907.

Carpenter, George N. *History of the Eighth Regiment Vermont Volunteers, 1861–1865*. Boston: Press of Deland and Barta, 1886.

Clark, Lewis H. *Military History of Wayne County, N.Y.: The County in the Civil War*. Sodus, N.Y.: Lewis H. Clark, Hulett and Gaylord, 1881.

Farrar, Samuel Clarke. *The Twenty-Second Pennsylvania Cavalry and the Ringgold Battalion 1861–1865*. Pittsburgh: Twenty-Second Pennsylvania Ringgold Cavalry Association, 1911.

Gilson, John H. *Concise History of the One Hundred and Twenty-Sixth Regiment Ohio Volunteer Infantry, from the Date of Organization to the End of the Rebellion.* Salem: ?, 1883.

Gleason, William J. *Historical Sketch of the One Hundred and Fiftieth Regiment Ohio Volunteer Infantry: Roster of the Regiment,* n.p., 1899.

Goodhart, Briscoe. *History of the Independent Loudoun Virginia Rangers, U.S. Vol. Cav. (Scouts), 1862–65.* Washington: McGill and Wallace, 1896.

Hard, Abner. *History of the Eighth Cavalry Regiment Illinois Volunteers During the Great Rebellion.* Aurora, Ill.: By Author, 1868.

Hayes, Edwin M. *History of the Tenth Vermont.* Rutland: Tuttle, 1894.

Howell, Hellen A., compiler. *Chronicles of the One Hundred Fifty-First Regiment New York State Volunteer Infantry, 1862–1865.* Albion, N.Y., ?.

Irwin, Richard B. *History of the Nineteenth Army Corps.* New York: G. P. Putnam's Sons, 1893.

Lewis, Osceola. *History of the One Hundred and Thirty-Eighth Pennsylvania.* Norristown: Wills, Tredell and Jenkins, 1866.

Newcomer, C. Armour. *Cole's Cavalry or Three Years in the Saddle in the Shenandoah Valley.* Baltimore: Cushing and Company, 1895.

Prowell, George R. *History of the Eighty-Seventh Regiment, Pennsylvania Volunteers.* York: Press of the York Daily, 1901.

Roe, Alfredt Seyle. *History of the Ninth New York Heavy Artillery.* Worcester, Mass.: By Author, 1899.

Swinfen, David B. *Ruggle's Regiment: The One Hundred and Twenty-Second New York Volunteers in the American Civil War.* Hanover and London: University Press of New England, 1982.

Terrill, J. Newton. *Campaigns of the Fourteenth Regiment New Jersey Volunteers.* New Brunswick: Daily Home News Press, 1884.

Walker, Aldace F. *The Vermont Brigade in the Shenandoah Valley, 1864.* Burlington: Free Press Association, 1869.

Wild, Frederick W. *Memoirs and History of Captain F. W. Alexander's Baltimore Battery of Light Artillery.* Baltimore: Press of the Maryland School for Boys, 1912.

Secondary Sources—Books

Abbott, R. H. *Ohio's Civil War Governors.* Columbus: ?, 1962.

Ackinclose, Timothy. *Sabres and Pistols; The Civil War Career of Colonel Harry Gilmor, C.S.A.* Baltimore: Toomey Press, 1996.

Alexander, Theodore et al., editors. *Southern Revenge: Civil War History of Chambersburg, Pennsylvania.* Shippensburg, Pa.: White Mane Publishing Company for Greater Chambersburg Chamber of Commerce, 1989.

Ambrose, Stephen E. *Halleck: Lincoln's Chief of Staff*. Baton Rouge: Louisiana State University Press, 1955.

Andrews, J. Cutler. *The North Reports the Civil War*. Pittsburgh: University of Pittsburgh Press, 1955.

———. *The South Reports the Civil War*. Princeton: Princeton University Press, 1970.

Ballard, Colin R. *The Military Genius of Abraham Lincoln*. Cleveland and New York: World, 1952.

Bean, W. G. *Stonewall's Man: Sandie Pendleton*. Wilmington, N.C.: Broadfoot Publishing Company, 1987.

Benton, E. J. *The Movement for Peace Without a Victory During the Civil War*. [Western Reserve Historical Publication 99]. Cleveland: Western Reserve Historical Society, 1918.

Beitzell, Edwin W. *Point Lookout Prison Camp for Confederates*. Abell, Md.: By Author, 1972.

Bok, Edward M. *The Americanization of Edward Bok*. New York: C. Scribner's Sons, 1920.

Browning, Robert M., Jr. *From Cape Charles to Cape Fear: The North Atlantic Blockading Squadron During the Civil War*. Tuscaloosa, Ala.: University of Alabama Press, 1993.

Bushong, Millard K. *Old Jube: A Biography of General Jubal A. Early*. Boyce, Va.: Carr Publishing Company, 1955.

Catton, Bruce. *A Stillness at Appomattox*. Garden City, N.Y.: Doubleday, 1954.

———. *Never Call Retreat*. [Centennial History of the Civil War]. Garden City, N.Y.: Doubleday, 1965.

Coker, Brad. *The Battle of Monocacy*. [Honors Monograph Series, College of Liberal Arts, University of Baltimore]. Baltimore: University of Baltimore, 1982.

Colt, Margaretta Barton. *Defend the Valley: A Shenandoah Family in the Civil War*. New York: Random House, 1994.

Cooling, Benjamin Franklin, and Walton H. Owen. *Mr. Lincoln's Forts: A Guide to the Civil War Defenses of Washington*. Shippensburg, Pa.: White Mane Publishing Company, 1988.

———. *Jubal Early's Raid, 1864*. Baltimore: Nautical and Aviation Publishing Company, 1989.

———. *Symbol, Sword, and Shield: Defending Washington During the Civil War*. Hamden, Conn.: Archon, 1975 and Shippensburg, Pa.: White Mane Publishing Company, 1991.

Cotton, Robert, and Mary Ellen Hayward. *Maryland in the Civil War: A House Divided*. Baltimore: Maryland Historical Society, 1994.

Cramer, John Henry. *Lincoln Under Enemy Fire: The Complete Account of His Experience During Early's Attack on Washington.* Baton Rouge: Louisiana State University Press, 1948.

Davidson, Isobel. *Real Stories from Baltimore County History.* Hatboro, Pa.: Tradition Press, 1967.

Davis, William C. *Breckinridge: Statesman, Soldier, Symbol.* Baton Rouge: Louisiana State University Press, 1974.

Denison, George T. *Modern Cavalry.* London: Bosworth, 1868.

Dilts, James D. *The Great Road: The Building of the Baltimore and Ohio, the Nation's First Railroad, 1828–1853.* Stanford: Stanford University Press, 1993.

Farquhar, Roger Brook. *Historical Montgomery County, Maryland—Old Homes and History.* Baltimore: Monumental Printing Company, 1952.

Farquhar, W. H. *Annals of Sandy Spring or Twenty Years History of a Rural County in Maryland.* Baltimore: Cashings and Bailey, 1884. 2 volumes.

Freeman, Douglas Southall. *Lee's Lieutenants.* New York: Charles Scribner's Sons, 1942–1944. 3 volumes.

———. *R. E. Lee: a Biography.* New York: Charles Scribners, 1934. 4 volumes.

Gallagher, Cary W. *Stephen Dodson Ramseur, Lee's Gallant General.* Chapel Hill: University of North Carolina Press, 1935.

Getty, Mildred Newbold. *Grace Episcopal Church, 1857–1957.* Silver Spring: Privately published, 1957.

Goldsborough, E.Y. *Early's Great Raid...Battle of Monocacy.* n.p., 1898 and Frederick, Md.: The Historical Society of Frederick County, 1989.

Gordon, Paul and Rita. *A Playground of the Civil War: Frederick County, Maryland.* Frederick: The Heritage Partnership, 1994.

Grove, William Jarboe. *History of Carrollton Manor, Frederick County, Maryland.* Frederick: Marken and Bielfeld, 1928.

Hagerman, Edward. *The American Civil War and the Origins of Modern Warfare.* Bloomington, Ind.: Indiana University Press, 1988.

Hale, Laura Virginia. *Four Valient Years in the Lower Shenandoah Valley, 1861–1865.* Strasburg, Va.: Shenandoah Publishing House, 1968.

Halsey, Don P. *Historic and Heroic Lynchburg.* Lynchburg, Va.: J. P. Bell and Company, 1935.

Hesseltine, W. B., editor. *The Tragic Conflict.* New York: 1962.

Jones, Virgil Carrington. *Gray Ghosts and Rebel Raiders.* New York: Henry Holt and Company, 1956.

———. *Ranger Mosby.* Chapel Hill: University of North Carolina Press, 1944.

Judge, Joseph. *Season of Fire: The Confederate Strike on Washington.* Berryville, Va.: Rockbridge Publishing Company, 1994.

Keller, S. Roger. *Events of the Civil War in Washington County Maryland.* Shippensburg, Pa.: Burd Street Press, 1995.

Klein, Frederick Shriver, editor. *Just South of Gettysburg: Carroll County, Maryland in the Civil War.* Westminster, Md.: Carroll County Historical Society, 1963.

Lee, Richard M. *Mr. Lincoln's City: an Illustrated Guide to the Civil War Sites of Washington.* McLean, Va.: BPM Publications, 1981.

Leech, Margaret. *Reveille in Washington, 1860–1865.* New York: Harper and Brothers, 1941.

Lewis, Thomas A. and the editors of Time-Life Books. *The Shenandoah in Flames: The Valley Campaign of 1864.* Alexandria, Va.: Time-Life Books, 1987.

Lossing, Benson J. *Pictorial History of the Civil War in the United States of America.* Hartford, Conn.: T. Belknap, 1868. 3 volumes.

Manakee, Harold R. *Maryland in the Civil War.* Baltimore: Maryland Historical Society, 1961.

Martin, Samuel J. *The Road to Glory: Confederate General Richard S. Ewell.* Indianapolis: Guild Press of Indiana, Inc. 1991.

McKee, Irving. *"Ben-Hur" Wallace: The Life of General Lew Wallace.* Berkeley: University of California Press, 1947.

McPherson, James M. *Battle Cry of Freedom: The Civil War Era.* [Oxford History of the United States] New York: Oxford University Press, 1988.

Meaney, Peter J. *The Civil War Engagement at Cool Sprint, July 18, 1864.* Berryville, Va.: Privately printed, ca. 1980.

Michel, Robert E. *Colonel Harry Gilmor's Raid Around Baltimore.* Baltimore: Erbe Publishers, 1976.

Morris, George S., and Susan L. Foutz. *Lynchburg in the Civil War: The City— The People—The Battle.* [Virginia Civil War Battles and Leaders Series]. Lynchburg: H. E. Howard, Inc., 1984.

Nevins, Allan. *The War for the Union.* New York: Charles Scribner's Sons, 1971. 4 volumes.

Newman, Harry Wright. *Maryland and the Confederacy.* Annapolis: By Author, 1976.

Nicolay, John G. *A Short Life of Abraham Lincoln.* New York: Century, 1907.

————, and John Hay. *Abraham Lincoln: a History.* New York: Century, 1904. 10 volumes.

Osborne, Charles C. *Jubal: The Life and Times of General Jubal A. Early.* Chapel Hill: Algonquin Books, 1992.

Parish, Peter J. *The American Civil War.* New York: Holmes and Meier, 1975.

Plank, Will. *Banners and Bugles: a Record of Ulster County, New York and the Mid-Hudson Region in the Civil War*. Marlborough, N.Y.: Centennial Press, 1963.

Plum, William R. *The Military Telegraph During the Civil War in the United States*. Chicago: Jansen, McClurg, and Company, 1882. 2 volumes.

Pollard, Edward A. *The Lost Cause: a New Southern History of the War of the Confederates*. New York: E. B. Treat and Company, 1867.

Pond, George E. *The Shenandoah in the Civil War*. [Scribner's Campaigns of the Civil War]. New York: Charles Scribner's Sons, 1883.

Reid, Whitelaw. *Ohio in the War: Her Statesmen, Her Generals, and Soldiers*. Cincinnati: Moore, Wilstach, and Baldwin, 1868.

Roseboom, E. H. *A History of Ohio: The Civil War Era, 1850–1873*. Columbus: ?, 1944.

Sandburg, Carl. *Abraham Lincoln: The War Years*. New York: ?, 1939.

Scharf. J. Thomas. *History of Baltimore City and County*. Philadelphia: Louis H. Everts, 1881.

———. *History of Western Maryland: Being a History of Montgomery, Carroll, Washington, Allegheny, and Garrett Counties*. Philadelphia: Louis H. Everts, 1882 and Baltimore: Regional Publishing Company, 1968 edition. 2 volumes.

Schildt, John W. *Drums Along the Monocacy*. Chewsville, Md.: Antietam Publications, Md., 1992.

Shingleton, Royce Gordon. *John Tyler Wood, Sea Ghost of the Confederacy*. Athens, Ga.: University of Georgia Press, 1979.

Sibley, F. Ray, Jr. *The Confederate Order of Battle, Volume I, The Army of Northern Virginia*. Shippensburg, Pa.: White Mane Publishing Company, 1996.

Smith, Elbert B. *Francis Preston Blair*. New York: Free Press, 1980.

Souvenir of Historic Frederick. Frederick: Marken and Bielfeld, 1925.

Stackpole, Edward J. *Sheridan in the Shenandoah: Jubal Early's Nemesis*. Harrisburg, Pa.: The Stackpole Company, 1961.

Stepp, John W., compiler and editor, with I. William Hill. *Mirror of the War: The Washington Star Reports the Civil War*. New York: Castle Books, Inc. for The Evening Star Newspapers Company, 1961.

Strode, Hudson. *Jefferson Davis: The Tragic Hero: The Last Twenty-Five Years 1864–1889*. New York: Harcourt, Brace, and World, 1964.

Summers, Festus P. *The Baltimore and Ohio in the Civil War*. Gettysburg: Stan Clark Military Books, Inc., 1993 edition.

Toomey, Daniel Carroll. *The Civil War in Maryland*. Baltimore: Toomey Press, 1983.

Vandiver, Frank. *Jubal's Raid: General Early's Famous Attack on Washington in 1864*. New York: McGraw-Hill, 1960.

U.S. Department of the Army. *The Medal of Honor*. Washington: Government Printing Office, 1948.

Warner, Ezra J. *Generals in Blue: Lives of the Union Commanders*. Baton Rouge: Louisiana State University Press, 1964.

———. *Generals in Gray: Lives of the Confederate Commanders*. Baton Rouge: Louisiana State University Press, 1959.

Welcher, Frank J. *The Union Army: Organization and Operations; Volume I: The Eastern Theater*. Bloomington: Indiana University Press, 1989.

Wenger, Warren D. *Monocacy: The Defeat that Saved Washington, D.C.* Bridgeton, N.J.: Eugene Printing, 1996.

Wert, Jeffry D. *From Winchester to Cedar Creek: The Shenandoah Valley Campaign of 1864*. Carlisle, Pa., South Mountain Press, 1987, and New York: Simon and Schuster, 1989.

———. *Mosby's Rangers*. New York: Simon and Schuster, 1990.

Whitmore, Nancy F., and Timothy L. Cannon. *Frederick: A Pictorial History*. Norfolk, Va.: Donning and Company, 1981.

Williams, T. Harry. *Lincoln and His Generals*. New York: Alfred A. Knopf, 1952.

Williams, T. J. C. and Folger McKinsey, et al. *History of Frederick County, Maryland*. Baltimore: L. T. Titsworth, 1910, and Regional Publishing Company, 1967 edition. 2 volumes.

Worthington, Glenn H. *Fighting For Time or the Battle That Saved Washington and Mayhap the Union*. Frederick: Frederick County Historical Society, 1932, and Shippensburg, Pa.: Beidel Printing House, 1985.

Wubben, W. B. *War Government, Federal and State, 1861–1865*. New York: n.p., 1906.

Secondary Sources—Articles

Albro, Walt. "The Forgotten Battle for the Capital," *Civil War Times Illustrated*. 33 (January/February 1993), Number 1, pp. 40–43, 56–61.

Alexander, Ted. "McCausland's Raid and the Burning of Chambersburg," *Blue and Gray Magazine*, XI (August 1994), Number 6, pp. 11–18, 46–64.

———. "'Old Jube' Fools the Yankees; Jubal Early's Diversions to Support McCausland's Raid," *Blue and Gray Magazine*, XI (August 1994), Number 6, pp. 19–20.

Alvord, Henry E. "Early's Attack on Washington, July 1864," District of Columbia Commandery. Military Order of the Loyal Legion of the United States. *War Papers*. Numbers 26, 1897.

Black, Wilfred, editor. "Civil War Letters of George Washington McMillen and Jefferson O. McMillen 122d Regiment, O.V.I," *West Virginia History*, 32 (April 1971) Number 3, pp. 171–193.

Carey, Richard. "When Gilmor Threatened Baltimore," Baltimore *Sun*, December 1, 1929.

———. "Colonel David Ramsay Clendenin," in William H. Powell and Edward Shippen. *Officers of the Army and Navy (Regular) Who Served in the Civil War*. Philadelphia: L. R. Hamersly, 1892, p. 88.

Conradis, Albert E. "The Battle of Monocacy: The Battle That Saved Washington from Capture," in Frederick County Civil War Centennial, Inc. *To Commemorate the One Hundredth Anniversary of the Battle of Monocacy: The Battle That Saved Washington*. Frederick: Frederick Civil War Centennial, Inc., 1964, pp. 8–60.

Cooling, Benjamin Franklin. "Monocacy—The Battle That Saved Washington," *Blue and Gray Magazine*, X (December 1992), Number 3, pp. 8–14, 16–18, 48–60.

———. "Civil War Deterrent: the Defenses of Washington," *Military Affairs*, XXIX (Winter 1966), Number 4, pp. 164–178.

Cowen, Benjamin R. "The One Hundred Days Men of Ohio," W. H. Chamberlain et al., editors. Ohio Commandery, Military Order of the Loyal Legion of the United States. *Sketches of War History 1861–1865*. Cincinnati: Robert Clarke Company, V, 1903, pp. 361–363.

Cox, William V. "The Defenses of Washington: General Early's Advance on the Capital and the Battle of Fort Stevens, July 11 and 12, 1864," *Records of the Columbia Historical Society*, IV (1901), pp. 1–31.

———. "Fort Stevens, Where Lincoln Was Under Fire," in Marcus Benjamin, compiler and editor. *Washington During Wartime: a Series of Papers Showing the Military, Political, and Social Phases During 1861 to 1865*. Washington: Bryon S. Adams, 1902, pp. 53–70.

Decker, Harry L. "Pendleton, Artillery Genius Under Lee, Was Pastor of All Saints Church Here," in Frederick County Civil War Centennial, Inc. *To Commemorate the One Hundredth Anniversary of the Battle of Monocacy, "The Battle That Saved Washington."* Frederick: Frederick Civil War Centennial, Inc., 1964, pp. 56–60.

Delaplaine, Edward S. "General Early's Levy on Frederick," in Frederick County Civil War Centennial, Inc. *To Commemorate the One Hundredth Anniversary of the Battle of Monocacy, "The Battle That Saved Washington."* Frederick: Frederick Civil War Centennial, Inc., 1964, pp. 42–55.

Duncan, Richard R. "Maryland's Reaction to Early's Raid in 1864: A Summer of Bitterness," *Maryland Historical Magazine*, 64 (Fall 1969), Number 3, pp. 248–279.

Engleman, Robert. "Fellowship of the Rings," Washington *Post*, June 25, 1989.

Feis, William B. "A Union Military Intelligence Failure: Jubal Early's Raid, June 13–July 14, 1864," *Civil War History*, 36 (September 1990), Number 3, pp. 209–225.

————. "Neutralizing the Valley: the Role of Military Intelligence in the Defeat of Jubal Early's Army of the Valley, 1864–1865," *Civil War History*, XXXIX (September 1993), Number 3, pp. 198–215.

Gallagher, Gary. "Monocacy" in Francis H. Kennedy, editor. *The Civil War Battlefield Guide*. Boston: Houghton Mifflin, 1990, pp. 235–238.

Getty, Mildred Newbold. "The Silver Spring Area, Part I," *Montgomery County Story*, XII (November 1968) Number 1, pp. 1–8.

Hamilton, Clay, and Charles T. Jacobs. "Greenbrier Civil War Soldier Buried in Maryland," Lewisburg (West Virginia). *The West Virginia Daily News*, October 11, 1983.

Hicks, Frederick. "Lincoln, Wright, and Holmes at Fort Stevens," *Journal of the Illinois State Historical Society*, 39 (September 1946), Number 3, pp. 323–332.

Lee, Blair. "The Day Confederates marched into Montgomery County History," *The Montgomery Journal*, June 28, 1989.

Lewis, Thomas A. "There in the Heat of July," *Smithsonian*, 19 (July 1988), Number 4, pp. 66–75.

McElroy, John. "Fort Stevens as National Park Favored as Tribute to Lincoln," Washington *Star*, June 27, 1933.

"Memorial Park on Monocacy Battlefield," *Confederate Veteran*, XXXVI (February 1928), Number 2, p. 44.

Morseberger, Robert E. "The Battle That Saved Washington," *Civil War Times Illustrated*, XXIII (May 1974), Number 2, pp. 12–17, 20–27.

"Oberlin and the Civil War," *Oberlin Today*, 22 (First Quarter 1964), Number 1, pp. 3–11.

Reagan, Ronald. "Why We Should Always Remember; The Lessons of the D-Day Invasion for a World Still Stalked by Evil," *The Washington Post*, June 5, 1994, Outlook Section, C-1.

Ruffner, Kevin. "'More Trouble than a Brigade': Harry Gilmor's 2d Maryland Cavalry in the Shenandoah Valley," *Maryland Historical Magazine*, 89 (Winter 1994), Number 1, pp. 389–411.

Savage, Kirk. "The Politics of Memory: Black Emancipation and the Civil War Monument," in John R. Gillis, editor. *Commemorations: the Politics of National Identity*. Princeton: Princeton University Press, 1994, pp. 127–149.

Smith, Edward. "When the Confederates Came to the Capital," Washington *Post*, July 9, 1989.

Smith, Everard H. "Chambersburg: Anatomy of A Confederate Reprisal," *The American Historical Review*, 96 (April 1991), Number 2, pp. 432–455.

Stackpole, Edward J. "The Day the Rebels Could Have Marched into the White House," Civil War *Times*, II (February–March 1961), Number 10, pp. 5–6, 19.

Stinson, Byron. "The Invalid Corps," *Civil War Times Illustrated*, X (May 1971), Number 2, pp. 20–27.

"The Civil War as Reported by the Star, One Hundred Years Ago, Confederates Menace Capital," Washington *Star*, July 12, 1964.

Vincent, Thomas McCurdy. "Early's March on Washington," in Marcus Benjamin, compiler and editor. *Washington During War Time: a Series of Papers Showing the Military, Political, and Social Phases During 1861 to 1865*. Washington: Byron S. Adams, 1902, pp. 47–52.

Wert, Jeffry E. "The Snicker's Gap War," *Civil War Times Illustrated*, XVII (July 1978), Number 4, pp. 30–40.

Wesley, Edward. "Rebels in Frederick: Battle Expected at Monocacy," *Fredericktonian*, January 16, 1978.

"When Early Came," Washington *Evening Star*, October 12, 1895.

Wilson, Edward S. "The Lynchburg Campaign," in W. H. Chamberlin, editor. Military Order of the Loyal Legion of the United States, Ohio Commandery. *Sketches of War History, 1861–1865*. Cincinnati: Robert Clarke Company, 1896, IV, pp. 133–146.

Wilson, W. Emerson. "City Prepares to Fight Invaders," Wilmington, Delaware *Morning News*, July 15, 1964.

Worthington, Glenn H. "The Battle of Monocacy," *Confederate Veteran*, XXXVI (January 1928), Number 1, pp. 20–23.

Secondary Sources—Unpublished

Beamer, Carl Brent. "Gray Ghostbusters: Eastern Theatre Union Counterguerrilla Operations in the Civil War, 1861–1865." Ph.D. dissertation, Ohio State University, 1988, and Ann Arbor: University Microfilms, 1989.

Bearss, Edwin C. "Documentation Troop Movement Maps, Battle of the Monocacy," U.S. National Park Service, 1979.

Brough J. "The Defenders of the Country and Its Enemies: the Chicago Platform Dissected," speech at Circleville, Ohio, September 3, 1864, Cincinnati, 1864.

Eckert, Ralph Lowell. "John Brown Gordon: Soldier, Southerner, American." Ph.D. dissertation, Louisiana State University, 1983, 2 volumes, and Ann Arbor: University Microfilms, 1984.

Fenton, Charles Wendell. "Early's Raid on Washington," Army War College, March 1916.

Gatchel, Theodore Dodge. "Early's Raid on Washington, June–July 1864," M.A. thesis, The American University, 1933.

Hampton, Wade. "The Raid on Point Lookout: a Study in Desperation," Research papers, The American University, August 1970, copy, Maryland Historical Society.

Johnson, Ronald W. "Gambrill Mill Site Evaluation and Brief Special History Study, Monocacy National Battlefield," National Park Service, 1984.

Macdonald, Patrick. "Structural Survey of Boscobel House and Gambrill Mill - Monocacy National Battlefield." National Park Service, 1984.

Minney, Elton D. "The Battle of Monocacy: an Individual Study Project," Army War College, 1988.

Pickering, Abner. "Early's Raid in 1864, Including the Battle of the Monocacy," Army War College, 1913-1914.

Porter, Charles W., Harry Langley, W. C. Little, "Report of Field Investigations Relating to the Monocacy National Battlefield Project." National Park Service, May 14, 1940.

Shufelt, Susan. "Historical Architecture Survey of Boscobel House, Monocacy National Battlefield." National Park Service, May 1984.

Smith, Everard Hall. "The General and the Valley: Union Generalship During the Threat to Washington in 1864." Ph.D. dissertation, University of North Carolina at Chapel Hill, 1977 and Ann Arbor: University Microfilms, 1977.

Thompson, Harry T. "A Report on the Monocacy Battlefield," National Park Service, November 23, 1937.

INDEX